Human Communication

Human Communication

Third Edition

Michael Burgoon
Frank G. Hunsaker
Edwin J. Dawson

SAGE Publications
International Educational and Professional Publisher
Thousand Oaks   London   New Delhi

For information address:

SAGE Publications, Inc.
2455 Teller Road
Thousand Oaks, California 91320

SAGE Publications Ltd.
6 Bonhill Street
London EC2A 4PU
United Kingdom

SAGE Publications India Pvt. Ltd.
M-32 Market
Greater Kailash I
New Delhi 110 048 India

Printed in the United States of America

Library of Congress Cataloging-in-Publication Data

Main entry under title:

Burgoon, Michael.
    Human communication / Michael Burgoon, Frank G. Hunsaker, Edwin J. Dawson.—3rd ed.
      p. cm.
    Includes bibliographical references and index.
    ISBN 0-8039-5076-4 (cl.) —ISBN 0-8039-5077-2 (pbk.)
    1. Communication. I. Hunsaker, Frank G. II. Dawson, Edwin J.
    III. Title.
    P90.B85 1994
    302.2—dc20   93-29323

94 95 96 97 98 10 9 8 7 6 5 4 3 2

Sage Production Editor: Astrid Virding

Contents

Preface

The writing of an introductory book is somewhat like the making of a movie in that text is not written and scenes originally are not filmed in the order that the reader or viewer will see them in the final product. So this Preface to *Human Communication* was, like almost all other openings of a text or scholarly book, written *after* the manuscript was already completed and in the hands of the publisher. By the time the author is compelled by the house editor to complete such a task, the author is often weary with the writing process and anxious to have things completed. But the compliance of the author is obtained, and a preface is written with multiple purposes, including (a) framing the content of the book so that the reader will know what is to come; (b) providing a synopsis of the book so that would-be purchasers or professors can be enticed to buy a copy of the book or adopt the text for classroom use, even if they do not have the time to read the book as produced; and (c) providing the publisher's marketing department with some idea of what the book is about so that they will not have to read much beyond the preface. Of course, these prefaces almost always end like an acceptance speech at the Academy Awards, with all kinds of people being acknowledged and thanked for their very real contributions to everything that occurred. Well, that is my preface to this Preface, so I will turn to the task of now doing what was expected of me, more or less.

Human Communication is meant to provide an introduction to the foundations of theory and research in the emerging discipline of communication. This book is well suited to a beginning level communication course for some universities. As such, it joins the ranks of a host of other books that might be used as texts for such a purpose. Some of those books focus on communication studies, especially introductory courses, as primarily performance-oriented courses where emphases are placed on such things as public speaking, small group discussion, or even experiential interpersonal communication activities. That is clearly not the primary focus of this book, so this book would probably not be satisfactory as the sole text in such a course.

Other books, usually called "fundamentals of communication" textbooks, attempt to incorporate much of the performance aspects of books similar to those described above, with chapters on public speaking and group discussion, while also including everything from general communication, to interpersonal communication, to a chapter on organizational communication, and even to the social effects of the mass media. In other iterations, I have written books that look much like the "fundamentals" text that I just described. But this edition of *Human Communication* is not that type of book. This book will either supplement or be supplemented by something else if that kind of combining of performance studies and communication sciences is required. There is absolutely no reason why a supplement for this book could not be the intelligence and experience of the professor in the class, but a number of publishing houses seem unwilling to bet on that and strive to make sure everything appears between the bound covers of their newly produced book. Because this book does not provide all of that fundamentals material, perhaps that means that in some institutions this book would best serve a more advanced theory and research course that might appear in the sophomore or junior year of some curricula.

This book is divided into two part, each containing five chapters. Part I provides an introduction to the assumptions we make about communication, key elements in the process of communication, and factors that inhibit our success in communicating with others. Such a format is far from unique and many textbooks open with similar goals. Chapter 1, however, provides our unique perspective on how one ought to approach the study of communication or begin to analyze communication problems. This chapter sets the tone for much of what is to follow. We debunk some of the myths that people hold about communication and then lay out our assumptions about how the process of communication works. Chapters 2, 3, and 4 examine the research evidence available on several important factors in the process of communication. These three chapters contain foundational evidence that will help the reader better understand the problem areas we approach in Part II.

Chapter 5, "Nonverbal Communication," is the most comprehensive research-based chapter in Part I. We think this material is very important for any intelligent introduction to the discipline, *but* the authors of this book felt uniquely unqualified to write such a chapter. Thus after yet another impartial, nationwide search for the most qualified scholars to contribute expertise in the area of nonverbal communication, Professors Judee K. Burgoon and Laura Guerrero, both of the University of Arizona, were selected to write this chapter. They graciously consented, and we think *Human Communication* is a much better book because of their participation.

Part II also has five chapters but is somewhat different in style, complexity, and focus from Part I. I have long argued that a *functional* approach to the study of communication represents a superior pedagogical format as compared with the *contextual* approach, which usually begins with dyadic communication, moves then to groups, then to public speaking, and ends with either organizational or mass communication. It has never been clear to me that there are so many differences in communication across these contexts to warrant such a standard organizational pattern in our books, our professional organizations, and, most important, our thinking. Rather, I believe that people communicate with others to satisfy some functional goal. Communicators have a purpose for communicating with others and it appears to me that we ought to examine the research about such purposive communication.

Part II of this book begins with two chapters on the persuasive function of communication. It is clear from all that we know, in terms of practical experience and research evidence, that people spend a great deal of their time attempting to influence others to believe, feel, think, or act as they do. That, of course, is our definition of the persuasive function of communication and theories of, and research about, persuasion are presented in Chapters 6 and 7.

We also believe that decision making, establishing and terminating close personal relationships, and conflict management are crucial functions that should be included in an introduction to the discipline of communication. The final three chapters of the book (Chapters 8, 9, and 10) are devoted to those functional themes and provide a synthesis of important theory and research.

It is unimaginable to me that anyone could write an introductory book that could not be criticized for what it included or for what it failed to include. Because this is not the first time I have engaged in such a writing task, I am fully prepared for such criticism of this third edition of *Human Communication*. The aspirations for this book are limited (and some will say in praise and others in biting criticism that the authors certainly lived up to their initial aspirations with the end product). We wanted to produce a relatively brief introduction to the discipline that met several standards upon which we, as authors, are in full agreement.

Obviously, we wanted to organize the book around the functional approach to communication. We did that. We also wanted to have a book that was relatively current in reviewing the extant scholarly research literature that supports our observations, summaries, and conclusions. That is somewhat of a problem for introductory textbook writers, however. Research included in texts often has not stood the test of time. We end up teaching students, often for years or decades, things the rest of the discipline no longer believes to be true. We attempted to reach a balance between the quest for currency and our own assessment of whether such a test of time was likely to be met by current research activity. Thus the latest convention paper or most current publication in any given area may not be included in our discussion of a given content area. Sometimes that is quite intentional.

Again, we have no particular opposition to professors using this book and providing their own input on the most current thinking in any of these areas.

It will be abundantly clear that this book relies primarily on empirical evidence from the allied social sciences, including, but not limited to, communication. We make no apologies for the fact that we are social scientists and have more faith in one kind of evidence (empirical data) than others that might be used in an introductory book about communication. Moreover, it was our intent to borrow heavily from important knowledge in the other social sciences as neither the study nor the practice of communication exists in isolation from other social phenomena.

A natural result of our intellectual commitments is that *Human Communication* is much more descriptive than prescriptive. We spend more time telling you the kinds of things that will likely happen if you communicate in a specific way than how you really should communicate. Most of that kind of summarization is descriptive. Some is speculative. We hope we have made it clear to the reader when we are describing and when we are speculating. But again, we are mostly attempting to describe, and that is also intentional and is as we think it should be in an introductory book.

We also wanted to write a book that demonstrated respect for the reader, whether he or she be a professional or a beginning student. To comprehend the vocabulary of communication fully (or any other discipline), you just might need a dictionary, so I suggest you buy one rather than complain about not knowing what some words mean. I certainly found such a tool to be of value when I was a student and I still use one today. Many major publishers today force an author to produce text that is at the tenth-grade level (that is a high school sophomore!). This text will not meet such a standard and no such injunction was offered by our publisher. We think many introductory books underestimate the intelligence of students and professionals and a conscious attempt was made not to make that error in *Human Communication*. In that same vein, although we hope we do not bore the reader with our writing, we saw this task not as writing primarily to entertain but to inform. This book is not like many college textbooks of the day. It is not full of photographs, four-color graphs, and "cute" cartoons. We have not included experiential exercises or designed a course within these covers. All of this is by design. We wanted to provide a literate book that would stand or fall on the substance of the ideas presented. As scientists, we are willing to wait for the empirical evidence of whether such an approach is viable in the marketplace (either of dollars or ideas).

There seems to be no end to the number of publishers willing to publish almost any kind of book in the introductory communication market. I had a number of choices and never seriously considered any other than Sage. Sara and George McCune, the founders of Sage Publications, Inc., have done a great deal to bring intellectual respectability to the entire discipline of communication. They risked substantial financial resources in a bet on the viability of this discipline. I think they won their bet, and many are grateful for all that both have done for the discipline. Sage is an "author's house" where you are allowed to write your book. They have a value for scholarly integrity and it shows in their products. For those reasons, I "pitched" this book to Sara, she responded with enthusiasm, and we made a deal. I am glad we did. Sophy Craze, whom I have still not met in person, was the editor assigned to make all this happen. She was just right for me as an author: She gave me assistance when I needed it and did not when I did not need or want it.

I have been fortunate to be a part of two really grand experiments in the discipline of communication, both of which greatly influenced this book. The first was being a student and then a faculty member at Michigan State University. I was there as a student when this new scientific approach to the study of communication was taking the discipline by storm. I went back as a faculty member and wrote an earlier version of this book. I was fortunate to work with a number of very good students there. In many ways, I will always be *of* Michigan State University. The second was participating in the development of a quality program in the communication sciences at the University of Arizona. Members of the faculty at Arizona, such as William Bailey, David Buller, Judee Burgoon, William Crano, Henry Kenski, Calvin Morrill, Lee Sigelman, and David Williams, made Arizona a really good place to work, learn, and prosper intellectually. Professional assistance from Sandra Froman, James Mackie, and David Ben-Asher helped maintain what we were all trying to build in the program. We have also been most fortunate to have had a wonderful group of graduate students in the program at the University of Arizona. Although I understand that when the history of this discipline is written this particular book will be little noted or long remembered, it is my belief (and hope) that the programs at Michigan State University and the University of Arizona will indeed greatly influence such a historical account.

My coauthors, Frank Hunsaker and Edwin Dawson, have a number of people they would like to thank. I think you know who you are. For me, I will simply end this preface with the same statement that I have used in a number of books before: I again thank all of those people who care about me and human communication, in whichever order.

—Michael Burgoon
Tucson, Arizona

Part I

THE VARIABLES IN THE COMMUNICATION PROCESS

The first part of this book builds the framework for better understanding the complex process of human communication. Several assumptions and misconceptions about the nature of human communication are explored. We suggest that some conceptions of communication are more valuable than others as tools for improving our skills as communicators and for understanding this very complex activity. We also offer several models of communication as well as discuss the use of models as an aid in understanding.

Several important variables that affect human communication will be discussed early in this book. Characteristics of both the source and receiver that affect the likelihood of success in any given communication event and some of the common variables that inhibit effective communication will be explored. Finally, the nature and functions of our nonverbal communication will be examined. Throughout, suggestions will be made as to how one goes about managing these important variables in order to be a more effective communicator.

1

An Introduction to Human Communication

Someone once insightfully said that a fish would be the last to discover the existence of water. What this person probably meant by the statement is that, because water is such a pervasive and important part of a fish's environment, its existence would not even be noticed unless it were absent. In many ways, the manner in which people perceive communication is analogous to a fish's awareness of water. Communication, like water to a fish, surrounds us. We constantly communicate with others and, except for the biological functions that sustain us, there is no activity more pervasive and critical than communication. Yet people invariably take communication for granted. We hear many of our students at the beginning of each term question our insistence that communication is a highly complex and difficult process. "After all," the students say, "we have been communicating for nearly 20 years, and we have gotten by without your help so far." We would not be so presumptuous as to suggest that people should read our book, or another like it, to get by. Our purpose is merely to convey to you that there is more to communication than meets the eye.

In so doing, we feel that it is necessary and imperative to dispel some of the more common myths about communication. If we were attempting to write a book about differential calculus, we could be relatively sure of two things: (a) that the majority of our readers would be virtually uninitiated in the subject and (b) that few would dismiss the complexity of the subject on the basis of many years of exposure to it. In short, we are suggesting that just because we are writing about the communication process and just because people have been exposed to it for a number of years, it does not follow that any of us know all there is to know. This process still has many intricacies that go unnoticed without our undivided and complete attention.

In the past, we have appealed to our students for that attention to the communication process. We have also attempted to assist them in systematically analyzing it and considering the numerous factors that come to bear in different communication situations. Some came to the conclusion, as we hope you will, that they were communication experts *only* to the extent that they had engaged in the communication process for a number of years. Others, unfortunately, though agreeing that there are many names, terms, processes, approaches, and effects that they had never heard of before, insisted that we were making the process more complex than it is. They felt that they could "get by" simply by getting out there and "relating to people." We do not wish to argue this point. Those who are unmotivated or think that they have all the answers, in terms of communicating with others, will find little of value in this book.

We feel that it is important to step back from the communication process and attempt to analyze it systematically and logically. Through such an analysis, people might be better able to recognize, comprehend, and apply many of the principles in the communication process. In so doing, they actually might improve their communication effectiveness instead of just "getting by." Moreover, by increasing communication competencies, people ought to be able to "relate to others" more frequently and more effectively if they choose.

No one exists in a vacuum. Everyone belongs to a spiraling hierarchy composed of interpersonal bonds, family, groups, and organizations. The pervasiveness of communication in this hierarchy is but one indication of the importance of this process in our lives. Through communication, people can exert some control over their physical and social environments. Changes in the social system, the establishment of personal bonds, the successful management of conflict, personal rewards and gratifications, and the accomplishment of mutual goals are possible only through some sort of communication behavior. The social system itself is an accomplishment, or creation, of communication. Communication is pervasive and important; people shape it and it shapes them. It is our assumption that most people will want to learn more about this vital aspect of human behavior, and it is with this thought that we begin.

Myths About Human Communication

Perhaps it will be helpful to examine first some of the myths that many people believe about human communication. Some of these myths have been popularized by the media, by business organizations, by some educators, and, in some cases, by enthusiasts trying to stress the importance of communication skills. We need to let you know what we personally believe from the outset.

All of the Problems of This World Are Communication Problems. It would be difficult to pinpoint when this myth about human communication became pervasive in our culture. However, the popular phrase from the 1960s movie *Cool Hand Luke,* "what we have here is a failure to communicate," became a catch phrase that identified communication as the nexus of all of humankind's problems. Others have picked up that slogan and are willing to apply it to any problem area in which two or more human beings seem to find themselves. Not all problems can be traced to some kind of a failure to communicate. We would argue that during the Gulf War, the problems experienced by United Nations' forces and Iraq's armed forces were not communication problems. In fact, President Bush proved quite effective in his ability to communicate with Saddam Hussein. The "smart bombs" that so utterly neutralized Iraq's ability to wage war clearly communicated the allied forces' position regarding

Iraq's invasion of Kuwait. We hope the point we want to make is clear. People differ in their attitudes, beliefs, and values, and that leads them to behave in different ways. Those different patterns of behavior often cause problems in human relationships. We are not willing to concede that people's thinking and behaving differently are necessarily a problem of communication. All of the communication we might be able to produce may leave one unconverted and unconvinced. We doubt that such a state of affairs would constitute a failure to communicate. People can well understand someone's position and reject the validity of it.

All of the Problems in This World Can Be Solved by More and Better Communication. This myth is the logical corollary of the first. Just as all people's problems are not necessarily related to their communication skills, we believe that more and better communication is not a panacea for all the problems in the world. It is painfully obvious in this society that more communication does not necessarily solve problems. In fact, people are so saturated with communication and information that they would be better served to learn when communication *can* facilitate problem solving and when it *cannot*. Perhaps it is disappointing for those in our profession to realize that everything is not within our domain of expertise; we could certainly become financially independent if it were so. Companies that plan to invest a great deal of money in promoting "better communication" will be sorely disappointed in the results if the basis of their problems is not related to communication. Educators must know that not all of the problems between teacher and student can or will be solved just by improving communication. These kinds of examples are apparent in many situations. There are problems between people and problems inherent in systems that have nothing to do with the ability to communicate and that, therefore, cannot be solved by increasing the amount of communication.

In a recent consulting experience, this point was made very clear to us. A large company had recently developed a product that would lead to a safer consumer product if they could convince manufacturers to use it. This safety product had a number of desirable characteristics, at least from the point of view of the developing company, and it should have been a marketable commodity. However, the manufacturers simply would not purchase it. The executives of this major company were convinced that they obviously had a "communication problem." They truly felt that if they could just convey how important and good their product was, the manufacturers would be eager to purchase large quantities. They retained a communication consultant (one of the authors) to help them devise a communication strategy to solve the problem. It was quickly discovered that there really was not a communication problem at all. The manufacturers were actually aware of how much the new product would add to consumer safety and were convinced that this was a real breakthrough in technology. They had decided, however, that they just did not want to spend the money required to purchase the item in question because there was not that much importance attached to consumer safety.

This myth needs to be dispelled in terms of interpersonal relationships as well. One of the authors firmly believes that if he could compel married couples in this country to engage in "more and better communication," he could increase the divorce rate by 50%! Most couples develop communication patterns that are both functional and satisfying. It often proves detrimental to attempt to alter existing patterns under the guise that "more and better" communication will solve all relational problems. Although we would not argue that communicating with relational partners will ultimately be ineffective in solving relational problems, we do suggest that relying solely on "more and better" communication may prevent couples from confronting more fundamental problems in their relationship. People often assume that if others disagree with them or are unwilling to behave as they desire, the others simply must not understand. If they do not understand, it is necessary to communicate some more with them. This is just not how things are. There is no necessary relationship between the amount of communication and anything else. More communication will not always solve problems and, in fact, sometimes can make things worse. People who dislike each other can often grow to dislike each other even more simply by continuing to communicate. They find out how really different and intolerable the other individual is.

We also object to the notion that even though *quantity* of communication is not a predictor of whether a problem will be solved, somehow if the *quality* of that communication is increased, things will get better. Things do not necessarily happen this way. In our first example, the quality of communication between the product developer and the manufacturers probably had little to do with the final outcome. It would have been impossible to improve much on the quality of communication because the manufacturers were truly convinced of the worth of the product. They understood and even believed everything that was said. They just did not think it important enough to warrant action. "It is not how much we communicate but what is said" is misleading; some problems will never be solvable through communication attempts.

Communication Is Without Costs. Many people believe that there are no costs associated with communicating; so, therefore, they assume that any effort to communicate is worth trying. This belief is not really true. We would argue that communication efforts should be considered employing a "cost-benefit" analysis. Attempting to communicate effectively with other people takes a great deal of effort and energy. Communication is hard work. Organizations must think of costs in terms of dollars, but individuals must actively consider how much time they are willing to invest in any given situation to maximize communication outcomes. We have all known people who do not know when to give up on trying to communicate about something. People have to learn to analyze situations to determine when the cost of communicating is worth the energy expended striving to communicate. If someone has very different political views from your own, abhors your present lifestyle, or is generally unpleasant to be around, it is well to consider the benefits of attempting to communicate with that person compared to the costs involved. Sometimes it is more "cost efficient" to communicate with such a person as little as possible. It is our hope that this book will help people decide for themselves when communication is worth the effort required; clearly, we think it *is* in many circumstances.

Communication Often Breaks Down. Machines break down; communication does not. All of us have probably heard someone describe a situation in which he or she felt that "communication had broken down." The explosion of the Space Shuttle *Challenger* and the tragic loss the seven lives aboard accentuates the dangers of buying into this myth. Throughout the investigation into the causes of this disaster, officials from Morton Thiokol, the company that designed the O-rings used in the booster rocket that exploded, repeatedly argued that the communication between engineers from Morton Thiokol and NASA had "broken down" and that somehow the responsibility for the disaster could be attributed to that communication "breakdown." Further investigations found that this was not the case. A number of Morton Thiokol engineers argued forcefully to delay the shuttle launch precisely because of potential malfunctioning of the O-rings. The fateful decision to override these warnings was apparently influenced by officials at both Morton Thiokol and NASA who felt tremendous pressure to launch as scheduled. Communication was present, but was not effective. It did not "break down."

Communication attempts can be successful or unsuccessful. We can be effective or ineffective in our attempts to communicate, but we simply cannot envision communication breaking down. We will suggest later in this chapter that the very nature of communication makes it an ongoing process in which it is difficult, if not impossible, to identify a beginning and/or end. In fact, it has been suggested that it is "impossible to not communicate" (Watzlawick, Beavin, & Jackson, 1967). It is more than just a semantic game that leads us to deplore strongly the use of the term *breakdown* to describe communication. We have often heard people revert to the too simple explanation that communication had broken down to describe a situation in which there was a problem. Has communication "broken down" if one cannot convince a person to believe as one does? Obviously, we have already said we do not think that failure to influence is even a communication problem in specific cases. Communication occurred; the outcome was just not what was expected or desired.

The use of the word *breakdown* provides little information. It does not provide any information that would allow people to solve a problem or avoid a similar situation in the future. To the extent that they accept such superficial descriptions of communication problems, people tend to limit their ability to analyze, adapt to, and change communication situations. Therefore, we will not use this term to describe communication problems between people. Maybe our aversion to this term is related to the fact that the authors own automobiles that are often in need of repair and are therefore used to a more precise, identifiable usage of the term *breakdown*.

Communication Is Either Good or Bad. We will not suggest that communication itself has inherent qualities. We would not even claim that possessing many skills in communicating would satisfy our notion of what is good. Communication must be judged as a tool that can be used for good or bad ends. We shall say more about communication as a tool in this chapter and throughout the book. Let us say here that our suggestions about effective communication are as valuable to the would-be scam artist as they are to the sincere individual. People can use communication to become demagogues, to incite riots, and to initiate wars. They can also use it as a tool to serve humanity or to grow and develop as individuals. There are some individuals who we hope will not come to possess more effective communication strategies because they might not use them for the proper ends. That is a decision that is not left for us to make, however. Perhaps there is one comforting thought about this question. If people in general truly understand the process of communication, perhaps they can be effective in using the tool in desirable ways *and* in resisting those who use it in ways found to be unacceptable.

Communication Is About Producing More Effective Messages. For too long people have equated effective communication with the ability to *produce* messages that would persuade, entertain, inform, or do a variety of other things. We do not argue with the assertions that effective production of communication is an important attribute and that people can and should be competent at doing this. However, we think that any definition of the competent communicator must also include message *consumption*. A person who is elegant in elocution but does not listen to or understand others cannot be called an effective communicator. We must develop skills that emphasize both message production and message consumption. To that end, we have devoted our efforts in this book.[1] But first we must understand the nature of the communication process.

The Nature of the Communication Process

In the first weeks of life an infant begins to learn the complex process of communication. Babies cry when they want food or attention, and they quickly learn that this crying behavior is a way of exerting control over their environment. It is also known that, early in life, infants respond to and are able to discriminate human speech sounds from other forms of noise. Later a child will learn to talk, and verbal communication will be added to his or her repertoire of gestures and sounds. But the process of learning to communicate does not stop in early childhood. People are constantly relearning and redefining their means of communication so that they can adapt to changing circumstances in their personal lives or the world around them. Communication is a constantly changing, dynamic function, involving exchange and interaction. One theorist has suggested that every sentence should begin and end with the word *and* to make people aware of the ongoing nature of their communication activities (Fabun, 1968). Although such a suggestion was probably not meant to be taken literally, people should be aware of the dynamic properties of the process of human communication.

When we say that communication is a process, we mean that *communication has no easily defined beginning or end; it is dynamic and not static; when one stops the process, communication ceases to exist.* Perhaps it would be helpful to examine a simple biological analogy—the digestive system—to underscore these important notions of process. To explain digestion, we could list the elements of the digestive process as just the organs involved: the mouth, stomach, small and large intestines, pancreas, and liver. But these elements alone do not constitute the actual process of digestion. For example, the stomach cannot digest meat proteins until the meat has been broken down in the mouth and then worked on by the enzyme pepsin. In turn, pepsin cannot perform its function without the aid of hydrochloric acid. All of these elements of the digestive process must work together, interacting and changing to meet different needs. Similar to digestion, the process of communication also involves change, interaction, adaptation, and an ongoing function.

Another major consideration of this process notion, as has been mentioned, is that once one stops the process, what is being studied no longer exists. When the biological function of digestion ceases, there is no process to study. Communication is a process because when it stops, it no longer exists (Cronkhite, 1976). Unlike machines that can be disassembled and put back together, communication occurs, or it does not occur. When the process is arrested, it is difficult to analyze communication, for there is little left to study. This, of course, means that communication is ideally studied while it is occurring. The difficulties in actually studying such a process are immense but worthwhile.

The Transactional Nature of Communication

Whatever your goals in life, you will eventually find it necessary and advantageous to learn to communicate more effectively. If you are interviewed for a job, you will have an immediate need to communicate your skills, intelligence, and desire to work. If you are beginning a dating relationship, you may wish to communicate the acceptance or rejection of your partner's actions. If you hold a managerial position in a corporation, you will need to communicate your business ideas to your subordinates and superiors. In short, you will be forced to come to grips with the fact that all communication is transactional in nature. *When we say that communication is transactional, we mean that a change in any one element in the process can alter all elements of communication.*

When one communicates with another person, there must be some relaying or sharing of meaning between the two. The communication affects both source and receiver and can affect future messages that will be produced. If you are trying to communicate with a friend, you might be called the *source* of communication and the friend might be called the *receiver*. One of the first things that you look for when relaying your message is the reaction of your friend. Is there an interest in what you are saying? Does your message seem to be understood? You look for visual responses (a smile or an eye movement, for example) and then a verbal response to your message. When the receiver reacts to a message sent by a source, the receiver provides cues for the source about the way the message is being received. These cues are known as *feedback*. Without feedback it is difficult to judge with any degree of accuracy how effective any communication transaction is. As you can no doubt see, the distinctions between source and receiver are arbitrary labels at best. People are *simultaneously* acting as source and receiver in many communication situations. A person is giving feedback, talking, responding, acting, and reacting continually through a communication event. Each person is constantly *participating* in the communication activity. All of these things can *alter* the other elements in the process and create a completely different communication event. That is what we mean by transaction.

The responses that a receiver makes to a source can change the speaker. Given enough negative feedback about one's beliefs and attitudes, pressure to change is obviously present. The entire relationship between two people can change as a result of just one message. An insensitive or rude comment can severely damage a friendship. Adding or removing one or more persons from a conversation also changes the entire nature of the communication event. When you communicate with another individual, you are adding to the history of the communication relationship. You will be somewhat different as a result of that communication, and it will no doubt affect the way you communicate in the future. Communication cannot be erased because it affects the participants; the essence of understanding the transactional nature of communication is to understand how any element in the process of communication can alter the entire communication relationship.

The Affective Nature of Communication

There is an old riddle that asks the question, "If a tree falls in a forest and no one is present to hear it fall, has sound really been made?" In other words, if no one is around to hear the crash, might it be supposed that the sound did not exist at all? Communication, whether it is nonverbal or verbal, cannot exist if there is no one around to receive the signals. Everything that people are willing to label as "communication" has an impact on someone. Of course, this is obvious from what we said about the transactional nature of communication, and we do not wish to belabor the point. However, we do wish to stress that much of the response to communication is affective and is involved with people's emotions and feelings. People do make subjective evaluations of the communication of others and respond to them on the basis of how they themselves are affected. We must also stress that people have affective or emotional responses to communication from others and that, too, helps determine the nature of future communication. Communication must have an impact on *someone,* or it simply is not communication.

The Personal Nature of Communication

Words are important to communication because they are convenient symbols by which we can share meaning. A word, however, is not the thing it represents, and a symbol is something that stands for something else. Likewise, the meaning or "message" is not in a word but in the people who use the word. *Meaning* is that which is intended, as by language. Examining a common word such as *chair* illustrates this point. What kind of *chair* do you visualize when you hear this word? Do you see a large, overstuffed living room chair; a hard, wooden dining room chair; or a metal folding chair? If you heard someone say, "They gave him the chair," would you know what is meant? Would the message have the same meaning if the person being talked about was in one case a college professor and in another case a murderer?

Because meanings are in people, communication is as personal as the individuals who use it. It is impossible to separate self from the communication process because all our experiences, attitudes, and emotions are involved and will affect the way we send and interpret messages. According to Kenneth Boulding, every individual has a unique "image" of self—a special way of viewing the world that is the result of all his or her personal experiences since childhood. The image of self that people have affects their communication activities:

Our image is in itself resistant to change. When it receives messages which conflict with it, its first impulse is to reject them as in some sense untrue. Suppose, for instance, that somebody tells us something which is inconsistent with our picture of a certain person. Our first impulse is to reject the proffered information as false. As we continue to receive messages which contradict our image, however, we begin to have doubts, and then one day we receive a message which overthrows our previous image and we revise it completely. The person, for instance, whom we saw as a trusted friend is now seen to be a hypocrite and a deceiver. (Boulding, 1956, pp. 8-9)

The purpose of any communication is to achieve shared meanings, but the symbolic nature of communication makes this difficult to accomplish. Not only is language symbolic—each word carrying varied connotations for different people—but it also is a process that is constantly changing. Consider, for example, an excerpt from George Washington's inaugural speech in 1789:

All I dare hope is that, if in executing this task I have been too much swayed by a grateful remembrance of former instances, or by an affectionate sensibility to this transcendent proof of the confidence of my fellow-citizens, and have thence too little consulted my incapacity as well as disinclination for the weighty and untried cares before me, my error will be palliated by the motives which misled me, and its consequences be judged by my country with some share of the partiality with which they originated.

Now compare the excerpt with one from President Clinton's inaugural speech in 1993 and see how much our use of language has changed:

Americans deserve better, and in this city today there are people who want to do better. And so I say to all of you here, let us resolve to reform our politics so that power and privilege no longer shout down the voice of the people. Let us put aside personal advantage so that we can feel the pain and see the promise of America. Let us resolve to make our Government a place for what Franklin Roosevelt called bold, persistent experimentation, a Government for our tomorrows, not our yesterdays. Let us give this capital back to the people to whom it belongs.

Language is not the only element of communication that is subject to change. It is very doubtful that George Washington would have understood the meaning of the much-used sign from World War II of "V" for victory, (or, from the Vietnam War era, for peace). Such signs, gestures, and behavioral cues, all integral parts of nonverbal communication, are also abstractions of reality. Each has different symbolic meanings for different people. Because communication is a personal process, a shared code (or codes) of symbols is required for people to understand each other, and some standardized usages do exist.

The Instrumental Function of Communication

We said earlier that communication is a tool that people use to achieve certain ends. That statement underscores the instrumental nature of the process of communication. Communication serves as an instrument by which people gain control over their physical and social environment. People can use communication for a variety of purposes that we will deal with in this book. Using the available means of persuasion to gain compliance is one function of communication that has gained considerable attention from antiquity to the present. When people attempt to change the attitudes and/or behaviors of others, communication becomes the vehicle of change. In fact, Berlo (1960) suggests that it is useful to view all communication as persuasive in nature. We understand how such a perspective can be taken. One could suggest that we are trying to "persuade" people to like us, to view us as credible, to accept our point of view, or to do a variety of other things. We have taken the position, however, that communication can serve a variety of functions. Looking at everything through this perspective of persuasion limits our understanding of the multifunctional nature of communication. There are certain communication situations in which an obvious intent to persuade is present, and we believe it useful to view communication as a tool to gain compliance in those specific contexts.

In other situations, however, the conscious intent to persuade is not present. We think communication used to develop social relationships and to manage conflicts is best viewed from something other than an advocacy point of view. We offer other models of analysis of those functions that we find useful. People also enter into situations with an instrumental purpose to make decisions, gain information, entertain, inform, and achieve a number of other outcomes. We treat all of those as separate functions and suggest ways in which communication can serve as an instrument to help us obtain desired outcomes. We do take the position that *instrumental communication is a strategic activity.* People can plan in advance and adopt strategies that are likely to make them more effective in a variety of contexts. They can also devise strategies to ensure that communication will serve a variety of functions for them. Some people eschew the word *manipulation* when describing human communication. We do not share such a strong aversion to the term, for we know that communication can be used to manipulate others. However, we have claimed that manipulation can be for good or bad ends. If people do devise strategies to use communication in an instrumental fashion, we also know, as we have said, that people devise strategies to resist influence and manipulation. Much of this book is devoted to the instrumental purposes of communication.

The Consummatory Function of Communication

The distinctions between the instrumental and consummatory purposes of communication are not always easy to make. McCroskey (1972) refers to expressive communication as communication that is not necessarily meant to affect another person. He suggests that such communication reflects people's feelings whereas instrumental communication may or may not represent true feelings. Berlo (1960) suggests that communication with *consummatory purposes has immediate reward value to the communicator.* He suggests that producing a composition may have consummatory values because the communicator enjoys the composition process. He further adds that presenting a composition to an audience so that they might share the communicator's satisfaction would also be an example of communication with primarily a consummatory purpose. We do not totally accept either definition of consummatory communication. *We would define* consummatory purpose *as any communication activity that has the goal of satisfying the communicator without any necessary intent to affect anyone else.* People may engage in conversation just because they enjoy talking. Talking satisfies certain felt needs. Others benefit by simply verbalizing ideas and notions with another. Many people enjoy performing, not for the impact it *might* have on an audience, but because they find a certain amount of joy in communicating. We would take exception with the McCroskey definition because we think that people often express "real" feelings and frequently say things that they do not necessarily believe just because it is satisfying. We have a close friend who obviously enjoys telling stories, and he could not care less whether they are "real" or "true." He just likes telling them. We also believe that the Berlo example of affecting an audience in a positive way would not qualify as consummatory communication under our present definition. The intent was obviously to produce a positive impact on others. The act of communicating can provide catharsis and/or gratification to the communicator without intent to affect others.

We must now return to our discussion of the transactional nature of communication, for we have said that all communication does affect all elements in the communication process. *Just because there was no intent (that is, purpose) to have an impact does not in any way imply that no impact will occur.* In fact, communication *will* have impact. A good performance, a well-written composition, or a cathartic conversation will become a part of the communication history of the participants. These will likely affect how others perceive a person and communicate with that person in future encounters. Moreover, it is our feeling that many communication transactions have both instrumental and consummatory goals. We think it is useful, however, to examine what the major purpose of the communicator is in a given situation in order to make distinctions concerning whether the communication was primarily intended to be instrumental or consummatory.

Defining the Communication Process

Not surprisingly, there are numerous definitions of *communication* (Dance & Larson, 1976). Most people, however, agree with the assumptions that have been stated so far: that communication is a dynamic process; that the communication process is a transaction that will affect both the sender and the receiver; and that communication is a personal, symbolic process requiring a shared code or codes of abstractions. Beyond these basic shared assumptions, communication theorists differ on how they are willing to define *communication*.

The basic disagreements revolve around the notion of *intent*. Does communication have to be an intentional behavior designed to produce some effect? People have devised what have been called "source-oriented definitions" that answer this question affirmatively. Such definitions would suggest that communication includes all activities in which a person (the source) intentionally transmits stimuli to evoke a response (Miller, 1966). Miller and Steinberg (1975) state this position even more strongly when they say:

> We have chosen to restrict our discussion of communication to intentional symbolic transactions: those in which at least one of the parties transmits a message to another with the purpose of modifying the other's behavior (such as getting him to do or not to do something or to believe or not to believe something). By our definition, intent to communicate and intent to influence are synonymous. If there is no intent, there is no message. (p. 35)

Attaching the concept of intentionality in this manner tends to make one view all communication activities as instrumental in nature; more specifically, it leads one to view all communication as persuasive. Such a view focuses attention on certain variables in the process, such as the content of a speech or message, the way it is delivered, and its persuasiveness. Much of the writing using such a definition focuses on the production of effective messages.

Another way of viewing communication has brought forth what others have called "receiver-oriented definitions" of communication. These definitions view communication as all activities in which a person (the receiver) responds to a stimulus (Stevens, 1950). Cronkhite (1976) offers a broad definition of *communication* that is similar to the preceding one when he suggests that human communication has occurred when a human being responds to a symbol. He suggests that communication can be produced intentionally or unintentionally and responded to in an intentional or unintentional manner. This definition is so broad that it only rules out nonsymbolic behavior as communication. Cronkhite even suggests that people can communicate with themselves by reading their own writing or listening to their voices on tape.

We do not find these broad definitions of *communication* to be very useful in our examination of the process. They are sometimes so general that *anything* that one does can be called communication. In this book, we are not going to consider any behavior communication unless it involves two or more people. Some people will obviously find fault with that decision. We find no reason to invent terms such as intrapersonal communication or communication with one's self. It is obvious to us that people think, reflect, carry on internal dialogues with themselves, read their own writing, or listen to themselves on tape. But to call these activities communication would violate the assumptions about communication that we hold. Obviously, intrapersonal variables are important factors in how one communicates. We can think things over and convince ourselves, but that is really not how we prefer to use the term *communication*.

We do not, however, dismiss definitions that emphasize the receiver out-of-hand. Such definitions place emphasis on how the receiver perceives and interprets symbolic behavior. In fact, we devote a great deal of this text to such an analysis. Source-oriented definitions have been criticized as too narrow because they exclude nonintentional, but nevertheless message-carrying activities. Receiver-oriented definitions have been criticized because they fail to make a distinction between communication and other kinds of behavior. A source-oriented view stresses certain variables, such as effective production, whereas the receiver-oriented definitions stress different variables, such as the receiver and the meaning a message has for him or her. Surely both approaches can be of value to the student of communication.

An examination of Fig. 1.1 might help in developing our view of communication:

In Figure 1.1 we have no difficulty in labeling Cell A as communication. Most definitions of communication would agree that when a source intends to direct symbolic behavior toward someone and a receiver perceives that intent was present, we can say that there has been communication. Please note that *this does not mean that either party has to agree on the nature of the intent of the communica-*

	Source has an intent to communicate	Source does not have an intent to communicate
Receiver perceives an intent to communicate	A. Communication	B. Ascribed communication
Receiver does not perceive an intent to communicate	C. Communication attempt	D. Behavior

Figure 1.1. Communication and Intention Matrix

tion. A source might be attempting to share information (intent) while the receiver might believe that the source was attempting to be coercive (perceived intent). Obviously, there will be communication problems in such an event. Such a situation, however, would be consistent with our notion of communication.

We also have little trouble dismissing Cell D as communication. If you do not intend to communicate with another and that person does not perceive such an intent on your part, none of the conditions of communication have been met. If you pass someone in the hall and do not intend to communicate and that person does not perceive that you intended to communicate, you have simply passed in the hall. Some behavior occurred, but it had no symbolic meaning to either party.

The other two cells in the diagram present more difficulty. In Cell B the communicator does not intend to communicate, but someone else believes such an intent was present. Receiver-oriented approaches would definitely say that such an event was communication. People ascribed meaning to some symbol. The source-oriented people would deny such an assertion. We are not going to argue as to whether or not that such a situation is communication. You can decide for yourself. We do know that such situations are common and can cause problems for people and can alter the nature of their future communication. Many nonverbal behaviors occur below the level of awareness of people; however, other people ascribe meanings to them. If you frown, fail to recognize someone, say things in a strange way, or any number of other things, it can affect the receiver's perceptions of you and your motives. To the extent that you are oblivious to these personal traits, you are likely to have difficulties with people, and those problems can affect the communication relationship. *The problems are a lack of awareness or lack of understanding of how your behaviors affect others.* People who wish to be effective communicators must become more sensitive to the impact of their behaviors (whether intentional or not) on other people. We can maximize the behaviors that we know are effective, or live with the negative results of behaviors that tend to be perceived as negative and/or inappropriate.

Cell C also presents a problem for us. Obviously, an attempt to communicate has been made, but whether such an attempt would meet everyone's definition of communication is not all that important to us. Clearly, this area deserves study because people need to learn strategies for using communication for instrumental purposes. The *problem in this situation is failure to be understood.* We will spend a considerable amount of time, especially in Chapter 4, differentiating between failure to understand and failure to be understood. These failures require different communication strategies to correct the problem. Let us just note that *if* the purpose of the communication event was *purely consummatory* in nature, the source might not care whether the receiver perceived intent even if the source did; the event or the act of communicating itself could satisfy the source. Obviously, such a situation occurs rarely, and receivers are likely to perceive that some intent was there, or no communication would have occurred in their presence.

So, in summary, we think the question of intent and perceived intent is important to the extent that it focuses on problems that can be solved with different communication strategies. We believe situations represented by Cells A, B, and C deserve our attention as we explore the process of effective communication. Perhaps we would be wise to briefly state our definition of communication:

> 2 = Communication is symbolic behavior that occurs between two or more participating individuals. It has the characteristics of being a process, it is transactional in nature, and it is affective. It is a purposive, goal-directed behavior that can have instrumental or consummatory ends.

Models of Communication

By now it should be obvious that even though communication is too often taken for granted as a simple, daily part of the lives of all of us, complexities do emerge. Although communication has been defined and its characteristics described, we still need to suggest *a method for focusing on the analysis* of the structures and functions of human communication. It will probably be helpful to represent communication in the form of a model, thereby enabling us to visualize and analyze different aspects of the process.

A model, as we will use the term in this book, is a visual representation. Just as a map of the world—a model illustrating the continents, oceans, and mountains—helps us to conceptualize the relationships of one to the other, a communication model can be a helpful, if symbolic, representation of this process.

One of the difficulties involved in constructing and using a model of a process is that we must freeze and isolate the elements involved. In our earlier example of the digestive process, we alluded to the problems of just diagramming the various organs or elements involved in digestion. Such a model does not show the process in action. A model by its nature is a static representation that arrests a process at one point. A model is also an abstraction, and simplification is inherent in abstracting. This presents another problem. In proposing a model of communication, we are, no doubt, presenting an oversimplified view of a very complex process. We have seen how many elements are involved in some simple communication activities. It would be impossible to represent all of the elements of communication in one model.

Despite the limitations inherent in models and the difficulty involved in using them, there are many good reasons to use models in an analysis of the communication process. Models help focus one's attention on various aspects of the process. This can be a useful teaching device, for it allows one to consider what a specific model includes and what others leave out. Models can also be used in practical ways to analyze real problems and prevent the occurrence of future problems. Just as economic models can be used to formulate national policy, communication models can be used to suggest methods of solving or avoiding problems. It is also possible to change various elements of models to test ways that such a change might affect other elements. It is possible to make such predictions and experiment with the relationships between elements in models in ways that are impossible in real situations. A model may also serve as a subjective view of the process, expressing one person's unique way of viewing communication. Moreover, models allow one to visualize and analyze separate parts of the process that may be difficult to analyze in other ways. In fact, the very simplification that we cited as a drawback is also an asset. Models are used to clarify and simplify complex systems. Models can use an observer's perspective and, with it, the capacity to understand why communication problems occur and how they can be avoided.

Different models have greater or lesser use in different situations. One model may be very adequate for studying one function of communication whereas we may find another perspective is better when analyzing another function. A visual representation can often assist us in conceptualizing what we thought was a complex process. Many people have provided insights on the nature of communication that provide a beginning point in identifying the necessary elements and provide questions that must be answered in order to develop models of human communication. We will briefly discuss two of those people who have obviously made contributions and influenced later attempts to construct communication models.

The Greek philosopher Aristotle was very concerned with communication. He examined and labeled several basic elements of the communication process, which were later expanded into a classical model. For Aristotle, the key elements in the process were simply the speaker, the speech, and the audience.

Aristotle focused on rhetorical communication, or the art of persuasive speaking, because this was a necessary skill in his day—used in the courts, the legislature, and the popular assemblies. Because all of these forms of public speaking involved persuasion, Aristotle was interested in discovering the most effective means of persuasion in speech.

According to Aristotle, the factors that played a role in determining the persuasive effects of a speech were its contents, its arrangement, and the manner in which it was delivered. Aristotle was also aware of the role of the audience. "Persuasion is effected through the audience," he said, "when they are brought by the speech into a state of emotion" (Cooper, 1960). Other elements that effected persuasion included the character (*ethos*) of the speaker and the arguments he made in the speech.

In 1948, Harold Laswell, a social scientist, proposed a model of communication that analyzed the process in terms of the functions performed by it in human societies. Laswell isolated and defined three definite functions: (1) *Surveillance* of the environment, alerting members of a community to dangers and opportunities in the environment. (2) *Correlation* of the different parts of society in making a response to the environment. (3) *Transmission* of the social heritage from one generation to another.

Laswell maintained that there were groups of specialists who were responsible for carrying out these functions. For example, political leaders and diplomats belong to the first group of surveyors of the environment. Educators, journalists, and speakers help correlate or gather the responses of the people to new information. Family members and school educators pass on the social heritage.

Laswell (1948) recognized that not all communication is "two-way," with a smooth flow of information and feedback occurring between sender and receiver. In our complex society, much information is filtered through message controllers—editors, censors, or propagandists—who receive the information and then pass it on to the public with some modifications or distortions. According to Laswell, one vital function of communication is to provide information about other world powers because we as a nation depend on communication as a means of preserving our own strength. Therefore, he concludes, it is essential for an organized society to discover and control any factors that may interfere with efficient communication. He suggested that a simple way to describe the communication process was to answer the following questions:

Who
Says What
In Which Channel
To Whom
With What Effect?

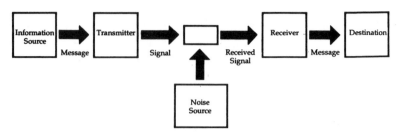

Figure 1.2. The Shannon-Weaver Model

An Information-Centered Model of Communication

Many models of communication have been concerned with how information passes from one point to another. Probably the best known of the models was developed by Shannon and Weaver (1949). Shannon was an engineer at Bell Telephone, and he was concerned with the accurate transmission of messages over the telephone. Weaver extended Shannon's concept to apply to all types of communication.

Perhaps you remember playing a game called "Telephone" when you were a child. A message was passed from child to child, and the information in the message was usually quite distorted when it arrived at the last person in the chain. The Shannon-Weaver model is concerned with the same problem: accurate message transmission. It envisions a source who encodes or creates a message and transmits it through a channel to a receiver who decodes or recreates the message (see Figure 1.2).

A key concept introduced in the Shannon-Weaver model is *noise*— that is, any additional and unwanted stimuli that can disrupt the accuracy of the message being transmitted. Noise can be the static interference on a phone call or loud music at a party or a siren outside one's window. According to Shannon and Weaver, noise is always present in the channel to be picked up by the receiver along with the message. Communication experts have extended this concept to include "psychological" as well as physical noise. Psychological noise refers to the interference of a person's own thoughts and feelings that disrupt the accurate reception of a message. We have all experienced moments when our daydreams (psychological noise) have caused us to miss a message completely.

The Shannon-Weaver model is fundamentally a linear model of communication that visualizes communication as a one-way process. Because communication is a transactional process, as we have repeatedly said, this model has some problems in application. Even if one were to add feedback from receiver to source, this representation still ignores much of the simultaneity and transactive nature of the process of communication. Moreover, this model does not deal with the different contexts in which communication can occur. It probably has some drawbacks in the contexts of the small group, public speaking, and mass communication. Another problem with this model is that it fails to specify attributes of the source, message, channel, and receiver that might be important in the total process of communication.

The SMCR Model

David Berlo (1960) proposed a model that emphasized how attributes of the four major elements (source, message, channel, and receiver) affect communication. This SMCR model solves some of the problems of the Shannon-Weaver model by such an inclusion.

As defined by Berlo, the *source* is the creator of the message—that is, some group or person with a reason for engaging in communication. The message is the translation of ideas into a symbolic code, such as language or gestures; the channel is the medium through which the message is carried; and the receiver is the person (or group) who is the target of communication.

Berlo's model also specifies the need for encoders and decoders in the communication process. The encoder is responsible for expressing the source's purpose in the form of a message. In face-to-face situations, the encoding function is performed by the vocal mechanisms, muscle systems, and other artifacts such as appearance, dress, and environment that produce verbal and nonverbal messages. However, it is possible to separate the encoder from the source. Although we have been serving as the source of communication in preparing the text, typewriter, typesetters, and a host of other people have assisted in the final encoding or message production. The decoding mechanism operates in a similar manner. In most instances, the decoder is the set of sensory skills of the receiver. In

certain situations, however, decoders are present in the process that
are not the intended receivers. In large organizations, people can be
responsible for decoding messages prior to passing them to executives. Often only message summaries will be sent to people whom
one desires to receive a message in its entirety.

In face-to-face, small-group, and public-address situations, the
channel is the air through which sound waves travel. In mass communication, there are many channels: television, radio, newspapers,
books, and magazines. Berlo's model also describes some personal
factors that may have an affect on the communication process.
These elements are the communication skills, attitudes, knowledge,
social system, and cultural environment of both the source and the
receiver.

The SMCR can be criticized on many of the same grounds that we
earlier used to suggest problems with the Shannon-Weaver model.
This model again is concerned with transmitting information from
one source to a receiver. The effects of feedback are minimized in
the model, and the simultaneous behavior of people as sources and
receivers is not adequately covered. In fairness to Berlo, he does
recognize these notions in his work, but his model fails to account
fully for the dynamic nature of communication. This model also has
limited utility in dealing with communication in different contexts.
This model represents a beginning point, however, and we have
chosen to organize Part I of this book around some of the elements
contained in this model. We can examine source and receiver attributes, behaviors, and perceptions and analyze their effects on the
process of communication. The next four chapters will do just that.
As we move into different contexts and functions, we will apply
models that we think are more useful.

The Westley-MacLean Model

We want to end our discussion of models by including a model
of communication that has been widely used in different contexts.
This model is useful because it demonstrates the utility of developing more complex models that handle communication in various
situations. Westley and MacLean (1957) formulated a model that

covered both dyadic and mass communication and also included feedback as an integral part of the communication process. In fact, one of the distinctions that Westley and MacLean make between dyadic (or two people) and mass communication depends primarily on differences in feedback. In face-to-face communication, there is immediate feedback from the receiver. Many kinds of stimuli pass between the receiver and the source in dyadic communication, and the source has the advantage of learning the receiver's responses almost immediately.

In mass communication, feedback is usually delayed and minimized. This is simple to understand if you picture a typical mass communication situation, such as a televised presidential speech. The president may be successful in delivering his message to millions of viewers, but he receives no immediate feedback from his listeners because he can neither see nor hear their reactions. The feedback or reaction of the receivers to this message may be delayed for days or weeks until the general reaction of the public has been recorded. But even this is minimized feedback because each individual's reactions are unknown to the source.

Basically there are five elements in the Westley-MacLean model: objects of orientation, a message, a source, a receiver, and feedback. The source (A) focuses on a particular object or event in the environment (X) and creates a message about it (X') which is transmited to a receiver (B). The receiver, in turn, sends feedback (f_{BA}) about the message to the source (see Figure 1.3).

In a mass communication situation, Westley and MacLean (1957) add another element, C (see Figure 1.4). C is a "gatekeeper" or opinion leader who receives messages (X') from the sources of mass media (A_S) or focuses on objects of orientation (X_3, X_4) in the environment. Using this information, the gatekeeper then creates his or her own message (X), which is then transmitted to the receiver (B). This provides a kind of filtering system, because the receivers do not get their information directly from a source, but rather from a person who selects information from many sources. For example, if you had an interest in animal communication, you might read several books and watch a few television documentaries about the subject. During a conversation with a friend, you might mention

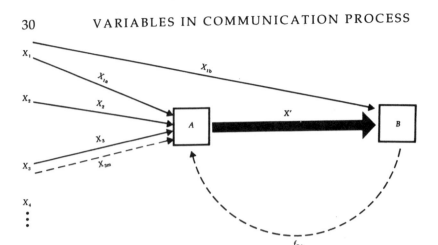

Figure 1.3. The Westley-MacLean Model for Dyadic Communication

something about an experiment to teach chimpanzees to use sign language. In doing this, you are filtering information. But, more importantly, you are providing your friend with an extended environment because you are making your friend focus on an object of orientation that was not in his or her environment or that was previously unnoticed. In mass communication, feedback may flow in three directions: from the receiver to the gatekeeper, from the receiver to the mass media source, and from the opinion leader to the mass media source.

Westley and MacLean do not confine their model to the level of the individual. In fact, they stress that the receiver may be a group or social institution. According to Westley and MacLean, any individual, group, or system has a need to send and receive messages as a means of orientation to the environment.

The Westley and MacLean (1957) model encompasses several important concepts: feedback, the differences and similarities of interpersonal and mass communication, and the importance of opinion leaders as an additional element in mass communication.

All of these models have different levels of utility, depending on the situation. All stress the importance of people and the symbolic behavior they use in the communication process. We now turn to a chapter-by-chapter analysis of the elements of communication

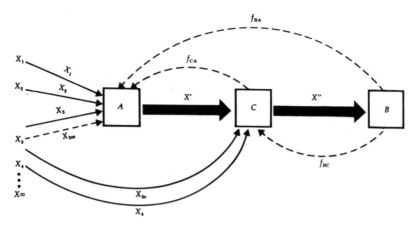

Figure 1.4. Westley-MacLean Model for Mass Communication

Summary

1. Communication is a pervasive activity that serves many important functions in a society and in our personal lives. The process of communication enables people to exert control over their environment.

2. There are several common conceptions about communication that *we do not believe*: (a) all problems are problems of communication, (b) all problems can be solved by more or better communication, (c) communication is without costs, (d) communication often breaks down, (e) communication is either good or bad, and (f) the study of communication is about producing more effective messages.

3. Communication is a process that is constantly changing. Moreover, when you stop the process, communication no longer exists.

4. Communication is transactional in that when one element in the process is changed, changes in all elements can occur. The source and the receiver constantly are having an impact on each other through symbolic behavior.

5. Communication involves subjective evaluations, and it is affective. Emotional responses affect the way we communicate with others and, in turn, how others communicate with us.

6. Communication is a process that involves a shared code, or codes, of verbal and nonverbal symbols. The meanings of symbols

are in the people who use them, not in the symbols themselves; meanings are in people.

7. Communication is instrumental in that we use it as a tool to affect other people and to control our environment. It is a strategic activity that we use to serve a variety of purposes. Communication can also have a consummatory purpose in that the act of communication itself can provide satisfaction to a communicator. Most communication events can have both consummatory and instrumental purposes.

8. Communication may be defined from the perspective of either a source or a receiver. Source-oriented definitions include as communication any activity in which a source deliberately transmits stimuli to evoke a response. Receiver-oriented definitions include as communication any activity in which the receiver responds to a stimulus. A source-oriented view focuses on the production of effective messages by the speaker. A receiver-oriented view focuses on the message's meaning to the receiver.

9. The question of whether communication has to be intentional or not is important. When the receiver has an intent to communicate and the receiver perceives such an intent, we have no trouble calling that communication. When there is not an intent to communicate on the part of the source and the receiver perceives no intent, we have no trouble in calling that noncommunication behavior. It is more difficult to decide in other cases. When a source has no intent to communicate but a receiver perceives there is one, we have ascribed communication and a failure to understand. When a source has intent to communicate that is not perceived by the receiver, we have a communication attempt and a failure to be understood.

10. A model is a visual representation that helps us conceptualize the relationship of various elements involved in a process such as communication. Models, by their nature, are simplified abstractions that isolate the elements and freeze the action of a process. Although models present a distorted view of a process, they are helpful because they can clarify complex systems.

11. From Aristotle's writings it is possible to extrapolate a classical model of rhetorical communication that contains three elements: the speaker, the message, and the audience. Aristotle also maintained that the construction of the message and the character of the speaker played an important part in persuading an audience.

12. According to Laswell (1948), communication has three functions: surveillance of the environment, correlation of different social groups, and transmission of the social heritage. Laswell describes communication with the following questions: Who/Says What/In Which Channel/To Whom/With What Effect?

13. The Shannon-Weaver model is concerned with the accurate transmission of a message. This model presents a source who sends a message through a channel to a receiver. *Noise* is any additional stimuli in the channel that can disrupt the accurate reception of the message.

14. Berlo's (1960) SMCR model contains four major elements: source, message, channel, and receiver. This model also focuses on the encoding and decoding functions that take place during communication. It specifies five personal factors that will affect communicators: their communication skills, attitudes, knowledge, social system, and cultural environment.

15. In the Westley-MacLean model, the source (A) creates a message (X') about an object of orientation (X) in his or her environment. The source then sends the message to a receiver (B) who transmits feedback (fBA) about the message to the source. This model introduces a filter system in mass communication situations. A gatekeeper (C) selects information from the many sources of mass media (As) or from objects in his or her environment (Xs), creates a message, and sends it to other people (Bs).

Note

1. Although we have seen some of these myths recently appearing in other books, *we* would like to acknowledge our scholarly debt to Dr. Michael Scott, from whom we first heard these enumerated.

References

Berlo, D. K. (1960). *The process of communication*. New York: Holt, Rinehart & Winston.
Boulding, K. E. (1956). *The image: Knowledge in life and society*. Ann Arbor: University of Michigan Press.
Cooper, L. (1960). *Rhetoric of Aristotle*. New York: Appleton-Century-Crofts.
Cronkhite, G. (1976). *Communication and awareness*. Menlo Park, CA: Cummings.

Dance, F. E. X., & Larson, C. E. (1976). *The functions of human communication—A theoretical approach.* New York: Holt, Rinehart & Winston.

Fabun, D. (1968). *Communications, the transfer of meaning.* Beverly Hills, CA: Glenco.

Laswell, H. D. (1948). The structure and function of communication in society. In L. Bryson (Ed.), *The communication of ideas* (pp. 37-51). New York: Harper & Row.

McCroskey, J. C. (1972). *An introduction to rhetorical communication* (2nd ed.). Englewood Cliffs, NJ: Prentice Hall.

Miller, G. R. (1966). On defining communication: Another stab. *Journal of Communication, 26,* 88-89.

Miller, G. R., & Steinberg, M. (1975). *Between people.* Palo Alto, CA: Science Research Associates.

Shannon, C. E., & Weaver, W. (1949). *The mathematical theory of communication.* Urbana: University of Illinois Press.

Stevens, S. S. (1950). Introduction: A definition of communication. *Journal of the Acoustical Society of America, 22,* 687.

Watzlawick, P., Beavin, J., & Jackson, D. (1967). *Pragmatics of human communication.* New York: Norton.

Westley, B. H., & MacLean, M. S., Jr. (1957). A conceptual model for communication research. *Journalism Quarterly, 34,* 31-38.

2

Source Variables

Henry David Thoreau wrote, "It takes two to speak the truth— one to speak, and another to hear." In emphasizing this view of communication, Thoreau pointed out the interdependence of the participants in the process. Each participant in the process of communication affects and is affected by the other people involved. This chapter and the next are devoted to an analysis of variables that affect people engaged in communication. Because the source and receiver are so interdependent and do mutually affect one another, it might seem to some that devoting one chapter to source variables and the other to receiver variables is at best arbitrary. In most situations, people play a variety of roles and often act as both source and receiver. People are constantly sending messages and, in turn, being bombarded with communication. In a typical trans- action, it is probably not at all clear who might be called a source and who might be called a receiver. *We think it is valuable, however, to attempt to isolate some of the variables that operate when we judge the attributes of a communicator.* Even if the distinction between source and receiver is somewhat artificial, it is useful to consider how other people judge us when we attempt to communicate with them. In the final analysis, a speaker's effectiveness is a judgment made by the receiver.

At first glance, the situation seems a dispiriting one. A speaker can certainly work to improve the content and delivery of a public speech: A careful outline can be prepared, research on the accuracy and completeness of the facts can be accomplished, a thorough analysis of the audience may be conducted, and one can practice the words that will be spoken. People in dyadic and small-group communication situations can spend time and effort being concerned and informed communicators. People in mass media institutions can spend millions of dollars attempting to communicate effectively. But what can people do to insure that listeners will believe that they are speaking skillfully? Can sources influence the way the receivers of communication perceive them?

A careful study of source variables in communication indicates that there are steps that speakers can take (short of plastic surgery and complete personality rehabilitation) to enhance other's perceptions of them as effective communicators. People can adapt their communication strategies in ways that will increase the likelihood of being perceived positively by their intended receivers. The *situation* is obviously an important determinant of the kinds of behavior required on the part of the source to be perceived as an effective communicator. People must behave differently when talking with one person or a few people as compared with their behavior when making a speech to a large group of people. Moreover, the *function* that sources wish their communication to serve affects strategies designed to impress receivers positively. For example, one desired outcome of a communicator might be to persuade another to change his or her behavior. At another time, the same communicator may intend to create a favorable impression on a new acquaintance. Although these are both attempts to influence others, strategies involved in persuading people to modify their behavior differ from those used in making new friends. Although there are many different variables that will affect perceptions of the source of communication, there are also many regularities in the way people judge communicators.

Certain judgments are made about communicators regardless of the context or function of communication. This chapter will examine some of the common judgments that receivers make about communicators.

This examination of source variables reveals problems that people face in most communication situations, while at the same time suggesting some solutions to these problems and setting out guidelines to achieve more effective communication. We will examine how people judge the credibility of a communicator and make some suggestions as to how one can be perceived as more credible and, therefore, more effective as a communicator across contexts. We will also examine how judgments of similarity and dissimilarity affect the communication process. Suggestions on how optimal levels of perceived similarity can positively affect communication will be offered. Finally, we will examine two different perspectives on the effects of power in communication and the sources of power that people can evoke that are important predictors of communication effectiveness.

Credibility

We are all aware that some people are more effective communicators than others. Many times the reasons for this effectiveness are not readily apparent to the people involved. When people can persuade others, or are naturally likable, or are able to settle disputes, they are usually held in high regard by others. When we cannot explain why these people have the impact they do, we often claim that they simply possess "charisma." Because it is hard to identify those variables that make one person charismatic, the use of a word such as *charisma* is not very helpful to those of us who wish to obtain greater understanding of human communication. It is also difficult to help someone become more charismatic, and thus a more effective communicator. Therefore, we must look at specific attributes of sources, including their communication behaviors, to understand the meaning of this ambiguous term.

From antiquity to the present, scholars have recognized that people make decisions about a source that promote or inhibit effective communication. Aristotle claimed that *ethos*, or the quality we call "credibility," is a critical and potent characteristic that a source must possess in order to be an effective persuader. Plato, Cicero, and Quintilian all wrote of the importance of source credibility, but differed somewhat in their definitions of that quality.

A considerable amount of experimental research attests to the importance of source credibility in the communication transaction. Sources with high credibility are more effective in producing a variety of desired outcomes than those with low credibility. In fact, the credibility of a communicator may be the best single predictor of the course or direction of most communication transactions. Of course, no communicator possesses an inherent quality called credibility. Source credibility, similar to beauty, is something that exists "in the eye of the beholder." *The receiver must confer credibility on a speaker, or it does not exist.* Because credibility is a perceived phenomenon, suggestions for establishing or enhancing this quality depend on many situational and personal variables.

There are numerous characteristics that sources bring to all their communication transactions. These characteristics include such qualities as gender, age, ethnicity, and socioeconomic status (SES). Some of these characteristics, or at least the way they are perceived, may not be within the source's control. All receivers are unique individuals, and the way they perceive a source is based on their previous communication experiences. Despite his exemplary performance during the Gulf War, a racially prejudiced person may be incapable of perceiving Colin Powell, Chairman of the Joint Chiefs of Staff, as a highly credible source. In the movie *Twins*, Danny DeVito perceived his twin brother, Arnold Schwartzenegger, as tall, whereas Patrick Ewing, who is more than 7 feet tall, probably would not share this perception. In other words, two people, when talking to the same person, may respond to that person quite differently as a result of their prior experience and individual perceptions. Nevertheless, research demonstrates that a speaker can, to some extent, control these factors and thereby become a more effective communicator. Knowledge of the way a receiver perceives a speaker's credibility can provide helpful insights into the communication process.

Dimensions of Source Credibility

Contemporary communication scholars have systematically analyzed what constitutes a credible speaker. Results indicate that people tend to evaluate a communication source on at least five specific dimensions (McCroskey, Jensen, & Valencia, 1973). Two of these dimensions—*competence*, or the source's knowledge of the subject, and *character*, or the apparent trustworthiness of the source—were identified by early writers and have withstood the test of time. Recent research supports the importance of these two dimensions and also suggests that people evaluate a speaker's credibility on the basis of his or her composure, sociability, and extroversion.

Each of these dimensions acts independently to influence the source's effectiveness as a communicator. For example, it is possible to decide that a person has great expertise on a particular topic and still believe that he or she is untrustworthy. Similarly, a person can be very likable and composed but be judged by others as having little competence on a specific subject. In any given situation, one decision may be more important than the others and be a better predictor of communication effectiveness. In a social situation, you may not care whether a person is extremely knowledgeable about Elizabethan drama so long as you enjoy talking with the person. However, if you are injured, it may matter little if your doctor is sociable and outgoing; you simply want someone who is competent to treat your broken arm.

The Dimension of Competence. It is common in most communication situations for a receiver to judge a source's competence on the subject being discussed. In fact, research indicates that perceptions of competence may be the single most important predictor of how people differentiate between credible and noncredible sources (Berlo, Lemert, & Mertz, 1969; McCroskey et al., 1973). This is especially true in those situations in which the function of communication is to persuade or inform. If a speaker is not perceived to be competent or knowledgeable on a topic, it makes little difference how trustworthy, composed, sociable, or extroverted he or she happens to be; people will remain unpersuaded and uninformed. If the function of communication is the development of social relationships, perceived competence of the source may be less important. However, there is evidence to suggest that, in general, knowledgeable people are often sought out for interactions. People make judgments about competence along a variety of dimensions, such as level of education, accessibility to current or pertinent information, or direct experience with the subject of interest. Whether or not receivers themselves are competent to judge the source's competence makes little difference; they will inevitably make such a judgment, and it will affect their communication. Overall, speakers who can increase other's perceptions of their competence have a higher probability of being effective in a variety of communication situations.

There are a number of ways sources may increase their perceived competence. In public speaking situations, it is common for speakers to be introduced to the audience by another person. If the person making the introduction refers to the speaker's title, such as doctor or professor, or labels the speaker as "a leading expert," this may enhance the audience's perception of the source's competence. Speakers may also indicate expertise on a topic by referring to previous experience with the subject, by mentioning other highly competent people with whom they are associated, by careful preparation, or by skillful use of evidence. Communicators must walk a very fine line when making reference to their own competence. Generally speaking, receivers are put off by speakers who "toot their own horn" in attempts to establish perceptions of competence. It is more effective to have others establish the speaker's competence. Speakers who are forced to establish their own competence must use subtle means, so as not to appear as though they are bragging. To do so runs the risk of creating a "boomerang effect" in which the audience attributes less competence to the speaker.

If receivers perceive a source to be low in competence, there is little likelihood that the speaker will be effective, regardless of his or her actual expertise on the subject being discussed. A good example of this involves a group of students who were invited to hear a lecture on life among the Ashanti. The speaker, an Anglo woman, was given an introduction specifically designed to ensure that she was perceived as competent; the audience was told that the source was born in Africa and raised among the Ashanti. Nevertheless, the predominantly African American audience was extremely unreceptive. The speaker was thoroughly familiar with the African experience of the Ashanti. She could converse easily and at length with the Ashanti people about shared cultural experiences; in fact, the native Africans perceived her to be "one of them" despite her skin color. But the audience of African American students had a very different perception of her competence to speak on what *they perceived to be the* "African experience." Communication was difficult because although the speaker knew what it was like to be an Ashanti, she did not know what it was like to be an African American, and the audience doubted her competence to speak on the announced topic.

Clearly, the woman's skin color was not in her control, but she could have taken steps to change the audience's perceptions. For example, she might have been perceived as more competent if she had directly confronted the situation and admitted to the audience that she did not understand the African American experience but could provide information about Africa that might be of interest. Sometimes an admission of lack of competence in one area is perceived as an indication of other kinds of competence.

Many research studies have demonstrated the importance of perceived competence. A great deal of that research has been done on the persuasion function of communication, and we will discuss that research in Chapter 6. Suffice it to say, however, that when people attribute messages to sources whom they consider highly credible, more attitude change will occur. In classic studies, the same voice and the same persuasive message have been attributed to a highly competent source (e.g., the surgeon general, a doctor, a research professor) or to a source of low competence (e.g., a high school student, a convict). In these studies, the message has been considerably more persuasive when the people believed it was from a highly competent source. Of course, the social position of doctor or convict does not in and of itself connote a competent or incompetent source. The persuasiveness of a message is enhanced when the content of the message matches those particular qualities of the source. For example, a doctor may be perceived as a very competent source when addressing the issue of cancer related to smoking cigarettes, and persuasiveness will be enhanced. If the doctor's attempts to persuade an audience concern conflicts that occur in prison, however, his or her perceived competence should be less than that of a convict. In other situations, it has been shown that people direct more communication toward people they perceive to be competent and are more willing to receive communication from such persons. Moreover, people who are perceived as competent are likely to emerge as leaders in group situations. Obviously, perceived competence is an important variable that affects communication situations.

In most situations, a source cannot be perceived as "too competent." An ideal source would be one who is highly competent to discuss the topic under consideration. The perception of competence, however, is itself a multidimensional process involving several variables. For example, a nuclear physicist heading a research project may be so brilliant that effectively expressing ideas to subordinates is difficult. In such a instance, the research assistants may perceive the physicist as highly competent on one dimension (mastery of subject matter) but incompetent on another (ability to express ideas). On the basis of this example, one might caution speakers to determine carefully those variables most important to their audiences if they are to be effective.

The Dimension of Character. The popular rejoinder "You're a good man, Charlie Brown," is an estimate of character perceived as goodness, decency, or trustworthiness. The dimension of character has a strong influence on a receiver's perception of source credibility. The term *credibility gap*, popularized in the early 1960s, refers almost solely to this dimension. Government officials were saying one thing, and later press accounts indicated they were doing the opposite. Recent problems in government have made people generally skeptical about the character of our national leaders. Colonel Oliver North, an adviser to President Reagan on matters of national security, was convicted of perjury for his testimony before a Senate committee investigating alleged government involvement in illegal arms deals with Iran. Incidents such as this explain why political leaders often have to adapt their communication strategies to put more stress on the character dimension, and much political rhetoric is aimed at changing people's images of the trustworthiness of elected leaders.

When people believe a communicator to be of low character or trustworthiness, they are less likely to listen to, let alone be influenced by, the message. Many people will terminate conversations or avoid situations in which they might be forced to communicate with someone who does not meet their personal standards of character. To some extent, we judge competence on the basis of objective qualifications (education, work experience, and other credentials), but perceptions of character are most often highly personal judgments about the source. Those judgments can be based upon first-hand experience with the source, but often judgments are made before any direct contact.

In Gallup polls taken throughout the 1960s, 1970s, and 1980s, CBS newscaster Walter Cronkite was repeatedly identified by respondents as "the most trusted man in the United States." One can only speculate as to the reasons for these findings. People obviously felt that he was an honest reporter who did not bias the news he reported with his own feelings and whose character could not be compromised. Therefore, when Cronkite said one thing and the government said another, the position reported by Cronkite would probably be believed by the majority of people who heard both massages.

Another former network newscaster created some controversy when he appeared in a commercial for an airline. Executives from the airline probably did not believe the newscaster would be seen as competent to discuss the construction of airplanes; however, they were betting the American people believed him to be of high character and would be persuaded by the commercials. Other newscasters criticized this arrangement, claiming that his lack of objectivity concerning the airline would damage the perceived objectivity of all newscasters. In fact, newscasters have turned down lucrative assignments to avoid having to do commercials as part of their duties.

The question of how to establish and maintain perceptions of high character is difficult to answer. Obviously, any past experience that calls into question a person's integrity reduces perceived character. People who change their positions on issues over time can be seen as less trustworthy, even if the change itself is a reasonable one. It is doubtful that an ideal source would be anything other than of high character. Obviously, the best advice for ensuring perceptions of high character is to be consistently honest. To the extent that people are perceived to be of high character, they will be more effective communicators. It is certainly a goal worth seeking.

The Dimension of Composure. A person who is composed, especially under conditions of considerable stress, is perceived to be more credible than a person who lacks composure. Research indicates that a speaker who is nervous or produces a number of nonfluencies (stammering and "uhs" and "ers") is less credible and less able to persuade others (Miller & Hewgill, 1964). Some public speaking students are immediately perceived as more credible in the early part of the course because they are composed during the stressful first speeches. Many people we perceive as "good public speakers" are not more competent or of higher character but are more composed.

To increase one's perceived composure, the novice public speaker can practice delivery to reduce nonfluencies and apparent nervousness. Fidgeting, shuffling of papers, and other distracting behavior often reduce a speaker's perceived composure. In American culture, extreme displays of emotion are also perceived as lack of poise. Many political commentators attribute Senator Muskie's defeat in the presidential primaries of 1972 to a moment when he lost his composure and publicly cried because of newspaper attacks on his wife. It is hard to predict, however, the effect that an individual instance of lack of composure will have. The environment in which these events occur may greatly alter the outcome. We obviously do not expect our friends to be totally composed at all times, nor do they necessarily become less credible to us because they occasionally emote instead of reason. In fact, few of us would be attracted to someone who was totally composed in all circumstances. However, we probably would not be happy with a person who could not retain composure when the situation called for it. Much research suggests that we value the ability to remain composed and that in many, but not all, communication situations the composed communicator is more effective.

The Dimension of Sociability. Sources that project likableness to their receivers are regarded as sociable. If you think about it, this makes perfect sense. People who like each other tend to spend more time communicating with each other and are more likely to be influenced by each other. Research shows that our interpersonal communication contacts are very influential in shaping and changing our attitudes on a variety of issues. Peers influence our political behavior, help determine the products we consume, and shape our thinking in numerous ways. Recent trends in advertising try to present advocates of consumer products as likable people; much of "image advertising" in politics is also designed to do just this. We tend to like people who give us the feeling that they like and respect us, and we are less likely to be influenced by those who do not. Therefore, we are more likely to attend to and be influenced by those whom we perceive as sociable.

There is more to sociability than just interpersonal liking. Although we may not have a friendship with, or a deep liking for, a person, if that person is cooperative and friendly in task situations, he or she will be perceived as more sociable. People who go about their work in a cheerful, friendly manner are likely to be preferred co-workers. All of these things combine to make a person appear to be more approachable and communicative. In all likelihood, people whom we consider unsociable will not be a part of our communication activities and will have little influence on us.

Many people expect more than just platitudes about being friendly and sociable as ways to be more effective communicators. Most of us would sincerely desire to improve our social relationships and, in effect, be perceived as sociable persons. We think that this function of communication is an extremely important one, and we have devoted an entire chapter to this in Part II of this book. This brief discussion of the dimension of sociability is offered only to stress that it is an important part of how people judge sources of communication.

The Dimension of Extroversion. The outgoing person who engages readily in communication situations is considered to be an extrovert. The person who is talkative and not timid in communication activities is sometimes said to be a dynamic speaker—and *may* be an effective communicator. A person who is too extroverted, however, may talk too much and take over conversations. We have all been in situations in which very dynamic, extroverted people

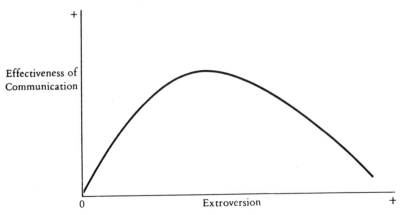

Figure 2.1. Relationship of Extroversion and Communicating Effectiveness

so dominated the scene that we felt like an unnecessary part of the conversation (few who know the authors of this text will believe such a statement). Although the optimum amount of source extroversion varies from receiver to receiver, people generally prefer to communicate with people who possess this attribute in moderation (Burgoon, 1976).

A person who is too introverted may make communication so tedious and effortful that we simply give up. It is hard work to communicate with a person who has little to say. On the other hand, people who show no sensitivity to our need to participate in the communication and are enamored only with the sound of their own voices are not likely to be preferred. We like people who can strike a balance. In most social situations, there is a fine line between being "the life of the party" and "a smashing bore." Figure 2.1 may help clarify the relationship between extroversion and effective communication.

As extroversion increases, people enjoy talking with, and listening to, a dynamic person. An extroverted person holds their attention and is generally interesting. However, at some point—and this point varies with people and situations—increased extroversion annoys people and makes them either dislike the person or withdraw from the situation.

The Dynamics of Source Credibility

Perceptions of a source's credibility are subject to change. Often a source comes to the communication situation with some degree of credibility already established. The degree of credibility perceived in the source prior to any specific communication event is called *initial credibility*. When we say that a speaker's "reputation has preceded him," we are commenting on this initial credibility. For example, a world-famous Arctic explorer talking before a group of professional geographers could expect to have a high degree of initial credibility with this audience. The speaker with a high degree of initial credibility is likely to use a very different communication strategy from that of persons who are seeking to establish or enhance their credibility.

During any communication event, the source's credibility may be reevaluated and either heightened or lowered in the receiver's mind. This assessment or modification of initial credibility is called "transactional credibility." Because people react to many different verbal and nonverbal behaviors, they continually assess a speaker and make evaluative changes during a communication transaction. For example, if an Arctic explorer told an audience of geographers about having a poor sense of direction and having to rely on a hired guide, the audience members would probably reduce their initial perceptions of the speaker's credibility. Sources may also improve their credibility during a transaction by not behaving as expected. Civil behavior on the part of a very militant person may be so unexpected that it catches an audience by surprise and makes the person appear to be very "reasonable" or credible and, therefore, persuasive. What a speaker says and does is continually being processed and evaluated by the people with whom he or she is communicating. If sources are aware of the criteria by which they are being judged, better decisions will be made about what can be done to insure continued perceptions of high credibility.

Terminal credibility is the receiver's perception of a source at the completion of a communication event. For example, if a known militant speaker unexpectedly is polite and composed throughout giving a speech, the audience's evaluation of that person would be different at the end of the speech than at the beginning. The relationship between receiver's expectations regarding a source's communication will be discussed in greater detail in Chapter 6. Suffice to say, all of us have entered a conversation with low regard for someone and left with a completely altered perception. Terminal credibility is important because it will influence a person's initial credibility if that person should communicate again with the same receiver.

People's perceptions of others change between communication events. Receivers might change their attitudes or values and be less receptive to a given source the next time they communicate. It is also possible that external variables will cause a receiver to change the evaluation of a source between communication events. We learn about people by receiving new and different information from other sources; this information may, in turn, alter our perceptions. Sometimes this change is positive and allows us to make more valid judgments, but sometimes we allow rumor and innuendo to alter our perceptions. Therefore, it is important to evaluate the sources of information about other people as well as the people with whom we communicate.

Other things may change a receiver's perception of a source's credibility. A person may have a high terminal credibility in a previous encounter because the topic of conversation was one that he or she was competent to discuss. In the next communication transaction, this same source may discuss a subject about which he or she has little knowledge. This may affect the receiver's perception of the speaker's competence in a negative way. However, a source who had high terminal credibility at an earlier time on a completely different topic may be held in high esteem on unrelated topics. This "halo effect" operates in a variety of situations. For example, a student who writes a good first examination paper may have an easier time in the rest of the course because of the early establishment of credibility. Clearly, credibility is ever-changing between and within communication events, topics, and people. But even though this variable is subject to change, it deserves serious attention from those wishing to be effective communicators.

Source-Receiver Similarity and Communication

Do opposites attract, or does like attract like? This age-old question is related to another perception that people have of communicators. We spent some time thinking about what we were going to call this basis of judgment in this edition of our book for we fear that social scientists have been overzealous in using and sometimes inventing "50-cent words" to replace more commonly used terms. *Homophily* refers to the degree to which interacting individuals are similar in certain attributes. Similar to others, we plead guilty of using this term in an earlier edition of this book and find with some amusement that the term is more properly spelled with a *y* instead of an *i*. We decided, however, to retain the use of the term in this edition because this concept (and spelling) is widely used by educators in our discipline, and we think you might run into it in other places.

Attributes that lead to homophily may include demographic characteristics such as age, education, and socioeconomic status; or they may include attitudes, beliefs, and values. If another person were completely identical to you (which is, of course, impossible), he or she would be completely homophilous with you. Some twins might come close to meeting this definition. At the opposite end of the similarity continuum is *heterophily,* or dissimilarity. The degree to which someone differs from us in various attributes is the degree of heterophily between us.

Because homophily-heterophily involves a variety of attributes, we can be both homophilous and heterophilous with another person at the same time. An electrician and a physician are heterophilous along the dimension of occupation, but homophilous on political attitudes if they both vote Republican and oppose higher taxes. Two college students may be highly homo-philous in terms of age, race, education, status, and background but heterophilous in beliefs if one is convinced that marijuana is physically harmful and the other believes it is completely safe. Their heterophily may involve only one belief or it may involve several. The homophily-heterophily relationship of any two people is highly complex. Knowing their level of similarity on one attribute does not necessarily make it possible to predict their similarity on another.

It is important to recognize that the homophilous or hetero-philous relationship between a source and a receiver is just that—a relationship. Homophily, like credibility, is not something inherent in a source or receiver. It can only be measured by the relationship of the two people involved. The perceptive communicator will understand the need to determine on what attributes a person or people are similar or dissimilar. In the next chapter we spend a consid-erable amount of time discussing methods of such analysis and make suggestions for adapting communications strategies based on those differences. The context in which communication occurs is obviously an important determinant of how much information can be obtained about similarity-dissimilarity. In dyadic contexts it is easier to assess the one other person involved. In public speaking and mass communication contexts, it may be impossible to recog-nize degrees of similarity and dissimilarity on several dimensions with *each* one of the receivers.

Determining Similarity-Dissimilarity

Generally, there are two ways of measuring similarity: one objec-tive and one subjective. An objective measure is the amount of similarity that is apparent to an impartial observer. The same IQ score or the same yearly income would be two objective measure-ments of similarity. Subjective measures, however, are those based on the perceptions of the participants. In any communication trans-action, both source and receiver act in light of their perceptions of each other rather than on some objective indicator of their level of dis-similarity. If sources believe that they have much higher status than their receivers, no amount of objective measurements and observa-tions revealing equality will make the communication relationship similar.

This is not to suggest that subjective and objective measurements of similarity are totally unrelated. In many cases, there is a great deal of agreement between the similarity perceived by an impartial observer and that of the participants in the communication transac-tion. In other cases, however, there are significant differences be-tween subjective and objective measurements. People often overes-timate similarity between themselves and people they like. People engaged in conflict situations may overestimate the amount of difference between themselves and the persons with whom they are having problems. An impartial observer is often valuable in pointing out that the differences between the combatants is not as marked as the participants perceive them to be.

The Relationship of Similarity-Dissimilarity to Communication

The amount of similarity between a source and receiver will affect their communication transactions in two important ways. First, it determines who will communicate with whom, and second, how successful that communication will be. When we have a choice of whom we will communicate with, we tend to choose someone similar to ourselves. People of the same status who live close to each other or who work together interact more (Collins & Guetzkow, 1964). Iowa farmers may talk about agricultural innovation to persons who share similar interests and attitudes (Warland, 1970) whereas inner-city residents may discuss family planning with persons of the same age, family size, and status (Palamore, 1972). This tendency for voluntary communication patterns to be similar makes sense: People who are similar share common interests that provide topics for communication.

As might be expected, similarity may lead to more effective communication (Rogers & Shoemaker, 1971). The degree of effectiveness depends on the degree of similarity. Complete similarity produces a static state; people who are in agreement may have little to talk about. On the other hand, people who are extremely dissimilar may lack the common experiences or vocabulary necessary for effective communication. A Hindu and an American may have difficulty discussing the nutritive value of beef because of their different attitudes toward cows. An industrial executive may be unable to discuss company business with a local plant worker due to a lack of common vocabulary, background, or perspective. The best degree of similarity is, therefore, what has been labeled *optimal heterophily* (Rogers & Shoemaker, 1971). Optimal heterophily is slight dissimilarity. If two people are similar on several attributes but dissimilar on the subject of discussion, they will be more likely

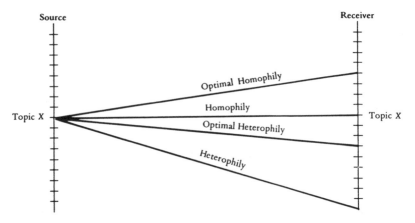

Figure 2.2. Model of Homophily-Heterophily Between Source and Receiver

to communicate effectively. They will have the common ground for understanding with enough difference to produce a dynamic, beneficial interaction. Figure 2.2 illustrates the different possible combinations of similarity.

Another consideration related to optimal heterophily is the relevance of similar and dissimilar attributes. Optimal heterophily need only exist on those attributes that are relevant to the issue of concern. A receiver's age may be a very important characteristic for the source when discussing political views, but a dissimilarity in age is unlikely to affect a discussion of the best types of fishing lures. To insure effective communication, a source should identify relevant attributes and emphasize similarities on these dimensions. This is not a simple task, for what is relevant to one person may be irrelevant to another.

Our perceptions of similarity can also affect our perceptions of the credibility of the source. For example, if we perceive a person to be very dissimilar in terms of amount of knowledge of a topic (i.e., he or she knows more), we are likely to rate that person very high on the competence dimension of credibility. Under such conditions, a dissimilar relationship between source and receiver may be acceptable, even desirable. Dissimilar sources are often consulted for information because of their perceived competence. In many cases, this increased perception of competence based upon differences in sources and receivers facilitates learning and increases the influence of the source.

Thus any notion of what constitutes optimal heterophily must take into account the function that the communication is meant to serve.

We will discuss the relationship between similarity and the development of satisfactory social relationships in detail in a later chapter. In the case of developing friendships and social relationships, communication is more effective when people are similar. There are a variety of ways, which we will discuss later, a person can maximize the probability of developing satisfactory social relationships based upon communication strategies that stress similarities. We also know that people will tend to view people who are similar more positively on some of the other dimensions of source credibility. For example, it makes sense to suggest that most people are more likely to see people who are similar as more sociable and probably more trustworthy.

In summary, dissimilarity and similarity must be considered in terms of what purpose the communication is to serve. Sometimes differences between source and receiver will lead to desirable outcomes such as learning and persuasion. In other cases, people will have more effective communication transactions when interacting with similar individuals.

It appears that if people begin with an optimally heterophilous relationship, communication has a high probability of success. But what about the situations in which the initial relationship is dissimilar? Communication with people from whom we are different cannot be avoided. In fact, many of our daily communication activities can be classified as heterophilous: teacher to student, parent to child, and employer to employee. The problem of heterophilous relationships has long confronted agencies, such as the Peace Corps, that are attempting to bring about social change. How does a clearly dissimilar source convince a Peruvian peasant to adopt water-boiling techniques or Pakistanis to adopt birth control methods? How do you gain acceptance of your grading proposals by a faculty committee or persuade your employer to give you a raise?

Compensations for Dissimilarity

There are several ways of compensating for or overcoming dissimilarity. One of the most effective is frequent interaction, which can increase attraction and perceptions of similarity. For example, students living on the same dormitory floor can overcome initial dissimilarities through frequent conversation. If the initial dissimilarities are too severe, however, communication attempts may not only be unrewarding but may discourage future communication. An Indonesian visitor who condemns Americans for the wastefulness and excessive use of pollution-causing disposable paper products will probably be too different from the owner of a paper products company for effective communication to take place.

Another way to compensate for differences is for a source to develop empathy, or the ability to project oneself into another person's role as the receiver. Developing empathy is often a difficult task in heterophilous relationships because differences suggest that each person has had little experience with the other's role. If people can place themselves in the same circumstances as others, they are more likely to develop empathy. This is why Peace Corps volunteers undergo extensive training in the customs and language of the country in which they are to live. To be effective communicators in such a situation, they must live like the natives.

A source may compensate for differences in a communication situation by paying close attention to the feedback of receivers. Of course, feedback may be necessary to indicate to the source that differences do exist; people tend to assume that others are similar to them until proved otherwise. When dissimilarities do exist, these differences need to be recognized so that misunderstandings do not develop. Thus feedback provides the source with necessary information about his or her receivers. By attending closely to feedback, the source can better understand the receiver's language patterns, norms, beliefs, and behavior and also can develop more empathy. Social workers in the inner city or on an Indian reservation must be especially attuned to the unique vocabulary and habits of their clientele if they are to communicate in any meaningful way.

Degrees of similarity are an important consideration for a source. The extent to which a communicator is similar to another will affect his or her choice of receivers, the effectiveness of the communication, and the receivers' perception of his or her credibility. We must stress that no one statement can be made on strategies to alter perceptions of similarity. In some cases it will serve the purpose of the source to be perceived as different from intended receivers. In fact, it may be necessary to be so perceived in order to achieve the desired outcomes of the interaction. In these circumstances, communication strategies designed to highlight these differences are advised. In other cases, similarity between source and receiver will lead to desirable outcomes. In several later chapters we will discuss how adaptations can be made that will alter perceptions of similarity to serve different functions.

Power as a Source Variable

Although power is often ignored in discussions of human relationships, it affects many of our daily communication activities. The fact that teachers can assign passing or failing grades, that parents can give or withhold support money, or that employers can promote or dismiss workers influences the nature of the communication that takes place between interactants. It is important to our discussion of power to advance two different perspectives concerning how power comes to play a part in the relationship between a source and a receiver. First, power can be seen as arising from connections between people. Power in this sense is a property of the *structure* of social relationships. Second, another equally viable perspective describes power as a *perceived phenomenon* in which power is bestowed by a receiver upon the source in attempts to satisfy various needs. Both perspectives have received considerable attention by researchers interested in understanding how people can and do exert control over others. We will first discuss the structural perspective of power.

Power as a Structural Attribute

When people enter communication situations there exists a socially defined structure that is derived from the individuals involved and their level of mutual dependency. Consider a job interview between a prospective employee and an employer. There are certain structural characteristics to this meeting that influence their relationship, as well as affect their patterns of communication. Obviously, the employer is in a position to fulfill the desires of a prospective employee by offering him or her a job. Regardless of the outcome, the employer has relatively little to lose from engaging in this interaction. The prospective employee, however, is completely dependent upon the employer for a chance at employment. It is the structural characteristics of the interview setting that determines which person wields the power. Power, in this social context, is synonymous with the other person's dependence (Emerson, 1962). In other words, the dependence of the prospective employee on the employer is equal to the power of the employer over the employee.

In this sense, power is a function of the power/dependence relationship of the two people involved. How can we assess the power dynamics in a such a circumstance? To do so, we must first understand the goals each person has in the transaction and how dependent each is upon the other to achieve these goals. The goals of the prospective employee are to make a good impression and be offered a job. Clearly, the would-be employee is extremely dependent in this situation. The employer has a different, though related, goal, that is, gaining the information necessary to decide whether this person is the most appropriate candidate to fill the position. Although the employer may feel some dependency in relation to the prospective employee, the dependency is minimal in comparison. By assessing the goals and the dependency level of each participant, we would conclude that the interviewer is in the position of power advantage, yet both have some level of power in the relationship. The employer is dependent upon the prospective employee to divulge certain information and to cooperate with the questions in order to make an optimal decision. This power relationship is considered imbalanced because one person has a power advantage. It is important to remember that this power imbalance is a structural attribute of the exchange relation and not contingent upon personal preferences or perceptions.

Other factors that influence power/dependence relationships are the alternatives that people have in achieving their goals. If the prospective employee has been job hunting for a long time and this interview seems like the last chance at employment, the lack of alternatives increases dependency on the employer and, in turn, his or her power *in this transaction*. If the employee has other options that may lead to employment, however, this will decrease the dependency on this interviewer, thus decreasing his or her power.

Power relationships will affect the structure of the behavioral interactions of those involved. Research has shown that in an imbalanced power relationship sources who have the power advantage will increase their power use over time by either receiving an increase of rewards from the other or decreasing the amount of reward given, while still receiving rewards. Take a common situation of two college students sharing an apartment. Bill wants to have someone around so he does not have to live alone. Dave does not have this same need to live with anyone else, but because they are friends, he agrees to let Bill move into the apartment. Dave is less dependent upon Bill and therefore has the power advantage in this relationship. Over time, Dave will likely be able to increase his influence over Bill by having him do such things as more household chores and running more of the errands. At the same time, Dave will not have to give any more rewards to Bill, other than allowing him to live with him. This power imbalance will continue to increase until a balance is reached where Bill gets no more from Dave than Bill can receive from an alternate relationship. In this case, the inequity in the relationship will probably cause Bill to find a new place to live where the rewards given equal the rewards received.

Just as power in a relationship can be said to be imbalanced, it can also be balanced. Two people are in a power-balanced relationship when the dependence of one person equals the dependence of the other. For example, two supervisors in an organization may have positions in which their respective subordinates are dependent upon them for rewards. When these two supervisors interact with each other, however, neither is more dependent upon the other to achieve their goals. It is likely that they both depend upon the other to do their job correctly so that the organization runs smoothly. Therefore, the structure of the relationship between these two "equals" creates a balance of power, or mutual dependence.

Throughout this section we have been stressing notions such as "at this time" and "in this particular transaction" for an important reason. Power is a product of social relationships. Power as a structural attribute relies on the exchange relationships between individuals during a particular transaction. The employer only has power *as it relates to* the prospective employee at that specific time. The employer does not "have" or "possess" power as an individual attribute but only in relation to connections with another person. Dave has power over Bill, yet Bill also has power over Dave in their particular relationship. This relational perspective of power characterizes communication as two way, and the source of a message can only utilize a power advantage (or disadvantage) as it is realized within a particular situation. Power/dependency is a dynamic process that changes as relationships change. These changes affect, and are affected by, the communication between people. The concepts relevant to this perspective and their effects on communication will be discussed in greater detail in Chapter 9 under the heading of "Social Exchange Theory."

Power as a Perceived Attribute

Power, similar to credibility and similarity, can also be seen as a perceived phenomenon: It exists in a source only to the extent that a receiver perceives it to be there. When a receiver perceives that a source possesses some type of power, specific patterns of communication behavior can be predicted. There are several types of power that can be attributed to a source (French & Raven, 1968).

The Components and Types of Power

A source brings to a communication situation certain personal resources that may be perceived as power elements by the receiver. Among these resources of power are such personal qualities as wealth, prestige, skill, information, and physical strength. Thus if the mayor of a city asked a resident to head an anti-litter campaign, that citizen might accept the mayor's offer because he or she perceives the mayor to have power by virtue of prestige and/or position. A complete list of the resources of power available to a source in a communication situation is impossible to construct because many different qualities may be perceived (or not perceived) as a power element by the receiver. People who earn $10,000 a year may be so "impressed" by a president of a corporation who earns

$250,000 a year that they might follow the president's advice to invest their life savings in a particular stock. In a similar situation, however, a person of great wealth may not be very impressed by the corporate president and would not follow that advice. The resources of power available to a source are relative to the receiver's perception in a particular communication situation.

In any communication interaction, a receiver has certain unique physical, psychological, and social needs. A source's potential for satisfying the needs of the receiver provides the motivational bases for power to operate in a communication situation. Motivational bases are the reasons we have for allowing people to exert control over us; they are the needs we desire to have satisfied by the source of communication. Thus a citizen who agrees to head the anti-litter campaign may be satisfying a personal need to be a community leader. A need to be held in favor might also influence the citizen to say "yes" to the mayor's request. Workers who agree to invest their savings may be satisfying a need to be associated with people of higher status or to make a "fast buck." Clearly, resources of power are contingent upon the needs of a particular receiver or group of receivers. These two components of power (resources and needs or motive bases) combine to create five distinct types of power in a communication transaction.

Reward Power. A source's ability to provide rewards if a receiver complies with the source's request is called *reward power* (French & Raven, 1968). The rewards administered by the source may be concrete, such as money or gifts, or they may be intangible rewards, such as praise and affection. An employer who gives his or her sales personnel bonuses based on their performance is exercising reward power. Of course, the actual reward offered must be perceived by the receiver as worthwhile, or it will have little impact. To one salesperson, a week's vacation in the Bahamas may not be worth the extra effort needed to secure the bonus. To another, simply being "Numero Uno" may be a sufficient reward for working the extra hours necessary to top the other members of the sales force. To a great extent, the exercise of reward power is dependent on the source's ability to assess the needs of the receiver accurately.

In addition to perceiving a reward as worthwhile, the receiver must see the reward as being within the source's power to bestow. For example, a person seeking public office who offers another person a position in his or her administration in return for campaign work must be seen by the receiver as having a chance to fulfill the promise. If the receiver thinks there is no possibility that the candidate will win (and if winning is the only base of power the source might have), it is unlikely that the receiver will comply with the candidate's request to work in the campaign. In other words, a promise is not likely to motivate a receiver if it is perceived as empty.

As one would expect, the ability of the source to induce compliance increases as the magnitude of the reward increases. A sales manager who offers the position of assistant manager as a reward to the best sales person will likely have more power than one who offers a week's salary as a reward. Of course, this is dependent on each salesperson's perception of the reward as worthwhile and within the sales manager's power to bestow. The successful use of reward power may further increase the source's power because the receiver will likely attach more significance to promises of future rewards. Therefore, if the sales manager does promote the best salesperson to the position of assistant manager, other salespeople will likely see future promises of rewards as highly probable. In other words, the manager's credibility along the character dimension will be enhanced, making him or her more effective in the future. Conversely, if the sales manager fails to live up to a promise, his or her credibility will probably be diminished, and the ability to exercise reward power over the sales force is likely to be decreased.

Coercive Power. Coercive power refers to the ability of a source to administer negative sanctions (punishment) if the receiver does not comply with the source's request (McGuire, 1969). For example, American hostages in Iran were forced to make "confessions" and "repudiations" through the threat of torture and even death. From this perspective, coercive power may be seen as a negative form of reward power. However, coercive power may also involve the threat to withhold reward, as in the case of a manager who threatens to withhold the raise of a salesperson who does not maintain a minimal level of performance.

The fact that the source in many communication situations may exert either rewards or punishment leads to an inevitable question: Which is more effective? Studies have shown that positive and negative sanctions are equally effective in inducing overt compliance to the source's request (McGuire, 1969). It is important to note, however, that the use of either kind of power may have profound impact on other variables in the communication interaction. For example, the use of reward power is likely to increase the attraction of a receiver to a source, whereas the use of coercive power tends to decrease this attraction. The manager who administers only negative sanctions to staff members will probably be disliked and may very well find it difficult to retain employees. Further, the use of negative sanctions requires more surveillance or scrutiny by an administrator. The manager who employs coercive power will find that he or she must devote a great deal of time to "catching" workers who are not compliant. Needless to say, this will probably have a detrimental effect on company morale and may affect the manager's ability to perform other functions that support his or her role relationship with subordinates. A receiver also may react negatively to the use of reward power if it is perceived as bribery or as compromising one's integrity. Most of us have been in situations in which we came to resent people trying to force our compliance by "buying" us. Even with these potential problems of reward power, most people will still find this type of power far superior to relying on coercion.

Referent Power. If the source in a communication situation makes an appeal to a receiver to "do this for me," the source is exercising referent power. In such an instance, the source is appealing to the receiver's wish to please the source. At the basis of referent power is the feeling of identification that the receiver perceives in the relationship with the source. For referent power to exist, the receiver must want to be like the source. Most people have, at one time or another, imitated the behavior or "parroted" the beliefs or attitudes of someone whom they found attractive. Most parents can attest to the existence of referent power. For example, when the leader of a group of teenagers adopts a new style of clothing, the other members of the group are likely to conform.

Referent power differs from reward and coercive power in the motive for compliance. For example, musicians in an orchestra may "play their hearts out" to please the conductor and get a raise in pay. The conductor in such a situation is exercising reward power over the musician. Then, too, the musicians may play well after the conductor has noted that their technique is rusty and needs improvement if they are to keep a job in the orchestra. In this situation, the conductor is exercising coercive power. However, if the musicians play their best because they wants to be liked by the orchestra leader, then the conductor is exercising referent power.

The use of referent power in a highly structured organization such as a corporation may cause long-term problems. The manager who is well liked by subordinates may be able to get them to perform well by asking them to "do this for me." The manager's success, however, may result in a promotion to a different position. In such a case, the manager's replacement may find the subordinates difficult to manage because he or she does not have referent power over them.

Expert Power. The concept of *expert power* is closely related to the competence dimension of source credibility discussed earlier in this chapter. A person in a communication situation may have power because the receiver *perceives* the source as possessing superior knowledge or expertise on a particular subject. At this time we must make a clear distinction between *expert power* and *informational influence.* Influence may result simply from information provided by a source. Information may be presented that is logical, rational, and consistent with the receiver's prior beliefs. The information itself may motivate the receiver to act. Expert power derives from the reputation of the source, whereas in informational influence "it is the content of the communication that is important, not the nature of the influencing agent" (Raven, 1965, p. 372). We will devote two chapters to influence processes, but this distinction is important to our present discussion. An example of expert power should make this distinction clear. A patient is likely to accept a doctor's diagnosis and follow instructions even though the patient is not given any more information about the nature of the illness or the treatment. Thus expert power can bring about compliance without affecting a receiver's understanding, attitudes, or beliefs. Vesting expert power in a person can drastically alter our communication with people. For example, many people are afraid to question a doctor (or other expert sources) for fear of appearing unintelligent. Such unchallenged acceptance is not always in the best interest of the receiver.

A receiver tends to perceive a source's expertise in relation to his or her own knowledge of the subject of interest (French & Raven, 1968). For example, a person who perceives him- or herself as the best golfer at the country club is more likely to accept advice from Payne Stewart than from a caddy—even though both say exactly the same thing, "Keep your head down!" The power accorded an expert source varies from topic to topic. Although millions of parents may consider Dr. Ruth Westheimer an expert on human sexuality, she is not necessarily considered an expert on political issues. Therefore, she is likely to have little influence on people's choice of a presidential candidate. In fact, it has been shown that a source's ability to exert power may be diminished by a source's attempt to influence receivers on a topic outside his or her area of expertise. Some people may reject Dr. Westheimer's recommendations on sexual behavior because of her political affiliations.

Similar to referent power, expert power is bestowed upon specific individuals. This may cause problems within an organization that relies heavily on an expert's judgment without questioning or understanding the content of the communication. For example, the staff of an engineering department of a manufacturer may rely on the expertise of a single person to solve technical problems. The rest of the staff may merely accept orders because the person has the reputation of being bright and right; this would be deference to expert power. If the expert should leave, they would be unable to carry on because they were not in the habit of asking the expert's reasons for giving certain orders. Another problem associated with heavy reliance on expert power is that experts are not always right. Unquestioning acceptance of communication without regard to content can be fraught with peril.

Legitimate Power. Legitimate power stems from the internalized values of receivers that affirm that the source has a "right" to influence them. When irate parents tell their recalcitrant child to go to bed "because we said so," they are exercising legitimate power. The child is likely to comply because values that have been reinforced for many years state that parents have the right to control their children. Similarly, Roman Catholics or Jews feel "obliged" to comply with the advice of their priest or rabbi on religious matters because this person has legitimate power over them.

Persons holding certain positions within highly structured organizations or social institutions may be accorded the right to prescribe other people's behavior. Thus a judge has the right to place a prisoner on probation, a teacher has the right to assign homework, and a supervisor has the right to request an employee to perform certain tasks. In such instances, the receiver—the prisoner, student, or worker —is obliged to comply with the source, not by virtue of the source's personality, but by virtue of the office the source holds.

To some extent, the use of legitimate power may direct the nature and flow of communication between people. In the military, officers may legitimately demand certain behaviors from those under their command. However, no subordinate may prescribe the behavior of a superior. Likewise, the statement, "The Cabots speak only to the Lowells and the Lowells speak only to God," defines the communication lines within a particular social structure—that of upper class Bostonians.

The range of legitimate power that a source can exert over a receiver varies from situation to situation and may change over time. When legitimate power is based on mutually shared cultural values, the source's influence is usually broad. Thus, for many years, husbands were able to dictate their wife's behavior in practically every area of life. They could tell their wives whom to talk to, where they could and could not go, and what they should wear. This was possible because both shared the cultural belief that the wives were subordinate to husbands. Parents have broad legitimate power over their children, because children are still seen as extensions of their parents. In most instances legitimate power is rather narrowly defined by the context of the communication situation. Supervisors have the right to tell their employees what work tasks to perform but do not have the right to tell them which candidates to vote for in an election. In fact, if sources attempt to exert influence in an area in which they do not have legitimate power, they may decrease any ability to influence in all other areas, including those in which they have the right to influence.

Legitimate power typically involves the exercise of other types of power. Thus a judge may be perceived as having legitimate power to exercise coercive power over a prisoner; an employer may be perceived as having the right to exercise reward power over employees. Of course, a receiver may also perceive a source's power to be illegitimate. Thus a student in a required course may resent a professor's attempt to use referent power, because the student may have felt "forced" to take the course. A student may accept the professor's use of referent power, however, if the course is an elective.

Conditions That Maximize the Effectiveness of Power

A receiver makes at least three separate decisions that affect whether a source can effectively exert power in a relationship (McGuire, 1969). All three of these decisions are based upon the receiver's perceptions. The first decision is based on *perceived control,* or the receiver's decision as to whether the source can apply positive sanctions (rewards) or negative sanctions (punishments) if the request of the source is not followed by compliance. For example, if a stranger in street clothes tells you and your friends not to stand on the corner, you and your friends will probably ignore the request unless the stranger pulls out a police badge and threatens to arrest you. Even though you might perceive the request to be an exercise in illegitimate power, you still might comply because you perceive the person to have control of possible punishments. Conversely, if a receiver believes a source has power (even if the source does not), the receiver is likely to comply with the source's requests. Thus if you and your friends *thought* the stranger to be a plainclothes detective, you would probably comply with the request to "move along" without a challenge.

The notion of perceived control is obviously very important when a source attempts to exercise reward or coercive power because these two types of power are based solely on the ability to control behavior that is contingent on possible sanctions. People will often engage in ingratiating communication strategies either to avoid punishment or receive rewards. But the moment that a source loses the ability to control and/or the needs of the receiver change, the communication patterns will also change. Relationships built solely on control rarely continue when ability to control is lost.

The second decision is based on *perceived concern*, or the receiver's decision as to whether the source really cares if the receiver complies with the request. Many times people make requests of others that they do not really expect to be fulfilled. Often they could not personally care less whether the receiver complies or not. There are many rules in colleges and universities that seem to have little basis in rationality. However, we are often forced to tell our students that they must obey those rules. We obviously cannot take the daring step of telling them they do not have to follow the administrator's dicta, but, in many cases we really do not care what behaviors follow. When the receiver perceives a lack of concern, there is little likelihood that compliance will occur. If there is perceived concern, however, the receiver will likely carefully consider a decision not to comply. If a person has control of rewards and punishments and is concerned about compliance, the receiver is likely to respond as requested. If a person asks another person to behave in a certain way "for me" (referent power) and it is obviously important to the source, a receiver will probable comply if the relationship is valued.

A final decision of the receiver is based upon *perceived scrutiny*. The receiver must decide if the source has the ability to observe whether he or she has complied with the source's request. Suppose, for instance, an English professor assigns the class a novel to read, stating that the students will not be tested on content of the book but the class will discuss it at the next meeting. A student who planned to attend the next class might well read the book for a variety of reasons. One of those reasons might be that the professor would have a chance to find out if the assignment was fulfilled. However, a student who had no intention of attending the next class might not read the text because the professor would have no way of ever knowing whether the assignment was completed or not. We learned with some amusement that students at the University of Arizona have been ignoring required courses in physical education because they knew that the college offices did not have the manpower to check on whether the requirement had been fulfilled. The college administrators obviously have the power to control the situation because they can hold up graduation. They at least profess to be concerned that students meet the course requirements, but they were not surveying the situation to see that compliance occurred.

As we stated earlier, one of the main problems in using reward or coercive power is the need for constant surveillance. If we do not communicate with people and give them good reasons for behaving in a certain way but instead rely simply on rewards or threats, we cannot expect the desired behaviors to continue unless we are constantly watching and scrutinizing the situation. This need for surveillance leads to an unfortunate self-fulfilling prophecy in many instances. We have heard supervisors say that their employees are lazy and the threat of unemployment is the only basis of power that is effective. They cite as evidence the fact that unless the workers are closely supervised, they will not perform their duties. Obviously, if people have no internal reasons for compliance and are simply going along to avoid punishment, we cannot reasonably expect them to continue working when the threat of punishment no longer exists. Giving good reasons for compliance may be as important a power base as any we know.

Summary

1. An important variable in any communication situation is source credibility. Receivers make judgments about sources that can have an important impact on what is communicated and how it is received. Credibility is a perceptual phenomenon. A source is only credible if receivers believes it to be so.

2. There are five decisions that a receiver makes about a source; these are known as the dimensions of credibility. These decision points are *competence*, or the source's perceived knowledge of the subject; *character*, or the apparent trustworthiness of the source; *composure*, or the extent to which the communicator tends to be in

control in situations that produce stress; *sociability,* or the degree to which the source seems likable and friendly; and *extroversion,* or an outgoing personality. Each of these dimensions acts independently to influence the source's effectiveness as a communicator.

3. A wise communicator will try to become very competent, composed, sociable, and of good character. Research indicates that people who are moderately extroverted are more positively evaluated than people who are extremely high or low in this dimension.

4. Because source credibility is attributed by receivers, it is subject to change over time. At the beginning of a communication transaction, the receiver assesses the source's "initial credibility." During the communication transaction, a receiver may modify his or her initial impression; we have called this "transactional credibility." After the communication has ended, the receiver is left with a final perception of the source, which is called "terminal credibility." To emphasize the process nature of communication, we might point out that terminal credibility acts as initial credibility the next time the participants interact.

5. Another variable in the communication transaction is *homophily,* or the degree of perceived similarity between source and receiver. *Heterophily* refers to the degree of perceived dissimilarity among the interactants. The nature of the relationship and the function of communication determine the optimal degree of homophily-heterophily. In some conditions in which the function of communication is persuasion or information acquisition, heterophily may serve the source. In social relationships, people who are homophilous tend to spend more time communicating. Frequent interaction, the development of empathy, and close attention to feedback help overcome problems associated with great degrees of dissimilarity.

6. Power is also an important variable. If a receiver perceives a source to have power, the nature of communication will change. The components of power are the resources possessed by a source that will satisfy some felt need of the receiver.

7. A source may be perceived to have at least one of five different types of power. *Reward power* is the ability of the source to apply positive sanctions. *Coercive power* is the ability to deliver negative sanctions. *Referent power* is the ability to appeal to a receiver's wish to please or be like the source. *Expert power* is accorded to a source

when the receiver believes that the source has superior knowledge on a topic. This is distinguished from informational influence in that a source with expert power gains compliance not because of the content of the communication but rather because of his or her reputation. *Legitimate power* stems from the internalized values of the receiver that affirm the source's right to exert control over the situation.

8. The receiver makes three decisions about the source that affect the use of power in communication situation. *Perceived control* involves whether or not the source has the ability to apply sanctions. If the source has no ability to deliver sanctions, certain types of power-based appeals will be ineffective. If there is no *perceived concern* (i.e., the receiver's decision as to whether the source really cares if the request is complied with or not), the source will not influence behavior. Finally, there is *perceived scrutiny*, or the receiver's decision whether the source has the ability to determine if the request has been fulfilled.

References

Berlo, D. K., Lemert, J. B., & Mertz, R. (1969). Dimensions for evaluating the acceptability of message sources. *Public Opinion Quarterly, 33*, 563-576.

Burgoon, J. K. (1976). The ideal source: A reexamination of source credibility measurement. *Central States Speech Journal, 27*, 200-206.

Collins, B. E., & Guetzkow, H. (1964). *A social psychology of group processes for decision making.* New York: John Wiley.

Emerson, R. M. (1962). Power-dependence relations. *American Sociological Review, 27*, 31-34.

French, J. R. P., Jr., & Raven, B. (1968). The bases of social power. In D. Cartwright & A. Zander (Eds.), *Group dynamics* (pp. 259-268). New York: Harper & Row.

McCroskey, J. C., Jensen, T., & Valencia, C. (1973, May). *Measurement of the credibility of peers and spouses.* Paper presented at the International Communication Association Convention, Montreal.

McGuire, W. T. (1969). The nature of attitudes and attitude change. In G. Lindsey & E. Aronson (Eds.), *The handbook of social psychology* (2nd ed., Vol. 3, pp. 194-196). Reading, MA: Addison-Wesley.

Miller, G. R., & Hewgill, M. A. (1964). The effects of variations in nonfluency on audience ratings of source credibility. *Quarterly Journal of Speech, 50*, 36-44.

Palamore, J. (1972). The Chicago snowball: A study of the flow and diffusion of family planning information. In D. J. Bogue (Ed.), *Sociological contributions to family planning research.* Chicago: University of Chicago Community and Family Study Center.

Raven, B. H. (1965). Social influence and power. In I. D. Steiner & M. Fishbein (Eds.), *Current studies in social psychology* (p. 372). New York: Holt, Rinehart & Winston.

Rogers, E. M., & Shoemaker, F. F. (1971). *Communication of innovations: A cross-cultural approach.* New York: Free Press.

Warland, R. H. (1970). *Personal influence: The degree of similarity of those who interact.* Unpublished master's thesis, Iowa State University.

3

Receiver Variables

M essage reception unfortunately is often thought of as a pas-sive activity. People frequently equate physical presence with message reception. Educators, to some extent, may be responsible for this notion because they place an inordinate amount of em-phasis on speaker characteristics and effective message construc-tion. Common sense and theory, however, would dictate that the receiver is just as important as the source in the communication process. Even the most dynamic speaker using the most eloquent logic will be rendered ineffective if there is no one to receive the message. Although no thoughtful person is willing to contest the idea that the decoding or receiving of a message is a different process from constructing or transmitting it, most people overlook the fact that both activities are precisely that—active processes.

Face-to-face communication provides a good perspective for view-ing the transactional nature of the relationship between a source and a receiver. As we noted earlier, during the course of a conversation, participants typically *exchange* messages. That is, each participant acts as both a source and a receiver, both encoding and decoding messages as the situation demands. A similar exchange occurs in small-group situations, in which a number of individuals engage in group discussion, sending and receiving messages in turn. Participants in public communication situations also share these two roles during a presentation when the speaker responds to verbal and nonverbal cues from the audience, or when members of the audience are encouraged to ask questions immediately after the presentation.

We turn our attention now to focus on the receiver as an important element of the communication process. By the nature of their responses to the speaker and the message, receivers will greatly influence communication transactions. Not only do receivers help determine the topic and the level of interaction, but they often decide whether or not the interaction will proceed any further. Receivers also shape the interaction by deciding how much attention to give to the source or content of the message. It is not uncommon for a receiver to set the tone of an entire conversation by choosing to "hear" only certain elements of the message. Many of us know someone who seldom initiates conversation, but successfully controls the interaction by either refusing to talk or by deftly changing the topic. These types of people are not very accommodating communicators.

Accommodation between the source and receiver is essential if an interaction is to be effective. Just as the receiver adapts to the source, the source must also adapt messages to the receiver. Each receiver is unique in terms of age, sex, personality, intelligence, skills, and experiences. These characteristics, which are brought to every communication situation, will have some repercussions in the transaction. Accommodations made by the source, based on these receiver characteristics, can foster feelings of trust and mutual sharing between the interactants, which, in turn, will likely make the communication more effective.

Accommodation, however, is not always easy to accomplish. Both receivers and sources vary greatly in personal attributes. Therefore, effective communicators will attempt to gather knowledge about those with whom they communicate. This is often easier said than done. It would be absurd to open our conversations by interrogating the other participant about personal attributes or, prior to a speech, pass out a questionnaire to an audience to assess their backgrounds and interests. Perhaps the best we can do is to make *predictions* and *generalizations* about the receiver or audience based upon past experiences, even though these may not always be effective or accurate. Forming a generalization and making a prediction about a given receiver or audience constitutes making an *audience analysis*. However, as the size of an audience increases, there is a greater likelihood that our generalizations will be inaccurate and invalid. Nonetheless, most communication scholars are in agreement about the necessity of relying on generalizations.

> As soon as a speaker attempts to influence the thoughts and actions of two or more people simultaneously, he faces a dilemma. Although he realizes that acceptance of his viewpoint is a personal and singular process, the speaker cannot consider independently and at the same time each listener in his audience. The communicator has no choice but to draw general conclusions about the similarities and differences in alignment of the separate auditors who collectively form his audience. (Martin & Colburn, 1972, p. 71)

Obviously, a skilled analysis of the audience is one for which the predictions and generalizations are sufficient. The following discussion focuses on demographics variables and communicator characteristics that research has shown to have significant affects on the communication process.

Receiver Demographic Characteristics

Awareness and understanding of receiver characteristics increases the possibility that messages may have the desired effect, whether that purpose is to inform, persuade, or entertain. Obviously the number of receivers varies depending on the context. A small number of receivers are found in face-to-face and small-group situations, whereas receivers can number in the thousands or even millions in the mass communication experience. Because of the vast number of receivers who respond in a mass communication or large-group situation, the audience in such instances can best be analyzed according to sociodemographic characteristics such as age, gender, ethnicity, and socioeconomic status (SES).

Age

The ancient expression, "Now that I am an adult I put away the things of a child," expresses in many ways the differences between children and adults in their persuasibility and the ability to adapt messages toward a receiver. Researchers have found that children, particularly between the ages of 6 and 11, use very few outward indications of whether they understand a given message. Receiver reinforcing remarks, called "back channeling" cues consist of receiver messages such as "uh-huh," "yeah," "um-humm," and other indications that the source's message is getting across. Not until children reach the eighth grade do they generally begin back channeling. This lack of back channeling may impede the ability of speakers to realize whether their message is having the desired effect. When speaking to children, therefore, it is advisable to openly ask whether the message is being understood instead of assuming that because the children are not making negative remarks they are in agreement.

Research into the persuasibility of older people has been almost nonexistent until recently. Two early studies suggest that as age increases, a person's susceptibility to persuasion decreases (Janis & Rife, 1959; Marple, 1933). Psychological research on the relationship between age and suggestibility to hypnosis provides some tangential support for this hypothesis (McGuire, 1969). Gerontological theorists, however, recognize that certain changes that occur as people grow older are not attributable solely to age. For example, a commonly held belief is that older people have deficiencies in their cognitive reasoning. It has been found that cognitive decline in old age is primarily a result of high blood pressure, an ailment that can strike at any age. Further, longitudinal research has shown that personality characteristics, such as openness, extroversion, and neuroticism, remain predominantly stable as people mature from their early 30s until well into their 80s (Costa et al., 1986). This is not to suggest that personality changes do not occur as people grow older, but the changes are not due simply to aging and tend to be normative changes as a result of life experiences (Helson & Moane, 1987). It would be unwise for a speaker to assume that an audience of older people will be closed-minded, or that they lack intelligence simply because they are old.

There are certain changes that do occur in later life that influence communication effectiveness. Generally, older persons experience declines in eyesight (starting around the age of 40), problems in hearing high-frequency sounds, and a decreased ability to discriminate between consonants such as "f," "g," "s," "t," and "z." Older people also have more difficulty understanding speakers who talk at a fast rate. These physiological changes associated with aging can influence communication. Speakers may need to increase their volume and speak slower when talking to an elderly audience. Many people who have hearing difficulty compensate through the interpretation of visual cues such as lip reading. There is a tendency, however, to choose language patterns that overcompensate for hearing impairments. When speaking with older adults, people are inclined to use simple concrete words or a type of "baby talk" that can lead to feelings of anxiousness with the elderly adult. These types of speech patterns are insulting, they obviously create barriers to effective communication, and they create affective and relational messages that can hinder the desired purpose of the communication.

It is clear that the age of an audience is a demographic characteristic that the source should assess. Obviously, different age groups will show an interest in different subject matter. A group of high-school students may be vitally interested in a panel discussion on the merits of a liberal arts versus a business education, but the subject is likely to have little appeal to 45-year-old executives. Politicians have often considered the age of their audience when deciding among campaign issues. A smart politician is likely to campaign for better housing and medical care for the elderly when addressing a group of senior citizens, whereas he may switch his topic to federal assistance for education when speaking at a college campus.

There is also considerable evidence that the rewarding or inhibiting effects of simple verbal expressions of approval or disapproval vary with age and other related factors (Stevenson, 1965). The effectiveness of praise and approval diminishes with maturity, and the information value of social reinforcement becomes more important with age (Gerwirtz, 1954). The effective communicator might wish to keep these factors in mind when interacting in either interpersonal, small-group, or public communication settings.

Gender

Early communication research was interested in biological sex as a determinant for the different effects of various messages. Many of these studies assumed that because men and women differ biologically, differences in perceptions and reactions should also differ. Differences in communication patterns were studied in light of these biological differences until the mid-1970s when the ancient concept of *androgyny* was reintroduced. Androgyny allows gender characteristics to be conceptualized as comprising both masculine and feminine dimensions rather than simply opposites. Psychological gender roles replaced the common biological distinctions in communication research. This focus also was fraught with confusion regarding which characteristics should be considered feminine or masculine, and subsequently many findings were met with skepticism. One study demonstrated that psychological gender has more predictive utility than biological sex (Montgomery & Burgoon, 1977). Renewed interest of the communication implications of proposed differences between males and females has spawned excellent texts and research programs although very few findings are conclusive. In spite of the confusion and contradictory findings in the literature, some research results concerning the influence of gender on message reception are worth noting (for an excellent reading on gender and communication, see Pearson, Turner, & Todd-Mancillas, 1991).

People often attribute certain qualities to women and men on the basis of sexual stereotypes: softness, emotionality, aggressiveness, confidence, and levels of persuasibility. Areas of interest for communication researchers include gender differences in perceptions. Some research indicates that males and females do differ in their preferences in the complexity of messages, with females preferring more complexity than males (Andrews, 1985). Research in literary theory indicates that men are more literal than women, and current research in perceptual differences (Fabes & Laner, 1986) supports the long-standing notion that men and women perceive each other differently. Various studies argue that there are pervasive cultural and societal expectations for male and female behaviors (Burgoon, 1989). Whether or not these stereotypical beliefs are grounded in empirical evidence is moot. What is important to consider when speaking to an audience is that myths about sex-role differences are as important as actual differences because these beliefs may give rise to differences in male and female behavior. We "expect" emotional women and rational men. Many writers and educators believe that such sex-role standards produce unnecessary internal conflicts, are incompatible with both individual and societal interests because they are unnecessarily restrictive, and lead to the reinforcement of these stereotypes. People are now more willing to accept less rigidly defined roles. The views that people have on the roles of men and women will, no doubt, affect our communication with them.

Many communication researchers have tested the hypothesis that women are easier to persuade than men. In one study, a group of college students at the University of Washington listened to a short persuasive speech opposing further expansion of federal government power in health and education. They were then tested for the degree of attitude change caused by the speeches. The results showed that the female students were persuaded by the speech to a greater degree than the male students. In addition, the women transferred the effects of the persuasive appeal to general and nonrelevant items more than men did. Specifically, the female subjects showed more attitude change on statements such as, "Government power has already been expanded too far," and "Government price control would result in unfair discrimination" (Scheidel, 1963).

A considerable number of experiments support the claim that women are generally more persuadable than men. However, when other variables are introduced, the results are not as clear-cut. One study with college students focused on the relationship between frustration, sex, and persuasibility. The subjects in the "frustrated" group were told that they were inferior students; those in the "ego-satisfied" group were told that they were superior students. The subjects were then tested to determine the degree of attitude change toward the topics of the persuasive messages. The results show that frustrated females change attitudes more than frustrated males. However, in the "ego-satisfied" group, no significant differences appeared between male and female subjects (Carmichael,

1970). In an early experiment, there was no difference in persuasibility between male and female receivers when the speaker was a woman (Knower, 1935).

Montgomery and Burgoon (1977) argue that early studies noting differences in persuasibility may be due to the specific topics used. Studies that use "male-oriented" topics or that focus on attitudes of little import may demonstrate more attitude change in women. Keeping in mind the shortcomings of research findings on gender and communication, it can be stated that women receivers "tend" to be more willing listeners than men, they are better encoders and decoders of public messages, and women generally give more constructive feedback than men. It is important to apply this information concerning sex roles to make finer discriminations about our audience. Research on androgyny indicates that many people are able to take on the best characteristics of both sexes and are not bound to traditional sex roles. Women are not necessarily persuadable, and men are not always rational. Therefore, the wise communicator will consider people's views of sex roles in determining the most appropriate communication strategy.

Social and Economic Status

Studies in the field of communication have indicated that the social and economic background of the audience will have a significant impact upon its response to a speaker and his or her message (for an especially good discussion of this problem, see Daniels, 1970). A poor person and a wealthy person are likely to be so heterophilous on such a wide range of attributes that effective communication may be hampered. Each interactant in such a situation comes from a different culture; each has had different experiences; each holds different attitudes, values, and goals. In short, the lack of a common frame of reference may make communication between the two extremely difficult.

The communication problems that arise when people of different social and economic backgrounds interact become evident upon a consideration of a hypothetical, though not unrealistic, communication situation. Suppose a well-meaning (and well-dressed) social worker comes to an economically deprived neighborhood once a week to talk to teenagers about career guidance. The social worker is a well-educated, upper middle-class Anglo-American from an affluent neighborhood. The teenagers are predominantly high-school dropouts, or indifferent students of lower middle-class parents. Before the social worker even speaks, he or she is at a disadvantage. First, the social worker is probably unfamiliar with the verbal and non-verbal dialect and customs of the group; to them, he or she is an outsider. Second, the social worker's values are not the same as theirs. He or she was raised in a culture that favored education and rewarded good marks in school. The teenagers grew up in a culture that reinforced the importance of living for the moment—after all, who knows what tomorrow may bring, especially to the poor. The teenagers are also likely to be hostile and mistrusting of the social worker because to them it may seem as if everything had been handed to him or her.

Clearly, the differences in the social and economic backgrounds of the social worker and the teenagers will cause communication problems. Conversely, if the communicator and receivers are homophilous in their social and economic backgrounds and if they share common life experiences, more communication is likely to occur, and the communication attempts probably will be more successful. This is one reason why many programs in poor neighborhoods have had greater success when using community members as leaders.

Ethnic Factors

It would seem logical that communication between interactants of the same race or ethnic group would be more effective than communication between people of different races or ethnic groups. Prejudice and hostility between different groups may account for some of the communication problems. In addition, members of different races and ethnic groups are often from different social and economic background. Cultural differences are an inherent part of racial and ethnic differences.

Once again the principles of homophily and heterophily come into play. People are more attracted to those who are like themselves than to those who are different. People perceive African Americans to be different from Anglo-Americans, Puerto Ricans to be different from WASPs, and Latinos to be different from Italians. The fact that members of different racial and ethnic groups are less likely to interact facilitates misunderstanding and the maintenance of stereotypes.

One of the authors had the opportunity to teach on a traditional Lakota Indian Reservation. He was acutely aware that many of the students would not look directly at him when working with them on an individual basis. He thought that the students either did not care for his style of teaching, or they lacked confidence in themselves. Upon asking another teacher, who was a tribal member, to explain this curious behavior, he was informed that many of the students who were raised in culturally traditional households were taught that looking directly at a person in authority was a sign of disrespect. These students were in fact paying respect to this *wasíchu* (a Lakota term for the white race, pronounced "wa-shee-choo") and not displaying the stereotypical unassertive behavior that is commonly associated with some Native American groups.

Intelligence

Many of the studies that have attempted to determine the relationship between intelligence and persuasibility have been beset by measurement problems. In one early study, unsupported propaganda statements effected less attitude change in people with high intelligence than in people with low intelligence (Wegrocki, 1934). In another study conducted among army recruits, it was found that educated subjects were more persuadable than subjects with little education when the speech was a logical one (Hovland, Lumsdaine, & Sheffield, 1949). However, one must question the validity of using formal education as a measurement of intelligence. In general, there seems to be no evidence to support the hypothesis that intelligence and persuasibility are related in either a positive or negative way.

Members of a well-educated audience may possess many advantages as receivers: They are usually knowledgeable on a wide range of topics, their vocabulary is good, and their message comprehension is also likely to be good. Because well-educated people tend to be knowledgeable, they also tend to be critical of unsupported messages. However, one cannot assume that there is any relationship between a person's critical ability and his or her persuasibility. Certain message patterns have a greater impact when attempting to persuade individuals with higher levels of education than those with less formal education. Chapter 7 will discuss in detail the effect of messages on persuasibility.

Psychological Characteristics of a Receiver

Demographic analysis of an audience may be useful to a source in some situations, but it is also beneficial to view receivers as individuals possessing a unique personality that will affect their response to a message. For example, extroversion, shyness, hostility, or anxiety can be characteristics of one's personality that remain fairly stable from situation to situation. It seemed logical, therefore, to a number of communication theorists that one should be able to predict a person's response to a message on the basis of a particular personality trait. Indeed, a considerable amount of time and effort has been devoted to determining the relationships between certain personality traits and persuasibility. The findings may be of use to the source of a message because they provide some insights into the nature of the decoding process.

Self-Esteem

Each of us has a personal concept of self, formed partially from our own perceptions and partially from the feedback received from others in social situations. The evaluation you make of yourself provides the basis for concepts of self-esteem. Self-esteem is considered the part of yourself that evaluates the self-concept. The closer the match between your idealized self and the perceptions of your real self, the higher your level of self-esteem. Individuals with high self-esteem generally consider themselves to be superior to others on a number of counts. Research has consistently shown that high self-esteem individuals will be less influenced by a failure experience, owing to their tendency to use avoidance defenses, whereas low self-esteem individuals will be more influenced by failure experiences (Nesbitt & Gordon, 1967). This finding clearly points to the caution that must be exercised in delivering negative feedback to another person.

Self-esteem is a personality variable that will greatly affect the way a person receives and reacts to a message. Individuals with low self-esteem are generally easier to persuade than those with high self-esteem (Janis & Field, 1959). Persons with low self-esteem are conformists by nature; they have little confidence in their own opinions and are persuaded easily by someone else's ideas. Individuals with high self-esteem have greater confidence in their opinions and find it easier to challenge the ideas of others. This makes them less susceptible to persuasion.

Relationships between self-esteem and persuasibility may also be discussed in terms of defensive behavior. One experimenter found that persons high in self-esteem use avoidance mechanisms that lead them to reject threatening persuasive appeals (Leventhal & Perloe, 1962). In the study, a group of Yale students with high self-esteem rejected a persuasive communication that presented very negative statements about army life because the topic was threatening to their concept of self and their lifestyle. Students with high self-esteem were influenced more by an optimistic message that enhanced their self-image by presenting favorable attitudes about army life. Subjects with low self-esteem, however, used defense mechanisms that led them to reject the optimistic appeal and accept the threatening one. On the basis of these findings, it would seem likely that a student with low self-esteem would reject a professor's optimistic statement that the student will be able to pass the next examination with enough studying. Conversely, a student with high self-esteem is likely to reject the same professor's pessimistic statement that the student will probably fail the examination.

In several experiments, the self-esteem of subjects has been manipulated to determine the effects that changes in this variable have on a person's resistance to persuasion. Studies have shown that increasing a person's self-esteem before listening to a persuasive appeal makes the person less persuadable (for a complete discussion, see Miller & Burgoon, 1973). This appears to be true even if the success experience prior to the persuasive appeal had nothing to do with the content of the message. These findings seem logical and consistent with others because providing people with a success experience is likely to increase their confidence, thereby making them less vulnerable to the persuasive attempts of others. However, these results seem applicable only when the persuasive message is a simple one. When the message is complex, it is difficult to make predictions about the persuasibility of receivers.

Aggressiveness and Hostility

The personality dimension of aggressiveness is closely related to self-esteem. An aggressive individual can be defined in terms of irritability, negativism, resentment, and suspicion (Infante, 1987). Aggressive persons may vary along these dimensions. Logically, aggressive individuals also tend to be high in self-esteem. This has led some communication theorists to speculate that aggressive people are probably less persuadable than unaggressive people. Several research investigations have supported this hypothesis (Abelson & Lesser, 1959).

When aggressive persons are frustrated, they are likely to become hostile. A hostile receiver is one who is antagonistic and un- friendly toward the source. The relationship among aggression, frustration, and hostility leads some communication researchers to suggest that raising a receiver's level of hostility by abusive treatment prior to a persuasive appeal will make the receiver less persuadable. The results of several experiments demonstrate that the relationship between the receiver's hostility level and his or her persuasibility is not quite that simple. A receiver who has been annoyed prior to hearing a persuasive appeal is more receptive to appeals that call for harsh actions and less receptive to appeals that call for neutral or good actions. In other words, the content of the message seems to affect the persuasibility of a hostile receiver. Thus a student whose required course has just been eliminated due to a lack of university funds is likely to be more persuaded by an appeal to march on the university president's office than one that suggests that students should make the best of the situation.

Anxiety

Anxiety level will affect one's need to interact or affiliate with others. In a classic experiment, Schachter (1959) demonstrated that anxiety-producing situations can increase an individual's need to affiliate with others and can alter preexisting criteria for choosing companions. Increased affiliative behavior will lead to alterations in communication behavior and will affect the degree of persuasibility. *Anxiety* is a state of worry, tension, and apprehension about the unknown. Early studies that focused on the question of whether or not anxiety affected the receiver's persuasibility resulted in confusing and contradictory findings. One study showed receivers with high anxiety to be more persuadable than receivers with low anxiety (Nunnally & Bobren, 1959). Another study found the opposite to be true (Janis & Feshbach, 1965). As in the case of hostility, anxiety and persuasibility seem related to the content of the persuasive appeal (Miller & Burgoon, 1973).

Receiver anxiety is related to a fear of misinterpreting or an inability to adjust psychologically to messages sent by others (Wheeless, 1975). Wheeless created the Receiver Apprehension Test (RAT) to measure levels of receiver apprehension. When receivers with chronically high anxiety are exposed to an anxiety-producing message, they tend to become less persuadable (Miller & Burgoon, 1973). This behavior acts as a distraction to the proposed message. A measure of cognitive effort is exerted attempting to cope with the anxiety, which impedes the receivers' ability to process additional information from the messages. Thus smokers who are very anxious about their health are likely to reject a strong fear appeal that attempts to persuade them to stop smoking. When receivers with low anxiety are exposed to anxiety-producing messages, however, they tend to become more persuadable. In such cases, the message stimulates the receiver, causing more attention to be paid to its content and thereby enhancing the possibility of attitude change. If receivers with low anxiety hear the same strong fear appeal to stop smoking, they are more likely to be persuaded by it.

Prior Attitudes

Every receiver brings to the communication situation a set of prior attitudes, or preconceived notions, that are the result of past learning experiences. Suppose a white Southerner was raised on the theory that blacks are intellectually inferior to whites. If while listening to a speech given by Charles Rangel, an African American congressman from New York, prior attitudes about blacks might interfere with accurate message perception. No matter how intelligently Representative Rangel speaks, the listener may still see the speech as further evidence of black inferiority because of prior attitudes and reactions based on stereotypes.

Research in the fields of psychology and communication clearly demonstrates that people who have strong attitudes and beliefs about a particular topic behave in ways that reinforce their opinions (Brewer & Crano, in press; Hillis & Crano, 1973). They may do this by seeking out messages that confirm their beliefs and avoiding messages that challenge their opinions; they may "misperceive" messages that are discrepant, or different from, their own views; or they may disparage the source of the message or the message itself. In other words, people with strong prior attitudes on a topic are difficult to persuade, and the more extreme their attitudes, the less persuadable they become.

The extent to which a receiver is involved in or committed to his prior opinions will influence his persuasibility. In one study, a group of boys and girls was exposed to two messages (Eagly & Manus, 1966). One message argued for stricter school rules for boys; the other argued for more school control over the type of clothing girls could wear. The boys in the experiment disparaged the relevant message (stricter school rules for boys) and the speaker more than the girls did; the girls disparaged the message they were involved in more than the boys did. Similarly, people who have made a public commitment to a position are more difficult to persuade than those who have not made such a commitment (Gerard, 1964). Thus the wise communicator avoids pushing receivers into a situation in which they feel compelled to take a strong stand on the issue under debate.

Directly related to the prior attitudes of receivers is the degree of attitude similarity between them and the source. Receivers will favor a source they think has attitudes similar to their own. They will view that source as more intelligent, better informed, and better adjusted than one with dissimilar attitudes (Byrne, 1961). Simply speaking, we tend to like people who have views similar to our own and we are generally more responsive to a message from a source we perceive as similar to ourselves. This is often the case among friends and may help to explain why people find it easier to communicate with their friends than with strangers.

Machiavellianism

Since Niccoli Machiavelli wrote *The Prince* in 1532, the term *Machiavellianism* has come to connote the use of guile, deceit, and opportunism in interpersonal relations. The Machiavellian, or Mach, is an individual who manipulates others for his or her own purposes (Christie & Geis, 1970). The high Mach, according to Christie and Geis, has a personality that is devoid of interest in interpersonal relationships, is unconcerned with group morality, has limited commitment to anything other than self, and possesses a distorted perception of reality due to the influence of personal needs. The low Mach has opposite attributes, although these persons have a tendency to spend time communicating about irrelevant topics in group situations.

Christie and Geis (1970) have found that high Machs are consistent in behaving manipulatively in interactions with peers when studied in the laboratory, and they assume that most of the interpersonal manipulation that occurs outside of the laboratory is verbally mediated. As far as low Machs are concerned, they appear to be more susceptible to emotional involvement in interactions on an interpersonal level and tend to be somewhat easily manipulated.

In game situations, the high Mach does not assume that the other members in the game will be loyal, and does not feel betrayed when they are not. If the stakes are high enough, the high Mach has little difficulty advocating a position contrary to personal beliefs, as long as this will insure success in the game (Burgoon, Miller, & Tubbs, 1972). In another study, Burgoon (1971) found that high Machs are more successful in unstructured groups in which face-to-face communication with other group members is possible. In other words, the high Mach has a superior talent for improvisation in terms of thinking on his or her feet when others are present. Thus the high Mach will usually perform in a more persuasive manner than low Machs in dyadic and small-group communication contexts. The Mach is persuaded less but persuades more. Adapting to such a personality trait is important for a communicator.

Variations in Receiver Listening Ability

As we have stressed throughout this chapter, message reception is an essential and active component of the communication process. Listening is the primary receiver skill in any communication situation, and no two receivers possess the same listening skills. Perhaps the most obvious factor that might influence communication accuracy is the physical and psychological capability of both the sender and receiver to discharge their functions in the communication encounter. We will concentrate here on the physical and psychological factors affecting audience or receiver abilities to *hear, comprehend,* and *retain* communication messages. In other words, we are focusing our concerns on differences in receiver listening abilities.

Hearing, the first component of listening, is the physical ability to receive sounds. We will not belabor the point that a physical impairment will make it difficult, if not impossible, for a receiver to hear the spoken word. There are many physical maladies that affect an individual's hearing ability. The allied disciplines of speech audiology and pathology concern themselves with these physical impairments to hearing. In terms of an interpersonal communication perspective, we suggest that the speaker keep in mind that many people have some difficulty hearing. Speech clinicians point out that many people with hearing disorders are not aware that they have an impairment. Although it may not be possible to ascertain whether or not a receiver suffers from such a problem, some knowledge of the incidence of this problem may explain some receiver behavior.

Comprehension, the ability to interpret and understand the spoken word, is the next component of listening. Clearly, a person who cannot hear a verbal message also will be unable to comprehend it. A receiver will be limited in his or her ability to comprehend a verbal message if the message variables are too complex, if the receiver has a limited vocabulary or intelligence level, or if the speaker has difficulty articulating messages. Attention to the demographic and personality variables we discussed above should be sufficient to compensate for vocabulary, complexity, and intelligence. The receiver should keep in mind that articulatory difficulties may be either chronic or temporary. It is not uncommon for physical exhaustion, high anxiety level, or prolonged speaking to temporarily impair a communicator's speaking ability. All of these factors have some effect on the receiver's comprehension level and ultimately detract from communication accuracy. The receiver can adjust to factors such as poor *vocal quality* (hoarseness, harshness, nasality, breathiness), poor *pitch patterns*, and other *nonfluencies*. With the exception of extreme cases, there is an initial period of getting used to such sounds. After this period of adjustment, listening comprehension does not seem to be significantly affected. Receivers can adapt to stuttering so that message comprehension will not be significantly impaired (Petrie, 1963).

The third component of listening, *retention*, is the ability to remember what has been said. Good listening skills, particularly the ability to recall information, are especially critical to college students, who depend on lectures and discussions for a great deal of their information. Studies at the University of Minnesota have revealed that students often recall better than they understand. To discover the reasons why recall is often superior to comprehension in students, experimenters hypothesized that if students anticipated what they were looking for in a speech, their comprehension and retention of the material would be increased. During the experiment, two groups of first-year students listened to the same speech and were then questioned on its content. In one group, however, the material was prefaced by anticipatory, or goal-setting, comments that directed the students to look for certain items in the material. The results confirmed the hypothesis that anticipation is an important part of effective listening (Brown, 1959).

Experiments such as these point to a need for specific training in listening. These experiments are helpful in isolating variables that contribute to good listening skills. For many years educators thought that improving reading ability automatically improved listening ability. On the basis of continued research we now know that there is not necessarily a direct relationship between reading ability and listening skills.

Everyone enjoys listening to a clever and entertaining speaker discussing an interesting topic, but what happens when the speaker is humorless, the topic boring, and the vocabulary difficult? In such a situation, the inexperienced listener is likely to turn off all listening powers and begin daydreaming or napping. This is an effective escape mechanism but not very helpful in increasing a person's knowledge or improving listening skills. Nearly every student has been embarrassed when asked a question by the teacher while feigning attention. In addition to helping to avoid embarrassment, awareness of some common barriers to effective listening can prove invaluable to most college students.

Barriers to Effective Listening

Most people with poor listening habits lack formalized training in listening. The first step in correcting deficient listening habits is recognition of the common barriers to effective listening. However, recognition must be accompanied by a conscious intent to improve listening skills and a great deal of hard work in overcoming these problems. The following is an aggregation of some common obstacles to effective listening; we will leave the desire and diligence to you.

1. *Physical Impairments.* Some physical impairment, on the part of either the sender or the receiver, can hinder effective communication. Communicators can compensate for these deficiencies, and speech clinicians can help to alleviate or lessen the effects of such impairments.

2. *Disinterest.* Poor listeners frequently excuse themselves from reception of verbal messages because they are uninterested in the discussion. Although effective listeners may feel the same way about the topic, they will attempt to ferret out the necessary information. College students, particularly, do not have the luxury of being uninterested, unless, of course, their purpose of being college students serves a social rather than an academic end.

3. *Distracting Speaker Characteristics.* Individual differences are such that most of us will encounter communicators who annoy us. We may not like the way they dress, their particular style of delivery, the tone or pitch of their voice, or their gestures or mannerisms. In short, many people look for excuses not to listen. The good listener will ignore such factors and concentrate on the material.

4. *Inflammatory Language.* Although profanity is the most common type of inflammatory language, it is by no means the only type of language that throws listening behaviors into a frenzy. Suggestive terms; racial, ethnic, or sexual slurs; and unpopular or unfamiliar slang expressions may also raise objections in the receiver. Try to ignore such language and concentrate on the essence of the material, even though your objections may be considerable. Remember that people operate with differing sets of moral and ethical codes, not to mention different levels of common sense.

5. *Self-Debating.* It is a common fault of the poor listener to debate silently with the spoken ideas of the speaker. It is difficult to listen when one is attempting to pick apart a speaker's comments or think up a witty or clever reply. It is advisable not to argue with a message —listen to it. *After* the message is presented is the most effective time to weigh its merits.

6. *Physical and Psychological Distractions.* There are many physical distractions that impede effective listening. Noise, room temperature, lighting, furnishings, and the presence of others are but a few. Similarly, psychological factors, such as tension, anxiety, fatigue, and excessive emotion, can impede listening. Although we often have little control over environmental factors, we can prepare ourselves in advance when we know that our full attention is required for a listening situation. Good listeners will also insure that distractions from other inattentive listeners do not interfere with their ability to receive a verbal message. College students who pay to attend class should *never* permit others to disrupt their education by talking or creating distractions.

7. *Note-Taking.* Students especially are conditioned to take notes on everything said in a lecture. Many important points are lost in asking the person beside you what was just said. Moreover, many speakers are not organized enough to make note-taking possible. The effective listener will jot down *major points* and perhaps will emphasize other points with a parenthetical reference to some familiar experience or fact. The poor listener will try to take down every word that was spoken. An effective form of note taking is to fill in an outline of the major points *immediately* after the lecture or discussion.

8. *Fact Hunting.* Some people are conditioned to listen only for facts. Well-organized messages use facts to provide evidence for major themes or claims. By attending to facts only, however, you may miss the major points of the address. The wise listener will concentrate on major points and will leave the facts for later.

9. *False Security.* Americans, on the average, speak at approximately 125 words per minute, whereas the average thought process can accommodate many more words per minute. Roughly, the receiver can take in information nearly four times faster than the speaker can dispense it. Without realizing it consciously, most of us sense that we can let our mind wander for a brief, few seconds and still turn our attention back to the speaker in time to capture the next idea or topic. Unfortunately, or fortunately, depending on the speaker or the source of our inattention, we frequently do not return to the discussion in time to catch the next point. The good listener will use this speech-thought differential wisely to recapitulate or preview the verbal content.

10. *Effort Expended.* Listening effectively is hard work and requires an expenditure of effort commensurate with the difficulty of the material. The type of listening patterns appropriate for casual conversations or for talk shows, such as *The Arsenio Hall Show*, will hardly prepare one for a difficult physics lecture or a political debate. Effective listeners must practice their listening skills on some difficult material.

As we stated earlier, effective listening can be possible only when the receiver is motivated to listen to the communication. Listening is a difficult task requiring attention, energy, and skill. An effective listener must adjust to the vagaries of the speaker as well as to the physical surroundings in which the communication transaction takes place. It is easy for a person to focus attention on a speaker's physical appearance, a nearby conversation, or distracting environmental factors. But all of these distractions interfere with effective listening and accurate communication. The rewards of improved listening are many and varied. A good listener is not only a better student but will probably be a better employee, a more-informed voter, and a generally well-liked individual.

Feedback: The Receiver's Response

Rarely do we find ourselves conversing with a chair or a coffee table (especially when there are other people around). The reason seems obvious: These are inanimate objects. Yet a computer is an inanimate object, and we can engage in a kind of communication with it. The fundamental difference between a chair and a computer is that the latter can respond to us. This response of a receiver to the source's message is called *feedback,* and it is a vital part of the communication process.

Human feedback differs greatly from the feedback provided by a machine. A machine, such as a computer, is coded to answer certain questions in a specific manner, providing such information as "incorrect," "file not found," "error reading drive c:", or "insufficient disk space." When human receivers provide feedback for a source, they engage in a complex series of verbal and nonverbal behavior. A receiver may smile, frown, sigh, yawn, wiggle, nod the head in agreement or disagreement, and make a variety of verbal answers. These cues let the source know whether his or her message is being accurately received. These cues are one of the most powerful means to attempt control that the receiver has.

Feedback enables the source to correct and adjust the message to fit the needs of the receiver. Suppose a college professor is demonstrating a difficult principle to a class. Midway through the lecture negative responses from the students are noticed. Some yawn, others look confused, and several classmates are whispering and comparing notes. From the feedback being received, the professor concludes that the message is not getting through to the students. So the professor changes wordings and gestures in an attempt to improve the message. The receivers in this situation have exercised control over the source through feedback; consequently, the feedback was useful to the source by providing information that helped the source accomplish his or her objectives.

The significance of feedback in the communication process cannot be exaggerated. Feedback is the link between source and receiver that gives communication its transactional nature. Just as the receiver provides feedback for the source, the source responds and emits cues back to the receiver. The speaker adjusts to the receiver, but the receiver also adjusts to the speaker in a simultaneous process. Everyone involved in communication sends messages and emits feedback, so that they are linked together in a dynamic transaction.

The greatest advantage of face-to-face or small-group communication lies in the amount and type of feedback provided. Face-to-face communication provides a continuous flow of immediate feedback. The source can easily see and hear the responses of the receiver; this helps in evaluating the message's effectiveness. If the feedback indicates that the message is not coming through, the communicator has the opportunity to change tactics immediately.

In mass communication situations, however, feedback is often delayed because of the separation of source and receiver. Consider the magazine writer, the television performer, or a political candidate speaking over the radio. Each is a source with a message to get across to the public, and each is concerned about the way that message will be received. Yet these sources can neither see nor hear the reactions of their listeners; they may not even be sure that they actually have an audience. Any feedback they may receive is delayed, so they do not have the opportunity to adjust and retransmit their message immediately to the audience.

When feedback is delayed, the receiver's ability to respond to a message—and to create an impact through that response—is minimized. The receiver may write a letter to the source or even call the television or radio station, but the receiver will never be sure that the message is noted by the source. Nor can the source rely on the few random samples of received feedback as being indicative of the reaction of the entire audience.

The effects of feedback on learning situations were tested in a classic study by two communication experimenters, Harold Leavitt and Ronald Mueller (1951). In the experiment, specific material was communicated to four groups of students under different feedback conditions. In the zero feedback condition, the teacher sat behind a blackboard and allowed no questions from the students. In the visual audience condition, the students could see the teacher, but no verbal feedback was allowed. In the yes-no condition, the students were allowed to respond with only "yes" or "no." Finally, in free feedback, the students were permitted to ask questions and make comments as often as they wished. The results confirmed the beneficial effects of feedback in learning situations. Scores indicating how well students learned the material increased steadily from zero to free feedback conditions.

Not all feedback is perceived as good or helpful to the source. Every receiver has the ability to emit positive or negative feedback, and we have all consciously used this power to exert control over a source. Positive feedback encourages the continuation of a behavior, whereas negative feedback indicates that behaviors should be changed. If a man approaches a woman at a party and begins talking to her, the woman may emit positive feedback by smiling, using direct eye contact, and participating in the conversation. This positive feedback will encourage the man to continue his behaviors. Negative feedback might consist of yawning in the man's face, glancing around the room, and answering only direct questions in monosyllables. These negative feedback behaviors are intended to modify the man's behavior, possibly to leave the woman alone. Positive feedback is encouraging and rewarding to the source. A source receiving positive feedback is likely to repeat the actions that produced the feedback. Negative feedback may be unpleasant or punishing to the source and may cause a change in tactics.

Studies have shown that positive and negative feedback may have a tremendous impact on a speaker's delivery (Gardiner, 1971). Negative feedback tends to make a speaker less fluent than positive feedback. The communicator's rate of speaking has been found to increase with positive feedback and decrease with negative feedback. In one study, negative feedback produced a significant increase in the loudness of the speaker's voice, but positive feedback had no effect on volume. Negative feedback causes speakers to shorten their presentation, whereas positive feedback causes speakers to perceive their presentations as longer than they actually are. Negative feedback generally inhibits the delivery of a speaker.

Feedback may even affect the source's attitude toward the subject being discussed (Gardiner, 1971). It has been demonstrated that if a person receives positive feedback when defending a belief that is discrepant from his or her own, if is likely that the person will change attitudes about the topic. For example, suppose a student in a social problems course is required to make a speech on the legalization of marijuana. The student knows that the professor is against legalization and decides to argue this position, even though believing marijuana should be legalized. If the student receives praise from classmates and a good grade from the professor, the student is likely to change his or her own attitude and favor the position that marijuana should not be legalized. However, if a speaker receives negative feedback when arguing a position not believed in, the speaker probably will not change his or her opinion. When speakers argue from a position that is consistent with their own beliefs, both very positive and very negative feedback will strengthen their attitude.

People are dependent on communication for survival, and feedback is the essence of the communication process. Without feedback, we could never exchange ideas, test new theories, or even learn about each other. Our dependence on feedback is most poignantly illustrated when former prisoners of war speak of their years in isolation as the cruelest experience of all. Feedback also plays a vital role in our development, for our concept of self is formed and constantly challenged by our perception of the way others see us. Vital personal needs also are met by feedback. Each of us has the need to feel significant, worthwhile, and loved, and these needs can be met by positive supportive feedback.

Summary

1. The receiver is often considered the passive person in the communication process, although without the receiver there would be no transfer of meaning. To some extent, the receiver exerts a degree of control over the source, and both receiver and source must accommodate each other in the communication transaction.

2. A source must make certain generalizations and predictions about the audience. A demographic analysis of the audience can provide information with which to make such generalizations and predictions. Six demographic variables will aid in making these assumptions: age, sex, sex role, social and economic background, racial and ethnic factors, and intelligence. Although generalizations and predictions based on these variables may not always be accurate, sometimes they are all that a source has available.

3. It is often beneficial to view receivers as individuals who possess unique personality dimensions. An individual's personality usually remains fairly stable over time and may, therefore, affect the response to a message. A personality analysis of the receivers can improve predictions concerning audience reaction, and it can assist in making communications more effective with given receivers. People with high self-esteem are generally less persuadable than people with low self-esteem. Aggressive people are generally less persuadable than unaggressive people. The anxiety level of a receiver tends to interact with the content of the message, thereby affecting the receiver's persuasibility. Receivers with high anxiety tend to be less persuaded by anxiety-producing messages, whereas receivers with low anxiety tend to be more persuaded by anxiety-producing messages. Receivers with strong prior attitudes on a topic are less persuadable than receivers with neutral attitudes. Finally, a high degree of involvement in or commitment to an idea will make a receiver less receptive to a message that argues counter to the receiver's prior attitudes.

4. Machiavellianism has come to connote the use of guile, deceit, and opportunism in interpersonal relationships. The Machiavellian (Mach) is a person who manipulates others for some self-interest. This individual can have a significant effect on the communication situation. High Machs tend to be more successful and create a greater impact in face-to-face communication situations than do their less manipulative counterparts.

5. Listening, the essential receiver skill in any communication situation, involves hearing, comprehension, and retention. Most people have developed poor listening habits owing to a lack of formal training in listening. The source may effectively increase audience reception of the message by prefacing the speech or communication with goal-setting statements.

6. Feedback is the response of the receiver to the communication message of the source. It serves as the link between the interactants, giving communication a spontaneous and transactional nature. Feedback enables the source to judge the impact of a message and to adjust the message to meet the needs of the receiver or audience. Feedback may also affect the source's delivery and the attitudes concerning the topic being discussed. Feedback is much more prevalent in face-to-face and small-group situations than in public or mass communication settings, where it is usually minimal or delayed. The

effectiveness of communication generally increases as the amount of feedback increases.

References

Abelson R. P., & Lesser, G. S. (1959). The developmental theory of persuadability. In C. I. Hovland & I. L. Janis (Eds.), *Personality and persuasibility* (pp. 138-166). New Haven, CT: Yale University Press.

Andrews, P. H. (1985). *Upward directed persuasive communication and attribution of success and failure: Toward an understanding of the role of gender.* Paper presented at the annual conference of the Central States Speech Association, Indianapolis.

Brewer, M. B., & Crano, W. D. (in press). *Social psychology.* St. Paul, MN: West Educational Publishing.

Brown, C. T. (1959). Studies in listening comprehension. *Speech Monographs, 126,* 288-294.

Burgoon, M. (1971). The relationship between willingness to manipulate others and success in two different types of speech communication courses. *The Speech Teacher, 20,* 178-183.

Burgoon, M. (1989). Social influence. In H. Giles & P. Robinson (Eds.), *Handbook of language and social psychology* (pp. 51-72). London: John Wiley.

Burgoon, M., Miller, G. R., & Tubbs, S. L. (1972). Machiavellianism, justification, and attitude change following counterattitudinal advocacy. *Journal of Personality and Social Psychology, 22,* 366-371.

Byrne, D. (1961). Interpersonal attraction and attitude similarity. *Journal of Abnormal and Social Psychology, 62,* 713-715.

Carmichael, C. W. (1970). Frustration, sex and persuadability. *Western Speech, 34,* 300-307.

Christie, R., & Geis, F. (1970). *Studies in Machiavellianism.* New York: Academic Press.

Costa, P. T., Jr., McCrae, R. R., Sonderman, A. B., Barbano, H. E., Lebowitz, B., & Larson, D. M. (1986). Cross-sectional studies of personality in a national sample: 2. Stability in neuroticism, extraversion, and openness. *Psychology and Aging, 1,* 144-149.

Daniels, J. (1970). The poor: Aliens in an affluent society: Cross-cultural communications. *Today's Speech, 18,* 15-21.

Eagly, A. H., & Manus, M. (1966). Evaluation of message and communicator as a function of involvement. *Journal of Personality and Social Psychology, 3,* 483-485.

Fabes, R. A., & Laner, M. R. (1986). How the sexes perceive each other: Advantages and disadvantages. *Sex Roles, 15,* 129-143.

Gardiner, J. C. (1971). A synthesis of experimental studies on speech communication feedback. *Journal of Communication, 21,* 17-20.

Gerard, H. B. (1964). Conformity and commitment to the group. *Journal of Abnormal and Social Psychology, 68,* 209-211.

Gerwirtz, J. (1954). Three determinants of attention seeking in young children. *Monographs for the Society for Research in Child Development, 19,* 2.

Helson, R., & Moane, G. (1987). Personality change in women from college to midlife. *Journal of Personality and Social Psychology, 53,* 176-186.

Hillis, J., & Crano, W. D. (1973). An investigation of the additive effects of utility and attitudinal supportiveness in the selection of information. *Journal of Social Psychology, 89,* 257-269.

Hovland, C. A., Lumsdaine, A. A., & Sheffield, F. D. (1949). The effects of presenting "one side" versus "both sides" in changing opinions on a controversial subject. In *Experiments in mass communication: Vol. 3. Social psychology of World War II* (pp. 201-227). Princeton, NJ: Princeton University Press.

Infante, D. A. (1987). Aggressiveness. In J. C. McCroskey & J. Daly (Eds.), *Personality and interpersonal communication.* Newbury Park, CA: Sage.

Janis, I. L., & Field, P. B. (1959). A behavioral assessment of persuasibility. In C. I. Hovland & I. L. Janis (Eds.), *Personality and persuadability* (pp. 29-54). New Haven, CT: Yale University Press.

Janis, I. L., & Feshbach, S. (1965). Effects of fear-arousing communications. *Journal of Personality and Social Psychology, 1,* 17-27.

Janis, I. L., & Rife, D. (1959). Persuadability and emotional disorder. In C. A. Hovland & I. L. Janis (Eds.), *Personality and persuadability* (pp. 121-137). New Haven, CT: Yale University Press.

Knower, F. H. (1935). Experimental studies of change in attitudes: A study of the effect of oral argument on changes of attitude. *Journal of Social Psychology, 6,* 315-344.

Leavitt, H. J., & Mueller, R. A. (1951). Some effects of feedback on communication. *Human Relations, 4,* 401-410.

Leventhal, H., & Perloe, S. I. (1962). A relationship between self-esteem and persuasibility. *Journal of Abnormal and Social Psychology, 64,* 385-388.

Levine, J. M., & Murphy, G. (1943). The learning and forgetting of controversial material. *Journal of Abnormal and Social Psychology, 34,* 507-517.

Marple, C. (1933). The comparative susceptibility of three age levels to the suggestion of group versus expert opinion. *Journal of Social Psychology, 4,* 176-186.

Martin, H. M., & Colburn, C. W. (1972). *Communication and consensus.* San Francisco: Harcourt Brace Jovanovich.

McGuire, W. J. (1969). The nature of attitudes and attitude change. In G. Lindsey & E. Aronson (Eds.), *The handbook of social psychology* (2nd ed., Vol. 3, pp. 248-249). Reading, MA: Addison-Wesley.

Miller, G. R., & Burgoon, M. (1973). *New techniques of persuasion.* New York: Harper & Row.

Montgomery, C. L., & Burgoon, M. (1977). An experimental study of the interactive effects of sex and androgyny of attitude change. *Communications Monographs, 44,* 130-135.

Nesbitt, R. E., & Gordon, A. (1967). Self-esteem and susceptibility to social influence. *Journal of Personality and Social Psychology, 5,* 268-276.

Nunnally, J., & Bobren, H. (1959). Variables influencing the willingness to receive communications on mental health. *Journal of Personality, 27,* 38-46.

Pearson, J. C., Turner, L. H., & Todd-Mancillas, W. (1991). *Gender and communication* (2nd ed.). Dubuque, IA: William C. Brown.

Petrie, C. (1963). Informative speaking: A summary and bibliography of related research. *Speech Monographs, 30,* 79-91.

Schachter, S. (1959). *The psychology of affiliation.* Stanford, CA: Stanford University Press.

Scheidel, T. M. (1963). Sex and persuadability. *Speech Monographs, 30,* 353-358.

Stevenson, H. W. (1965). Social reinforcement of children's behavior. In L. P. Pipsitt & C. C. Spiker (Eds.), *Advances in child development* (Vol. 2). New York: Academic Press.

Wegrocki, H. J. (1934). The effect of prestige suggestibility on emotional attitude. *Journal of Social Psychology, 5,* 384-394.

Wheeless, L. R. (1975). An investigation of receiver apprehension and social context dimension of communication apprehension. *The Speech Teacher, 24,* 261-268.

4

Variables Inhibiting
Effective Communication

We believe that it is appropriate to extend our discussion of source and receiver variables in the communication process with mention of some other variables that effect communication. It is not uncommon, particularly after one reads about the dynamic and transactional interface between source and receiver, to assume that communication will occur smoothly if one takes into account the various factors that we just discussed. This is not the case at all, and we do not intend to convey this impression. We probably fail in communicating accurate reflections of our thoughts and feelings more often than we convey precise meanings.

As you will recall from our introductory remarks, our plan for this book is to follow the present discussion of communication variables with a section on the various functions that communication may serve. It also makes sense to reserve discussion of inhibiting factors that arise when one is attempting to persuade, to facilitate social relationships, or to manage conflict for a more detailed analysis of these communication functions. Given this rationale, we will briefly focus our attention in this chapter on some of the general factors that inhibit communication regardless of the context or purpose of that communication. We urge the reader to keep in mind that these obstacles, as well as those that we will introduce in later chapters, can and will influence all communication attempts to some degree.

Communication, as we have emphasized earlier, is a highly personal and individualized process, and, to some extent, we can trace many communication problems back to this fact. If we probe into the attitudes, perceptions, and psychological predispositions of communication participants and into the way they use language to express themselves, it sometimes seems implausible that communication can succeed on anything but the most elementary of levels. For even when people share a common cultural background, they are ultimately isolated from each other's reality by individual differences involving experiential factors, personality, morality, and philosophical orientations and also by the feelings and expectations they associate with words, the symbols of this reality. Each person is unique and responds to stimuli in a unique manner. These qualifications may seem a bit overwhelming and pessimistic, but they point to what we consider a sobering fact of life: Communication, at the very best, involves a compromise of meaning between individuals.

The Scientific View of Language

The scientific view of language rests upon a number of basic assumptions.[1] In taking a scientific view of language, we argue that the structure of language is based, to a great extent, on the fundamental concepts of abstraction and inference. Central to any understanding of the inhibiting factors in the communication process, therefore, is a thorough awareness of the symbolic nature of communication and language. We need to distinguish *language* from *speech*. Language is the most important aspect of speech, and in a sense, it is the cause of speech. However, it is not identical with speech. Our language is not simply the sum total of all the speech sounds made by speakers of English, although most of these speech sounds are determined by language in some way. There is an abstract structure that conforms to the system of the language, but a particular speaker deviates from that actual structure when speaking. Deviations occur in the way words are employed or in the type of words employed. Each of us uses language in ways that are unique. Effective communicators maintain grammatical correctness, yet are able to manipulate words in such a way as to create their own idiosyncratic meaning.

The Abstract Nature of Language

Words enable a language to be communicated to members of a particular social system because they are *symbols of abstract ideas or things*. By *abstract*, we mean that words vary in their degree of precision or vagueness. As we perceive an object or an idea, we naturally omit, summarize, and generalize about the nature or meaning of that object or idea. The meaning of the words we use, therefore, reflects these abstractions. Many communication problems arise when we fail to recognize this fundamental aspect of language by assuming that others share the same meanings that we have for words.

Symbols have no meaning in and of themselves. They require some type of interpretation, and hence, they are *arbitrary*. Therefore, there is *no inherent relationship between the form of the word and its meaning*. For example, if you are in a foreign country and know nothing of that country's language, you could not examine the form of a word and discover its meaning. Within any given language community, meanings are learned as part of the socialization process. For common meaning to be reached in communication, common meanings must be ascribed to symbols or words. People must be sensitive to the meanings that other people give to specific symbols. When people forget that words are symbols and require interpretation, however, they play roles out of *Alice in Wonderland* in assuming "when I use a word, it means just what I choose it to mean—neither more nor less." This obviously ignores the role of the other people involved in communication.

We make our world meaningful by interpreting symbols, that is, by creating meaning for words. As one philosopher observed:

> Man lives in a symbolic universe. . . . He does not confront reality immediately; he cannot see it, as it were, face to face . . . instead of dealing with things themselves, man is, in a sense, constantly conversing with himself. He has so enveloped himself in linguistic (symbolic) forms that he cannot see or know anything except by the interposition of this artificial medium. (Cassirer, 1944, p. 25)

Viewed from the scientific perspective, language is not reality itself but merely a representation of reality—an abstraction. Scientific theorists, such as John Condon (1975), emphasize that the "word is not the thing," in the same way that a "map is not the territory" (p. 129). Words, then, represent reality in the same sense that maps are representations of territory but not the territory itself. It is also true that the "map" does not represent *all* of the territory—a word cannot encompass the entire meaning of what it is intended to represent. Because words are arbitrary, they possess a level of ambiguity or vagueness. As concepts or ideas become more abstract, it becomes increasingly more difficult to interpret intended meanings.

Overall, the more abstract the term, the greater the likelihood of misunderstanding. For example, teachers often suggest to students that they should "study hard" to do well on an exam. In this situation, what type of studying will satisfy the admonition to "study hard"? Clearly, the meaning of "study hard" may differ for the student and the teacher. Does the teacher want the students to spend a great number of hours memorizing course materials or to spend enough time on relevant topics to be sure the course material is understood? It is often the case that students will come to their instructor after performing poorly on an exam and claim that they studied "hard," that they spent an entire night going over the material and trying to memorize it, only to discover that the exam was made up of essay questions requiring integration of relevant concepts and ideas. This misunderstanding between teacher and student expectations was due in part to the vagueness of language, in this case the meaning ascribed to studying "hard." Preparation for the exam would have been greatly facilitated had the instructor used more precise language in explaining what was meant by "study hard," and the student would have benefited from questioning the instructor about what was meant by those words.

The preceding example illustrates a fundamental problem related to the abstract nature of language—making erroneous inferences. *Inferences* are judgments made from evidence or assumptions. One important factor that often inhibits effective communication is our failure to distinguish between statements of inference and statements of observation or fact. It is not possible to make these distinctions based solely on the form of a statement because our language provides no grammatical, syntactical, or pronunciational distinctions between them. Thus it is not surprising that our failure to distinguish on these verbal levels contributes appreciably to the difficulty we have communicating. In short, we find it exceedingly easy to make inferences about reality as we perceive it and to utter inferential statements with the false assurance that we are dealing with facts as we observed them. For example, I can say "Mark is wearing a red shirt." This statement of observation or fact can be easily confirmed or refuted simply by looking at the shirt Mark is wearing. However, what if I were to say, "Mark is hungry." This statement goes beyond simple observation. I have now made an inference about Mark's behavior based upon the assumption that, in this case, his rapid consumption of food reflects his gustatorial state. In fact, Mark may not be hungry at all. He may be eating because he has an upset stomach, he wants to relieve stress, or he has an eating disorder. Although this example may be frivolous, erroneous inferences can, and do, lead to disastrous consequences.

The inference-observation dilemma also involves a degree of risk taking. Everyone is, of course, aware of taking a calculated risk. People frequently observe a situation, such as the amount of material to be covered on the final exam, and decide not to act on that situation (i.e., they may not study much of the material because it *may not* be on the final examination). In this example, they are inferring that the exam questions will be limited and that they can get away with not studying much of the material. Whether their hunch or inference is right or wrong, they are still aware of the potential outcomes of such behavior. Unfortunately, when we fail to recognize that we have made an inference (or conclusion from facts or premises) instead of

Table 4.1 Characteristics of Statements of Observation and of Inference

Statements of Observation
1. Can be made only after actually observing some behavior or occurrence
2. Must stay within the parameters of the observation
3. Are appropriate only for the actual observer
4. Approach certainty or sureness

Statements of Inference
1. Can be made at any time
2. Go beyond the parameters of actual observation; an inference can be made to the limits of one's imagination
3. Can be made by anyone, not just by the observer
4. State only degrees of probability or likelihood

an observation (or noting the occurrence of some observable phenomenon), we are not aware of the possible outcomes, which can sometimes prove costly, dangerous, or even fatal. The tragic explosion of the Space Shuttle *Challenger* appears to be due, in part, to a series of faulty inferences made by officials at NASA and Morton Thiokol, the manufacturer of the O-ring that malfunctioned in the early moments of the flight (Hirokawa, Gouran, & Martz, 1988). One especially questionable judgment was based on the inference that redundant, or back-up, systems would compensate for any failure in the primary O-ring system. This inference was based upon a long history of success in launching manned rockets, going back to the *Mercury* capsule flights of the early 1960s.

We need to stress that making inferences is a necessary and adaptive mode of information processing. We *must* make inferences throughout the day to make sense of our environment and, by and large, the inferences we make are valid and valuable. Inferences are at times the only recourse we have available to us. We are suggesting that inferences be *labeled* as inferences with a certain degree of probability associated with them. When inferences, especially incorrect ones, are considered to be actual observations, however, effective communication surely will suffer. Table 4.1 lists some of the characteristics of statements of observation and statements of inference.

One final issue regarding the abstract nature of language worth discussing is that much of the language we use is *equivocal*—it has two or more possible interpretations. Equivocal communication, then, is ambiguous and obscure and is often contradictory and evasive. Misunderstanding often arises when individuals mistakenly assume that their interpretation of a statement is the correct or intended one. For example, suppose your roommate asks for your opinion of a new, completely hideous hairstyle and you reply, "A lot of people can't wear their hair that way." Your roommate may be pleased with this response, believing that your impression was favorable when, out of politeness, you were trying desperately to evade an honest answer that would hurt your roommate's feelings. We often equivocate when we believe that a completely honest reply will result in unpleasant consequences. Further, equivocation allows us later to deny any "misinterpretation" of what we have said. Think of the ways that we and others gracefully decline invitations to social events we do not wish to attend or how we reply when asked about the appearance of a friend's newborn baby. Equivocating allows us to respond to direct requests without disclosing our true feelings or intentions.

Consider the following situation: Your date cannot (or will not) go out with you unless you find a date for his or her less than attractive friend. In an effort to save yourself from a boring evening at home, you ask one of your friends to go along with you on a blind date. Invariably your friend will ask you to describe his or her potential date before committing to go along. What do you do? The standard reply, of course, is, that the friend "has a wonderful personality." Chances are that this stock reply will tip your friend off. Thus a more strategic and clever equivocation might increase your chances of evading a direct response and persuading your friend to escort your date's friend.

This above example is, no doubt, somewhat trivial. However, equivocal communication is not always so. Devious communicators exploit others with messages that appear to answer questions, but in fact do not (for more information concerning equivocal communication, see Bavelas, Black, Chovil, & Mullett, 1990; Bowers, Elliott, & Desmond, 1977). The following is an exchange between a reporter and President Nixon's press secretary during the Watergate scandal:

Reporter: Has the President asked for any resignations so far, and have any been submitted to his desk?

Ziegler: I have repeatedly stated that there has been no change in the White House staff.

Reporter: But that was not the question. Has he asked for any resignations?

Ziegler: I understand the question, and I heard it the first time. Let me go through my answer. As I said, there is no change in the White House staff. There have been no resignations submitted.

Given the political situation at the time of this press conference, it is clear that Ziegler understood the question being asked, but, for political reasons, a direct response would have, at least in Ziegler's mind, had disastrous consequences. Yet, because of the nature of the situation he was in, Ziegler tried to appear to answer the question, when in fact he did not. We have no way of knowing, given Ziegler's responses, whether Nixon did or did not request resignations from any of his staff.

We will not argue that full disclosure of our beliefs and feelings is always the correct choice, although it would certainly reduce the amount of ambiguity found in equivocal communication. The degree and amount of open and full disclosure in which we are willing to engage is an individual choice that is determined by circumstances and the relationships of the interactants. Awareness of some of the vagaries of language and communication, however, will help communicators increase their effectiveness and pinpoint some of the miscommunications of others.

H. P. Grice (1975) provides a set of general principles that people are expected to observe if conversations are to move in a mutually understandable direction. Grice's Cooperative Principle contains the categories of Quantity, Quality, Relation, and Manner. *Quantity* refers to the amount of information that is expected to be provided so that meanings can be understood by both parties. Included within this category is the maxim that individuals should contribute the amount of information required for the purposes of the exchange; nothing more, nothing less. Not presenting enough information clearly leads to misunderstandings, and overinformativeness may lead to confusion and may also mislead the course of the conversation. The category of *quality* refers to the truthfulness of the information. Contributions to a conversation should be genuine; that is, not saying what you know to be false and not making comments on issues in which you lack adequate evidence. The category of *relation* concerns the relevance of information contributed to the conversation, given the restrictions of the previous discourse. *Manner* relates not to *what* is being said in a conversation, but rather *how* it is being said. Grice argues that people should avoid obscurity and ambiguity while presenting information in a brief and orderly manner.

These "maxims" of conversation are not meant to suggest that people actually follow these practices in their everyday communication with others. They do suggest what is reasonable for us to follow in order for people to cooperate in their communication exchanges. A participant may intentionally violate a maxim to mislead others, to obscure an issue, or to create ambiguity in conversation. We argue that when these conversational maxims are followed, the effectiveness of information exchange will be enhanced, as well as increasing communicators' ability to influence and direct the actions of others.

The Nature of Language

To understand the scientific approach to language and the connection between language and reality in communication, it is essential that we turn our attention to the fundamental nature of language. Various aspects of the environment are given names through language. Therefore, *language orders reality*. It is the principal vehicle for social communication; it is influenced by social structure and, consequently, influences human social order. It can be argued that a society is a product of its language. Language separates and specifies certain features of the environment that are relevant to a particular society's mutual concerns and interests. For example, Arabs are said to have thousands of words in their language connected in some way with the camel. Inhabitants of the Solomon Islands have nine different names for the coconut, but no name corresponding to our general word for coconut. However, they have only one word for the different meals of the day, whereas we employ several (Lewis, 1948).

We believe that you will appreciate the variables inhibiting effective communication better if you view the communication process as the symbolic representation of reality. Many factors that impede effective communication are a result of both misperceptions and interpretations about symbols. Also, communication is a selective process in terms of what people expose themselves to and how they use this information.

Communication and Perception

Communication is inexorably tied to the perceptions people have about their world and the other people inhabiting their world. It has also been suggested that both communication and perceptions are inextricably tied to language.

One of the earliest notions of language and society is the *Whorf-Sapir hypothesis*. The basic premise of this theory is that our modes of thinking, as well as the artifacts of our culture, are at the mercy of the language we speak and, particularly, of the grammar of that language (Whorf, 1957). This notion grew out of early anthropological studies of the languages of the Native Americans, often called Amerind languages. For example, Whorf argued that the Hopi Indians could never perceive the world in terms of Aristotelian philosophy because that philosophy, as well as the whole of European philosophy, demands a separation between objects (nouns) and action (verbs). This distinction cannot be expressed easily in the Hopi language because the Hopis tend to classify words in terms of duration. For example, in Hopi, "flame" is a verb, not a noun, and is classified as an event of brief duration. On the other hand, the Hopi perception of this object-event relationship is difficult for Indo-Europeans to comprehend. Whorf argued that in English, verbs are used to denote action, whereas in Hopi the distinction between nouns and verbs is a distinction based entirely on duration instead of being a distinction between action and things. The Whorf-Sapir hypothesis begs the question, "Do these language differences also reflect differences in perception?" If the Whorf-Sapir hypothesis is correct, the basic perception of nature is determined by our language.

We would argue, however, that these differences in language may simply reflect differences in *priorities*, not in *perceptions*. Although in our culture we do not have a variety of words to distinguish variations in "coconut," it does not necessarily follow that we are incapable of perceiving variations in coconuts in much the same way as the inhabitants of the Solomon Islands. For Solomon Islanders, the ability to differentiate coconuts through the use of different words is functional and highlights the priority that they assign to that fruit in their culture. Focusing on functional variations in language allows us to view cultural differences in word usage as reflecting the specific needs of those cultures rather than perceptual divergence precipitated by the language itself.

Perceptions have also been linked to *psychological dispositions*. Research suggests that logical or analytical thinking is not the predominant mode of human response but is a limited reaction under conditions of need. People often respond according to the *law of least effort*. In terms of communication behavior, this appears at the most fundamental level in the tendency to confuse words or language with the things or processes they name. This inability to grasp the difference between a symbol and its referent causes differing perceptions due to a failure to check back from language to experience and reality. One would expect to be able to establish common symbols or perceptions suitable for any communication situation; but people are not governed by objective and immutable laws of logic, and they are not a community of computerized minds. People are psychologically different and they often do not know exactly what they think or believe. Their efforts at communicating, therefore, are frequently misrepresentations of their feelings and perceptions. If we acknowledge that thinking is integral to communicating, we can readily see how people create their own barriers in the communication process.

Closely related to differing psychological dispositions in forming perceptions is the *limited experience factor*. Because language is symbolic in nature, it can only evoke meaning in a receiver if that receiver has experiences corresponding to that symbol. Even if we all spoke the same language, it would not alleviate problems tied to our different experiences. We live in private worlds, each with our own perceptions, emotions, and attitudes. To the extent that these perceptions arise from similar experiences with similar aspects of reality as experienced by others, communicators can share more than just a common language. But language itself, even when very exact and precise, is a very limited device for producing mutual understanding when it is not based in common experience. People, then, will employ differing degrees of selectivity in their communication behavior.

Communication and Selectivity

Generally people are unaware that communication is a very selective process; thus they are unaware that selectivity greatly affects their communication. The significance of selectivity becomes apparent when we consider a common communication situation, such as watching the evening news.

For the sake of clarification, let us focus for a while on a hypothetical individual, Chris, at home on a Tuesday evening at 7 p.m. Having finished dinner, Chris decides to relax and turn on the evening news. Of course, there is a choice among several networks, but, like most of us, Chris prefers one over all the others. In making her decision, Chris is selectively exposing herself to just one of a number of possible news programs. Having decided which channel to watch, Chris may pay attention only to certain news stories. She may, for example, attend to only the political and economic news of the day, avoiding entertainment and the weather—both of which bore her. Of those messages to which Chris pays attention, she will perceive and interpret each in a very personal way. For instance, being a liberal Democrat, she may interpret a story about a Republican-sponsored bill to increase federal expenditures for defense as just another indication of Republican insensitivity to domestic issues. Like anyone else, Chris's selectivity does not stop here. On the next day and those that follow, she will retain just a few of the messages that she received during the news program.

While highlighting the importance of selectivity in communication, the above example also displays the stop-gap nature of these selective processes. In short, we cannot pay attention to a message to which we are not exposed; we cannot perceive and interpret a message to which we have not attended; and we cannot retain a message that we have not perceived. Undoubtedly, the subject of selectivity deserves careful consideration in any discussion of effective ways to communicate.

Selective Exposure

From the variety of communication experiences available to them, people choose to expose themselves to communication that reaffirms preexisting ideas and attitudes, thereby bolstering their image of themselves and what they "know." Such behavior is founded on a basic aspect of human nature: The rationale behind almost all human activity is the strong need to protect, maintain, and enhance one's self-concept or -image. For example, during the 1992 election, many Democrats endorsing Governor Bill Clinton refused to expose themselves to information suggesting that President George Bush should lead the country for the next four years. It is likely that more Republicans watched President Bush's campaign advertisements than Democrats, and they did so to reaffirm the attitudes and opinions they had concerning George Bush. This issue of selective exposure and its relationship to persuasion and social influence will be discussed in greater detail in Chapter 7.

Because people tend to expose themselves selectively to messages that support their self-image, we would expect the converse of this principle also to be true; that is, people tend to avoid messages that challenge their preconceptions. For example, we would expect a person who has very traditional attitudes about the roles of men and women to avoid listening to the messages of feminist supporters because they are a threat to a self-concept that has been reinforced since childhood. However, some experts challenge the idea that people intentionally avoid exposure to messages that are unfavorable to their self-image. Indeed, evidence is scant, and, for the moment, *all that can be said with certainty is that people selectively expose themselves to messages that reinforce their already existing attitudes.*

Selective Attention

Information theorists tell us that although the eye can handle about 5 million bits of data per second, the brain is able to "compute" the information at a much slower rate. Obviously, at any given time, we must select the information to which we will give active attention or else nothing will make sense.

The information received is usually held for a short time in what may be called "short-term sensory storage"—something similar to a short-term memory bank—from which we draw according to our capacity to process sensory input. When we do draw from it, we may either respond to the data immediately or transfer the information to a more permanent memory bank (Egeth, 1967). For example, let us say that you are reading a newspaper and have focused almost all of your attention on an article that interests you a great deal. If a friend sitting nearby happens to say a few words to you, you will probably continue to focus on the article. However, the stimulus provided by your friend's voice has not been totally neglected; it may simply have been transferred by your sensory receptors to the memory bank. Minutes later, when you have completed the article, you will have the capacity to draw the message (simply that someone said something to you) out of storage and attend to whatever your friend had been trying to convey. Clearly, a person can give attention only to a limited number of stimuli at one particular time.

There are several factors that may interfere with a person's ability to attend to stimuli in the environment. The most obvious obstacles are caused by certain physiological impairments, such as poor eyesight, poor hearing, or color blindness. People with normal vision, for example, turn their attention to the color of the traffic light before crossing a street. People who are color-blind, however, will attend to different stimuli in the same situation. In all likelihood, they will check to see which light is the brightest—the top or the bottom. If it is the top light, it will be concluded that the light is red.

Certain physiological needs can also interfere with interpersonal communication. Suppose you are having an extremely busy day at the office with no time for anything but a few quick coffee breaks. Immediately after work, you are required to attend a seminar featuring several speakers discussing their view on modern business management. The topics may be of interest to you; in fact, you may be seeking specific information that you know they can provide. But try as you will to listen to what is being said, you can think of nothing but the dinner that is to follow. In this case, your physiological need (hunger) has forced you to focus selectively on "food" as the most important stimulus in your environment. This need has impaired your ability to attend to other desirable stimuli. To some extent, training facilitates our ability to attend to certain stimuli that we know we will need at a particular moment. An aeronautical engineer at the Kennedy Space Center is faced with an awesome array of dials, graphs, buttons, toggle switches, and computer readouts. Unless he or she knows what to look for—that is, unless there is conscious selection of certain stimuli (a process of selective attention that seems impossible to the untrained observed)—effective communication with co-workers will be impaired. On a less sophisticated level, a retail clerk who works for a department store may be trained to attend to certain facts, such as the customer's name and address, the account number, the price of items purchased, the amount of payments made, and the date.

Sometimes our past experience forces us to focus our attention on certain stimuli in our environment. This is fortunate for us, otherwise, like Nero, we might be fiddling while our own house burns. Stimuli that imply an immediate danger often narrow our attention in this way. If someone shouts, "Watch out for that car," we would not consciously have to choose to attend to that warning rather than choose to watch the dog dig up the lawn across the street or to look at an attractive sunset on the horizon. Through past experience and familiarity with similar information, we automatically select the warning as the most important of all stimuli available to us.

Sometimes, however, familiarity with certain information tends to make people negligent in their conscious selection of data. If students are familiar with the material being discussed in a lecture, they might be less attentive to the professor's words than if they had no knowledge of the subject. The professor's attempt to communicate is thus foiled by the students' assumption that they already know what the professor intends to say; the students' attention to the professor's message is limited to "one-ear listening."

A sender may employ various techniques to gain a receiver's attention. For many years, the volume level of television commercials was markedly higher than the volume of regular programming. To some extent, this focused viewer's attention on the advertiser's message. Consequently, the FCC outlawed this practice. Sometimes breaking the flow of one communication with another sender's message may mitigate the effectiveness of either message. Consider, for example, a television documentary on poverty that is interrupted by a commercial that urges the viewers to "live the good life" by vacationing on some Caribbean island. The airline's message may permanently disrupt the viewer's thoughts about the documentary message, and this may annoy the viewer to the point of refusing to refocus attention on the commercial message. There are, of course, some viewers whose attention may wane after the first 5 minutes of a program. In such cases, a commercial break may serve to draw their attention back from incidental stimuli—family, friends, a snack, or a beer—to the electronic messages on the television.

Some communicators also create obstacles by focusing our attention on some things to the exclusion of others. For example, when a salesperson emphasizes the solid construction of a car, its 2,000-cc overhead cam turbo-charged engine, fully synchronized five-speed transmission, rack-and-pinion steering, and award-winning design, that salesperson is riveting attention on what he or she considers the most important, and salesworthy, features of the car. However, in doing so, the salesperson is diverting attention from what may be the most practical consideration; Will the car fit the garage? If not, the customer who buys it may regard the salesperson's message as a failure because it did not provide an essential bit of information. From the salesperson's perspective, the communication will be viewed as a great success, unless, of course, the customer returns to the showroom with an angry complaint.

Sometimes noise will affect our attention in a communication situation. Experiments in which subjects were orally instructed to attend to only certain stimuli in the environment confirm this fact. In one series of tests, subjects simultaneously received two or more auditory messages. It was found that a message can be most easily heard in noise when the message and the noise come from two different locations (Hirsch, 1950). It was also demonstrated that the differences in the intensity of sounds aid in selectively attending to one message among several—even if the relevant message is softer (Egan, Carterette, & Thoring, 1954).

Some of these data are born out of our everyday experiences. For instance, two messages produced very close to each other and of equal volume intensity usually cancel each other out. One example is the mother who is trying to decipher the screams and protests of her two children, each of whom is accusing the other of spilling a glass of milk. In moments of high debate when the voices of two opposing groups are spiraling to an incredible noise level, it is often the softer words of some less emotional person that pierce through the noise and hold our attention.

Selective Perception

Perhaps the most workable definition of *perception* is that it is "the process of making sense out of experience—the imputing of meaning to experience" (Haney, 1967, p. 52). However, the process of perception is not as simple as this definition may at first seem. To begin with, different people do not experience the same stimuli in exactly the same way. Differences in environment; differences in sensory receptors; differences in internalized values, goals, and attitudes —all contribute to differences in the way a person perceives reality. Furthermore, language, the process by which we impute meaning, compounds the problems caused by these physiological and psychological differences. No two people invest a particular word with exactly the same meaning. To one person, the word *happy* may mean not being depressed; to another person, it may mean being overjoyed at some wondrous event that has taken place. The communication problems that result from these individual differences are often intensified by the fact that people tend to be unaware that differences do, in fact, exist. In short, we think that what we perceive is reality. How can there be differences?

Most people have experienced moments when their perceptions of a particular person or situation or object differed greatly from the perceptions of other people. For example, Dr. Elizabeth Jones may be perceived as an excellent surgeon by a man whose life was saved by a delicate heart operation that the doctor performed. The husband of a woman who died under Dr. Jones's scalpel may perceive the doctor as a quack whose license should be revoked. Dr. Jones's husband perceives her as a sensitive and dedicated professional and a loving wife. Her children view her as a strict mother whose gaze makes them uncomfortable. Will the real Dr. Jones please stand up? Of course, the point is that there is no real Dr. Jones. Each person thinks his or her private perception of Dr. Jones is the real woman.

A person's past experiences and expectations will affect the way stimuli in the environment are perceived. For example, if a critic you

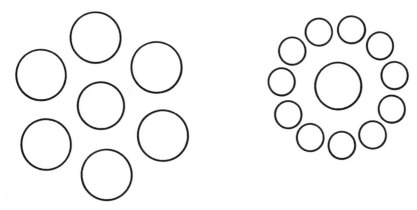

Figure 4.1. Environmental Factors May Affect a Person's Perception of Stimuli. Do the center circles in these figures appear to be the same size?

respect writes a brilliant review of a new film, the review is likely to create a favorable image of the movie in your mind. More important, this favorable impression will affect your actual perception of the film: If you expect to like the movie, you probably will.

People often forget that words, which function to define, label, or categorize, restrict our perceptions of other people, things, and situations. In one study, for example, two groups of subjects were shown identical drawings of ambiguous shapes, and each group was given a different "label" for the same drawing. When asked to reproduce the shapes, the subjects consistently drew the shapes more in accordance with the words used to describe them than with the actual shapes they saw.

One cannot help wondering how long progress has been retarded by the assignation of inappropriate names. How much time was lost and how many lives were squandered by the term *malaria*? Contracted from the Italian words *mala aria* ("bad air"), it perpetuated the erroneous notion that the disease was caused by the bad air of the swamps. And how many bright and willing scientists were inhibited from even dreaming of the possibility that the *atom* (from the Greek for "indivisible") *could* be split, largely because its *name* said it could *not* be divided (Haney, 1967, p. 143).

Selective Retention

The principle of selective retention states that people remember more accurately messages that are favorable to their self-image than messages that are unfavorable. In short, people remember the good things and forget the bad. An example of this can be seen in reunions held by former inmates of Auschwitz, during which they grow sentimental over remembered jokes, sounding just like old fraternity brothers at the annual class dinner.

It is rather difficult to discuss selective retention apart from attention and perception because all are functions of the same basic process. In fact, sometimes it is virtually impossible to assign degrees of importance to each function. For instance, if people are exposed to a political message and shortly thereafter present an incomplete or distorted report on what they have heard, we may wonder, were the "data" themselves incorrectly perceived, or was the retention incomplete or distorted? Or were both perception and retention inaccurate? If the time lapse between the perception and the report is lengthy, it becomes even more difficult to answer these questions.

The available research makes it difficult to make many conclusive statements about whether or not the retention of at least part of a message is improved if intense sensory stimuli accompany the message. Teachers, for example, often use visual aids to help their students remember the message they are listening to. Sometimes increasing the motivation for retention is helpful. Thus if a professor tells his or her students that remembering that day's lecture will assure them of passing the next exam, the students will probably be more mentally receptive, will concentrate more deeply, and will remember the lecture more fully and accurately. However, if the lecture seemed confusing to the students or involved material with which they had no prior contact, the degree and accuracy of the students' retention (and the success of the professor's communication) will be limited.

It would seem that retention in conjunction with other selective processes can be quite detrimental to effective communication. Our perceptions, as we have said, are, in part, influenced by our memory of past experiences and messages. If we do not retain messages that conflict with our basic self-image or if these messages become distorted in memory with the passage of time, our future perceptions will be narrowed or distorted. The cycle of behavior that results may be a difficult one to break, and consequently our communication efforts may be greatly hampered.

Summary

1. All communication involves a compromise of meaning among people because each individual responds to communication—symbols of reality—in unique and personal ways. Although language provides a shared system for interpreting symbols, each person invests a word with different meaning. Language may also facilitate misunderstanding because it leads us to view words as reality instead of as abstract symbols of reality.

2. Much of communication depends upon the particular language of the participants. The Whorf-Sapir hypothesis asserts that people's perception of the world is at the mercy of the language they speak. Language, as well as psychological disposition and previous experience, affect the perceptions that people bring into communication situations.

3. An important factor inhibiting effective communication is the tendency of people to fail in distinguishing between statements of inference and statements of observation. Risk taking is also part of the inference-observation confusion. Though people often take calculated risks, when people make inferences and take them for actual observations, they may not even be aware of the potential undesirable consequences. This can often lead to unpleasant or even fatal results.

4. The process of selectivity in communication operates such that people must be exposed to a message or else they cannot attend to it; they must attend to a message or they cannot perceive it; they must perceive a message or they cannot retain it. Various factors such as physiological impairments, psychological and physical needs, cultural background, and prior attitudes will affect each stage of this selectivity process.

5. Receiver's selectivity attends to only a limited number of stimuli at any one time. Physiological factors, psychological needs, and past experiences affect a person's ability to attend to stimuli in the

environment. Other variables that affect attention are the quantity and difficulty of incoming stimuli.

6. *Perception* is the process of imputing meaning to experience. Physiological, psychological, experiential, and semantic factors all impinge on people's perceptions. No two people will perceive the same stimuli in exactly the same way.

7. Individuals more accurately retain messages that are favorable to their self-image. A person also tends to forget unfavorable messages more quickly than favorable ones. The retention of at least part of a message seems to be improved if intense sensory stimuli accompany the message. Selective retention thus reinforces one's self-image.

Note

1. This is obviously an abbreviated treatment of language and communication presented in this chapter. We have avoided discussing the politicization of language introduced by people from various quarters in the discipline. Those with postmodern leanings will find much to dislike with our scientific conceptualization of language. For the purposes of this book, however, if language is not referential, it is impossible for us to develop fully the functional approach to communication taken in the last section of this book. We have deferred much of our discussion of language variables, empirical research in the effects of language variables, and linguistic devices used in the design of messages for the moment. A large body of language-related research is discussed in the chapters on social influence, relational communication, and conflict and communication.

References

Bavelas, J. B., Black, A., Chovil, N., & Mullett, J. (1990). *Equivocal communication.* Newbury Park, CA: Sage.

Bowers, J. W., Elliott, N. D., & Desmond, R. J. (1977). Exploiting pragmatic rules: Devious messages. *Human Communication Research, 3,* 235-242.

Cassirer, E. (1944). *An essay on man.* New Haven, CT: Yale University Press.

Condon, J. C., Jr. (1975). *Semantics and communication* (2nd ed.). New York: Macmillan.

Egan, J. P., Carterette, E. C., & Thoring, E. J. (1954). Some factors affecting multi-channel listening. *Journal of the Acoustical Society of America, 26,* 774-782.

Egeth, H. (1967). Selective attention. *Psychological Bulletin, 67,* 41-57.

Grice, H. P. (1975). Logic and conversation. In P. Cole & J. C. Morgan (Eds.), *Advances in experimental psychology* (Vol. 14, pp. 1-59). New York: Academic Press.

Haney, W. V. (1967). *Communication and organizational behavior.* Homewood, IL: Irwin.

Hirokawa, R. Y., Gouran, D. S., & Martz, A. E. (1988). Understanding sources of faulty group decision making: A lesson from the *Challenger* disaster. *Small Group Behavior, 19,* 441-463.

Hirsch, I. J. (1950). The relation between localization and intelligibility. *Journal of the Acoustical Society of America, 22,* 196-200.

Lewis, M. (1948). *Language in society.* New York: Social Science Research Council.

Whorf, B. L. (1957). *Language, thought and reality.* New York: John Wiley.

5

Nonverbal Communication

JUDEE K. BURGOON

LAURA K. GUERRERO

A local graffiti board carries the inscription, "You hear my words but you miss my meaning." This statement, which reflects the notion that there is more to meaning than just words themselves, is really a plea for awareness of nonverbal communication—those messages that take a form other than words. Such messages are a frequently overlooked aspect of communication; yet, they are very powerful. They are our first and only means of communication in infancy. Even when we have mastered the verbal language system, we continue to rely on such things as gestures, glances, touches, and voice qualities to carry much of the meaning in our transactions with others. In fact, one estimate is that more than 60% of the social meaning in interpersonal interchange is transmitted nonverbally (Burgoon, Buller, & Woodall, 1989). When someone says, "I could tell from his eyes that he was angry" or "Her voice made it clear that we were finished talking," he or she is actually responding to nonverbal communication. Adults also give great weight to nonverbal cues when verbal and nonverbal messages are contradictory. Imagine talking to a friend who insists she is not angry yet her lips are pursed and she moves away every time you try to get close to her. Are you more likely to believe her words or her actions?

Despite the important role that nonverbal messages play in our day-to-day interactions, few people are conscious of the ways in which they use such messages or how they respond to the nonverbal cues of others. It is ironic that people spend 12 years in school systematically studying verbal language, but almost no time is devoted to the study of the syntax or vocabulary of nonverbal behavior. The result is that our ability to send and interpret nonverbal messages is generally inadequate. We hope that this chapter will begin to remedy that deficit by bringing more nonverbal behaviors into conscious awareness. Once people become aware of such behaviors, they are usually better able to bring them under conscious control.

One word of advice, however. Before you jump to the conclusion that much of what we know about nonverbal communication is intuitive, think twice. It is true that some of it is intuitive, but many aspects only seem so with the benefit of hindsight. Take, for example, posture and liking. When students read that people typically have only *moderately* relaxed postures with those they like, but have the *most* relaxed posture around individuals they dislike, that seems plausible because a person doesn't feel the need to appear interested or maintain an attractive posture around disliked others. But before knowing that relationship, most students predict that people will be most relaxed with those they like. This is just one example of the many nonintuitive and counterintuitive ways in which nonverbal cues operate. It should underscore for you the fact that not all nonverbal communication is readily and easily understood. Many behaviors have the same meaning, some behaviors have several different meanings, and some behaviors have no meaning. All of this indicates that nonverbal communication is a rather complex enterprise. Contrary to popular belief, it is not possible to "read another person like a book." But it is possible to become more observant of one's own nonverbal discourse and more attuned to the meanings of others.

The Nonverbal Codes

Nonverbal communication has many modes of expression. Research suggests that there are seven commonly used "codes" or mediums for conveying messages (see Table 5.1). Each of these codes has some unique properties that influence the communication roles it performs. Research also suggests that these nonverbal codes combine to fulfill many communicative functions within daily interaction. We will examine the properties of the codes first, and then turn to the various communication functions the nonverbal codes serve.

Proxemics

Proxemics, or the ways in which people structure and use space in their daily lives, is one of the key codes of nonverbal communication. The distances we maintain between ourselves and others and our reactions to inappropriate spacing have a potent impact on the communication process. A well-known example that illustrates the importance of proxemics comes from an embassy cocktail party. A newly arrived American diplomat was carrying on a conversation with his Arab host. As was the custom in his country, the Arab moved up very close to the American. This made the American very uncomfortable; so he retreated a few feet. Not used to such a distance, the Arab moved in again, and again the American retreated. This comedy of advance and retreat continued until the Arab had literally chased the American across the length of the room. The American's impression of the Arab was that he was pushy, whereas the Arab regarded the American as cold and aloof. Clearly, each person had sent unintentional messages through the use of space.

Dimensions of Proxemics. This example highlights one of the underlying concepts of proxemics: the human need for certain amounts of space. People seem to have two different types of spatial needs, the first of which is *territoriality*, which consists of a need for and defense of territory. Similar to other animals, humans apparently carve out territories. Likewise, a family's home and property are its territory, which means that these are not openly accessible to strangers or intruders. Often teenagers hang signs proclaiming

Table 5.1 Nonverbal Codes and Some Associated Message Elements

The Nonverbal Communication System

Proxemics	Haptics	Chronemics	Kinesics	Physical Appearance	Vocalics	Artifacts
*personal space	*positive affect	*urgency	*gaze	*body shape	*tempo	*size
*conversational distance	*playful	*duration	*facial expression	*weight	*tempo variety	*volume of space
*territory	*control	*waiting time	*smiling	*height	*pitch	*style
*lean	*ritualistic	*lead time	*gestures	*hair & skin color	*pitch variety	*materials
*body orientation	*hybrid	*punctuality	*head movements	*grooming	*loudness	*lighting
*seating arrangement	*task-related	*monochronic/polychronic use of time	*posture	*clothing color	*resonance	*temperature
	*accidental	*displaced/diffused point pattern	*postural relaxation	*clothing style	*dialect	*ventilation
	*aggressive		*postural asymmetry	*adornments	*tension	*color
	*affection		*random trunk & limb movement	*cosmetics	*fluency	*art
	withdrawal		*gait		*pauses	*decor
					*articulation	*furniture arrangement
					*breathiness	

"Stay Out" or "Enter at Your Own Risk" on their bedroom doors in an attempt to protect the privacy of their territory. Altman (1975) classified territory into three types: *primary, secondary,* and *public.* Primary territory is central to the lives of the occupants, is occupied consistently, and often reflects the owner's personality and identity. Physical and psychological retreat often takes place in primary territories. Bedrooms, offices, and homes are examples of primary territories. While primary territories are private, secondary territories are semi-public in nature. Informal rules of membership govern who occupies the space. For example, a college hangout tends to be occupied by the same group of people. Often the entrance of a "new face" causes comment. Finally, everyone has free access to public territory. We would expect to see all kinds of people at beaches or grocery stores. Yet interestingly, even within such public territories, people follow proxemic norms. Students in a nonverbal class once did a quasi-experiment, watching people's proxemic norms from the top of a cliff overlooking a busy section of a San Diego beach. They noticed that people would look for the biggest "open spot" to lay their beach towels down. After a while, the students could predict fairly accurately where the next group of beach-goers would decide to sit.

One thing to keep in mind when classifying territory as primary, secondary, or public is that the same place can have different meanings to different people. The bar on the popular television series, *Cheers,* for example, may be secondary territory to most of the customers who frequent it, but for Norm and Cliff it is a primary territory.

The physical and social effects of inadequate territory are illuminated by various studies of overcrowded conditions. A classic study with rats found that even when there was plenty of food and water available in their environment, the rats became aggressive, neurotic, sexually deviant, and ill when their territory was reduced by overpopulation (Calhoun, 1962). Sociological studies have found similar results among inhabitants of heavily populated urban areas (Davis, 1971). The avoidance of communication and the heated confrontations that characterize residents of particularly congested areas may be partially attributable to inadequate territory. Perhaps in an effort to avoid such adverse effects, individuals often take precautions to protect and defend their territories. For instance, people may create *boundary markers* such as fences or screens to mark their territories visibly. Siblings who paint a line across their bedroom floor to separate their "space" are using such a device. Another way to protect territory is to use *central markers*. Setting a book down on a table or laying a coat on a chair are ways of marking the "center" of a territory. If you attend aerobic classes you have probably noted this phenomenon. Participants often lay their towels on the ground to reserve their spot before picking up their mats and weights.

The second type of spatial needs that humans require is *personal space*. Personal space differs from territory in that it is not a fixed geographic area. Rather, it is an invisible "bubble" of space that individuals carry with them. Depending on the situation, a person's need for space may expand or contract; personal space has no rigid boundary. In a formal situation, people feel much more need for personal space than if the situation is an intimate one. A multitude of factors combine to determine a person's needs or preferences for space. These preferences are responsible for cultural proxemic norms, which are the standards of behavior that society considers correct.

Personal Space Preferences and Norms. Gender partly determines a person's choice of distance in an interaction. In general, two females will sit or stand closer to each other than they will to males; males, in turn, will sit or stand closer to the opposite sex than they will to each other. The *race* of the interactants may also affect distance. Not surprisingly, people usually adopt closer distances in same-race than mixed-race interactions. Another factor is *status*. As a sign of respect, we generally stand further away from people who are of higher status. It is easy to tell by watching subordinates approach a seated business executive just what the status relationship is; those who stand in the doorway are likely to be of much lower status than those who walk up to the edge of the desk. Or notice the degree of deference students show professors in the distance they maintain. Closely related to status is the effect of *age*. We often stand closer to our peers than to persons who are older or younger. Another determinant of our use of space is *personality*. Extroverts are willing to be closer to others than those who are shy and introverted (Andersen & Sull, 1985). Aggression may be connected to personal space needs. In a prison study, two groups of men were tested on their reactions to people closing in on them. The prisoners were instructed to say "Stop" when they felt that the invader was too close. Men who had a history of violence required personal space zones that were four times the size of the space zones needed by men who did not (Fast, 1971).

Yet another factor determining spatial preference is *ethnic and cultural background*. Anthropological observations indicate that standards of spatial use vary greatly in different societies. For most North Americans, the average conversational distance when standing ranges from 18 to 28 inches; distances closer than 18 inches are presumably reserved for intimate interactions (Hall, 1966; Willis, 1966). In comparison with people in many other cultures, North Americans tend to maintain greater distances from one another. This difference has created some embarrassing situations in the past for North American travelers in Italy and Latin America who misinterpreted the friendly advances of the natives. There is some evidence now, however, that these cultural differences are becoming less noticeable (Forston & Larson, 1968). It is possible that international travel and the mass media are helping to standardize personal distance practices.

Overriding many of the above variables is *personal attraction*. As would be expected, people approach much closer to someone they find attractive; people are also much more willing to tolerate the approach of an attractive person. Similar to the effect of attraction is the degree of acquaintanceship. People maintain a greater distance from strangers than from acquaintances and the distance between friends is smallest (Little, 1965). This makes sense because we are more likely to develop friendships with people we find attractive.

Other influences on personal distance are such situational variables as the *topic*, the definition of the *social situation*, and the *person's psychological state*. All of these factors affect a person's spatial needs at a given moment. For example, students expecting to receive praise will sit closer to a professor than students who expect to receive an unfavorable report of their class progress (Leipold, 1963). Similarly, people are likely to stand closer in an informal situation than in a formal one because the nature of the social event has altered their personal space needs. Most people have experienced moments when they were so upset that they preferred others, even intimate friends, to keep their distance.

Responses to Personal Space Invasion. In many situations, people feel
they have less space than is needed. To cope with such situations,
people may communicate their discomfort in a variety of ways.
To see some of these first hand, try this simple experiment: Find
a fellow student seated alone at a large library table; then sit down
in the seat immediately next to him or her. Chances are that the
person will first try to counteract your intrusion by avoiding eye
contact, shifting body orientation away from you, and creating
"barriers" with such objects as books or coats. If that fails, he or
she may glare at you. If all else fails, the person may take flight.
Responses will differ from individual to individual, but nearly all
will show signs of discomfort (Baxter & Deanovitch, 1970; Felipe
& Sommer, 1966; Patterson, Mullens, & Romano, 1971). In such
places as a crowded elevator or bus, a different response pattern
is likely to occur. People have learned that in such instances,
invasion of their personal space is necessary. They cope with the
situation by treating other people around them as nonpersons or
objects. The next time you find yourself in such a place, notice the
absence of eye contact and the rigid posture of the other people.
This behavior helps to reduce some of the tension created by
strangers who are in a space zone usually reserved for intimates. As
explained by Robert Sommer (1969), a nonperson cannot invade
someone's personal space anymore than a tree or chair can. It is
common under certain conditions to treat another person like an
object, as part of the background.

It is clear that people have strong spatial needs and strong reactions to violations of their personal space or territory. As a result,
proxemic variations can serve as a very powerful communication
vehicle. The ways in which people define and defend territories, the
distances they adopt from others, and the arrangements of space
that they create can all act as messages.

Haptics

Proxemics can be thought of as an approach-avoidance continuum.
At the approach end is *haptics,* or touch. As a form of communication, haptics has received increasing attention in nonverbal research
over the past decade. Our need for touch seems to be powerful. We

know, for instance, that monkeys raised without any contact with other monkeys will spend hours clinging to a cloth-covered wire figure, preferring it to an uncovered figure that supplies food. Humpback whale mothers use their fins to caress their baby calves. This need for contact can also be seen in human babies raised in orphanages and institutions. In many orphanages, babies are left for hours by themselves, lying in their beds in an environment with almost no sensory stimulation. They are rarely touched or held for any length of time. Such babies first become apathetic and lifeless, then develop bizarre behaviors; many even die. If human contact is so essential in early life, it seems reasonable to conclude that touch can have significant communicative value.

Touch in the North American Culture. Despite the apparent value and utility of touch, it is discouraged as a mode of communication in North American culture. In fact, we are classified as a noncontact culture (Hall, 1966). Our clothing styles and taboos about revealing our bodies reflect our inhibited view of touch. Boys learn at an early age that touching is not masculine, especially among males. One attraction of contact sports for boys may be that it is one of the few situations in which body contact is condoned. The rituals of huddling in close contact and slapping on the basketball court demonstrate the recognized value of touch in communicating solidarity, supportiveness, and enthusiasm.

For girls, touching is more acceptable. A girl may hug her father or mother without disapproval. It is permissible (though uncommon) for girls to hold hands or put their arms around one another, but unfavorable insinuations would be made about boys who did the same thing. It is possible that all findings on proxemic preferences, especially on sex differences, really indicate our fear and avoidance of touch. Thus males sit the farthest apart from each other because touching would be inappropriate.

This avoidance of touch is taught at an early age. As children, we are frequently told not to touch other objects, "improper" parts of Mommy's or Daddy's body, and even parts of our own body. To compensate for reduced tactile stimulation, we formalize acceptable forms of tactile interaction. The handshake, social dancing, the perfunctory kiss: All of these are acceptable means of communicating by touch. Touching certain parts of the body is also acceptable, if the touches are not prolonged. Brushing an arm or putting a hand on someone's shoulder is permissible, but touching the abdomen or thigh is not, except in overtly sexual situations.

Touch as Communication. Touch can convey a myriad of meanings, ranging from care and concern to anger and violence. Researchers have grouped adult touch into categories based upon the meaning attached to haptic behavior. One such study found seven primary forms of adult touch: positive affect, playful, control, ritualistic, hybrid, task-related, and accidental (Jones & Yarbrough, 1985). *Positive affect* touch includes haptic behavior designed to express support, appreciation, inclusion, affection, and/or sexual interest. Putting an arm around a friend to comfort is one form of touch that conveys positive affect. *Playful* touch occurs when someone tries to lighten a situation through playful affection, such as tickling, or through playful aggression, such as mock wrestling. *Control* touches serve mainly to direct behavior, gain compliance, or gain attention. Tapping someone on the back to initiate conversation is one example. *Ritualistic* touch, often in the form of a handshake or brief hug, is common during greetings and departures. *Hybrid* touch combines elements from positive affect and ritualistic touch. Hugging and kissing as a way of saying "hello" or "good-bye" exemplify hybrid touch. *Task-related* and *accidental* touch may be considered contact rather than communication. A dentist has to touch you to examine your teeth, but you are unlikely to feel that any meaning has been conveyed by such a touch. Similarly, if Michael Jordan and Scottie Pippen accidentally bump into one another during a Bulls game they are unlikely to attribute much meaning to the touch.

As you read through the above categories of touch, you may have noticed the omission of negative forms of haptic communication. One study on children (Guerrero & Ebesu, 1993) identified two forms of touch that convey negative affect: *aggression* and *affection withdrawal*. Aggressive touch comprises hitting, kicking, pushing, and tripping. Affection withdrawal includes touch designed to shun attempts at affection, such as removing someone's arm from around your shoulders or pushing someone's hand away from yours.

The meaning of touch, whether it be positive or negative, is conveyed through five different dimensions underlying haptic behavior. First, the *location* of touch is important. Researchers have found that handholding and face touching express more intimacy, composure, and informality than many other forms of touch (Burgoon, 1991) and that sexually implicit forms of touch, such as touches to the lower body, express more relational commitment than do holding hands or putting arms around one another (Johnson & Edwards, 1991). Second, the *duration* of touch is a key feature. Touches that are long and lingering express more warmth and caring than do briefer touches. *Intensity* of touch is also relevant. A hit can be playful when soft and violent when hard. A handshake can convey either power or submissiveness based upon its strength. *Frequency* of touch is one of the most commonly studied dimensions of haptic communication. A romantic couple may display affection by touching continuously or by engaging in multiple discrete touches. Finally, the *instrument of touch* conveys a message. Do you decide to be bold and touch that "special someone" by putting a hand on his arm or do you decide to be a bit more indirect by letting your arm casually brush against his? All five of these dimensions work together to define the quality and meaning of a given touch.

The power of communication through touch has been studied in several applied settings. In one hospital, nurses who touched their patients found the patients had better attitudes toward them and increased their verbal output (Agulera, 1967). Encounter groups emphasize touching as a way of breaking down communication barriers. Through touch, members become more aware of each other and supposedly more sensitive to each other's needs. By allowing others to touch them, they make themselves vulnerable, which is a prerequisite to building trust.

If touch is so potent, why is it often suppressed in our society? One explanation is that as societies progress, they substitute for touch other signs and symbols, such as language. From this perspective, touch, like drums, is regarded as a sign of a primitive society; refinement and "sophistication" thus dictate a reduction in such personal, ambiguous forms of communication as touch. But our society is not likely to eliminate haptic communication totally. In fact, a trend toward more touching seems to be taking hold. The recognition by clinical psychologists of the value of touching, the impact of the encounter movement, changing gender roles, and the increasing sexual awareness of young people may be contributing to more acceptance of touching behavior. It may become possible for men to display affection openly through touch, as is already done in other cultures. Then perhaps even the phrase "a touching scene" will take on a new meaning.

Chronemics

An interesting but often overlooked dimension of nonverbal communication is chronemics, or our use of time. Our notions of time, how we "use" it, the timing of events, our emotional responses to time, even the length of our pauses all contribute to the communicative effect of time. Our music gives strong evidence of the meanings conveyed by time. Just recall a few phrases from some musical favorites: "If I could save time in a bottle"; "To everything, turn, turn, turn, there is a season, turn, turn, turn"; "I love you more today than yesterday, but not as much as tomorrow." Or consider such expressions as "dead time," "time on our hands," "lead time," and "making time." Clearly, we are time-conscious and conscious of the meanings conveyed by the way we deal with time.

Our sensitivity to time in this culture is partly revealed through our reliance on clocks. Notice how few people you meet in a single day who do not wear a watch. We are so obsessed with time, in fact, that we become genuinely disturbed if a few minutes are "wasted." After all, "time is money." We view time as a commodity to be spent, earned, saved, or wasted. We also divide time into small increments; we are even conscious of passing seconds.

In contrast, many other cultures have less concrete notions of time. In some, time is a vague sense of the present. It is "here and now," and punctuality is not valued. The Sioux Indians have this orientation. In their language, there are no words for "late" and "waiting." Among the Pueblo Indians, things take place "when the time is right," whenever that may be. Such cultural differences in peoples' attitudes toward time have caused many communication problems. The federal government lost thousands of dollars on construction projects because the Hopi Indians did not have a concept of a "fixed date" by which a house or road would be completed. Many American businessmen have told angry tales of having to wait a half hour or longer to see an Arab or a Latin American associate. To North Americans, a waiting period of this length is an insult, but in other cultures it is appropriate.

Cultural Time Systems. The ways in which cultures use time can be divided into three sets: *technical, formal,* and *informal* (Hall, 1959). Technical time is used in certain professions such as astronomy, but the terminology (solar, sidereal, and anamolistic year) carries little meaning for the layperson. Formal time is our traditional, conscious time structure. It includes our division of time into days, months, years, and seasons. Our uses of cycles of time, such as day and night; our valuation of time; our perceptions of its depth, duration, and tangibility are all part of our formal time system. Edward Hall commented on the importance of formal time patterns:

> The American never questions the fact that time should be planned and future events fitted into a schedule. He thinks that people should look forward to the future and not dwell too much in the past. His future is not very far ahead of him. Results must be obtained in the foreseeable future—one or two years or, at most, five or ten. (1959, p. 134)

Promises to meet deadlines and appointments are taken very seriously. There are real penalties for being late and for not keeping commitments in time.

Informal time is the set that causes the most difficulty because it is the loosely defined and out-of-consciousness time system. Phrases such as "in a moment" and "forever and ever," as well as humorous clichés such as "see ya' later, alligator" reflect the informal time system. Whereas the vocabulary of informal time is generally the same as that of formal time, its meaning is more ambiguous because it is dependent on the context rather than on clear-cut definitions. The phrase "see ya' later," for example, may mean "I'll see you in six months" when conversing with your dentist, but "I'll see you tomorrow" when conversing with your best friend. Moreover, the informal manner in which it is learned means that we are usually not consciously aware of it. It is the features of our informal time system that are most often implicated as message elements.

Message Elements. One message element is *urgency*. Nowhere is it spelled out what it means to be "urgent" in our culture. But if you received a phone call at 2 in the morning, you would undoubtedly assume that the call was urgent, whereas a call received at two in the afternoon would be routine. How we use time signals the importance of something. Another element of our informal time system is *duration*, a particularly potent element in our culture. Everyone has their own definition of what is a short, long, or impossibly long period of time. With North Americans' heightened sensitivity to the passage of time, "forever" may actually be a relatively short period, technically speaking. Five minutes may be impossibly long if a person is waiting for test results. *Waiting time* itself is an important message element. It was once fashionable for young women to keep their dates waiting as they finished getting ready. The length of time the man had to wait sent a definite message about the young woman's eagerness to start the date. Similarly, we may expect to wait to see the CEO but be perturbed if we have to sit around waiting for an equal-status colleague. Because we attribute meanings to the amount of time we have to wait to see someone, it is possible to tell people nonverbally what we think of them through this mode.

Similar to waiting time, *punctuality* can convey our feelings about someone. If you are always late meeting a friend, it may signal a lack of respect or attraction. Punctuality in formal situations, such as job interviews, is crucial. Arriving very early may communicate that you are overzealous; arriving late may cost you the job.

Monochronism and *polychronism* can carry potent messages. When time is used monochronically, people perform one task at a time. In contrast, those using time polychronically can engage in multiple activities at once. North American culture is characterized as primarily monochronistic in its use of time. If someone watches television and writes a shopping list while you are trying to talk to him or her, you are likely to feel slighted.

The *timing and sequencing* of activities and statements are two additional chronemic variables that have message potential. When something takes place and what order things follow are important. A hostess may plan a dinner party on a Saturday night because she knows no one will have to work the next day, or she may plan it for a week night because she knows everyone will have to leave early in the evening. Each choice carries a different meaning. Similarly, with dating situations, the timing and order of events may be critical: When do you first kiss? How far in advance do you call for a date? How late do you stay out on a second date? In verbal communication, the placement of pauses and punchlines is of equal importance. The success of comedians such as Billy Crystal and Whoopi Goldberg has been due partly to their excellent sense of timing.

One final consideration is the time pattern an individual generally follows. Americans seem to follow one of two time patterns. Some people habitually operate in a *diffused point pattern*: They arrive somewhere around the appointed time. They may be early or late, but they have some built-in maximum range of acceptability and are usually consistent in either their early or late arrival pattern. In contrast, those who operate on the *displaced point pattern* see the appointed time as a fixed boundary that cannot be violated. These are the people who usually come at the scheduled time or earlier. Whereas people have tendencies to follow either the diffused or the displaced point pattern, the nature of an event may also determine which pattern is used. The diffused point pattern is perfectly acceptable for a shopping trip; for a business appointment, it is appropriate to arrive early or on time but never late (5 minutes beyond the scheduled time being considered late). Conversely, an invitation to a cocktail party at 6:00 p.m. may mean one is expected to arrive at 7:00 p.m. or later. If dinner is to be served, however, it is required that one arrive promptly at 6:00 p.m. or, at the very latest, 6:15 p.m.

Misjudgments and misuses of these informal time systems can lead others to interpret our nonverbal behavior inaccurately. The person who is habitually late on the job expresses lack of interest, disorganization, and disrespect for the employer. The party guest who stays long after the others have departed may communicate insensitivity and selfishness by dallying. We know of one instance where, instead of staying late, a couple arrived 2 hours early for a party and could not be dissuaded by their hosts, who were in the throes of last-minute cleanup, that they were not welcome. Obviously, such violations of the informal "rules" of our culture are bound to carry strong messages, whether intended or not. It is just this feature of time—the fact that we do not openly identify or discuss the rules and the meanings attached to them—that permits chronemics to operate as a subtle but powerful code.

Kinesics

A more traditionally studied code of nonverbal communication is kinesics, or the visual aspects of behavior. Included under this heading are movement and posture, gestures, facial expressions, and eye behavior. These modes of behavior have long been recognized as carrying meaning in an interaction. At the turn of the century, a movement even developed—the elocutionary movement—to teach people how to convey emotions through various body positions, facial expressions, and gestures. For instance, the upturned palms signified supplication; the out-turned hand at the brow showed distress or fear. These artificial behaviors can be seen in the old silent movies. Although people may ridicule such overdramatizing, certain kinesic behaviors are still being prescribed in speech classes today. Consider a few excerpts from a public speaking chapter in a contemporary communication text (DeVito, 1988):

> In saying, "Come here," there will be movements of the head, of the hands and arms, and of the entire body that motion the listener in your direction. . . . When speaking from a stationary microphone or when movement is otherwise restricted . . . you can give the illusion of movement by stepping back or forward or flexing the upper torso so that it appears that you are moving a great deal more than you in fact are. . . . Use gross movements to emphasize transitions and to emphasize the introduction of a new important assertion. (p. 372)

These recommendations underline the belief that kinesic behavior is important. This is a fair assumption, for research has demonstrated that, when compared to other nonverbal codes or to the verbal code, kinesic cues usually carry the greater portion of the meaning being transmitted.

Functions of Kinesic Behaviors. Ekman and Friesen (1969b) devised a system for classifying kinesic behaviors in terms of the functions that they fulfill within the communication process. Under this system, there are five major types of kinesic behaviors: emblems, illustrators, affect displays, adaptors, and regulators. *Emblems* have direct verbal translations and, thus, can be substituted for verbal communication. In fact, many emblems may have developed because it is sometimes impossible or inappropriate to communicate verbally. For example, if you are in church and put your finger over your lips to tell a child to be quiet, you have set a good example by being silent as you communicated the message. Also, imagine waving good-bye to someone as they board a plane. It would be inappropriate in such a situation to scream "good-bye" instead of communicating the message nonverbally. *Illustrators* accompany language and help describe or accent what is being said. Sketching a spiral staircase in the air or pretending to swing an invisible bat are examples of two kinds of illustrators. *Affect displays* convey emotions, usually through facial expressions such as smiling. *Adaptors* are kinesic behaviors that are often idiosyncratic and help individuals adapt to stress or satisfy personal needs. These behaviors, which include scratching, tapping a pen, nervously wringing your hands, and playing with jewelry, are usually not intended to communicate a message. *Regulators*, the final type of kinesic behavior, help to initiate, maintain, structure, and conclude interaction. Turn-taking and leave-taking cues fall under this category.

Message Elements. One of the reasons kinesic cues can fulfill so many functions and carry so much information is because there are so many different features that can be varied as message elements. Every part of the body, from the eyebrows and eyes to the legs and feet, can be manipulated, and this gives rise to endless possible combinations of features. Birdwhistell (1970) has even estimated that there are 250,000 expressions possible in the face region alone. Fortunately, not all of these minute differences in expressions are meaningful. It appears from the research to date that kinesic cues are used in rather systematic ways. Many experts even believe that kinesic patterns follow rules, much like our verbal language system does. Hence, it is possible to reduce the vast number of kinesic cues to a smaller, more manageable set of meaningful behaviors. Altogether there seem to be 50 or 60 distinguishable body movements, with 33 of them in the head and face region alone (Birdwhistell, 1970). Interpretation of such cues is further aided by the fact that kinesic cues are norm-governed; that is, people follow consistent patterns in their use of kinesic cues.

Kinesic Norms. As with proxemics, a wide range of factors determine kinesic norms. Perhaps the most noticeable one is gender. Men walk differently and even carry books differently from women. Males and females also have characteristically different ways of sitting. Notice, for instance, differences in the way men and women cross their legs. In general, women use fewer gestures and large body movements than men but engage in more eye contact (Hall, 1985). People have strong stereotypes of masculine and feminine behavior. As a result, the man who deviates from the norm may be regarded as effeminate or homosexual, when his kinesic behaviors may actually have been learned because they were appropriate for his ethnic background or because they were comfortable. Similarly, women who deviate may be considered unattractive or domineering.

A second consideration is *race*. K. R. Johnson (1972), in his examination of kinesic patterns among African Americans, has commented on the unique walk adopted by some young men to signal masculinity and sensuality. This walk can be described as a slow, casual, rhythmic stroll. Johnson (1972) also identified a unique form of posturing used by African American females to communicate anger or hostility: hands are placed on the hips and weight is shifted back on the heels with the buttocks extended. Other more subtle kinesic differences have been found. Burgoon et al. (1989) summarized research indicating opposite eye contact patterns for speakers and listeners as a function of race. Within Anglo dyads, speakers tend to look at listeners only intermittently, while listeners are expected to look at the speaker fairly continuously in order to signal attention. Conversely, in African American dyads, speakers maintain constant gaze while listeners are expected to look at speakers only occasionally.

Byers and Byers (1972) argued that this racial difference can cause problems in classrooms where Anglo teachers expect African American and Puerto Rican students to look at them when they are speaking. Such differences may also cause difficulties in the workplace.

Ethnic and cultural background also make a difference. Sitting and standing patterns in the United States vary radically from those used in many African and Middle Eastern countries. Cultures may dictate different behavioral patterns that are appropriate for various types of situations. For instance, in Ireland great displays of grief are expected at funerals, whereas in Japan, widows are expected to maintain a stoic smile.

Cultures also differ in the meanings they assign to the same behavior. For example, Southern Italians and Greeks indicate "no" by tilting their heads up in a rapid motion similar to the way many other cultures, including ours, signal "yes." The problems that can occur when two cultures assign different meanings to the same kinesic cue are illustrated in the following example: When one vice president traveled through Latin America on a goodwill tour, he stepped off the plane and held up his hand in the A- OK sign (thumb and forefinger touching to form a circle) to show that he was happy to be there. To his dismay, the crowd booed him. They were equally dismayed by his behavior. He had made what was considered in their country an obscene gesture. Similarly, a Soviet premier visiting the United States exited his plane with his hands clenched over his head, a Russian sign signifying gratefulness for a warm welcome. The U.S. crowd, however, saw the gesture as an arrogant signal meant to convey Soviet superiority. Obviously, such kinesic confusion can impede the communication process and lead to grave misunderstandings.

Despite the considerable confusion and misunderstanding that is possible with kinesic cues, they still remain one of the most effective and heavily relied on nonverbal codes, in part because they are so noticeable, in part because people trust visual information, and in part because there is an infinite number of cues that can be combined to produce precise messages. Kinesic behaviors will, therefore, play a dominant role in all the communication functions to be discussed.

Physical Appearance

Another visual dimension of nonverbal communication is the physical appearance of the human body. Our preoccupation with appearance was wryly noted by the Earl of Chesterfield:

> Women who are either indisputably beautiful, or indisputably ugly, are best flattered upon the score of their understandings; but those who are in a state of mediocrity are best flattered upon their beauty, or at least their graces; for every woman who is not absolutely ugly thinks herself handsome. (Stanhope, 1780)

Men and women are both very conscious of their own appearance and that of others. In fact, physical attraction is often the key determinant of whether people will choose to become acquainted. One study (Walster, Aronson, Abrahams, & Rottman, 1966) found that the biggest predictor of whether people were satisfied with a computer date was the physical attractiveness of their partner; we choose dating partners who are within our own "range" of physical attractiveness. Thus if you consider yourself to be fairly attractive, but not outrageously gorgeous, you are likely to seek a partner who is also moderately but not highly attractive. Why? According to this line of research people strive to maximize the attractiveness of their partners while minimizing their chances of rejection. Studies seem to confirm this, showing that the most attractive woman at a party is less likely to be asked to dance than her moderately attractive counterpart.

Dimensions of Physical Appearance. A number of appearance features influence communication. Natural features such as body *type*, *height*, and *skin color* are not ones we can manipulate at will to send messages, but they may create perceptions and stereotypes that affect how other nonverbal behaviors are interpreted. Our bodies may be categorized as one of three general types:

1. the *endomorph*, which is soft, round, and fat;
2. the *mesomorph*, which is bony, muscular, and athletic; and
3. the *ectomorph*, which is tall, thin, and fragile.

Research has clearly shown that people stereotype our personality on the basis of our body types. Some personality attitudes connected with the endomorph are sluggishness, tolerance, affability, warmth, affection, generosity, complacency, and kindness. Adjectives applicable to the mesomorph are dominant, cheerful, reckless, argumentative, hot-tempered, optimistic, enthusiastic, confident, and efficient. The ectomorph is characterized as detached, introspective, serious, cautious, meticulous, thoughtful, sensitive, tactful, shy, and suspicious.

Body shape, height, and weight have a definite impact on others. For example, endomorphs are frequently discriminated against in seeking jobs, whereas tall men seem to win out consistently over short men for jobs (Knapp & Hall, 1992). In fact, a University of Pittsburgh survey of graduates found that men taller than six feet two inches in height receive higher starting salaries than men shorter than six feet. The reason these bodily features create such reactions may be a function of physical attractiveness. Our stereotyped image of the hero is someone who is tall and athletic rather than short and fat. The stereotyped heroine is moderately tall and sleek. These stereotypes are perpetuated by the mass media in their selection of people who fit the "image" of a movie or television star. People who deviate from these images may, therefore, be perceived as less attractive.

A second relevant dimension is *skin*. Skin color, texture, and the presence of such things as wrinkles, blemishes, scars, and freckles can all have an effect on our impressions of others and our interest in interacting with them. Think of all the media speculation and uproar about Michael Jackson's change in appearance between the early and late 1980s. When interviewed by Oprah Winfrey in 1993, Jackson hotly denied altering his skin color to appear more white, insisting that he suffered from a skin disease. Jackson also emphasized that he had undergone "very little" plastic surgery and was proud to be an African American. This exchange between Jackson and Winfrey points to the power of physical appearance cues such as skin color and facial structure. *Hair*—its color, length, style, texture, and cleanliness—has similar effects. Most bearded, long-haired men can testify to experiences of discrimination because of their appearance. Whether or not such an appearance is intended as defiance or rejection of society's values, it is interpreted as such by older generations. The reaction to long hair has been so strong that violent incidents have been known to occur.

Three other important dimensions are *clothing, accessories,* and *cosmetics.* Numerous studies have examined the various features of dress that have some communication value. Everything from the texture, color, and design of fabrics used to the stylishness and neatness of a garment or outfit can make a difference. People's preferences for and uses of these features are related to their personality and social background. Observers apparently recognize this fact because a person's typical dress is interpreted as a message about his or her lifestyle, values, personality, and attitudes toward others. An employer is likely to perceive signals of disrespect from the employee who always shows up in jeans or signals of availability from the female secretary who wears short skirts and tight-fitting sweaters. Accessories may also carry meaning. The presence or absence of jewelry and its style may indicate age, wealth, and status. Just the wearing of glasses has its effects: People who wear glasses are rated more intelligent, dependable, industrious, conventional, shy, and religious but less attractive and sophisticated. Makeup also affects our perceptions of others. McKeachie (1952) found that women who wore lipstick were perceived as more frivolous, less talkative, more placid, more conscientious, and, surprisingly, less interested in the opposite sex. Today it is more likely that lipstick and other makeup would be a sign of greater interest in the opposite sex. The color of clothing also makes a difference. Women wearing bright red, for example, are viewed as sexier and more extroverted than women wearing more neutral tones. One study on the color of sports uniforms found that not only did people perceive teams in black as "tougher" and "meaner" than teams wearing other colors, but teams in black were actually penalized more than teams wearing other colors (Frank & Gilovich, 1988).

Physical Appearance as Communication. Although it should be clear that physical appearance cues produce strong reactions in others, physical appearance as a code is more limited than some of the other nonverbal codes. This is because during any interaction it cannot be altered easily and because, across the history of any relationship, it has its major impact in the early stages of the relationship. Once people become acquainted, they tend to rely less on the external information supplied by physical appearance and more on first-hand personal knowledge. Thus physical appearance is mostly effective at the beginnings of both conversations and long-term relationships. But as we shall see, those first impression effects can still be important.

Vocalics

Vocalics is concerned with the use of the voice in communication. It focuses on how we say something rather than what we say. It is, therefore, referred to as the vocal element of speech, as opposed to the verbal element, which is the words and their meanings. Actually, our vocal behavior is often critical to understanding the meanings of words. Consider the following question: "How could she do it?" Depending on whether the emphasis is on how, could, she, or do, the sentence carries different meanings. Or consider the following quote: "Woman without her man is powerless." What meaning did you attach to this sentence? If you are a woman you may be shaking your head and denying its validity. Now consider the same quote punctuated with commas, "Woman, without her, man is powerless." How did the pauses (represented by commas) change the meaning of the sentence? Now male readers are the ones likely to be shaking their heads! These examples show that our vocal behavior, which includes emphasizing words or inserting pauses, is instrumental to understanding our language. But vocalics does much more than serve as an auxilliary to language. Vocal cues are involved in all the communication functions to be discussed later in this chapter.

Dimensions of Vocalics. Vocalics is comprised of several features. Voice quality is the characteristic *tonal quality* of the voice, based on such factors as resonance, articulation, lip control, and rhythm control. *Intensity* refers to the pressure of sound waves and is perceived as loudness. *Tempo* refers to the speed at which a person speaks, which is partially affected by the length and location of pauses. *Pitch* is the fundamental frequency of the voice. *Fluency* refers to the absence of distractions such as repetitions, hesitations, stuttering, filled pauses ("ers," "ums"), and false starts. *Vocal patterns* include inflectional patterns, dialects, and other combinations of vocal elements that form identifiable patterns. The final area of vocalics focuses on *vocal characterizers*, such things as crying, laughing, yelling, sneezing, sighing, and snorting.

The combination of all these elements should produce in each of us a unique voice. Who could question the uniqueness of the voices of James Earl Jones, Marlene Dietrich, Howard Cosell, or Demi Moore? The fact that the FBI has begun using voice prints along with fingerprints to identify criminals confirms the singularity of our vocal behavior.

The Voice as a Code. Because each voice has distinctive properties, people view the voice much as they do a written signature—it is presumed to reveal a great deal about the speaker. People glean information from the voice about a person's physical and psychological makeup, his or her educational and social background, and a whole host of other characteristics. Similar to physical appearance, vocal cues are an important contributor to our first impressions of others and our expectations about their communication behavior. Vocal cues also promote stereotypes in much the same way that physical appearance cues do. Often these stereotypes vary depending upon the gender of the communicator. For example, a male speaker with a "breathy" voice is perceived as young and artistic while a female speaker with a "breathy" voice is seen as pretty, petite, effervescent, and high-strung. If you are a man with a "throaty" voice you are likely to be stereotyped as mature, sophisticated, and realistic; a woman with a "throaty" voice is viewed very differently—as unintelligent, unemotional, lazy, neurotic, apathetic, and uninteresting. Some vocal cues, however, tend to promote uniform perceptions regardless of the speaker's gender. Increased tempo, for instance, leads to perceptions of animation and extroversion while increased pitch variation leads to perceptions of dynamism.

But the voice performs a much wider range of communication functions than promoting stereotypes. The innumerable combinations of paralanguage features, coupled with the tremendous capacity of the human ear to detect subtle differences, make it possible for

vocalics to be a very flexible, multipurpose code. The voice is a key
carrier of emotional messages. It reflects our attitudes toward others
and our relationships with them. We use vocal cues to create certain
impressions and influence the actions of others. And besides clarifying verbal messages, vocalic cues may actually regulate the flow of
verbal communication. Thus vocalics is a very powerful nonverbal
code. It probably ranks second only to kinesics in terms of its significance in interactions.

Artifacts

The last nonverbal code that deserves mention is artifacts, which
includes the use of the environment and objects. A person's office
or home and its furnishings carry messages about the occupant.
Similarly, the kind of automobile a person drives may be chosen to
project a particular image. Furthermore, artifacts can significantly
affect interaction patterns. Artifacts have been broken down into three
general categories of *fixed*, *semi-fixed*, and *dynamic* environmental
elements (Hall, 1966). Fixed elements include those environmental
features that are relatively permanent, such as size, volume of space,
materials, and architectural style. If you have ever visited a large European city, such as Paris or Munich, you may have noticed that the
lay-outs of these cities are much different from that of Los Angeles
or Phoenix. Highrise apartments outnumber detachable homes even
as you head past the edges of the city proper; buildings are more
densely packed than in Western U.S. cities. Often people visiting a
large city for the first time feel caught up in the excitement and
business of so many people living and working so close together.
Other small-towners may feel trapped in a large city. Just as cities
may communicate a message about the type of population they
shelter, structural differences in homes often communicate messages about inhabitants. A sprawling one-story ranch-style home
creates a different impression than a two-story home. The size of a
room—large and airy or small and cozy—can also dictate the kinds
of activities in which a family can comfortably engage.

Semi-fixed environmental elements are changeable but they tend
to stay in place for lengthy periods of time. The lighting, temperature, ventilation, color, furnishings, and noise of an environment,

as well as the arrangement of furniture and objects are all important semi-fixed factors. Consider some different settings. A bar or restaurant is dimly lit, decorated with subdued colors. It features comfortable, intimately arranged chairs and tables to encourage its customers to linger. An office is usually brightly lit, properly ventilated, kept at a slightly cool temperature, painted in neutral (nondistracting and nonirritating) colors, and furnished with functional chairs and desks that are not conducive to relaxation. A church sanctuary has lofty inspiring ceilings, subdued colors that set an atmosphere of peace and reflection, or reds and purples that are rich in religious symbolism, and stiff uncomfortable pews to force attention to the minister. Each setting conveys a message about the kind of activity and interaction that is acceptable in that atmosphere. The owners or designers can thus manipulate settings to suit their preferences. The restaurant owner who wants quick turnover in clientele will raise the lights and purchase less comfortable furniture. One businessman has been designing chairs explicitly intended to discourage people from sitting too long. A famous hotel replaced all its comfortable lobby furniture with hard benches and chairs to encourage people to circulate among its shops rather than sit. The same principle is employed in airports.

Placement of furniture within a room may also carry a message. Notice, for example, where professors place their desks within their offices. Those who have their desks between themselves and the doorway have established a barrier that reduces their accessibility to students. The placement of furniture in a public setting can do much to increase or decrease interaction. Hospitals and other public institutions in which chairs have been lined up along the walls for the convenience of janitors inhibit interaction. Similarly, in a classroom with fixed rows of chairs, there is less overall interaction than with a circular arrangement. Conversely, in bars, where people are seated at tables in close proximity and in intimate arrangements, interaction is frequent and personal.

Color has powerful effects. Prison walls are sometimes painted in pastel pink to calm inmates. Fast food restaurants and discount stores are often painted a stimulating color of red to encourage quick customer turn-around. Color and light have also been found to be beneficial for treating depression. In cities such as Seattle, depression rates go up during the winter season. Some medical doctors who blame this increase in depression on the thick cloud cover and lack of sun prescribe using brighter lights and arousing, pleasant colors in one's home environment.

Other semi-fixed features of the environment that have an impact are the attractiveness of its furnishings and the degree of sensory stimulation it provides. In one study, subjects rated photographs of people's faces significantly higher in attractiveness when the subjects were in a "beautiful" room than when they were in an "ugly" room (Mintz, 1956). Similarly, children in Germany were given IQ tests in either beautiful or ugly rooms. Those in the beautiful rooms scored 12 points higher than those in ugly rooms ("Blue Is Beautiful," 1973). Unattractive rooms are seen as fatiguing and displeasing, whereas attractive rooms tend to create feelings of well-being. The degree of sensory stimulation can further contribute to or detract from the atmosphere of a setting. There is a good deal of evidence to suggest that both understimulation and overstimulation are undesirable.

Finally, dynamic environmental elements refer to readily movable objects, such as art, flowers, tablecloths, and decorations. Decorating a house for holidays, putting candy bowls out when company visits, and lighting candles for a romantic dinner all demonstrate how dynamic artifacts can lend ambiance and set a mood.

Because we have control over the semifixed and dynamic artifacts in our environment, artifacts become an extension of ourselves. Our furnishings reflect our personalities and tastes. People who decorate in green say something different about themselves than those who decorate in pink. The memorabilia that populate people's desks or rooms, even their stationery, give clues about themselves. Status can be clearly communicated by the elegance of a person's office and its location. For instance, offices in corners with windows and those with their own private door connote more status than those located in the middle of a large room. Employees with large wooden desks clearly have more status than those with small metal ones. Business executives who recognize this can use their offices to convey messages of status.

Our environment both communicates and impinges upon the communication process. The way we design and use the elements in our environment transmits messages about ourselves and dictates the nature of the communication that will occur. Thus artifacts are responsible for defining the communication context. They help to determine how all the other nonverbal codes are to be interpreted.

Functions of Nonverbal Communication

It would be a mistake to assume that the nonverbal codes operate independently of one another or that they have distinctly different purposes. Rather, they are frequently dependent on one another to create the total meaning of a message. Although some of the codes are more specialized than others in what communication roles they fulfill, most of them perform the same communication functions and they act in combination to perform those functions. The functions can be grouped into seven categories:

1. message production and processing,
2. impression formation and management,
3. relational communication,
4. expressive communication,
5. mixed messages and deception,
6. interaction management, and
7. social influence.

Message Production and Processing

Have you ever noticed that people gesture and smile when talking on the telephone? At first this might seem odd since the receiver cannot see the nonverbal cues. Yet researchers have found that when individuals are asked to explain a complicated procedure to someone who cannot see them, they are still likely to use nonverbal cues. Why? First, when describing something, particularly when it is rather complex, nonverbal communication may help the sender formulate and verbalize the message. For instance, if you are giving someone directions to your new apartment, sketching the path in the air may help you find the right words to describe it. Second, nonverbal communication is so intricately woven with verbal communication that it may become automatic to use the two channels together. When nonverbal and verbal communication work together to create messages, understanding is often strengthened.

There are at least five ways in which nonverbal cues work in conjunction with the verbal message (Ekman & Friesen, 1969b). One is *redundancy*. Nonverbal behavior frequently repeats what is being said verbally. For example, if an instructor tells you that you have 5 minutes to finish a test and simultaneously holds up five fingers, he or she is providing nonverbal redundancy. A second function of nonverbal behavior is *accentuation*, the highlighting or emphasizing of a verbal message. Pounding a desk top during a speech to make a point more emphatic is one example. On a less dramatic level, moving closer to someone who has expressed interest in you highlights the message of friendliness that may have first been signaled with the eyes. *Elaboration* is a third way in which nonverbal cues aid the verbal message. By modifying or expanding upon the verbal message, such cues clarify the total meaning. The smiles and gestures of returning travelers discussing their trip provide added information. The lingering touch after a fight may carry a much stronger plea for reconciliation than the difficult words of apology preceding this nonverbal behavior. Fourth, nonverbal behaviors may provide a *contradiction* of the verbal message. Such contradictions may be intentional or unintentional. If a person sarcastically says, "That is the most brilliant performance I have ever seen," he or she is intentionally contradicting the verbal statement through the tone of voice. Such contradictions may add intensity to the overall meaning. However, many times the contradictions are actually accidental betrayals of true feelings, as in the case of the person who unconvincingly raves about an unwanted gift. Finally, nonverbal cues may at times provide *substitution* for portions of the verbal message. Typically, emblems are used for this purpose. Nonverbal substitution may be used when the verbal channel is restricted, as in the case of trying to communicate across a noisy room. Substitution may occur when the verbal channel seems less capable of expressing the meaning, as in the case of showing disapproval of what someone is saying. Nonverbal cues can also heighten attention to the verbal message through contrast. A stern glance following the verbal statement, "Is that clear?" may be all that is necessary to make the point.

Nonverbal cues also facilitate attention and recall. Vocal variety, in terms of tempo, pitch, and intensity, heightens attention and comprehension. A moderately fast-paced speaking rate secures attention, while slower speaking rates give listeners time to daydream. This makes sense because the average person speaks at a rate of 120 to 150 words per minute, yet the average receiver can process words twice as fast without any loss of comprehension. Some advertisers have capitalized on this aspect of vocalics by increasing the speed of their radio commercials to achieve more audience recall.

The environment is also key in securing attention and stimulating recall. Administrators once believed that windowless classrooms would block noise and distractions and therefore help students concentrate on their studies. Instead, windowless classrooms left students feeling bored and unstimulated. Students became "clock-watchers." Open classrooms with large windows or too much activity often have the opposite effect—students may become overstimulated and anxious. A classroom that is neither too complex nor too distracting is optimal for comprehension and recall.

The nonverbal cues used by teachers also have an effect on student learning. One study found that students of teachers who used immediacy cues, such as eye contact, smiling, physical proximity, and gesturing, reported learning more than students of teachers who did not use such cues (Andersen, 1986). Teachers and other speakers can also stimulate attention and recall through the use of illustrators and emblems. In particular, gestures that serve to visually represent words aid in comprehension. So if you cannot convince your boss that you have "too much work to do" with words alone, try illustrating what a "tall" stack of papers you have on your desk with a gesture!

In many ways this first function of nonverbal communication, message production and processing, lays the foundation for the other functions. As will be shown in the succeeding sections, nonverbal cues help us make first impressions, express ourselves, communicate relational messages, and influence others.

Impression Formation and Management

A second function of nonverbal communication is the presentation of self, or the image that we present to others. The judgments receivers make from the images we present is the impression formation half of the equation. The ways we as senders deliberately manipulate the images we project is the impression management half of the equation. It is Erving Goffman's (1959) contention that human behavior can be viewed as a drama. Much of our behavior is a matter of playing roles for others, just as actors play roles. When we are "on stage," we create a front for others. That front may change from audience to audience. We may have one set of behaviors that fit the role of friend and another set of behaviors that are appropriate for the role of lover. You, no doubt, show different facets of your personality to your family from the facets you show to an employer.

Nonverbal behaviors are relevant to self-presentation in that successful performances of our roles are dependent on the degree to which nonverbal messages are well coordinated with each other and with the verbal level of interaction. Nonverbal cues are also responsible for creating someone's initial expectations of what roles we are likely to play. Research has demonstrated that nonverbal information heavily colors first impressions. Those first impressions may lead to a successful or unsuccessful self-presentation, depending on whether the sender intends to create those perceptions or not.

Two nonverbal codes that are especially responsible for initial impressions are physical appearance and vocalics. The relationship between these two codes and personality has been noted earlier. People judge our personality from body type alone. Our body shape is one feature over which we have little control when it comes to managing an impression. But we do have control over apparel, which is a major influence on first impressions when people are previously unacquainted. Clothing has been found to be significantly related to the perceived status and social roles of others (Gorden, Tengler, & Infante, 1982; Knowles, 1973). An executive who wears a $200 designer suit to the office is likely to be perceived as high in status. A clerk wearing the same suit may be seen instead as status-seeking. Clothing is also taken as an indicant of personality. Women rated high on good appearance are seen as more sociable and more intelligent (Silverman, 1945). Dress may even influence perceptions of the political philosophy of the wearer. In a study limited to college students, persons who were dressed "less conventionally" have been classified as radical, left-wing, and prone to marijuana use. Conversely, figures dressed "conventionally" have been perceived as career oriented and favoring the traditional "fun and football" culture (Kelley, 1969). Vocal cues lead to the same kinds of judgments. Listeners make judgments about a person's socioeconomic status, education, and occupation from voice cues alone and often with high accuracy (Addington, 1968; Ellis, 1967; Harms, 1961). Even when people try to disguise their status, their vocal patterns may give it away.

Credibility is also conveyed by vocal cues. Studies have shown that moderately fast speaking rates, lack of vocalized pauses (e.g., "ums," "ers"), vocal variety, and moderately high intensity combine to create an impression of a confident and competent speaker (Buller & Aune, 1988). In job interviews, vocalic and physical appearance cues combine to create a strong impression. Vocational consultants often advise their clients to dress in "the image of the company" by emulating the dress of prospective co-workers. Interviewees also make favorable impressions when they speak in confident voices, switch turns smoothly, give medium length responses, and display high involvement (Coker & Burgoon, 1987; Gifford, Ng, & Wilkinson, 1985).

Once in a job, nonverbal communication can be used to project a professional image. The white-coated doctor who walks briskly and speaks with an "air of authority" is attempting to inspire confidence in us. The politician who uses energetic, expansive gestures may be trying to convince us that he or she is both dynamic and insightful. Even such a seemingly minor feature as dialect may affect our evaluation of someone's credibility. For example, the female New Yorker is seen as more dynamic but less sociable in comparison with the female Southerner who is seen as the least composed of any of five regional speakers. The New York and General American dialects are perceived as indicators of more competence than the Northeastern, Southeastern, and Southern dialects (Toomb, Quiggins, Moore, MacNeill, & Liddell, 1972). This may explain why radio broadcasters work hard to achieve General American (dialect-free) speech.

Once people move beyond the initial stages of acquaintanceship, physical appearance cues become less important to the impression being created, and greater reliance is placed on the other codes. Dress may still act to identify the role a person is performing, but other codes that have the potential of being varied during an interaction become much more useful. Depending on what kind of impression a person is trying to manage, all the cues that are used as relational messages may be brought into play to manipulate that image consciously. Thus the student who wants to communicate friendliness and interest in class may sit closer to the front, lean forward during lectures, engage in frequent eye contact, and smile a lot. Of course, the performance may fail if done to excess, for excessive behaviors are seen as insincere.

Relational Communication

Relational messages are messages that define the nature of the relationship between two or more people. Any communication may have two levels: the "content" level—the information and ideas being exchanged—and the "relational" level—the information regarding how partners feel about each other and the relationship. When people signal their intentions and expectations toward others, when they reveal the degree to which they like someone or grant that person status and power, they are communicating at the relational level.

Nonverbal codes are constantly in use expressing relational messages while the verbal band is being used for other purposes. It is often easier and less risky to define relationships through nonverbal messages than to commit ourselves verbally. Thus we rely heavily on the combined nonverbal codes to send and receive messages of liking, approval, trust, dominance, and so forth.

One category of relational messages that has received considerable attention in the nonverbal literature is *liking and attraction*. Our bodies communicate much about our feelings toward others. Liking is conveyed by *conversational involvement* cues that show that a person is interested in the partner and the conversation at hand. Five types of conversational involvement cues have been delineated (Burgoon

& Newton, 1991; Coker & Burgoon, 1987). First, *immediacy cues*, such as touch, close proxemic distancing, and forward leans, signal approach as well as both physical and psychological closeness. If we lean forward or face a person directly, we probably like the person; conversely, if we lean back or turn our face away we may dislike the person. Vocal animation, vocal variety, and gestural animation contribute to the second dimension of conversational involvement —*expressiveness*. *Altercentrism*, the third facet of conversational involvement, refers to focusing on the partner. Nonverbal cues signaling warmth, friendliness, and general participation in the interaction convey altercentrism. *Smooth interaction management* in the form of fewer silences, shorter latencies, and more body coordination is the fourth mode of communicating involvement. People often mirror the sitting or standing positions of someone they like or agree with. Finally, a *moderately low level of social anxiety* signals involvement. A person's degree of muscular relaxation further connotes liking; people are moderately relaxed with those they like.

Our liking of others is additionally reflected in the way we include them within a communication circle. When we wish to affiliate with others, we often use our body to form an inclusive unit. We may cross our legs and orient our bodies toward the person we wish to include. We may also engage in *tactile tie signs*, such as holding hands or putting arms around one another. While doing this, we may also use our arms and legs as barriers to others we want to exclude from the interaction. Most people use direct eye contact to cement the bond further. They avoid eye contact with those who attempt to intrude, or they alternatively glare at them.

The subtle nature of nonverbal messages makes them particularly useful when one wishes to escalate a relationship. In contrast to verbal messages, individuals can deny the meaning of many nonverbal messages and, therefore, save themselves from embarrassment if rejected. A. E. Scheflen (1965), a psychologist, has demonstrated that there are consistent patterns of human courtship behavior. The term *quasi-courtship behavior* refers to the flirting games that go on between men and women, whether or not they are interested in each other. In many instances, it is merely a ritual in which both parties agree implicitly that it will not go beyond an understood point. They simply engage in the behavior to assert their own sexual attractiveness. In other instances, it serves as a prelude to more intimate relations. Quasi-courtship behavior then becomes a means of determining another's availability and approachability.

The ritual frequently begins with intermittent eye contact, which creates emotional arousal. Women hold their thighs together, walk with the upper arms against their body, and tilt their pelvises slightly forward. Men stand with their thighs apart, hold their arms away from their body, swing them as they walk, and carry their pelvises slightly back. Attraction is further evidenced by heightened muscle tone and erect postures. Men pull their stomachs in, whereas women throw their chests out to emphasize their breasts. Both sexes engage in preening behavior: tugging at socks, rearranging clothes and makeup, stroking hair, and glancing in mirrors. If a woman is open to a man's advances, she may cross her legs to expose a thigh, unfold her arms, engage in flirting glances, and roll her hips. Both men and women may open more buttons on their shirt or blouse than they usually do.

In the advanced stages, men and women increase proximity. If seated, they will close others out by their shoulder and leg positions. Once an intimate distance has been established, touching is likely to occur. A man may brush a woman's arm; a woman may touch a man's thigh. If contact progresses beyond this stage, chances are it is no longer quasi-courtship behavior.

A second major type of relational message for which nonverbal cues are enlisted is the communication of *status and power*. Artifacts and clothing are frequently called upon to signal status and power. Plush offices, luxury automobiles, and custom-tailored clothes are taken as measures of a person's importance. Eye contact may reveal a person's position in a group. The individual who receives the most eye contact from others is usually the one with the most power. Initiating touch and having the prerogative to violate proxemic norms are also indicative of power and status. Yet another code that may be used in a subtle way to communicate status is chronemics. One person who had a keen understanding of this use of time was Harry Truman. When he was president, an important editor who came to see him was kept waiting 45 minutes. When an aide informed Truman that the editor was becoming impatient, Truman replied that when he was junior senator from Missouri, that same editor had kept him "cooling his heels" in the outer office for an hour and a half. As far as he was concerned, the "SOB" had 45 minutes to go.

Expressive Communication

Our emotional states are usually revealed through the body, face, and eyes. Body positions typically indicate a person's general mood or gross affective state, whereas the face gives clues to specific feelings. Research on facial expressions of emotion has typically divided affect displays into two groups: *primary affect displays* and *affect blends*. Primary affect displays are universally recognized and distinct from one another. Researchers have discovered that Western cultures and primitive tribes alike use the same basic facial displays for certain primary emotions such as anger, disgust, happiness, sadness, surprise, and fear (Ekman, 1971; Izard, 1977). Anger, for example, is expressed facially with lowered eyebrows, tightly pressed lips, and a harsh stare; disgust is expressed with a wrinkled nose, lowered brow, and curled upper lip (see Table 5.2). Such primary affect displays are recognized across different cultures. Most people are also fairly accurate in deciding whether a person feels pleasant or unpleasant, relaxed or aroused. Beyond that, however, it becomes more difficult to make accurate judgments. For instance, a person may have difficulty distinguishing between rage and resentment, happiness and amusement, or pride and confidence. These types of emotional expressions are sometimes labeled *affect blends* because they combine kinesic cues connected to multiple emotions. The eyes may fly open in surprise while the lips curve open in an elated smile. Jealousy is an example of a blend affect. Researchers have found that individuals experiencing jealousy often display a "flash" of emotion, with their faces registering fleeting traces of anger, sadness, hurt, and disappointment within a single moment (Ellis & Weinstein, 1986).

Although our faces are often transparent when we feel strong emotions, there are times when we exercise some control over our affect displays. Paul Ekman and Wallace Friesen (1969b) proposed five *display rules* that help regulate how much or how little emotion we allow others to see. One such display rule is *intensification*, or the exaggeration of affect. Imagine receiving a gift from someone you

Table 5.2 Kinesic and Vocal Behaviors Associated With Primary Affect Displays

Primary Emotion	Associated Behaviors
Anger	Kinesic: brows drawn and lowered, lips either tightly pressed together or slightly squared shape, hostile stare Vocalic: fast tempo, loud, high pitch
Disgust	Kinesic: wrinkled nose, lowered brow, upper lip raised, chin raised Vocalic: slow tempo, small pitch variation
Happiness	Kinesic: smiling, raised cheeks, dimples, eyes crinkle at corners Vocalic: fast tempo, pitch variation, vocal animation
Sadness	Kinesic: frown, lips parted, inner brow raised, brows drawn together, gaze aversion Vocalic: slow tempo, low pitch
Surprise	Kinesic: raised brows, slightly raised open eyelids, white of eye shows above the iris, open mouth Vocalic: fast tempo, high pitch level
Fear	Kinesic: raised brows, open mouth, lips tense and drawn Vocalic: fast tempo, high pitch, little pitch variation

really like. The gift is okay and you are pleased, but you act even happier about the gift than you really are. You have used intensification. Now imagine that you really hate the gift, but pretend that you love it. In this case you have used the display rule called *masking* because you covered up one emotion with a different emotion. There are also times when we use *deintensification*. For example, if you are really angry at a child you might curb your reaction. *Neutralization* is another way to regulate emotion. Consider the following situation. Your best friend studies twice as long as you for a midterm. The grades come back and you get an "A." You're ecstatic, but you look over your shoulder and see that your friend only earned a "C" so you put a noncommittal expression on your face and say, "I did okay." In this case, you pretend not to feel an emotion when you actually do. The final type of display rule, *simulation*, involves the reverse process—you pretend to feel an emotion when you actually do not. Often it is appropriate to feign happiness when someone shares good news or concern when someone is upset, but in reality you don't really feel any emotion.

Other kinesic cues, such as eye contact and gestures, can also be indicative of emotion. Depression, for example, is often marked by gaze aversion, fewer illustrators, and slower body movements. Anxiety is often leaked through increases in fidgeting and motor behavior. Anger can lead to clenched fists and forceful hand movements (Siegman, 1985).

The use of display rules, although often effective, can backfire. Consider the following real-life cases. During a 1988 presidential debate, Michael Dukakis, the Democratic candidate, was asked if he would approve of capital punishment if his wife was brutally raped and killed. In an effort to appear unwavering in his political views, Dukakis answered the question without revealing any emotion. Later critics claimed that this unemotional response left viewers wondering how a man running for president could be so unmoved. Similarly, President Bush was criticized for smiling while discussing depressing statistics (e.g., babies born addicted to drugs, high-school dropout rates) during a televised address. Bush's advisers informed the press that Bush was afraid he would get overemotional so he smiled to lighten the mood. Obviously, his strategy was not completely successful.

Kinesic cues are not the only indicators of emotions. Vocal behavior also provides clues to a person's emotional state. In fact, the voice is second only to the face in terms of emotional expression. A loud, high-pitched, fast, irregular, clipped voice may communicate anger, whereas a slow, slurred, soft voice with irregular pauses and downward inflections may signal sadness (Davitz, 1964). Yet many individual differences exist in communicating the same emotion. Moreover, the same emotion can be expressed in different ways at different times. A person may shout one time when angry and whisper intensely another time. People also differ in their sensitivity and accuracy in judging vocal cues. Consequently, no firm statements can be made about which vocal behaviors are universally symbolic, except perhaps laughing and crying.

Mixed Messages and Deception

When verbal and nonverbal messages contradict one another, or when two nonverbal messages (e.g., smiling while crossing your arms defensively over your chest) are at odds with one another, a mixed message has occurred. Such messages can result in either increased understanding or confusion. A sarcastic response may provide the wit needed to lighten a conflict situation or may hurt someone's feelings. Imagine a little girl telling you that she thinks she is ugly. You jokingly respond with, "Oh, yeah, you're such an ugly thing," and she starts crying. This happened to one of the authors, who momentarily forgot that children, unlike adults, tend to believe the verbal message over the nonverbal message. Yet even for adults, determining the true meaning behind a mixed message can be difficult. Adults tend to rely most heavily on visual cues, followed by vocal cues. Verbal cues are generally relied upon least. Visual primacy is strongest, however, when part of the message is communicated by the face and when positive rather than negative emotions accompany the message. One exception to the visual primacy rule occurs when the message being sent is persuasive. In this case, the verbal channel seems to hold the most weight.

One special form of mixed message that is particularly hard to decipher is deception. In fact, studies have found that adults can detect deception only slightly better than chance (Miller & Burgoon, 1982). *Deception* has been defined more broadly than "lying" and includes any intentional act that seeks to leave a receiver with an impression, belief, or understanding that the sender considers to be false (Zuckerman, DePaulo, & Rosenthal, 1981). Equivocations, exaggerations, and concealments are three of several behaviors that fit such a definition.

So what nonverbal cues are indicative of deception? Research has shown that many cues stereotypically thought to be associated with deception are not. Chances are that someone has asked you to "look me in the eyes and tell me the truth." Were you able to look in the person's eyes and still lie? Research suggests that you probably could. Because you knew eye gaze is stereotypically associated with truthfulness, you were prepared to control the amount of gaze you displayed.

This idea that people attempt to control nonverbal cues stereotypically associated with deception underlies the *leakage hypothesis*, which predicts that the body provides more clues that deception is occurring than does the face (Ekman & Friesen, 1969a). This is because people are more conscious of their facial movements and, therefore, do a better job controlling the face. The anxiety and arousal associated with deception is then leaked through the body, possibly through fidgeting and random leg movement. Some research has shown that the lower body is less controllable and more "leaky" than the upper body. Vocal cues also appear to leak information about deception more than the face. Together, results from several studies seem to point to a leakage hierarchy with lower body at the top (representing the least controllable channel), the face at the bottom, and the voice and upper body somewhere in the middle. Specific behaviors related to actual deception include: pupil dilation, blinking, adaptors, false smiles, speech errors, speech hesitations, and higher voice pitch (Burgoon et al., 1989; Zuckerman & Driver, 1985). Notice that the only facial cues associated with actual deception are hard to control and difficult for decoders to detect. Deceivers tend to show more discrepancy between verbal and nonverbal channels than do truthtellers. A successful performance truly depends on consistency among the nonverbal and verbal codes; deception often produces inconsistency. Thus although nonverbal behaviors may be enlisted to create various fronts, they may also be used by observers to peek behind the facade.

Interaction Management

A sixth major function of nonverbal communication is defining communication contexts and regulating the flow of interaction within those contexts. Probably the primary code responsible for defining the context is artifacts. The way in which an environment is designed, arranged, and furnished will set the general tone for communication. A formal environment will produce formal communication. A small, dimly lit space with comfortable furniture will produce more casual and intimate communication. The environment may also provide clues about what roles people are expected to take. A friend reports that when she went to see the president of her university about an affirmative action matter, she found herself ushered to a seat 20 feet from the president, who ensconced himself behind an enormous desk. It was clear to her that she was to take a subordinate role and he, a dominant one. Similarly, the presence of a silver tea service at a meeting between foreign diplomats means that any negotiations will be conducted in a very formal, polite fashion and only after the social amenities have been satisfied.

Nonverbal cues may also be used to regulate the flow of an interaction. Kinesics and vocalics are the predominant codes used for this purpose. People have several means of indicating when they are willing to listen and when they want to talk. Kinesic and vocalic cues have been found to differ according to four categories of *turn-taking* (Cappella, 1985). If you are the person talking, you may be involved in either *turn-yielding* or *turn-maintaining*. If you wish to yield your turn and let others begin talking you might lean back or lower your vocal pitch. When we use eye contact and a head movement, we tell another person that he or she may begin speaking. If, however, you wish to maintain your speaking turn, you might increase voice volume and tempo while decreasing silent pauses. Looking away or filling a pause with a gesture are other ways of preventing an interruption and maintaining control of the conversation.

If you are the listener, you can engage in *turn-requesting* or *turn-denying*. Leaning back may signal that you are listening, whereas leaning forward or raising a finger may signal that you want to talk. Another turn-requesting cue is rapid backchannelling. Backchannelling cues, such as "uh-huh" and "yeah" usually indicate that a speaker is attentively listening; but if these cues are sped up, they indicate that a speaker understands the point and wishes to control the floor. These same backchannelling cues, when delivered more slowly, can give a speaker reinforcement and serve to deny oneself a turn. Kinesic cues from the face and eyes may also indirectly control an interaction. Direct, continuous eye contact can signal desire for feedback and demand attention. As the face is such a good indicator of the way someone feels about us, it is natural that we look at the face frequently when we want feedback. This tends to force the other person's attention on ourselves and to induce nonverbal or verbal feedback.

Beyond kinesic and vocalic behaviors, proxemics may have a regulatory effect on interaction. Such things as shifts in distance can keep another person from speaking or signal a desire to end a conversation. If you want to cut off conversation with someone, you might take a step back, look at your watch, and then lean away. In this case, proxemic and kinesic cues have combined to help regulate the interaction.

Social Influence

The power of nonverbal communication can be used to influence others even when verbal communication fails. A particularly good example is the story of a frustrated Californian who had tried in vain to receive compensation for his faulty new automobile. The dealer and the manufacturer both failed to respond satisfactorily to his claims. Realizing the futility of his efforts, he resorted to symbolic communication to protest his treatment by painting big yellow lemons on the sides of his car and parking it in front of the dealer's office. Of course, nonverbal and verbal communication are often combined to create strong persuasive messages.

A variety of nonverbal strategies, ranging from affiliation and credibility cues to attractiveness appeals and violations of expectations, have been found to be effective in encouraging attitude change. Louder, faster, and more fluent voices, for example, are perceived as more persuasive. Such cues communicate confidence and credibility. Research has shown that when a speaker and receiver share speech tempo similarity, social attractiveness is enhanced and compliance is more likely. This same line of research (Buller & Aune, 1988; Buller, Le Poire, Aune, & Eloy, 1992) has shown that faster tempo increases perceptions of speaker dominance and competence. Similarly, a somewhat erect posture and rhythmic, forceful gestures can contribute to the impressions of confidence and credibility, thereby heightening persuasiveness. Facial expressions that show liking and approval also seem to have the same effect (Mehrabian & Williams, 1969).

Another nonverbal feature that adds to persuasiveness is physical attractiveness. One study had a female speaker dress in rather unattractive clothing and give herself an oily, unkept appearance. Not surprisingly, she was much less persuasive with her audience than when she wore attractive clothing, makeup, and a flattering hair style (Mills & Aronson, 1965). Physical appearance cues may operate in yet another way. They may lead to a violation of expectations. A "hippie-looking" speaker who argues for tax reform may actually be more convincing than a conservatively dressed speaker. The appearance cues may lead a receiver to expect either unintelligent or radical views from such a speaker. A rational presentation on a "conservative" topic, therefore, comes as a pleasant surprise. If this interpretation is correct, it is possible that students may actually be more influential with peers and teachers alike by dressing in a deviant fashion, so long as what is said then counters the expectations established by the dress.

Nonverbal cues play a significant role in the modification of the behavior of others. Nonverbal cues can be used in a variety of ways to manipulate the way others communicate and act. Some of the strategies that produce an impact are threat cues, appeals to power and status, and violations of expectations. The power of staring as a threat is illustrated by a study in which drivers who received stares from a pedestrian on a street corner actually crossed the intersection faster than those who did not receive stares (Ellsworth, Carlsmith, & Henson, 1972). Stares are threatening, and people will take actions to avoid them. Uniforms may implicitly suggest a threat as well, although uniforms also carry connotations of status. People typically comply with the requests of a uniformed individual, even when the requests are illegitimate. For instance, a person dressed in a nondescript uniform asked pedestrians to put a dime in a parking meter for a stranger's car. The vast majority complied (Bickman, 1974). Even when uniforms are not used, clothing so effectively communicates status that it can influence the actions of others. Notice the differences in treatment that well-dressed and casually dressed customers receive from waiters or salespeople.

On a more positive note, nonverbal affiliation and liking cues can alter effectively the way others behave. Such cues may encourage another person to acquire a new skill, to volunteer assistance when help is needed, and even to become more intimate in communication. For instance, touching usually leads to more disclosure of intimate information.

One last way in which nonverbal behaviors may modify the actions of others is through violations of norms and expectations. It was noted earlier that proxemic behavior is highly norm governed. People develop expectations about what distances others will adopt. A violation of the normative distance can, therefore, have some interesting effects. If you invade people's personal space, they may become more active nonverbally, use more vocalized pauses ("ums" and "ers"), and become more verbose and less flexible in verbal statements (Garner, 1972). Violations of dress expectations can also have detrimental consequences. One study done by two college students tested the effects of hair and dress on people's willingness to sign a harmless petition. In one situation, the male student had long hair and a beard, the female experimenter wore long hair and both had on "hippie" clothing. On the second occasion the male cut his hair and was clean shaven, the female wore her hair up, and both dressed "conservatively." Not surprisingly, significantly fewer people signed the petition of the "long hairs." The conclusion to be drawn is that violating expectations can have either positive or negative effects, depending on what kind of violation it is and what your purpose is. Positive violations may increase persuasion and lead to desired behavioral changes; negative violations may produce undesirable outcomes. In this area and many others, we are only beginning to understand the ways in which nonverbal communication operates and the power that it holds.

Summary

1. Nonverbal messages are a powerful part of the communication process. Because so much of nonverbal behavior operates outside of conscious awareness, most people fail to recognize the wide range of roles that such messages play. Misinterpretation is common.

2. Nonverbal communication may be classified according to the different codes or modes of expression that are used. The seven primary codes are proxemics, haptics, chronemics, kinesics, physical appearance, vocalics, and artifacts.

3. Proxemics is the study of how human beings structure and use space to communicate. People have two spatial needs: territorial and personal. Territory has been broken down into three categories of primary, secondary, and public. Sex, race, status, age, personality variables, cultural norms, personal attraction, and situational variables all affect an individual's spatial needs. People resent invasions of their personal space and have developed several response patterns to deal with such invasions.

4. Haptics is the study of a person's use of touch. Touch has significant communicative value, but in our society it has been discouraged
as a mode of communication except in intimate relationships. Several
different types of touch, including both positive and negative affect,
have been delineated. Additionally, five dimensions of location,
duration, intensity, frequency, and instrument of touch underlie
haptic behavior.

5. Chronemics is the study of how human beings use time. The
American use of time falls into three categories or sets: technical
time, or scientific breakdowns that have little bearing on nonverbal
communication; formal time, or the traditional, conscious divisions
of time such as years, months, and days; and informal time, which
is dependent on the context of a communication situation for its
definition. The American use of informal time follows two patterns:
the diffused point pattern, in which people arrive somewhere around
the appointed time, and the displaced point pattern, in which people
arrive at or before the appointed time. Chronemic message elements
include urgency, duration, waiting time, punctuality, and mono-
chronic versus polychronic use of time.

6. Kinesics, or the visual aspects of behavior, has long been
recognized as carrying meaning in a communication interaction.
Kinesic behaviors have been broken down into five broad classifications: emblems, illustrators, affect displays, adaptors, and regulators. Sex, race, culture, and social status often influence kinesic
behavior; however, every individual develops unique kinesic patterns. People use the body to communicate much about their feelings toward others. A person's emotional state may be revealed
through the body, face, eye movements, and gestures. Kinesic behavior may also provide clues to an individual's status and background.

7. Our physical appearance may also carry messages to another
person. People tend to stereotype our personalities on the basis of
our body type. In addition, dress, hair, accessories, and cosmetics
are often used as indicators of certain traits. Dress is most typically
seen as a message about a person's lifestyle and status. Physical
appearance as a nonverbal code is especially important in first
impressions.

8. Vocalics is the study of the vocal (as opposed to verbal)
aspects of speech. Because there are so many features of the voice
that can be varied, this code fills a broad range of communication

functions. It is relevant to such things as the way people signal the nature of their relationship with others, the regulation of interactions, the impressions that people try to create, and the learning and persuasion processes. As is the case with physical appearance cues, people often stereotype others based on vocalics.

9. Artifacts are a final nonverbal code that may both serve as a message vehicle and influence the communication transmitted through other codes. The design of an environment reflects the interests and personalities of the designer and the users of the space. Fixed features such as size, space volume, and architectural design, as well as semi-fixed features such as lighting, temperature, color, and furniture arrangement, help to dictate the kind of communication that will take place. Dynamic features, such as objects, may also carry messages.

10. The nonverbal codes act in combination to perform communication functions including message production and processing, impression formation and management, relational communication, expressive communication, mixed messages and deception, interaction management, and social influence.

11. Nonverbal messages can serve as verbal complements through redundancy, accentuation, elaboration, contradiction, or substitution. Vocalics and the environment can aid in facilitating attention and recall, as can the use of immediacy behaviors, illustrators, and emblems.

12. Another communication role that nonverbal behaviors perform is self-presentation: the impressions people form about others or attempt to create for others. Much of interaction can be viewed as a drama, with each person performing a role for an audience. Nonverbal cues are important in determining whether the front that is presented is successful or not. Initial impressions are influenced primarily by physical appearance and vocalics. Credibility judgments are influenced by all of the nonverbal codes.

13. Nonverbal communication sends relational messages of liking and attraction through conversational involvement and courtship cues. Similarly, nonverbal cues can signal power and status. Such messages can be conveyed by single or multiple nonverbal codes.

14. Our emotional states are revealed predominantly through the body, face, and eyes, and secondarily by the voice. Research on facial expressions examines both primary affect displays and affect blends.

Although we often show emotion spontaneously, there are times when we exercise control over emotional displays. There are five specific display rules that we use to help regulate how much or how little emotion we allow others to see: intensification, masking, deintensification, neutralization, and simulation.

15. When messages are mixed, adults tend to rely on visual codes over vocal codes and on vocal codes over verbal codes. One type of mixed message—deception—is particularly difficult to detect. Researchers have found that many nonverbal behaviors that are stereotypically associated with deception are unrelated to actual deception. A "leakage hierarchy" appears to exist, with the body providing more clues than the face that deception is occurring.

16. Yet another major function of nonverbal communication is the structuring of interactions. Environmental features are an important source of clues as to what roles people are expected to perform in any situation. Kinesic, vocalic, proxemic, and haptic cues are used to regulate the flow of interaction. They determine whose turn it is to speak, how long each person will speak, and sometimes even what the people will talk about.

17. Finally, nonverbal cues may be enlisted in efforts to enhance attitude change and to influence others. A number of strategies involving nonverbal behaviors can be used to manipulate the actions of others. Liking and approval cues, credibility appeals, power and status appeals, threat cues, attractiveness manipulations, attention arousal or distraction manipulations, and violations of expectations have all been found effective as modification techniques.

References

Addington, D. W. (1968). The relationship of selected vocal characteristics to personality perception. *Speech Monographs, 35*, 492-503.

Agulera, C. (1967). Relationships between physical contact and verbal interaction between nurses and patients. *Journal of Psychiatric Nursing, 5*, 5-21.

Altman, I. (1975). *The environment and social behavior*. Monterey, CA: Brooks-Cole.

Andersen, J. F. (1986). Instructor nonverbal communication: Listening to our silent messages. In J. M. Civikly (Ed.), *Communicating in college classrooms: New directions for teaching and learning* (pp. 41-49). San Francisco: Jossey-Bass.

Andersen, P. A., & Sull, K. K. (1985). Out of touch, out of reach: Tactile predispositions as predictors of interpersonal distance. *Western Journal of Speech Communication, 49*, 57-72.

Baxter, J. C., & Deanovitch, B. F. (1970). Anxiety effect of inappropriate crowding. *Journal of Consulting and Clinical Psychology, 35,* 174-178.

Bickman, L. (1974). The social power of a uniform. *Journal of Applied Social Psychology, 4,* 47-61.

Birdwhistell, R. L. (1970). *Kinesics and context.* Philadelphia: University of Pennsylvania Press.

Blue is beautiful. (1973, September 17). *Time,* p. 66.

Buller, D. B., & Aune, R. K. (1988). The effects of vocalics and nonverbal sensitivity on compliance: A speech accommodation theory explanation. *Human Communication Research, 14,* 301-332.

Buller, D. B., Le Poire, B. A., Aune, R. K., & Eloy, S. V. (1992). Social perceptions as mediators of the effect of speech rate similarity on compliance. *Human Communication Research, 19,* 286-311.

Burgoon, J. K. (1991). Relational message interpretations of touch, conversational distance, and posture. *Journal of Nonverbal Behavior, 15,* 233-259.

Burgoon, J. K., Buller, D. B., & Woodall, W. G. (1989). *Nonverbal communication: The unspoken dialogue.* New York: Harper & Row.

Burgoon, J. K., & Newton, D. A. (1991). Applying a social meaning model to relational message interpretations of conversational involvement. *Southern Communication Journal, 56,* 96-113.

Byers, P., & Byers, M. (1972). Nonverbal communication and the education of children. In C. B. Cazden, V. P. John, & D. Hymes (Eds.), *Foundation of language in the classroom* (pp. 3-31). New York: Teachers College Press.

Calhoun, J. B. (1962). Population density and social pathology. *Scientific American, 206,* 139-146.

Cappella, J. N. (1985). Controlling the floor in conversations. In A. W. Siegman & S. Feldstein (Eds.), *Multichannel integrations of nonverbal behavior* (pp. 69-104). Hillsdale, NJ: Lawrence Erlbaum.

Coker, D. A., & Burgoon, J. K. (1987). The nature of conversational involvement and nonverbal encoding patterns. *Human Communication Research, 13,* 463-494.

Davis, D. E. (1971). Physiological effects of continued crowding. In A. H. Esser (Ed.), *Behavior and environment* (pp. 133-147). New York: Plenum.

Davitz, J. R. (1964). *The communication of emotional meaning.* New York: McGraw-Hill.

DeVito, J. A. (1988). *Human communication: The basic course.* New York: Harper & Row.

Ekman, P. (1971). Universal and cultural differences in facial expressions of emotions. In J. K. Cole (Ed.), *Nebraska Symposium on Motivation* (pp. 207-283). Lincoln: University of Nebraska Press.

Ekman, P., & Friesen, W. V. (1969a). Nonverbal leakage clues to deception. *Psychiatry, 32,* 88-106.

Ekman, P., & Friesen, W. V. (1969b). The repertoire of nonverbal behavior: Categories, origins, usage, and coding. *Semiotica, 1,* 49-98.

Ellis, C., & Weinstein, E. (1986). Jealousy and the social psychology of emotional experience. *Journal of Social and Personal Relationships, 3,* 337-357.

Ellis, D. S. (1967). Speech and social status in America. *Social Forces, 45,* 431-451.

Ellsworth, P. C., Carlsmith, J. M., & Henson, A. (1972). The stare as a stimulus to flight in human subjects. *Journal of Personality and Social Psychology, 21,* 302-311.

Fast, J. (1971). *Body language.* New York: Pocket Books.

Felipe, N. J., & Sommer, R. (1966). Invasions of personal space. *Social Problems, 14,* 206-214.

Forston, R. F., & Larson, C. U. (1968). The dynamics of space: An experimental study in proxemic behavior among Latin Americans and North Americans. *Journal of Communication, 18,* 109-116.

Frank, M. S., & Gilovich, T. (1988). The dark side of self- and social perception: Black uniforms and aggression in professional sports. *Journal of Personality and Social Psychology, 54,* 74-85.

Garner, P. (1972). *The effects of personal space on interpersonal communication.* Unpublished master's thesis, Illinois State University.

Gifford, R., Ng, C. F., & Wilkinson, M. (1985). Nonverbal cues in the employment interview: Links between applicant qualities and interviewer judgments. *Journal of Applied Psychology, 70,* 729-736.

Goffman, E. (1959). *The presentation of self in everyday life.* Garden City, NY: Anchor Books/Doubleday.

Gorden, W. I., Tengler, C. D., & Infante, D. A. (1982). Women's clothing predispositions as predictors of dress at work, job satisfaction, and career advancement. *Southern Speech Communication Journal, 47,* 422-434.

Guerrero, L. K., & Ebesu, A. S. (1993, May). *While at play: An observational analysis of children's touch during interpersonal interaction.* Paper presented at the annual meeting of the International Communication Association, Washington, DC.

Hall, E. T. (1959). *Silent language.* Garden City, NY: Doubleday.

Hall, E. T. (1966). *The hidden dimension.* Garden City, NY: Doubleday.

Hall, J. A. (1985). Male and female nonverbal behavior. In A. W. Siegman & S. Feldstein (Eds.), *Multichannel integrations of nonverbal behavior* (pp. 195-226). Hillsdale, NJ: Lawrence Erlbaum.

Harms, L. S. (1961). Listener judgments of status cues in speech. *Quarterly Journal of Speech, 47,* 164-168.

Izard, C. E. (1977). *Human emotions.* New York: Plenum.

Johnson, K. L., & Edwards, R. (1991). The effects of gender and type of romantic touch on perceptions of relational commitment. *Journal of Nonverbal Behavior, 43,* 43-55.

Johnson, K. R. (1972). Black kinesics: Some nonverbal communication patterns in the black culture. In L. A. Samovar & R. E. Porter (Eds.), *Intercultural communication: A reader* (pp. 181-189). Belmont, CA: Wadsworth.

Jones, S. E., & Yarbrough, A. E. (1985). A naturalistic study of the meanings of touch. *Communication Monographs, 52,* 19-56.

Kelley, J. (1969, May). *Dress and non-verbal communication.* Paper presented at the annual meeting of the American Association for Public Opinion Research.

Knapp, M. L., & Hall, J. A. (1992). *Nonverbal communication in human interaction* (2nd ed.). New York: Holt, Rinehart & Winston.

Knowles, E. S. (1973). Boundaries around group interaction: The effect of group size and member status on boundary permeability. *Journal of Personality and Social Psychology, 26,* 327-331.

Leipold, W. E. (1963). *Psychological distance in a dyadic interview.* Unpublished doctoral dissertation, University of South Dakota.

Little, K. B. (1965). Personal space. *Journal of Experimental Social Psychology, 1,* 237-247.

McKeachie, W. (1952). Lipstick as a determiner of first impressions of personality: An experiment for the general psychology course. *Journal of Social Psychology, 36,* 241-244.

Mehrabian, A., & Williams, M. (1969). Nonverbal concomitants of perceived and intended persuasiveness. *Journal of Personality and Social Psychology, 13*, 37-58.

Miller, G. R., & Burgoon, J. K. (1982). Factors affecting witness credibility. In N. L. Kerr & R. M. Bray (Eds.), *The psychology of the courtroom* (pp. 169-194). New York: Academic Press.

Mills, J., & Aronson, E. (1965). Opinion change as a function of the communicator's attractiveness and desire to influence. *Journal of Personality and Social Psychology, 1*, 73-77.

Mintz, N. L. (1956). Effects of aesthetic surroundings: II. Prolonged and repeated experience in a "beautiful" and "ugly" room. *Journal of Psychology, 41*, 459-466.

Patterson, M. L., Mullens, S., & Romano, J. (1971). Compensatory reactions of spatial intrusion. *Sociometry, 34*, 1114-1121.

Scheflen, A. E. (1965). Quasi-courtship behavior in psychotherapy. *Psychiatry, 28*, 245-257.

Siegman, A. W. (1985). Expressive correlates of affective states and traits. In A. W. Siegman & S. Feldstein (Eds.), *Multichannel integrations of nonverbal behavior* (pp. 37-68). Hillsdale, NJ: Lawrence Erlbaum.

Silverman, S. S. (1945). *Clothing and appearance: Their psychological meaning for teen-age girls.* Research monograph, Bureau of Publications, Teachers College, Columbia University.

Sommer, R. (1969). *Personal space.* Englewood Cliffs, NJ: Prentice Hall.

Stanhope, P. E., Earl of Chesterfield. (1780, September 5). In a letter.

Toomb, J. K., Quiggins, J., Moore, D. L., MacNeill, J. B., & Liddell, C. M. (1972, April). *The effects of regional dialects on initial source credibility.* Paper presented at the annual meeting of the International Communication Association, Atlanta.

Walster, E., Aronson, V., Abrahams, D., & Rottman, L. (1966). Importance of physical attractiveness in dating behavior. *Journal of Personality and Social Psychology, 4*, 508-516.

Willis, F. N. (1966). Initial speaking distance as a function of the speaker's relationship. *Psychometric Science, 5*, 221-222.

Zuckerman, M., DePaulo, B. M., & Rosenthal, R. (1981). Verbal and nonverbal communication of deception. In L. Berkowitz (Ed.), *Advances in experimental social psychology* (Vol.14, pp. 1-59). New York: Academic Press.

Zuckerman, M., & Driver, R. E. (1985). Telling lies: Verbal and nonverbal correlates of deception. In A. W. Siegman & S. Feldstein (Eds.), *Multichannel integrations of nonverbal behavior* (pp. 129-148). Hillsdale, NJ: Lawrence Erlbaum.

COMMENTS ON THE FUNCTIONS OF HUMAN COMMUNICATION

In Part I we explored the nature of the communication process and the contexts in which communication occurs. In Part II some of the major functions of communication will be discussed. Perhaps it is best to begin with the caveat that not all of the possible functions that communication serves can be discussed in the brief space remaining. It is important, however, to focus on a few ways that people use communication to serve several specific needs—gaining compliance, establishing social relationships, making decisions, and managing conflict. It is our intention in the remainder of the book to focus on these functions of communication, rather than on specific contexts such as small-group, public speaking, or mediated communication. This decision reflects our belief that students will be best served by focusing on the goals and outcomes of communication: elements that are common to all contexts. These final chapters, then, will concentrate on the functions that occur across communication contexts. Although there are surely differing strategies for persuading someone in a face-to-face interaction, small-group, public speaking, or mediated communication setting, there are common elements that are applicable across all situations. The same can be said of communication and social relationships, decision making, and communication and conflict management. It is our hope that you will consider differing strategies for adapting the information contained in this final section to fit best the communication contexts in which you operate.

6

Persuasion:
Approaches to Gaining Compliance

It would be difficult to overestimate the role that persuasive communication has in our lives. The central function of most communication is to influence. The issue of influence is directly related to a definition we provided earlier—that communication is *purposive*, that is it directed toward the achievement of a goal. For example, students attempt to influence teachers to give high grades on their papers and exams, teachers try to persuade students that their classes have praxis, relational partners spend an exorbitant amount of time attempting to influence each other, and employees spend a great deal of their work-related conversations attempting to convince their superiors that they have what it takes to "make it." Most communication events are attempts to manipulate the environment around us. Our ability to get what we want in life is, to a large extent, is based upon our ability to manage the impressions others have of us—honesty, trustworthiness, capability, and so on.

If you had access to a transcript of your daily interactions, you would be surprised to note how many of your interactions are conscious attempts to shape, change, and/or reinforce someone's (or your own) attitudes, emotions, perceptual framework, and—ultimately—behavior.

Also of vital interest to all is our ability to say "no" to those who are attempting to influence us. Because we do not all have common goals, it is important to keep in mind that our attempts at persuasion and influence are often met with counter-persuasive attempts by those we are trying to influence. This underscores the transactional nature of communication and, especially, persuasion. Our attempts to control events and outcomes is closely tied to our abilities as communicators to persuade, accept influence from others, and resist persuasion when our own self-interests are at stake.

Persuasive communication sometimes fails to be effective even when logically and directly planned and heavily substantiated by reasons for change. Basketball great Earvin "Magic" Johnson, after being diagnosed HIV positive, returned (albeit briefly) to play for the Los Angeles Lakers. Health care professionals argued that the risk of other players contracting the HIV virus from Magic Johnson while on the court were infinitesimally small. Professional basketball players from around the league were given the latest medical information available concerning the risks of contracting the HIV virus by playing with Magic Johnson. Not all of the players were convinced by these persuasive messages. Questions, anxiety, concerns, and previously learned stereotyped images of HIV infected persons were too strong for any rational argument to persuade some players that playing with Magic Johnson was safe. Amid much controversy, Magic Johnson decided to retire from professional basketball. This example is matched by numerous other curiosities in the area of persuasive communication. Why, how, and in what ways people are persuaded to change—anything from their brand of toothpaste, to attitudes concerning segments of society, to their political party—are the primary emphases of several communication theories.

Defining the Persuasion Process

Theories of persuasion radiate from some central ideas about the nature of persuasion. To understand the role that theory plays in our investigation of persuasive communication, we need to begin with a workable definition of *persuasion*. It is important to point out that there are difficulties in using "hard and fast" definitions for *persuasion*, that is, specifying instances to which the concept applies. For example, a common definition contends that persuasive communication is "a conscious attempt by one individual to modify the attitudes, beliefs, or behaviors of another individual or group of individuals through the transmission of some message" (Bettinghaus, 1973, p. 10). From our perspective, one glaring problem with this FREE definition is the lack of acknowledgment that we can, and do, persuade ourselves. Another definition maintains that persuasion is "a successful, intentional effort at influencing another's mental state through communication in a circumstance in which the persuadee has some measure of freedom" (O'Keefe, 1990, p. 17). This definition includes the notion of conscious intent and focuses on persuasion as a communication phenomenon but emphasizes changes in mental states and fails to address the issue of changes in behavior. These examples are not offered with the intent to unduly criticize any attempt at defining *persuasion*. We simply want to emphasize that any definition of persuasion, no matter how carefully conceived, is open to criticism. One definition might be criticized as simply being "too broad" and including cases of persuasion that it should not, while others may receive criticism for being "too narrow in scope." For our purposes, we define *persuasion* as a conscious symbolic act intended to form, modify, or strengthen the beliefs, opinions, values, attitudes, and/or behaviors of another or ourselves. We will begin by addressing the issue of intent associated with defining a persuasive act and then discuss the relationship between changes in mental states (e.g., values, beliefs, attitudes, and opinions) and changes in behavior as they relate to persuasion.

It may be useful in terms of our definition of persuasion to reflect on the definition of *communication* we presented in Chapter 1. Just as we focused on the source's *intent* to communicate and the receiver's *perceptions* of the source's intent to communicate, we feel persuasion

	Source has an intent to persuade	Source does not have an intent to persuade
Receiver perceives an intent to persuade	A. Persuasion (possible forewarning)	B. Not persuasion (possible conformity)
Receiver does not perceive an intent to persuade	C. Persuasion (possible deception)	D. Ruled out as persuasion

Figure 6.1. Persuasion Grid

must be viewed in the same fashion. In fact, there is perhaps more agreement about the specific role of intent in the process of persuasion than in the communication process itself (Miller, Burgoon, & Burgoon, 1984). We strongly agree that central to any definition of persuasion is the notion of one (or more) person(s) consciously intending to influence another. The grid in Figure 6.1 is a modification of the communication grid presented in Chapter 1.

Figure 6.1 displays only those situations in which sources do or do not intend to persuade and receivers do or do not perceive the other's attempt to influence them via symbolic messages. This grid differs from the communication grid in that it requires that there be agreement between source and receiver on the general persuasive nature of the intention to communicate. Cell A is obviously persuasion. Not only does the source have a clear intention to persuade, but the receiver is cognizant of being the target of a persuasive attempt. Communication between a customer and a retail clerk is a typical example of Cell A.

A receiver's awareness of being the target of persuasion can significantly affect the outcome of persuasive attempts. A great deal of research has revealed that the targets of persuasion often develop resistance to persuasive attempts when forewarned of an impending persuasive effort. We will deal with inducing and overcoming resistance to persuasion later in this chapter. We do want to note here that there is potential for a boomerang effect to occur when a receiver becomes aware that a communicator is attempting to manipulate him or her, resulting in attitude and/or behavior changing in the opposite direction advocated by the source. Other studies, however, have revealed that persuaders who openly admit their attempts at influence may be seen as more credible and honest. If this credibility change occurs as a result of being forthcoming about the persuasive attempt, forewarned targets may be more persuadable (Burgoon & Miller, 1990).

Cell B defines a situation in which a source has no intention to influence, but the receiver is influenced by what the source says or does. Because the source does not have the intent to persuade, we do not consider this scenario to be a legitimate exemplar of persuasion, despite the fact that the receiver was influenced. Although this type of influence is of interest to social scientists and worthy of investigation, it is more appropriately studied as possible conformity rather than as persuasion. Our preference is to stay focused on the issue of intention when considering what is, and is not, persuasion.

Our perspective of persuasion is in line with the situation defined in Cell C. Here, the source has a unmistakable intention to influence a receiver of the communication, but the receiver fails to perceive that intention. As we have stated previously, because forewarning often prompts a defensive response that can produce the opposite of a desired persuasive effect, we contend that concealment of persuasive intent is often required for any hope of success. For example, teachers may desire to influence their students, to study hard or initiate independent research on a topic, a desire that might be best served by making the students think that the true purpose of the communication is to inform or educate. Further, some research indicates that people are likely to be influenced by overheard conversations in which they are not the targets of persuasion (Walster & Festinger, 1962). It appears to be the case that when people hear things they think they were not intended to hear, they are less defensive and, therefore, more likely to be influenced by the force of the arguments they perceived were intended for others or lacking the intent to persuade. However, because receivers in this context are unaware of the source's intentions, we would be remiss if we did address not at this time the issue of deception and persuasive communication.

Some people incorrectly think that all persuasion attempts are deceptive, or at least that persuasion necessitates some form of deception because the "true" intent to persuade may be concealed from the target of influence. They maintain that successful persuaders often must keep their "patsies" unaware of their intention to influence them. It is not our design to argue that deception is inherently good or bad. In the final analysis, the goodness or badness of deceptive communication is tied to the source's purpose. We *do* argue that deception, like all strategies of persuasion, has its costs and benefits, and it would be wise for any would-be persuader to be aware of some of the hazards of relying exclusively on deception as a means to influence others. First, as we have already noted, persuaders can often increase perceptions of their credibility by being forthright in disclosing their intent to influence others. They are seen as being honest and straightforward. Second, any communicator caught being deceptive will likely be ineffective in persuading the target audience to accept his or her arguments. There is no doubt that relationships can suffer disastrous consequences when either partner is caught being deceptive. The loss of trust that will likely ensue influences subsequent persuasive attempts and may ultimately result in the dissolution of the relationship. Although it is probably true that some people do not like to be persuaded, it is also true that most people resent being deceived even more. Third and finally, the idea that people in general resist persuasion simply for the sake of opposing change is unfounded. Many people enjoy being persuaded by good arguments (Roberts, 1924). We suggest that rather than keeping audiences in the dark through deceptive schemes, persuaders can be more effective if they can convince the target audience that, by the weight of their arguments, the most rational course of action is to be influenced.

We rule out Cell D as important to this discussion of persuasion. Where there is no intent from the source of a message to persuade, and no intent perceived by the receiver of the message, no persuasion occurs.

In summary, we adhere to a more restricted source-oriented perspective of persuasion as opposed to our more general view of communication. For our purposes we hold that the best way to study persuasion is to examine those situations in which both source and receiver are cognizant that persuasion is being attempted as well as situations in which, for whatever reason, the source's intention to persuade is not recognized by the target. The remainder of this chapter, then, will focus on situations during which a person wishes to influence others.

An important issue raised by our definition of *persuasion* centers on the nature of change necessary to label a communicative attempt as persuasive. Has an educational television station's fund-raising effort succeeded in persuading a viewer to contribute at the point when the viewer phones in a pledge for $50? Would you remain convinced that persuasion had occurred if the viewer never sent in the $50 check? Essentially, this problem focuses on the differences between attitude and behavior. Most people assume that attitude and behavior are related; in fact, a common definition of *attitude* is "a predisposition to behave in certain ways." Research indicates, however, that a person's attitude and behavior are often inconsistent. The educational television viewer may be persuaded to hold the attitude that watching public television without supporting the station financially is parasitic. But that viewer might still fail to send in a check—no matter how much guilt is felt.

One classic study demonstrated this inconsistency between a person's attitude and behavior (LaPiere, 1934). On the West Coast, at a time when many people held anti-Oriental attitudes, 92% of a group of hotel and restaurant clerks told researchers that they would not serve Chinese people. When a well-dressed Chinese couple arrived at the hotels and restaurants, however, in only one case were they refused service. Unfortunately, the attitude-behavior discrepancy also works the other way; many people express positive attitudes toward minority groups members, yet behave or treat them in negative ways.

Furthermore, changed behavior does not always indicate changed attitudes. While at college, many of us find ourselves in situations where socially expected behaviors conflict with our personal beliefs and values. For example, many of our students have revealed to us that they would prefer not to drink alcoholic beverages at parties or other social occasions, but they perceive that the negative relational consequences of not drinking are too great. In this situation, their behavior is not indicative of any change in their attitude about drinking alcohol, only that their attitude regarding the value placed on social relationships is a stronger influence on their behavior than their attitude concerning drinking alcohol.

A persuader who achieves conformity without attitude change is not much of a persuader, unless merely concerned with behavior. A politician who gets votes because of being viewed as "the lesser of two evils" might be content with that type of victory. Persuaders must decide whether they want to influence behavior, attitudes, or both. In summary, persuasion can be said to be successful when the changes intended by the source of communication are realized. In any given persuasion instance, there are several changes that might occur, and any one of these changes might be satisfactory to the person attempting to bring about change. It is only when we know something of the communicator's intent that we make judgments about the relative efficacy of persuasive communication.

In determining the kind of persuasion that has occurred, the communicator can only infer attitude change from behavior. We only infer people's attitudes by what they do and what they say. Making these inferences, however, is easier if one understands the variety of forms that change can take. Persuasive communication can lead to changes in opinions, beliefs, or values; these changes in turn lead to changes in perception, affect, cognition, or overt action.

Opinions are verbalized evaluations of people, things, or ideas. An opinion may be favorable, neutral, or unfavorable. If you read an editorial that persuaded you to say, "I now think that America's decision to send U.S. troops into Somalia to assure that food and resources get to the people is an honorable action," you would have undergone an opinion change. A *belief* is a conviction about truth or falsity. If you believe that the earth is flat and if you then are shown pictures of the earth taken by the astronauts and if these photographs change your mind, you have undergone a change in belief. Unlike an opinion, a belief is not evaluative. For example, "Many people voted for Bill Clinton for President of the United States" is a belief; "The people who voted for Bill Clinton for President were smart" is an opinion. A *value* is similar to an opinion, but it is more deeply held and more resistant to change. Values exert an enduring influence on a person's thinking and behavior. A good example of the difference between a value and an opinion is provided by the continuing controversy over the issue of abortion in this country. People on both sides of this complex issue profess holding the value of life in high regard. Rather than discuss the specific issues related to abortion, the point we wish to raise is that those favoring abortion and those who are opposed to abortion hold differing opinions based in part on a shared value of life. In short, each opinion can be differentiated from deeper religious, philosophical, or ethical values.

These three internal states—the holding of opinions, beliefs, and values—are the first targets of persuasive communication. Changes in these states can lead to changes in perception. For example, students who become convinced that a professor is discriminating against them are likely to perceive everything that happens in the classroom from this point of view. Changes in beliefs, opinions, and values can also lead to affective, or emotional, change. By appealing to emotions, persuasion can alter a person's mood, self-concept, and state of mind. Some persuasive messages try to produce affective change by inducing guilt and fear. For instance, a person who goes through a profound change in religious values may become fearful of "fire and brimstone." Sometimes affective change is the only goal of a persuader. For instance, a man may try to persuade a woman to love him. At other times, affective change is sought so that further change will result: A man may attempt to persuade a woman to love him so that she will marry him.

Cognitive change influences a person's rational thought processes. People change their behavior partly by considering alternatives and revising their ideas to adapt to new information. Parents who wish their child to give up smoking might begin by presenting factual evidence supporting the health risks associated with smoking. Cognitive change may also be desirable for its own sake. For example, a history teacher is (he or she hopes) helping the students achieve cognitive change as they move through the course. Changes in beliefs, opinions, or values can aid cognitive change, as in the case of a student who has to be convinced that a communication course is valuable before enrolling in it.

Overt action is observable behavior. Although overt action can be influenced by changes in a person's beliefs, opinions, or values, this is not always the case. For example, a person can use coercion to induce overt behavior that is unrelated to the beliefs, opinions, or values of another person. A teacher may induce students to study by threatening them with a failing grade, but the teacher may not necessarily change the students' opinions about the value of the subject matter.

Coercion, then, differs from persuasion in that targets of influence do not have a perception of choice regarding their behavior. Clearly, if one feels forced to modify behavior, one has been influenced. However, it is important to note that changes in overt behavior due to coercion are not indicative of changes in beliefs, opinions, or values, and therefore, the behavior will not likely continue once the threat is withdrawn.

Of course, attitude changes are not always reflected in overt behavior. A man may be convinced that the Republican candidate would make the best governor but still not go to the polls on Election Day. If people change both their internal state (beliefs, opinions, or values) and their behavior, then optimally effective persuasion has taken place. The most enduring change of this sort occurs when a person alters his or her behavior to conform with new values. A woman who becomes convinced that feminism gives her a way to understand pervasive political and personal grievances and who changes her way of life and her relationships with men and other women to reflect her new values will be relatively resistant to persuasive attempts that argue counter to those values.

Figure 6.2 summarizes the effects of persuasive communication. Persuaders must decide what they want to change, how to construct their appeal, and whether or not they have achieved the desired change. To a great extent, the persuaders' goals determine the kind of change they need to seek. One situation may warrant an attempt to change behavior; another situation may call for attitude change.

Approaches to Persuasion

There are many different approaches to understanding how one goes about changing people's opinions, beliefs, values, and/or behaviors. There are different models of persuasion that make very different assumptions about the underlying psychological mechanisms that explain why certain persuasive strategies are effective, and why others fail. These models make different assumptions about the nature of people, how information is processed, and how differing communication strategies ought to operate.

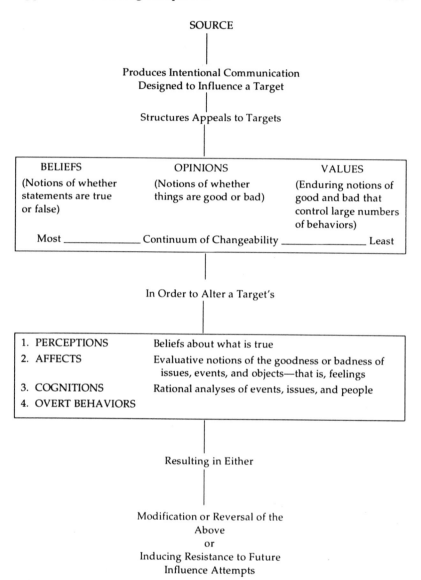

SOURCE

|

Produces Intentional Communication
Designed to Influence a Target

|

Structures Appeals to Targets

|

BELIEFS	OPINIONS	VALUES
(Notions of whether statements are true or false)	(Notions of whether things are good or bad)	(Enduring notions of good and bad that control large numbers of behaviors)
Most _____ Continuum of Changeability _____ Least		

|

In Order to Alter a Target's

|

1. PERCEPTIONS	Beliefs about what is true
2. AFFECTS	Evaluative notions of the goodness or badness of issues, events, and objects—that is, feelings
3. COGNITIONS	Rational analyses of events, issues, and people
4. OVERT BEHAVIORS	

|

Resulting in Either

|

Modification or Reversal of the
Above
or
Inducing Resistance to Future
Influence Attempts

Figure 6.2. Model of Persuasion

We will now present a number of theoretical perspectives that provide an explanatory framework from which we might understand some of the dynamics of persuasive communication: learning theories, consistency theories, Social Judgment Theory, the Elaboration Likelihood Model of Attitude Change, and Burgoon's Language Expectancy Theory. Learning theories of persuasion have been most concerned with how different reward contingencies can be used to shape desired behaviors. The concern of people interested in developing communication strategies from this perspective has been in creating messages that are most likely to create appropriate behavioral responses. There are a group of models of persuasion that have been labeled "consistency theories." These models have in common the assumption that people change attitudes in response to a perceived inconsistency among beliefs, attitudes, and behaviors, or a number of other things. When people experience this inconsistency, there is a drive to restore consistency by changing present attitudes, beliefs, values, and/or overt behaviors. People operating from this perspective have devised communication strategies designed to make inconsistencies apparent to people in the hopes that desired changes will result from the desire to restore consistency. Social Judgment Theory represents a departure from the first two general classifications of persuasion. It suggests that people make judgments about any persuasive communication on the basis of how much it deviates from their present position. Too much deviation from present beliefs can result in immediate rejection of the message. The Elaboration Likelihood Model focuses on the amount of thinking or "elaboration" individuals will engage in when presented with a persuasive appeal. Language Expectancy Theory is based on the assumption that through social and cultural norms people develop expectations about appropriate language use. Violations of these expectations can result in either increasing persuasive effectiveness or diminishing the persuasive impact of the message.

It is hoped that the reader will examine these different conceptions of persuasion in order to understand how different assumptions about the nature of people and how they process communication can lead to very different communication strategies. As will become obvious to all, these models of persuasion sometimes suggest contradictory ways of attempting to persuade people. There are many areas of agreement, however, among the differing perspectives. None of these models is *right*, and none of them is completely *wrong*. All have potential use in structuring persuasive communication, and it is hoped that the reader will try to make an application of these models to differing persuasive situations to determine which, if any, might be a useful way of understanding why people change. It is highly likely that some models will be appropriate in some persuasion situations and not in others.

Learning Theories

Infants are born without any opinions, beliefs, or values. Through the socialization process, they learn to respond to the environment, to behave acceptably, and yet, in their own self-interest, to accept certain ideas as true or false, good or bad. In fact, *learning* can be defined as the process of acquiring or changing behavior in response to individual encounters with people, events, and things.

Yet much that is said about persuasion, and about communication in general, implies that the person being persuaded already holds an opinion, belief, or value and that the communicator is simply trying to induce a switch—from Bush to Clinton, from pro-issue to anti-issue, from Pepsi to Coca-Cola. In many cases, however, the person being persuaded does not care any more about Bush, pro-issue, or Pepsi than about Clinton, anti-issue, or Coca-Cola. In other words, that person may have no feelings at all on the matter. The Exxon Company spent an enormous amount of money on an advertising campaign to familiarize people with its new corporate name, Exxon. The goal was clearly factual learning rather than attitude change. In such cases, the persuader needs to be aware of general principles of learning so that messages can be structured to be most effective.

Theories of learning center on the relationship between stimuli and responses (for further study on theories of learning, see Burgoon, Burgoon, Miller, & Sunnafrank, 1981; Hill, 1971; Smith, 1971). A stimulus, in this context, is anything that occurs in the communication transaction and is perceived by the receiver; a response is what the receiver does as a result of the stimulus. For example, a speech advocating a high tariff on foreign-made products might be a stimulus; an attitude change in the direction of the advocated position or a vote for a bill establishing such a tariff might be the response. A speaker's choice of words and delivery may function as stimuli. If the receiver perceives them as offensive, the response might be dislike for the speaker and resistance to the message. A pleasant spring day, the speaker's bow tie, the grinding of a garbage truck, the receiver's own emotional state, and other nonverbal or psychological factors may serve as stimuli that elicit responses.

The stimulus-response relationship can be manipulated in order to enhance learning. For instance, most learning theories assume that reinforcement is necessary to induce learning. There are two general kinds of reinforcement: positive and negative. Suppose someone came to your door and asked you to allow your name to be listed in an advertisement supporting a political candidate. If you were told that you would be listed as a "prominent" citizen along with the mayor, several movie stars, and other celebrities; that your participation would make you a patriotic person; and that you would be paid $10 for allowing your name to be used, you would be offered positive reinforcement or rewards. If you were told that anyone not allowing their name to be used will be considered unpatriotic and furthermore might find themselves under investigation by the Internal Revenue Service, you would be offered negative reinforcement; that is, you would be offered an opportunity to escape from an undesirable situation. Negative reinforcement is not the same as punishment. Negative reinforcement leaves open the door to the desired behavior; punishment takes place only after the receiver has behaved in an undesired way. If you rejected the offer to be listed in the ad and the next day found that you had been fired from your job because FBI agents had made some unsavory suggestions to your boss, that would be punishment.

Advertisers often use positive reinforcement to link products (stimuli) to increased sexuality, likability, and other supposedly desirable states in order to increase sales (desired response). They also use negative reinforcement, for example, by linking a mouthwash to escape from the supposedly undesirable state of having "morning breath." Both positive and negative reinforcers are likely to have impact on the receiver's behavior. If the communicator can demonstrate to a person the way he or she will be rewarded or will escape an undesirable state by complying with the communicator's request, behavior will probably change. Punishment, however, does not usually work so well. People who do not escape the undesirable state and who are punished tend to withdraw from the situation. In other words, the use of punishment might be very effective in insuring that an unwanted behavior ceases; however, using punishment alone does not necessarily produce other behaviors that might be desirable.

Most learning theories also assume that the time between response and reinforcement affects the speed of learning. If you know that by signing the political advertisement you will be paid $10 in cash on the spot, you might be more willing to sign than if you learned you would get a $10 tax rebate the following year. Negative reinforcement is also more effective if escape from the undesired state will be immediate. For instance, telling young people that they will live to be 70 years old instead of 68 years old if they stop smoking is not likely to be as effective as telling them that smokers are automatically disqualified from an athletic group they wish to join.

Furthermore, specific reinforcements tied to specific desired responses are more effective than vague ones. A speaker who tells you that your life will be better if you support the police is likely to be less persuasive than one who says you will not be mugged if you sign a petition to add 5,000 more police officers to the force. Therefore, learning theory suggests that a persuader should design the message to state the exact behavior desired and the exact reinforcement that will result.

Because people differ in their abilities and readiness to learn, repetition can induce learning. A persuader cannot be sure that everyone has understood the message; repetition helps him or her reach as many receivers as possible and helps solidify the learning of those who understood the first time. Probably everyone is familiar with the kind of organizational foul-up in which a manager claims to have told all his or her subordinates what was expected of them but it somehow did not get through. The importance of repetition is consistent with the idea that persuasion is most successful when it is part of a campaign; that is, one-shot attempts at persuasion often do not work, follow-up communication is needed. Repetition is especially important if the receivers are people with differing backgrounds, information, and abilities. However, even people with similar capacities to handle communication differ in their willingness to respond at a given time. Within a group of receivers, some may be distracted by personal problems, noise, other messages they have recently received, and any number of additional physical and psychological factors. Repetition can help to overcome these barriers to receptivity. It can also help the persuader overcome such obstacles as selective attention, distortion, and forgetfulness. Anyone who uses repetition to persuade must be careful not to hammer away with a message that is never going to be accepted. Speakers who assume that anyone who does not agree with them simply because the did not understand is a familiar irritant. "You don't seem to get my point" can only alienate someone who has already gotten the point and rejected it.

Learning theory also indicates that simple elements are more easily learned than complex ones. For instance, in early advertisements, aspirin was advertised as a way to relieve headaches. Each company claimed that its brand did the best job. As the campaigns progressed, each company presented more complex information about its product. Language teaching proceeds in a similar way. A beginning student first learns some basic words, then strings them together into simple sentences, and finally moves on to holding conversations or writing paragraphs. Mastering simple elements strengthens the receiver's willingness to respond to more difficult material.

One of the basic assumptions of the learning model is that persuasive messages should be structured to begin on a simple level; once the receiver understands and is rewarded for complying, responses can then be made to more complex messages. Another assumption of most learning theories is that people generalize their responses from one situation to another. The "coattails" of a victorious political candidate, for instance, may sweep into office some more obscure members of his or her party. Institutional advertising, which popularizes the name of a company that makes many products, is also aimed at the generalization response: "If you like our company's green beans, you'll love our ketchup." It is fortunate that generalization occurs as often as it does, because it is economical. Without generalization, a persuader might have to repeat his or her message in every situation. Learning in one situation, however, does not always transfer to others. People may love a company's green beans, but they may dislike the shape of its ketchup bottle. In that case, two separate communication efforts will have to be made. One cannot assume that generalization will always occur.

Learning theory also emphasizes the importance of feedback. Positive feedback can work as a form of reinforcement, rewarding the receivers and helping to ensure that they will continue to respond in the desired way. For example, a press agent whose job is to persuade writers and reporters to do stories about his or her client—for example, the blue-jeans industry—may reward the authors of favorable stories with praise for their fine abilities or with "freebies" (e.g., a new pair of jeans or tickets to a rock concert). Similarly, negative feedback can facilitate learning if it is perceived as constructive. The press agent might suggest that a writer whose story on the apparel industry failed to mention blue jeans now has an excellent opportunity to sell a follow-up story that does talk about jeans. However, if negative feedback is merely critical or does not give specific suggestions for improvement, it can be perceived as punishment and have undesirable results.

Learning theory does not offer the only explanation for human change. In fact, much about learning theory has been criticized for its stimulus-response model, which critics believe is a simplistic view of the nature of human beings. A good deal of such criticism has been focused on radical behaviorists, such as B. F. Skinner, who maintain that "attitudes" are only conditioned behavior, that we are the sum of our conditioning—no more. According to this school of behaviorism, all social problems could be solved if people were conditioned in desirable ways. In addition to raising questions about who would control the conditioning process, this theory also raises questions about the nature of the human species. Other theories about human change assume that people make decisions and engage in behavior that does not depend on the stimulus-response relationship. These theories deny that people merely respond to stimuli in their environment; in fact, some theories suggest that people do not always respond in the way that would bring them the best reward.

Consistency Theories

Although some learning theorists prefer to ignore variables within the receiver's mind that might interfere with the stimulus-response relationship, other persuasion theorists have focused on the mind as a "middleman" between the stimulus and the response. For example, cognitive theory sees the mind as a complex mechanism that organizes past learning and present stimuli into meaningful units. Thus the mind is not simply being bombarded with unrelated stimuli; it is always organizing information into patterns.

A mind operating in this fashion evaluates persuasive communication in terms of the way it fits into an organizational pattern. If a new communication fits into the pattern, the receiver's internal state remains balanced. For instance, if a man recently lost several thousand dollars because of shady and irresponsible dealings by his stockbroker and if he then hears a speech proposing stricter regulation of brokerage firms, he can fit the speaker's proposals into the pattern of his experience and feel comfortable with the conclusions. He does not need to be persuaded. His attitudes are probably already consistent with the positions being advocated by the message; that is, there is internal consistency. If the message does not conform to prior attitudes and/or presents a position opposing, or unfamiliar to, the receiver, internal inconsistency is likely to occur. For instance, if stockbrokers or investors who had been successful in the market heard the same speech advocating stricter control, they might have great difficulty in resolving the speaker's proposals with prior beliefs and experiences regardless of how logical the communicator was. Strategies must be employed to persuade the receiver; one such strategy would be to maximize internal inconsistency.

Given that internal inconsistency makes people uncomfortable, it is presumed that when a person disagrees with another who is liked or respected; when a person is asked to behave at odds with privately held opinions, beliefs, and values; or when attitudes are held that are incompatible, cognitive inconsistency occurs and change results. In our example, if the stockbroker respected the speaker, it might cause a great deal of inconsistency to disagree with the position being advocated. Another communication strategy might attempt to point out to the broker that the attitude of wanting to make money for

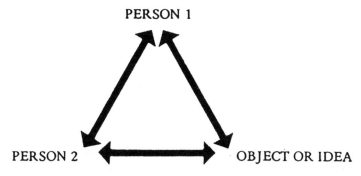

Figure 6.3. Balance Theory/Linkage Patterns

clients and yet protect them from unscrupulous hucksters is incompatible without a change in attitudes toward stricter market controls.

Balance theories assume that people are comfort-seeking animals who will strive to reduce internal inconsistency and that they are rationalizing beings who will find ways to justify changing attitudes and/or behaviors. The goal of the communication strategist is to point out inconsistencies while simultaneously providing ways of reducing inconsistencies by accepting new positions or exhibiting alternative behaviors that are, of course, more desirable to the persuader.

The earliest balance theories dealt with relationships between two persons and some object or idea (Heider, 1946). The relationships, or linkages, can be either favorable or unfavorable. When they cause internal inconsistency, one or more of the linkages can be changed to restore the balance. Figure 6.3 shows the basic patterns of linkage in balance theory.

Linkages between the people are favorable or unfavorable depending on credibility, attraction, interpersonal experience, or power relationships. Linkages between each person and the object or idea—that is, the topic of communication—can also be favorable or unfavorable, depending on each person's opinions, beliefs, and values. When the combinations of favorable-unfavorable linkages that appear in Figure 6.4 occur, a state of balance exists and no persuasion takes place.

In Situation A of Figure 6.4, Person 1 likes Person 2, is favorable toward the topic of communication, and knows that Person 2 agrees.

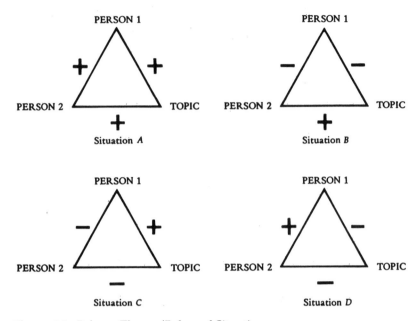

Figure 6.4. Balance Theory/Balanced Situations

For example, the cheated stockholder likes and agrees with the speaker advocating stricter control of brokerages. This combination of variables creates a state of balance, and persuasion is not needed. In Situation B, Person 1 is unfavorable toward both Person 2 and the topic and also knows that Person 2 disagrees. In this case, to pursue the stock market example, Person 1 might be a broker who has grown rich by questionable methods and who also dislikes the reformer's personality and politics. He or she would remain unpersuaded by Person 2, perhaps rationalizing that only a self-righteous and politically biased person would favor reforms. Again, balance remains secure. Similarly, balance is maintained in Situation C, in which Person 2 is disliked and takes an opposing position on the topic, and in Situation D, in which both parties like each other and oppose the topic.

In all the balance models shown in Figure 6.4, persuasion is not likely to occur because there is no internal inconsistency for either party—internal inconsistency is the motive for change. Without such imbalance, the two people remain comfortable with the linkages

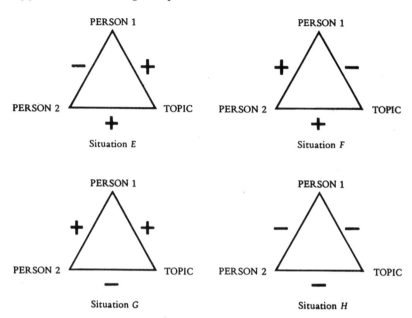

Figure 6.5. Balance Theory/Unbalanced Situations

between themselves and the issue and will seek to maintain that comfort. However, in the situations illustrated in Figure 6.5, the linkages are unbalanced and some type of change must occur.

In Situation E of Figure 6.5, Person 1, the cheated stockholder, dislikes the reformer but agrees about the need for reform. The stockholder will probably change his or her opinion of the speaker because people tend to like others who agree with them. If the feelings of dislike are very strong, however, the stockholder might just change his or her attitude toward the topic, deciding that someone he or she dislikes so intensely must be wrong and that the shady firm he or she bought stocks from must have been an exception to widespread integrity in the financial world. Yet another alternative would be for the stockholder to change his or her perception of the reformer's position, possibly by deciding that the reformer proposes only superficial changes that will not really work. Whatever the actual shift in the stockholder's position, the situation illustrated in Situation E must cause some alteration in attitudes because it is too uncomfortable for him or her to remain as is. Situations F and G are similar in that we feel uncomfortable when someone we like favors something we oppose or opposes something we favor.

In Situation H it is difficult to predict the change that will occur. We do not feel comfortable when people we dislike oppose what we oppose. We want to agree with our friends and disagree with our enemies. The receiver of persuasive communication in this situation might reevaluate the source and use the agreement as a basis of increased liking, or the receiver might change an opinion to disagree with the disliked source, or the receiver might change a perception of the source by denying the honesty of the communication. For instance, if a leading conservative suddenly made a speech favoring national health-care insurance, a liberal democratic listener might decide to like the conservative, decide he or she must have been wrong about national health-care insurance, or decide that the conservative has some devious reason for making this statement.

There is a handy rule of thumb for determining whether or not a communication situation is balanced or unbalanced. Anytime there is an odd number of negative signs on the triangle, the linkages are unbalanced, and change must occur. When there is an even number of negative signs (or no negative signs), the linkages are balanced and change does not occur.

Several principles allow one to predict the kind of change that will occur in an unbalanced situation (McGuire, 1966). If there is a contradiction between a receiver's feelings toward the source of the communication and the content of the communication, the attitude toward the content is more likely to change. In other words, it is more difficult to change one's view about a person than about an idea. This fact helps explain why a highly credible source is often so successful at persuasion; people prefer to alter their opinions on the subject rather than to alter their opinions of the person's credibility. In preferring to change that way, people are altering negative linkages rather than positive ones ("I like this person; so I'll change my dislike of the views"). If receivers feel very negatively toward the issue, however, they will resist changing their attitude toward it; more likely, they will change their attitude toward the source. Thus highly involving issues about which people are polarized are less likely to follow the negative sign-changing tendency.

Symmetry theory elaborates on the balance model and shows how communication affects internal consistency (Newcomb, 1953, 1956). According to symmetry theory, communication leads to more interpersonal similarity; that is, if you like another person, you desire to be similar to him or her and will, therefore, try to resolve disagreements. When you and someone you like disagree, you feel internal inconsistency and a pull toward symmetry. The strength of the pull depends on how much you like the person and how intensely you feel about the issue. The more these two factors conflict, the more pull you feel to resolve the conflict. This pull increases the likelihood that you and the other person will communicate about the issue. And as research shows, communication leads to increased similarity in views. Perhaps you and a close friend, for instance, will find ways to compromise on an issue or perhaps one of you will change your view after learning about the other's arguments and feelings. Symmetry theory differs from balance theory in that it not only suggests that change will occur, but also gives reasons why people end up shifting beliefs and changing behaviors. The central reason for the change is based on what we know about people's tendency to use communication as a vehicle to maintain similarity with valued others.

Congruity theory is a refinement of balance and symmetry theories (for a complete explanation of this research, see Osgood & Tannenbaum, 1955). It mathematically predicts both the amount and the direction of change that will occur in an unbalanced communication situation. One of the failings of balance theory is that it allows for only one change in a situation. For instance, in Situation E of Figure 6.5, if Person 1 changes an opinion of Person 2, balance is re- stored. Congruity theory allows for more subtle changes. For example, suppose Figure 6.6 reflects your attitudes toward the source of a communication (a respected friend) and toward his or her position (favoring assisted suicides for the terminally ill).

Your respected friend is rated very favorably on the scale (+3), and you moderately oppose (−2) his or her statement that those who are terminally ill should be allowed to receive assistance in committing suicide. According to congruity theory, you would probably change this unbalanced situation in two ways. First, you would become more favorable toward assisted suicides because someone you respect is in favor of it. At the same time, you will become less

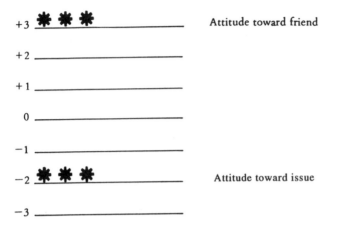

Figure 6.6 Congruity Theory / Attitude Scale

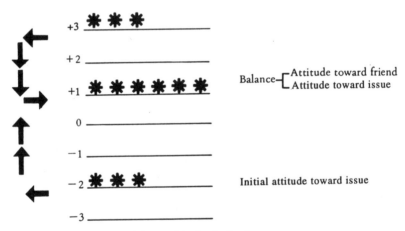

Figure 6.7. Congruity Theory / Attitude Scale

favorable toward the friend, because of speaking for an issue that you opposed. However, you will not change in an equal amount toward both source and issue; you will change most whichever attitude is least strongly held. Assuming that your attitude toward assisted suicides changed more than your attitude toward your friend, balance (with both attitudes occupying the same line on the scale) would be achieved in the way shown in Figure 6.7.

Congruity theory claims that attitudes toward both the source and the content of a message change as a result of communication.

Through relatively complex mathematical formulas, congruity theory can predict the magnitude and the direction of attitude change after communication. Congruity theory is considered to be a more sophisticated representation of the process of persuasive communication in that it recognizes more of the complexities involved in bringing about desired changes. It is very useful because it allows rather precise predictions about attitudes following persuasive communication. Perhaps a more important aspect of this model, for our purposes, is its recognition that multiple changes are likely to occur when people attempt to persuade others. It should be of interest that this model suggests that credibility will be reduced in some proportion when positions that people find unacceptable are advocated. It further posits that even though you might obtain the desired goal of persuading someone, that person will, in effect, see you differently. Furthermore, over time people can communicate in ways to restore lost esteem or credibility. This model poses an interesting question for you to consider: How important is it for you to persuade someone if it is, in fact, going to change that person's perception of you? Obviously, this varies from situation to situation, and at times it is certainly important enough for us to take certain personal risks in order to convince people of the validity of our positions. At other times, however, it might not be worth either the risk or the effort it would take to restore our credibility and esteem to prior levels. At any rate, this kind of question should be considered by the potential persuader.

Another consistency theory of persuasion that deserves special attention because of the unique perspective it takes on communication and persuasion is cognitive dissonance. Like the other models discussed, the *theory of cognitive dissonance* assumes that people feel uncomfortable when they hold opinions or ideas that are psychologically inconsistent; it is further assumed that when people experience this discomfort called *cognitive dissonance,* they will be motivated to change attitudes or behaviors to reduce that inconsistency (the original report of this theory is found in Festinger, 1957). These two assumptions are not radically different from the earlier models we have discussed. However, the theory of cognitive dissonance does depart from the earlier models in that it places particular attention on the kinds of behaviors that people engage in to justify and rationalize their changes in attitudes and behaviors *after they have been persuaded to accept a new opinion or to commit a behavior.* Remember that the earlier models put a great deal of emphasis on making inconsistencies apparent and then providing means to reduce those conflicts. This theory places emphasis on how people will support their new positions by way of a variety of communication techniques.

It is assumed that any time people make a decision to change their attitudes or to commit some type of behavior, they will experience some amount of cognitive dissonance. For example, a person who is faced with a decision about the kind of automobile to purchase is faced with some conflict in making a choice. Once the decision is made and a car purchased, however, dissonance is aroused. The person probably is somewhat unsure of whether or not the right decision was made and is aware that there are positive and negative aspects about both the purchased car and the car he or she decided not to buy. This feeling is presumed to be dissonant, and a variety of things can be done to resolve the problem. It has been found that people who purchase new automobiles tend to be more attentive to advertisements and information relating to the brand they bought. It is presumed that these people actively seek out information that supports their decision. There is less evidence to suggest that they will seek out negative information or avoid hearing good things about other makes of car, but there is no doubt about their desire for supportive information about the decision they have made.

One of the most important things about this theory is the unique and interesting research that has been done to test some of its assumptions. It is also important because it explains some human behavior that is not intuitively obvious to many of us. Perhaps reviewing some of the research is an enlightening way to demonstrate how people rationalize their behavior when it conflicts with previously held attitudes and how they move to support new attitudes that they have adopted. For example, if you were told that people had agreed to what most would consider an unpleasant task such as eating fried grasshoppers, it could probably be agreed that some persuasion had occurred. People were persuaded to commit a behavior at odds with their private opinions. However, what if the ultimate purpose was to persuade people to be more positive about fried grasshoppers? Would you expect people who had been persuaded to eat the grasshoppers by a high-credible and well-liked source also to change their attitudes more favorably toward grasshoppers than people who had initially agreed, at the urging of a low-credible or disliked source, to consume the disliked food? Most people would agree that the greatest attitude change *toward the grasshoppers* would be after agreeing to eat them when asked by the high-credible source. Research indicates, however, that just the opposite occurs, and dissonance theory has a very plausible explanation for these findings (Zimbardo, Weisenberg, & Firestone, 1969).

Although it might be more difficult for a low-credible source initially to persuade people to try the grasshoppers, once such a behavioral commitment was secured, people should experience a great deal of cognitive dissonance resulting from the discrepancy between their private opinions and their overt behaviors. They cannot reduce this dissonance by justifying the behavior on the basis of doing it because of their liking for the source because they do not like that person. The simplest way to reduce the dissonance is by changing their attitudes toward grasshoppers. They might say something like, "They really aren't so bad after all." However, the people who initially were persuaded by a highly credible individual to try the grasshoppers were not under the same pressures to change their attitudes toward the disliked object. Although cognitive dissonance still occurs because of the inconsistency between attitudes and behaviors, there are ways that the dissonance can be reduced that do not require changing attitudes toward the grasshoppers. The most likely outcome is for the receiver to justify the behavior by claiming that the grasshoppers were tried out of regard for the source and that anybody would do the same if asked. The receiver can comfortably continue to dislike eating grasshoppers given that justification.

Another example might help make the point about how people operate to reduce dissonance and support what they have been persuaded to do. Let us stress again that we are only discussing how people seek to support what they *have already been persuaded to do.* Suppose that someone persuaded you not to engage in an activity that you enjoyed. Let us further suppose that this persuasion was accompanied with a mild threat outlining the harms that would befall you if you went ahead and did the enjoyable task. Would you be likely to change your attitude toward the task itself more if the threat were mild than if the threat was severe and you were advised of the extremely harmful results of the behavior? The attitude toward the enjoyable task itself would be more likely to change if you refrained from doing it if you had been given a mild threat (Aronson & Carlsmith, 1963). Most of us would probably not agree with this without further explanation; dissonance theory offers that explanation. If the consequences of doing the task were not all that bad, there would be less likelihood of justifying the behavior by pointing out that you refrained only to avoid punishment. You would have to rationalize not doing it by some other method; the easiest way to avoid the feeling of dissonance would be to claim that "you really did not like the task that much anyway and that you could either take it or leave it." People who are given threats promising extreme punishments for continuing to do the task can simply reduce the dissonance caused by discrepancies between attitudes (enjoyment in doing the task) and behavior (not doing the activity) by claiming that, under the conditions, any reasonable person would not engage in the desired task. In the first case, actual attitudes toward the task have become negative, and the behavior has been extinguished. In the second instance, the behavior is extinguished, but the liking for the task has not necessarily changed. One can readily see how educational institutions and organizations of all kinds use punishment as a means of controlling behavior. Perhaps this theory further elaborates the earlier cited notions that behavior control does not always equal persuasion in the sense of changed opinions, beliefs, and values.

Any decision can potentially cause dissonance. Simply deciding on one course of action can cause you to have more favorable attitudes about the chosen alternative and more negative reactions toward what you chose not to do. Holding negative thoughts about chosen alternatives and positive thoughts about what you chose not to do is uncomfortable. One likely mode of resolution is to become even more positive about what you are doing and dismiss the negative while building up in your own mind even more reactions to that which you gave up. This is but a sampling of the research in this area. It is our hope that the use of this model of persuasion in explaining human conduct is apparent.

Dissonance can also be aroused by holding two conflicting attitudes or opinions. The potential persuader must keep this in mind when attempting to apply this knowledge. There is a possibility that whenever you convince someone to accept your position on a given issue, it may place the person in a conflicted position because the new attitude is at odds with positions already held. Awareness that people will need to reduce the dissonance created by holding incompatible positions may allow you to initiate persuasive measures to ensure that the mode of reduction will not result in others returning to the old position after you thought you had successfully persuaded them. To the extent that you continue to provide supportive information and view the persuasion effort as having to continue even after the initial attempt and/or commitment, success is more likely. You must also constantly keep in mind that there is a difference between behavioral compliance and true commitment to a position. To the extent that people are coerced into behaving a certain way and given no choice in the matter, there is little likelihood of internal acceptance of the behavior or changes in attitudes. When people feel responsible for their own actions and can provide reasons for acceptance of attitudes and behaviors, longer lasting change is likely to occur. More will be said in Chapter 7 about how one goes about structuring persuasive messages with these considerations in mind. The important addition that this model makes to the family of consistency theories is its emphasis on the things people go through after they have been persuaded. The other models are primarily concerned with accomplishing the initial persuasion and have little to say about what happens after people accept your position or agree to do the things you ask of them.

Social Judgment Theory

Social judgment theory differs from learning theory and consistency theories in several ways (Sherif, Sherif, & Nebergall, 1965). First, it views attitude change as a two-stage process. In the first stage, the receiver judges the relationship of a communication to his or her own currently held or most preferred attitude about an issue. For instance, if Susan X believes that the death penalty for convicted murderers is a good idea and if she hears someone argue that the death penalty is itself tantamount to condoning murder, she will judge the communication to be widely discrepant from her view. In

TABLE 6.1 Social Judgment Theory/Acceptance-Rejection Continuum

Latitude of Acceptance	Latitude of Noncommitment	Latitude of Rejection
1. The death penalty should be invoked for convicted murderers.	4. The death penalty should only be invoked if the victim is a juvenile.	5. Convicted murderers should pay restitution to the families of their victims.
2. The death penalty should be invoked only for premeditated murders.		6. Convicted murderers should face prison sentences.
3. The death penalty should be invoked only if committed during the perpetration of a felony.		7. All convicted murderers should receive psychiatric counseling in order to reassimilate them into society.

the second stage of attitude change, Susan X makes changes in her opinions, beliefs, or values. How much change she makes will depend on how much discrepancy she perceives between her view and the source's view.

Social judgment theory treats attitudes as more complex than favorable-unfavorable or positive-negative reactions. It claims that attitudes are best represented by a continuum as shown in Table 6.1.

The receiver has his or her own position on an issue; this is called the *prime attitude*. In the preceding example, the receiver believes that the death penalty should be invoked for convicted murderers. In addition to Susan X's prime attitude, she has a *latitude of acceptance*—a range of positions that she is willing to accept (1, 2, and 3). The *latitude of noncommitment* is a range of positions on which the receiver is neutral or has divided feelings (4). Finally, the range of positions that the receiver finds unacceptable (5, 6, and 7) forms the *latitude of rejection*.

The receiver's attitude continuum for this example is shown in Figure 6.8. According to social judgment theory, a persuasive message that falls within or slightly out of the latitude of acceptance is perceived by the receiver as being closer to the prime attitude than it really is (Sherif et al., 1965). Suppose a source argued in a well-prepared persuasive speech, for Statement 4, "The death penalty

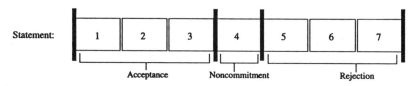

Figure 6.8. Acceptance-Rejection Continuum

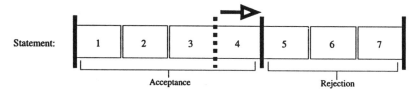

Figure 6.9. Acceptance-Rejection Continuum

should only be invoked if the victim is a juvenile." The receiver would tend to *assimilate* this position into his or her own latitude of acceptance. Then the attitude continuum would look like Figure 6.9.

With this new continuum, Statement 5 ("Convicted murderers should pay restitution to the families of their victims") is now close to the latitude of acceptance and might be assimilated into it after more persuasive communication.

If a source argues for a position that is in the receiver's latitude of rejection, however, it is seen as more discrepant than it actually is. If a source argued, for instance, that all convicted murderers should receive psychiatric counseling in order to reassimilate them into society, the receiver would contrast the source's statements with his or her own and remain unpersuaded. This *contrast effect* may lead in some instances to a *boomerang effect*. The receivers in the death penalty example, for instance, might be so repelled by the suggestion of reassimilation of convicted murderers that they would shrink their latitude of acceptance and decide that all positions except for their prime attitude are unacceptable. This situation is illustrated in Figure 6.10.

Social judgment theory also predicts the ways in which the receiver's ego-involvement affects his or her attitude change. High ego-involvement corresponds to a wide latitude of rejection; low ego-involvement corresponds to a wide latitude of noncommitment. For

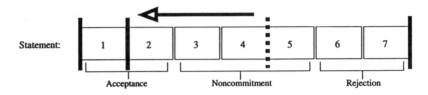

Figure 6.10. Acceptance-Rejection Continuum

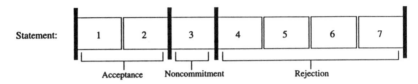

Figure 6.11. High Ego-Involved Receiver

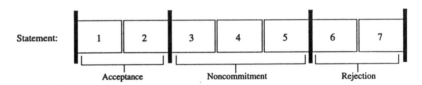

Figure 6.12. Low Ego-Involved Receiver

example, a person awaiting trial on a murder charge would be highly ego-involved on the subject of the death penalty. Then latitudes might appear as they do in Figure 6.11.

A person who has never been the victim of violent crime and who has nothing personal at stake in the issue might have latitudes such as those shown in Figure 6.12. (Note that ego-involvement does not affect the latitude of acceptance.)

Because an ego-involved person has a wide latitude of rejection, persuasive messages are more likely to fall into that range and be contrasted with the prime attitude. Thus attitude change is difficult. A receiver who lacks ego-involvement, however, has a wide latitude of noncommitment into which persuasive messages are likely to fall. Such messages can then be *assimilated* into the acceptable range, and persuasion is more successful. Common sense certainly supports the conclusion that people are more reluctant to change their attitudes on issues that are directly important to them.

Elaboration Likelihood Model

The Elaboration Likelihood Model (ELM) of persuasion is another approach that focuses on the ways in which people process information contained in persuasive communication (Petty & Cacioppo, 1986). According to this model, the impact of persuasive communication depends upon the amount of issue-relevant thinking, or elaboration, in which individuals will engage. Essentially, ELM posits that under different conditions, individuals will employ one of two types of elaboration—either *central* or *peripheral* routes to persuasion. Sometimes individuals engage in extensive elaboration or issue-relevant thinking about an issue. When we engage in this "central route" processing, we attend very carefully to the persuasive message and carefully examine the arguments contained within the message. Also, we will likely reflect on other issue-relevant concerns associated with the topic of the persuasive message. For example, if you were presented with an argument proposing that starting immediately, every undergraduate student must pass a mandatory comprehensive final examination before graduation, it is likely that this persuasive message will engender considerable issue-relevant thinking on your part. Because this proposal, if enacted, will have serious repercussions on you as a college student, you will spend considerable cognitive energy evaluating the message itself and reflecting on other considerations and consequences of the proposal. However, if the same argument were presented to you with the exception that the proposal would be enacted sometime after your expected graduation, it is unlikely that you would expend as much effort evaluating the message or considering the consequences of accepting the persuasive appeal. Under these conditions, information processing takes place through the "peripheral route" and little elaboration occurs.

When engaged in peripheral-route processing, an individual's motivation to engage in elaboration is low. The issue is probably not salient for the individual and the consequences of accepting the advocated position are not personally relevant. Under these circumstances, thinking about the persuasive message typically will be guided by some simple decision rule rather than by focusing on the strength of the argument itself. Receivers processing through the peripheral route will focus more on their affective responses to the source and their evaluations of the source of the message; that is, is the source attractive, likeable, or credible? Cues such as these that are associated with the source of the persuasive message primarily determine responses to the message when processing occurs through the peripheral route. For instance, consider the final comprehensive examination example proposed earlier. If you would be unaffected by the proposed implementation of this plan (because it would take place after you have graduated), your reaction to such an appeal most likely would be based on your affective evaluation of the person who delivered the message, rather than on the validity of the argument or the evidence it contained. Because the issue is not particularly relevant to you and because persuasion has occurred primarily because of your response to the source of the message, persuasive effects will probably not endure. That is to say, if you hear an argument against the proposal, it is quite possible that you will alter your response if you have a positive affective response to the source of that counterargument. Persuasive effects, then, are a function of peripheral cues rather than the quality of the message.

However, when engaged in central-route processing, an individual's motivation to engage in elaboration is high and the receiver has high involvement in the issue. Receivers who are highly involved in an issue will be affected by the quality of the arguments contained in the message and be persuaded more by strong arguments than by weak arguments. Here characteristics of the source of the message are less relevant. The importance of the issue will cause the individual to engage in considerable elaboration on the validity and the evidence contained in the argument. Under conditions of high elaboration (or central-route processing), persuasion occurs if the receiver agrees with the arguments and any change is based upon an evaluation of the message rather than an evaluation of the source of the message. When compared with persuasion that occurs through the peripheral route, persuasion due to central-route processing is more enduring, more resistant to counterargumentation, and more likely to be incorporated into the receivers value-belief system.

ELM has generated a considerable amount of research into attitude acquisition and change. It is an appealing and elegant model in that it accounts for effects of both the source and the message on persuasion. However, ELM has received criticism on several issues.

First, the notion that individuals engaged in central-route processing are persuaded more by "strong" rather than "weak" arguments is problematic. Petty and Cacioppo (1986), the creators of ELM, have been unable to define precisely what constitutes a weak versus a strong argument. In all of their studies (which, by the way, use the mandatory comprehensive exam problem), weak and strong arguments are defined empirically; that is, arguments for and against the mandatory exam are created and then tested with subjects in a laboratory. Those subjects in the high elaboration condition (i.e., subjects who were lead to believe that the mandatory final exam would be required of them) were then presented with arguments either for or against the proposal. Arguments that resulted in favorable thoughts were labeled "strong-argument" messages, while those that generated unfavorable thought were defined as "weak-argument" messages. This type of reasoning precludes an understanding of what it is about strong arguments that makes them persuasive under conditions of high elaboration. If a subject in the high elaboration condition is not persuaded by a strong argument, the conclusion is that the message (at least for that subject) is "weak" rather than "strong," not that the model is wrong.

Another criticism of the model is that it stipulates that people process messages only through central or peripheral routes; that is, that message processing is only possible by one of these two methods and no variations of either type of processing are considered. This presents a somewhat simplistic model of human information processing that we have difficulty fully accepting as a means of understanding the impact of messages on persuasive outcomes. Additional confusion about what constitutes elaboration of issues and the lack of generalizability of the model makes employing the tenets of ELM confusing. One important contribution that ELM gives to the study of persuasion, however, is its recognition that the amount and type of topic-relevant thinking varies by receiver. Messages focusing on issues of high relevance for a particular receiver will be scrutinized differently from messages concerning issues of low importance to the receiver. ELM has generated a wealth of research investigating these important issues and is a relatively new approach to investigating the effects of messages on persuasive outcomes.

Language Expectancy Theory

One of the few language-based theories of persuasion is Language Expectancy Theory (LET) (Burgoon, 1989; Burgoon & Miller, 1985). The logic that underlies LET argues that because language is a rule-governed symbolic system, people develop sociological and cultural norms and expectations about language use in given persuasive situations. In most communication transactions, language use confirms these norms and expectations, which enhances the normative status of those individuals engaged in those behaviors. For example, you probably have developed expectations about the language your close friends, parents, teachers, and so on, will use when they attempt to persuade you. Over time, because these expectations for language use by these individuals are usually confirmed, fairly rigid norms of the appropriate use of language develop and the normative status of these individuals becomes reinforced. LET asserts that communicators may intentionally or accidentally violate the norms governing language use, which in turn violates receivers' expectations. These violations of receivers' expectations will affect their receptivity to persuasive messages. Depending upon a variety of variables, violations of language expectations can either enhance or inhibit the effectiveness of persuasive messages. A key factor in persuasive effectiveness is whether the language choice of the source *positively* or *negatively* violates the target of persuasion's expectations.

Violations of Expectations

Central to the concept of positive and negative violations of language behaviors is the form in which the range of expectations exists. For ease of discussion, LET argues that the range of language behaviors falls within a bandwidth; here all language behaviors fall within a normative expected range. This bandwidth reflects expected language behaviors formed culturally (gender, age, ethnicity) and socially (occupation, role in society). For example, our expectations differ about the language men and women should use. Whether desirable or not, in our society men have a wider bandwidth of language choices available to them. In general, men's use of aggressive language does not violate normative expectations. However, the same cannot be said of women. Men who use aggressive language in persuasive attempts will often be seen as dynamic, confident, and in control. Women who use aggressive language, however, may be seen as being argumentative, uncooperative, and emotional, and thus run the risk of decreasing their persuasive effectiveness. It is argued that receivers have normative expectations about the use of fear appeals, opinionated language, and magnitude of language intensity. Although these language variables will be discussed at length in the next chapter, for a clearer understanding of LET a brief description of each is presented here. *Fear appeals* are persuasive messages designed to convince the persuadees that some great harm will befall them or someone important to them if the advocate's claim is not adopted. *Opinionated language* conveys two types of information: the claims that the persuader wants the target to accept, and the source's attitude about those who either agree or disagree with that claim. *Intense language* can be conceptualized as the degree to which a persuasive message deviates from neutrality. Clearly, opinionated language is one type of intense language, as are fear appeals and language that contains obscenity.

When a receiver perceives that the language used by a would-be persuader is culturally or socially inappropriate (i.e., falls outside the bandwidth of acceptable behaviors), a negative violation of language expectations occurs and predictably will inhibit the receiver's receptivity to the persuasive appeal. If the source's intention is to change the receiver's attitudes or behavior with the persuasive message, a negative violation will result in either a lack of change in attitude or behavior or, perhaps more profoundly, a change in attitude or a modification in behavior occurring in a direction opposite that desired by the source.

Predicting the effects of positive violations of expectations is somewhat more problematic. Essentially, a positive violation of expectations takes place when a source is expected to violate normative language use in a negative way, but in fact, conforms to appropriate language use. Although positive violations should increase the likelihood that a persuasive message will have the desired effect, at first glance positive violations of expectations should only occur when a source is initially evaluated negatively. This conceptualization of violations of expectations rules out the possibility that persuaders who construct messages in an expected manner can ever positively violate expectations and thereby increase their persuasive effectiveness. Therefore, Burgoon and Miller (1985) advanced the proposition that positive violations of expectations occur when persuaders are expected to depart from normative language use in a negative manner but instead conform to social norms governing language choices. Thus positive violations of expectations can occur when an expectation that a source will communicate outside the bandwidth of appropriate language use is infracted because the source has devised the message to fall within the acceptable range of behavior. Further, a positive violation of expectations occurs if a source who is initially evaluated positively enacts behavior outside the expected range of appropriate behavior in a positive direction; that is, the source communicates unexpectedly in a positively evaluated direction. For example, an average speaker who delivers an eloquent, cleverly crafted argument will likely benefit from the contrast between how the receiver expected him or her to perform and the actual performance. A great deal of social-influence research confirms that a discrepancy between an expected and enacted behavior is causally related to desired persuasive outcomes.

A great deal of research also supports the basic propositions presented in LET. It is posited that highly credible communicators have the freedom to select varied language strategies in developing persuasive messages, whereas low-credible speakers must conform to more limited language options if they wish to be effective. In addition, high-credible speakers can enhance the persuasive impact of their messages by using intense language. However, low-credible speakers (or those who are unsure of their perceived credibility with a given receiver) will usually be more persuasive if they employ appeals of low intensity. Although the effects of fear appeals have been widely investigated in relation to persuasive messages intended to change attitudes or modify behaviors, LET argues that irrelevant fear arousals often mediate receptivity to different levels of language intensity. For example, if you are aroused by induction of irrelevant fear or suffering from specific anxiety, you will be most receptive to persuasive messages containing low-intensity appeals but relatively unreceptive to highly intense persuasive appeals. The stress experienced by a speaker has an effect on the type of messages generated. Communicators under cognitive stress produce less intense, more ambivalent messages. Cognitive stress also results when speakers are forced to violate their own norms about appropriate communication behavior by encoding highly intense messages.

The final concept proposed by LET is the relationship between language intensity and attitude change. According to LET, there is a direct linear relationship between level of language intensity and attitude change following counterattitudinal advocacy. To facilitate a better understanding of counterattitudinal advocacy, an example might be helpful. Consider this situation. You are staunchly against smoking cigarettes. Upon graduation from college you receive a job offer from one of the major tobacco companies in the world at $100,000 a year (very generous for an entry-level position). Because you have thousands of dollars in student loans to repay, are planning to get married, and have no other impending job offers, you take the job. Undoubtedly, you will be required not only to stifle your own attitude against smoking, but also to adopt the "company line" regarding smoking, the sale of cigarettes, and so on. When you, acting as a representative for the tobacco company, make positive claims about cigarette smoking as a part of your job, you are engaging in counterattitudinal advocacy; that is, you are publicly avowing attitudes that you personally do not hold. Now, imagine the exact same situation, except that the salary offer is only $18,000 a year. According to LET, both of these situations would cause you to experience cognitive stress because you are violating your own set of normative expectations. In which of these situations do you think you would experience the most cognitive stress? Although research has shown that individuals faced with situations such as these tend to experience attitude changes in the direction of the publicly avowed statements, the smaller the incentive (in this case, salary) the greater the cognitive stress and the greater the attitudinal change in the direction of the counterattitudinal statements. In our example, it would be expected that although you might not come to hold cigarette smoking in positive regard, your negative attitude about cigarette smoking would change in the direction of the positive position that you are forced to take due to your job responsibilities; that is, you would be less opposed to the idea of smoking cigarettes, but the change would probably be greater if you were paid only $18,000!

It was our intention in this chapter to introduce you to a variety of theoretical perspectives that have been applied to persuasive communication. Although none of the theories presented here can explain how and why a particular approach to persuasion will or will not work, each in its own way describes conditions in which different aspects of human nature and behavior combine to create circumstances that can facilitate or inhibit persuasive communication. The next chapter will be devoted to explicating a variety of strategies and message variables that are critical to a more complete understanding of the persuasion process.

Summary

1. Most definitions of persuasion stress three elements: conscious intent, message transmission, and behavioral influence. Although people may persuade others unintentionally, the criterion of conscious intent facilitates the formal study of persuasion. A persuasive message may lead to changes in a person's attitude (beliefs, opinions, and values), which, in turn, may lead to changes in a person's perceptions, emotions, cognition, or overt action. An opinion is a favorable, unfavorable, or neutral evaluation of a person, thing, or idea. A belief is a nonevaluative conviction about the truth or falsity of something. A value is a deeply held opinion that exerts influence on a person's thinking or behavior.

2. Learning theory focuses on the relationship between stimuli and responses. A stimulus is anything that is perceived by the receiver; a response, then, is the receiver's reaction to the stimulus. According to various learning theories, the effectiveness of communication can be enhanced through the use of positive or negative reinforcement. Obviously, positive reinforcement involves rewarding people for making the appropriate or desired responses. Negative reinforcement involves threatening the receiver with an undesirable situation for making the wrong response. Negative reinforcement, however, is not the same as punishment. Punishment occurs *after* the receiver has responded in an undesired way; negative reinforcement provides the receiver with an opportunity to behave in the desired way. The time between the response and the reinforcement may affect the speed of learning. Specific reinforcements tied to specific

desired responses are more effective than vague ones. People generalize their responses from one situation to another. Feedback serves as positive or negative reinforcement in shaping attitudes and behaviors.

3. Three different consistency theories make similar assumptions about the persuasion process. Cognitive balance theory views the mind as a complex system that organizes past experiences and present stimuli into meaningful patterns. People tend to evaluate a persuasive message according to the way it fits into the patterns. If the message fits, the receiver's internal state remains balanced. If the message does not fit, the receiver is in a state of internal inconsistency. To establish balance, the receiver must change his or her attitude toward either the source or the message. Other things being equal, if there is a contradiction between the receiver's attitude toward the source and the message, the receiver's attitude toward the message is more likely to change. If the receiver feels very strongly about the topic, however, the attitude about the source is more likely to be changed. Symmetry theory modifies the balance theory by trying to explain the way communication affects internal inconsistency. Congruity theory claims that when internal inconsistency exists, attitudes toward both the source and the message change.

4. The theory of cognitive dissonance is an extension of earlier balance and consistency models of persuasion. Although this theory makes some of the same assumptions about the nature of the persuasion process, it is primarily concerned with all of the processes that people go through to rationalize or justify their behaviors after a decision or commitment has been made. There has been a considerable amount of research that suggests that dissonance does motivate people to seek reasons that will help them justify their behavior. The less justification that people have for behaving a certain way or for changing their attitudes, the more dissonance they will experience after committing the behavior. One way to reduce that dissonance is to believe even more strongly that one's new attitude is correct and that justification for change was present. When people have a great deal of justification for doing something or believing a specific way, they can go ahead and engage in the behaviors without actually changing attitudes to conform to those behaviors. They can simply claim that anybody under similar circumstances would have behaved the same way. They do not have conformity between beliefs and attitudes if the discrepancy can be justified.

5. Social judgment theory views attitude change as a two-step process. First, the receiver judges the relationship of a communication to personal attitudes, and second, makes changes in these attitudes. According to this theory, a person's attitudes about a topic are best represented by a continuum, ranging from the most acceptable to the least. The position a receiver finds most acceptable is called the prime attitude. A receiver also has a latitude of acceptance (positions that are acceptable), a latitude of non-commitment (positions about which he or she is neutral or divided), and a latitude of rejection (positions that are unacceptable). A persuasive message that falls within or slightly out of the latitude of acceptance is perceived by the receiver as closer to the prime attitude than it really is. Thus the receiver tends to assimilate this position into the latitude of acceptance. A position that falls within the receiver's latitude of rejection is seen as more discrepant than it actually is and creates a contrast effect. A receiver who is very ego-involved in the topic has a wide latitude of rejection into which a persuasive message may fall, whereas a receiver who is not ego-involved has a wide range of noncommitment. Because a receiver perceives messages as more similar and more discrepant than they actually are, persuasion is likely to be more successful with the receiver who is not ego-involved than with the one who is very ego-involved.

6. The Elaboration Likelihood Model (ELM) of persuasion argues that the effects of persuasive communication depend upon the amount of issue-relevant thinking, or "elaboration," in which individuals engage. Under different conditions, individuals will engage in either *central-* or *peripheral*-route processing of persuasive messages. In central-route processing, receivers focus on the validity and evidence contained in the persuasive message and other issue-relevant concerns. Central-route processing occurs when individuals are highly involved with the topic of interest. Attitude change that occurs through central-route processing is robust and more resistant to persuasive counterarguments. In peripheral-route processing, receivers tend to use simple decision rules that require little information processing as the basis for acceptance or rejection of the persuasive argument. These decision rules focus on extrinsic features of the communication situation, such as the characteristics of the source (i.e., attractiveness and credibility) while paying limited attention to message attributes. Attitude change under these conditions is less enduring and often easily changed by counterarguments.

7. Language Expectancy Theory (LET) argues that because language is a rule-governed symbolic system, people develop expectations about appropriate language usage in given persuasive situations. These expectations are based on cultural and societal norms of language behavior and form a bandwidth of appropriate communication behaviors for individuals. Persuasive effectiveness is influenced by the violations of expectations. Violations can either inhibit or enhance persuasive effectiveness. Negative violations occur when a source uses culturally or socially inappropriate language, which decreases his or her persuasive effectiveness. Positive violations occur when a source, who is expected to use either socially inappropriate language or to conform to normative language expectations, employs language that is evaluated in a positive manner. This type of violation will increase the persuasibility of the message.

References

Aronson, E., & Carlsmith, J. (1963). The effect of the severity of the threat on the devaluation of forbidden behavior. *Journal of Abnormal and Social Psychology, 66*, 584-588.

Bettinghaus, E. P. (1973). *Persuasive communication* (2nd ed.). New York: Holt, Rinehart & Winston.

Burgoon, J. K., Burgoon, M., Miller, G. R., & Sunnafrank, M. (1981). Learning theory approaches to persuasion. *Human Communication Research, 7,* 161-175.

Burgoon, M. (1989). Social influence. In H. Giles & P. Robinson (Eds.), *Handbook of language and social psychology* (pp.51-72). London: John Wiley.

Burgoon, M., & Miller, G. R. (1985). An expectancy interpretation of language and persuasion. In H. Giles & R. St.Clair (Eds.), *Recent advances in language, communication, and social psychology* (pp. 199-229). London: Lawrence Erlbaum.

Burgoon, M., & Miller, M. D. (1990). Communication and influence. In G. L. Dahnke & G. W. Clatterbuck (Eds.), *Human communication: Theory and research* (pp. 229-258). Belmont, CA: Wadsworth.

Festinger, L. (1957). *A theory of cognitive dissonance.* Stanford, CA: Stanford University Press.

Heider, F. (1946). Attitudes and cognitive organization. *Journal of Psychology, 21,* 107-112.

Hill, W. F. (1971). *Learning: A survey of psychological interpretation.* Scranton, PA: Chandler.

LaPiere, R. T. (1934). Attitudes vs. actions. *Social Forces, 13,* 230-237.

McGuire, W. J. (1966). The current status of cognitive consistency theories. In S. Feldman (Ed.), *Cognitive consistency: Motivational antecedents and behavioral consequents* (pp. 1-46). New York: Academic Press.

Miller, G. R., Burgoon, M., & Burgoon, J. K. (1984). Communication and compliance: An overview of the research on the process of persuasion. In C. Arnold

& J. W. Bowers (Eds.), *Handbook of rhetorical and communication theory* (pp. 400-474). Boston, MA: Allyn & Bacon.

Newcomb, T. M. (1953). An approach to the study of communicative acts. *Psychological Review, 60*, 393-404.

Newcomb, T. M. (1956). The predictions of interpersonal attraction. *American Psychologist, 11*, 575-586.

O'Keefe, D. J. (1990). *Persuasion: Theory and research.* Newbury Park, CA: Sage.

Osgood, C. E., & Tannenbaum, P. H. (1955). The principle of congruity in the prediction of attitude change. *Psychological Review, 62*, 42-55.

Petty, R. E., & Cacioppo, J. R. (1986). *Communication and persuasion: Central and peripheral routes to attitude change.* New York: Springer.

Roberts, W. R. (1924). Aristotle on public speaking. *Fortnightly Review*, pp. 122-116, 201-210.

Sherif, C. W., Sherif, M., & Nebergall, R. E. (1965). *Attitude and attitude change: The social judgment-involvement approach.* Philadelphia: W. B. Saunders.

Smith, M. D. (1971). *Theoretical foundations of learning and teaching.* Waltham, MA: Xerox College Publishers.

Walster, E., & Festinger, L. (1962). The effectiveness of overheard persuasive communications. *Journal of Abnormal and Social Psychology, 65*, 395-402.

Zimbardo, P., Weisenberg, M., & Firestone, I. (1969). Changing appetites for eating fried grasshopper. In P. Zimbardo (Ed.), *The cognitive control of motivation* (pp. 44-54). Chicago: Scott, Foresman.

7

Persuasion:
Applications and Message Strategies

The previous chapter discussed a number of the many models that attempt to explain *why* people change their attitudes and/or behaviors. Many of these models pose interesting questions and have generated intriguing explanations for human behavior. After reading the last chapter, several of our students have persuaded us that it is not enough simply to understand the underlying psychological motivations for change. They claimed that although they found the models interesting, it was unclear to them how they might use this information to make them better persuaders. In fact, one of them said that he did not really know any more about communication and how to use it to persuade than he did before reading the chapter. Given this negative reinforcement, our general feelings of inconsistency and the decision that this feedback was generally close to our latitudes of acceptance, we felt it necessary to resolve the cognitive dissonance associated with our desire to do a good job and the knowledge that our readers were not being adequately served; thus, we were persuaded to make some changes in this edition.

This chapter, therefore, attempts to acquaint you with some of the available research on how one goes about structuring effective persuasive messages. This synthesis represents our best understanding about what the research says, and we offer a description of what has been found to be most effective. Perhaps it is wise to elaborate briefly some of our assumptions about the material included in this chapter. First, we resisted several suggestions to include this material in a chapter on public speaking. Traditionally, some of the material in this chapter has been used in guides on how to be effective in persuading a group of people in some formal speaking situation. Although we think that many of the suggestions made in this chapter would be very useful to a speaker who wishes to persuade others, we think these suggestions have broader applicability than would be suggested if included in a chapter on public speaking. Frankly, we think that there are a variety of situations in which people wish to be effective persuaders. It is important for business executives to know what kind of messages are most likely to be accepted and retained by people when effective decision making is paramount. Anyone involved in an intimate relationship needs to know that some kinds of messages increase tension whereas others lessen it. During conflict situations it is important to have an idea about what type of communication likely will lead to desirable outcomes. Through practice and intelligent observation, a person can learn to communicate with messages that work.

A second issue needs to be discussed prior to our analysis of the available research. We do not think that all communication is persuasive by nature; that view is too simplistic. We also are not interested in simply training people to be manipulators. Many people find our strong emphasis on the persuasive function of communication to be somewhat irritating, if not offensive, and we are willing to speak to that issue. Persuasion is a pervasive part of our daily lives, and much of our communication is suasory in nature. The suggestions we make in this chapter are likely to be useful to the would-be huckster who wishes to use the tool of communication for ends that we might personally find reprehensible. There is another view that we find comforting, however. Knowledge of how to construct persuasive messages and how those messages are likely to affect people also should be a useful tool to help the knowledgeable person *resist persuasive claims that should not be accepted.* The power of this knowledge that would allow one to persuade is surely offset by the power to resist persuasive attempts when we understand the ways in which they are being used against us.

Finally, given the alternatives to persuasion—that is, the use or threat of force and violence—we believe that persuasion is an acceptable and desirable tool by which we can influence our social environment. If, through the information in this chapter, we are able to help you become a more effective persuader and consumer of influence messages, we may well be reducing the likelihood that you will resort to more socially undesirable alternatives to get what you want.

The Components of a Persuasive Message

We believe that one way to begin to understand how to go about constructing effective influence messages is by analyzing how people go about making critical decisions. If we can understand how people evaluate logical arguments, we are more likely to construct messages that will be seen as logical and increase the probability of those messages being persuasive. Toulmin (1959) has created a model of critical thinking that has great utility in persuasive discourse. He claims that arguments grow out of information (data) about a particular issue that leads to an inference or conclusion (claim). There is also a bridging statement, which he calls a *warrant*, that allows the data to be linked to the claim. Although Toulmin was not concerned primarily with creating persuasive messages, it is appropriate to argue that a persuasive message that facilitates this kind of critical thinking is most likely to be effective. Every persuasive message presents an idea or course of action that the communicator advocates; it then suggests reasons that listeners should agree with it. Thus it can be argued that most persuasive messages, in their simplest form, are made up of the three components in the Toulmin model: claim, warrant, and data. These elements work to reinforce each other in persuasive attempts. We shall elaborate further on these three elements.

Claim

A *claim* is any statement, implied or explicit, that a communicator wants his or her audience to accept or agree to. A particular claim can serve as the major point of several related arguments, or it may be used by the communicator in one part of an argument to support an assertion (claim) made in another part.

There are several kinds of claims that can be used in a message. In a *policy* claim, the speaker calls for a specific course of action. The statement, "Abortion should be available to women on demand," is an example of a policy claim. The speaker might make a *fact* claim: "In Sweden, abortion is available to women on demand." A *value* claim such as the following might be made: "The Swedish system that allows for abortions on demand is superior to the abortion policies in the United States." Regardless of the kind of claim used, the claim alone does not provide in itself a reason for audience acceptance.

Warrant

To persuade, the communicator must support each claim with two other message parts: a warrant and data. A *warrant* is a general belief or attitude stated in support of a claim. To be effective, a warrant must be implicitly accepted by the audience; otherwise, it remains just another claim. For example, a communicator who says, "Schools should not be racially integrated," is making a claim. The claim can then be supported with the general statement, "Blacks are genetically inferior to whites in mental ability." Such a statement would be a warrant. Members of the Ku Klux Klan might accept this warrant and so accept the claim. But it is highly likely that a convention of anthropologists or a group of African Americans might not believe the warrant and so would reject the claim as unwarranted. In this case, the warrant itself (that African Americans are mentally inferior) becomes a claim and needs a new warrant to justify it.

Many persuasive messages fail even when the claim is acceptable to the audience because the warrant is totally rejected. For instance, suppose someone who believes marijuana to be a dangerous drug goes to see a 1930s movie called *Reefer Madness*. It claims that marijuana is a dangerous drug, a claim the viewer is predisposed to support; it warrants that smoking marijuana leads to mental illness and violent crime. It may seem so absurdly exaggerated that the viewer rejects first the warrant, then the claim, deciding that marijuana could not be as dangerous as all that. An inappropriate warrant can actually be counterpersuasive.

Data

Data are specific beliefs stated in support of a claim. Similar to the warrant, the data must be accepted by the audience to be persuasive. McCroskey (1968) has suggested that there are three types of data: first order, second order, and third order.

First-order data are specific beliefs or knowledge shared by the communicator and the audience. It may be claimed, for example, that all cigarette advertising should be banned. Such a claim might be warranted by the generally accepted belief that cigarette smoking causes lung cancer. The communicator might then offer as data the information that cigarette advertising encourages smoking. The success or failure of this argument depends upon whether or not the data are first order; that is, whether or not they are a belief or an awareness of fact that the audience shares with the communicator. If they are not, the data themselves become a claim that the communicator will have to support by further argument.

Second-order data are beliefs held by the communicator but not necessarily known or shared by the audience. This type of data is often called "source assertion," because it asks the audience to accept something just because the speaker, or source, says it is so. The important message component in this case is the warrant that the speaker is a credible source. For example, a speaker might assert that consistently poor nutrition retards the mental development of children. If his or her credibility is high enough—let us say that the audience knows the speaker to be an established and respected member of the medical profession—the assertion itself becomes sufficient data. If the audience fully accepts the warrant (often implicit) that the speaker is a knowledgeable source, it will probably accept the speaker's claim without the need for further documentation. In this case, the second-order data, information previously known only to the speaker, becomes first-order data, which the audience also accepts as part of its beliefs or knowledge, and can be used in documenting further arguments. Of course, if the audience doubts the authority of the speaker, the data are useless.

When the communicator has low credibility and the audience does not share his or her views, *third-order* data must be used to persuade. This type of data is called "evidence." It comes from a third party, a source outside the communicator and the audience. Here is an example:

1. All cigarette advertising should be banned. (claim)
2. I am a truthful person. (warrant)
3. *The New York Times* said in an editorial that all cigarette advertising should be banned. (third-order data)
4. *The New York Times* is a credible source. (warrant)

As you can see, this example really consists of two separate persuasive messages. The first is:

1. *The New York Times* said in an editorial that all cigarette advertising should be banned. (claim)
2. I am a truthful person. (warrant)
3. I say that I read this editorial in *The New York Times*. (second-order data)

If that claim is accepted, it can be used as first-order data in a second message:

1. All cigarette advertising should be banned. (claim)
2. *The New York Times* is a credible source. (warrant)
3. *The New York Times* said in an editorial that all cigarette advertising should be banned. (now considered first-order data, because the audience accepts it)

Third-order data ask the audience to accept warrants for two separate claims. The audience must trust that the speaker is telling the truth about what he or she read in *The New York Times,* and it must trust *The New York Times.* If the communicator has low credibility or if the outside source is disliked or disbelieved by the audience, third-order data are not persuasive. Of course, no amount of credibility will persuade if the audience totally rejects the claim. For instance, an audience of Roman Catholic clergy will probably not accept a claim that abortion should be legalized, no matter how credible the speaker or data.

Although it is useful to understand these common message elements in persuasive discourse, to do so will not explain how to *construct* effective persuasive messages. So far, we have progressed only a short distance on our journey from theory to actual application of knowledge about how to gain compliance. There are several message variables that may or may not be present in any of the specific message elements that we have just discussed. Communicators must make several decisions in creating the most persuasive message possible. They must decide what to include in any given persuasive message, what kinds of feelings should be appealed to in the receiver, and finally, how to organize all of these elements.

Selecting Message Appeals That Are Persuasive

Aristotle specified three basic appeals that a communicator can make in a persuasive message. A speaker can use a logical argument (*logos*), an emotional argument (*pathos*), or an argument based on credibility (*ethos*). Contemporary communication experts have attempted to distinguish between logical and emotional appeals. A logical appeal is one that presents evidence in support of the acceptance of a claim or attempts to build an argument that is logically true. An emotional appeal focuses on the consequences that will result if a person accepts or rejects the communicator's claim. According to this schema, we would probably agree that an advertisement claiming that one should buy an automobile in August because a thousand dollars could be saved is appealing to our sense of logic. An advertisement that stresses the increased social status accruing to those people who buy a certain brand of automobile is an emotional appeal.

Unfortunately, not all messages are as easy to classify according to type of appeal as these two examples. Although it is clear that certain messages are more logical or more emotional than others, it is probably not very useful to view logical and emotional appeals as completely separate and distinct. Many persuasive messages contain both emotional and logical appeals. Cold hard statistics are often included on why the status-producing automobile is also a good buy because of its continued high resale value. Other messages, primarily based upon evidence and logical appeals, often include emotional reasons for accepting the claims being advanced. It is probably rare in conversation to use one type of appeal exclusively in a persuasive attempt; we rely on many types of appeals in our persuasive arsenal.

There are also other problems associated with analyzing emotional and logical appeals. The logic or emotion of an appeal is perceived by the receiver, and those perceptions are not always identical to the perceptions of the communication source. Though one might assume that receivers would be able to differentiate between logical and emotional appeals, there is evidence to suggest that this is not always the case (see, e.g., Lefford, 1946; Ruechelle, 1958). Research has shown that people cannot always tell whether arguments are logical or illogical. When people agree with the conclusion drawn by the communicator, they tend to claim that the argument was logical. This judgment is made whether or not the message is based on commonly accepted rules or logic. However, when people disagree with the position being advocated, they are able to detect the faulty reasoning in the persuasive message. One would probably expect that as people become more trained in the use of logic, these results would not be the same. Bettinghaus (1968) found that students who were trained in formal logic were indeed better able to detect faulty logic than students who had not been trained; however, even the trained students made more errors in detecting faulty logic in persuasive messages that they agreed with.

Although we cannot always decide in advance what appeals will be perceived by receivers as logical or emotional, we do know that appeals to logic and/or emotion can be effective persuaders. We also know that the communicator may face situations in which logical appeals are expected. For example, many people in formal public speaking situations are expected to appeal to the logic of their audience. When people are expecting a speaker to be logical, it is in the best interest of the speaker at least to give the appearance of being logical. Bettinghaus also found that when people used phrases such as "isn't it only logical . . . " people saw the message as more logical than emotional. As we noted in the previous chapter, there is a great deal of research to suggest that people develop expectations about the proper communication behavior of others, and, to the extent that those expectancies are not violated, the speaker can be effective.

Despite the difficulty involved in classifying different types of appeals, there are several factors that will influence the persuasiveness of a message regardless of the type of appeal used.

Appeals Based on Evidence

Is it important to present evidence (third-order data) to support a claim? The answer depends on the situation. Research has shown that sometimes evidence is very persuasive, whereas at other times different kinds of supporting material are more effective. It is possible to extract from the research some generalizations about the usefulness of evidence (for a detailed discussion of evidence, see McCroskey, 1969, 1970).

If a communicator has high credibility with an audience, there probably will be no need to present evidence. For example, suppose that President Clinton's chief economic adviser claims that the nation is headed for a depression. If you believe this is a credible source, you will probably accept the statement without hearing the statistics. Citing the evidence would not make her or him more persuasive to you because you already believe her or him. The adviser's position convinces you that she or he is an expert in her or his field.

But what if the speaker has low credibility? In that case, evidence is persuasive only if the audience was previously unaware of the data. If, in the example above, the economic adviser were a person you considered untrustworthy, you would want to hear strong evidence. If that adviser gave convincing statistics that you had not known before, you might accept the claim in spite of her or his low credibility. But suppose you were a student of economics who had read the same statistics and drawn a different conclusion. In that case, the adviser's use of evidence would not persuade you; it might even make you resist the claim more because you would suspect that the facts were being manipulated. In general, if an audience already knows of the evidence, it has probably made up its mind, and the communicator gains nothing by restating the evidence.

Research has also shown that evidence must be delivered clearly if it is to have maximum persuasive effect. This does not mean that speakers must use compulsively logical and straightforward approaches, for they may lose the audience by boring the members to death. But if there is no organic unity to the speaker's presentation, if statistics are haphazardly thrown at the audience, or if words are mumbled and droned in a relentless monotone, all the evidence in the world will not help. A poor delivery will not only make evidence useless, failing to persuade the audience of the particular argument being discussed at the time; it is very possible that it will also reduce the speaker's credibility in terms of future messages that may be present.

Apparently, a speaker runs risks in presenting evidence. It may have a neutral effect, swaying an audience neither one way nor the other, or it may actually hurt a speaker's chances of successfully conveying a message. What, then, is the ultimate value of evidence? Studies show that, whereas the immediate effect of evidence can be negligible, the long-range effects—for both high- and low-credible speakers—may be important. Over a period of time, audience attitudes may change slowly but decidedly if the listeners receive several doses of evidence in the messages conveyed to them. A good example is the political candidate who begins the campaign months in advance of election day. The cumulative effect of the evidence presented, especially in claims made against opponents, may eventually alter the attitudes of the voters. Another important effect of evidence is in making receivers more resistant to counterinfluence on the part of another potential persuader. Therefore, if we know that a person, over time, is likely to hear persuasive counterarguments, it would be wise to include evidence no matter how credible we are with that individual. It appears that evidence is often remembered and used when people hear other appeals arguing the opposite side of an issue.

There are two final points that should be made about the use of evidence. The first is that little research is available that distinguishes between "good" and "bad" evidence. However, it is probably common sense to suggest that evidence is more likely to be perceived as good evidence when it is relevant to the claim being advanced and properly linked to that claim by an appropriate warrant. The second point is that the sources of evidence also help people make judgments about the quality of the evidence. Evidence obtained from a source low in credibility can have an adverse effect on the persuasiveness of your message, and it can also reduce your credibility. Many times a person can increase communicative effectiveness, however, by relying on evidence and examples from other high-credible sources (Reinard, 1988).

Appeals Based on Fear

Many communicators try to persuade by stimulating fear in their audiences. Public health pamphlets, for example, predict a frightening future of blindness, sterility, paralysis, or the possibility of contracting the virus that leads to Acquired Immune Deficiency Syndrome (AIDS) as the reward for sexual promiscuity (or even occasional indiscretions) unless one takes the recommended precautions. Gun-control advocates talk of unleashed violence, and their opponents talk of first steps down the road to totalitarianism. Students in a driver's education course watch a state highway department film that graphically portrays the results of reckless or negligent driving, complete with blood and bodies and intimations of one's own mortality. Because people do react strongly to fear in everyday life, much research has been done to see if fear can be used to change attitudes.

A fear appeal says that harm will befall the listener or someone important to him or her unless the claim of the communicator is adopted. A strong fear appeal shows this harm dramatically. A film intended to make people stop smoking that shows a close-up of a cancerous lung being removed from a corpse is an example of a high fear appeal. A moderate fear appeal states the same message less dramatically, as in the case of a film that shows people smoking and then coughing. A low fear appeal states the message in a fairly calm way; for example, a printed advertisement claiming that scientists have established a link between smoking and lung cancer. It is important to note here that we are talking about the construction of messages that vary on the degree to which they contain vivid or frightening *consequences* associated with failure to accept the claim of the persuader, which is not necessarily isomorphic with the amount of fear that the receiver experiences after exposure to the message. Put another way, exposure to a film depicting "blood on the highway" contains frightening images that may or may not translate into a fearful affective response in the viewer. This distinction will be elaborated on further as we discuss findings from extant research on fear appeals. Fear appeals are those that evoke varying degrees of fear responses within receivers and are not necessarily those that depict the most frightening, vivid, or grotesque images. It is important to distinguish between these two different approaches to fear appeal research (O'Keefe, 1990). A communicator must decide what type of fear-arousing message will produce the desired effect.

Research findings on fear appeals in persuasive communication are conflicting. Some studies show that a strong fear appeal is best; others show that a moderate fear appeal is best. Such confusion means that factors other than the fear appeal itself are affecting the receiver's response to the message (for detailed discussions of fear appeals see Miller, 1963; Witte, 1992). The credibility of the source is one influence on the audience's reaction to a fear appeal. A high-credible source is more persuasive when using a strong fear appeal. A less credible source does better with a moderate fear appeal. If a doctor tells you that you will die of heart trouble within a year if you do not stop overeating, that should provide enough incentive for you to take action. If a well-meaning friend tells you the same thing, you may not be persuaded so quickly. Therefore, a communicator who plans to persuade through fear should first attempt to establish credibility in the eyes of the audience.

When the fear appeal threatens harm to someone important to the listener, a strong fear appeal is most effective. For instance, a claim that children undernourished on sugar-coated breakfast cereal and junk food may grow up with brain damage would be more persuasive than the claim that they may grow up failing to appreciate good food. When the fear appeals threaten loved ones, listeners cannot reason that they are hurting only themselves by rejecting the claim. Contemporary drunk driving public service announcements have been designed with this approach in mind. "Friends don't let friends drive drunk" changes the focus of the consequences of drunk driving from the target of the message to significant others and the harm that will befall them when engaged in this risky behavior.

A strong fear appeal with evidence is more effective than one without evidence and is stronger than any mild fear appeal, with or without evidence. In research studies, only the people who heard evidence kept their changed attitudes for longer than two weeks. Those who heard appeals without evidence quickly returned to their original belief. Thus an opponent of sugar-coated cereal and junk food who wants to change the nutritional attitudes of mothers should make claims that can be supported with convincing evidence. If there is no evidence for the brain-damage claim, a mild fear appeal would be better, citing evidence that supports the claim that bad eating habits formed in early childhood usually continue in adult life.

Research indicates that fear appeals will be more effective if they point to immediate negative consequences associated with not accepting the claim of the communicator. The more immediate the likely negative consequences, the more effective are strong fear appeals. Most smokers would likely respond to a fear appeal pointing out the link between smoking and lung cancer *if* they were convinced that they would develop lung cancer soon, for example, next month. That would be an immediate result of their refusal to give up tobacco. To the extent that negative outcomes are in the distant future, however, strong fear appeals tend to be ineffective as people dismiss the seriousness of the threat and/or refuse to attend to the fear-arousing messages. On the other hand, when there is an immediate threat, strong fear appeals can motivate people to take prompt actions.

Because fear appeals are persuasive messages intended to "scare" people into adopting the communicator's point of view regarding their behaviors, one additional aspect of creating effective fear appeal messages is the issue of target *efficacy* (Witte, 1992). The effectiveness of fear-arousing messages are enhanced if the recommended response is directly related to the target's ability to perform the advocated behavior. For example, a fear-arousing message intended to frighten at-risk groups, such as young, single college students, into practicing "safe sex" will likely fail with those in that audience who do not have a clear idea of which sexual activities are "safe" and which are "risky" and *how* to take the precautions necessary to avoid contracting sexually transmitted diseases.

Most of the research that we have reviewed and the examples we have advanced have been concerned with fear appeals that make threats to someone's physical well-being. There are other kinds of fear appeals that merit discussion because of their ability to motivate people to change attitudes and behaviors. The fear of social disapproval can be a significant persuader, and little has been done to link this threat to social well-being to other kinds of fear appeals. This kind of fear appeal can be very important in the interpersonal and small-group communication arena. Few of us are without fear of disapproval by liked and respected others; we want our friends to like us, and we have at least some fear of their criticism. Persuasive appeals can be structured to use that fear of social disapproval as the basis for changing people's attitudes. As we have said earlier, however, very strong fear appeals based on anxiety about social disapproval may have a backlash effect. If you threaten people who like and respect you with loss of your friendship unless they comply with your wishes, one possible outcome is for them to change their evaluations of you as a person. In Chapter 6, we discussed in detail how imbalances between sources and topic attitudes can lead to shifts in either or both source and topic attitudes.

The final point that should be discussed is the continued use of fear appeals over time. If a communicator continually uses fear as a motivator, people are likely to dismiss such claims at some point in time. This kind of communicator becomes a "prophet of doom" who is known for dire predictions. People who constantly use fear as a motivator run great risks in terms of their own credibility. Also, a person who continually threatens people with social disapproval runs the same risk. Fear, when used in proper proportions, can be an effective means of persuasion. Employing the wrong kinds of appeals or too much reliance on this technique can have outcomes that are undesirable to the potential persuader.

Appeals Varying in Language Intensity

Some of our closest friends and most respected colleagues believe we have obtained whatever modicum of success we have because people have confused the intensity of our claims with the validity of our positions. People have choices to make about kinds of language that will be used in any given persuasive message, and there is evidence to suggest that those language choices will have a great effect on whether the persuasion attempt succeeds. One important language variable that influences persuasion is *language intensity*. Language intensity can be rated by measuring the distance between a claim and a neutral position. For example, the claim, "Unions are *destroying* the newspaper industry," is certainly less neutral than saying, "Unions create *problems* in the newspaper industry." There are different ways to vary the intensity of language in a message (Bowers, 1964).

One way is to insert qualifiers. One kind of qualifier expresses probability. Take the statement "Recent Supreme Court decisions on the rights of accused criminals will *certainly* lead to more violent crime." This statement can be made less intense by replacing *certainly* with *perhaps*. Another kind of qualifier expresses extremity. If a presidential aide tell the press, "The president *vigorously condemns* bias in the news media," the attitude implied is obviously more intense and more threatening than if he or she says, "The president *frowns* upon bias in the news media."

A second way to increase intensity of language is to use metaphors, especially those with sexual or violent connotations. Claims such as, "The president is *raping* the Constitution," "The recent incursion by Iraq is a *molestation* of the country's territorial waters," "Public school teachers *suffocate* student creativity," or "Prejudice in the system has *brutalized* the minds of young children," go beyond a representation of the facts as they stand and attempt to persuade through the intensity of images.

Whether such high-intensity language does, in fact, achieve the speaker's goal is difficult to say. One study showed that very intense communicators seem more credible and that their messages seem clearer and more intelligent; however, the study did not indicate that such communicators were actually more effective in persuading people to accept the positions being advocated (McEwen & Greenberg, 1970). Other research has found that messages employing low levels of language intensity are actually more persuasive than those using highly intense language. Obviously there are some intervening factors that affect how language intensity operates in persuasive messages.

One such factor mediating the effects of language intensity is the expectations that receivers develop for what is "appropriate" communication behavior on the part of any given communicator. For example, it has been demonstrated that within this culture, different expectations about appropriate language behavior vary between male and female communicators. A number of studies conducted by the first author of this book found that male communicators were much more effective when they used highly intense language than were females saying the same thing (Burgoon & Burgoon, 1990; Burgoon & Stewart, 1975). Moreover, females were very persuasive when they used language low in intensity. One *possible* explanation for these findings has to do with cultural-level stereotypes that may or may not be useful. If a culture expects males to be aggressive and to demonstrate this by using forceful language, then males using highly intense language would not be violating expectations in any negative manner and would, therefore, be persuasive using language high in intensity. To the extent that aggression in females has not been accepted, however, females who chose highly intense language would be negatively violating expectations and, therefore, would not be as persuasive. It is also interesting to note that female receivers were *least* persuaded by females who used highly intense language and *most* persuaded by males using language high in intensity. Although it is no doubt true that these kinds of stereotypes are changing, these recent results indicate that there are sex differences associated with this language variable.

Another variable that affects decisions about the level of language intensity that is most effective in persuasive discourse is the involvement of the receivers on the particular issue being discussed. Listeners who are very involved in a given topic (e.g., reporters listening to an argument advocating naming of confidential sources) are especially likely to respond negatively to highly intense claims. With such audiences, a communicator will effect little attitude change with highly intense language. If a topic is less crucial to the receiver, more highly intense language can be used in the persuasive attempt.

There are several possible explanations for these findings. Our discussion of the consistency models in Chapter 6 provides one such explanation. If people find an issue very important and hear a source advocating the opposite of what they believe, the easiest move to restore balance is to derogate the communicator. Social judgment theory offers an explanation that also tends to make a lot of sense. Selecting messages very high in intensity will obviously place the communication far from the listener's latitude of acceptance. Therefore, the claims that the communicator makes are likely to be *contrasted* with the views that the receiver privately holds. To the extent that this contrast effect operates, people will resist accepting highly intense claims. If the issue is less important, the claims are more likely to fall in the expanded latitude of noncommitment (which is large on issues of little import) and this contrasting will not occur. People can, therefore, take more extreme positions. All of these explanations taken together suggest the cautious use of extremely intense language in persuasive attempts. As most of us are aware, there is a tendency for people in discussion situations to take even more extreme positions than they really hold when there is disagreement or criticism. Moreover, many public speakers will take unusually intense positions to illustrate their support of or opposition to an issue. There are certainly pitfalls associated with this strategy.

Opinionated language is similar to intense language and has similar effects. Generally speaking, opinionated language really expresses two separate messages: the claim and the speaker's attitude toward those who agree or disagree. Opinionated language may express rejection of those who disagree, as in the statement "Only criminals with something to hide would object to being stopped and frisked by a police officer." Or it may praise those who agree with or show acceptance of the communicator; for example, "People who favor stop-and-frisk laws are responsible citizens who are willing to put up with a slight inconvenience in the interests of justice." Statements such as "Stop-and-frisk laws are good" are non-opinionated, for they merely express a claim.

Research indicates that opinionated rejections are perceived as more intense than non-opinionated statements. They can be used effectively by highly credible sources. Less credible sources, however, do better with non-opinionated language (Miller & Lobe, 1967). Also non-opinionated language is likely to be more persuasive with an audience that is involved in the issue being discussed. A neutral audience is more persuaded by opinionated rejections.

Because these findings are so similar to those suggesting contrast effects for highly intense language, we can offer some general conclusions. When the audience thinks the communicator is credible, more intense language can be used to support a claim. But when the communicator is unsure of his or her credibility or knows it to be low and is advocating a position that is counter to beliefs that are important to the receiver, the communicator should, as a matter of strategy, choose less intense language. All of this suggests that the intuitive assumption that a passionate speaker is most persuasive needs reconsideration.

Making Strategic Decisions About What to Include in a Persuasive Message

As we have discussed them, most claims are only one side of an argument. The communicator must make a strategic decision as to whether or not it is best to cite opposing arguments. In a one-sided message, a claim is made and the communicator attempts to support it. In a two-sided message, the same claim can be made but there is at least the acknowledgment that opposing arguments exist, with some attempt to demonstrate why the claim being advocated is superior to those in opposition. The decision to present a one-sided or two-sided message depends on several factors residing with the people with whom one is communicating.

In cases in which an audience already agrees with the claims of a speaker, a one-sided argument will immediately increase or confirm that support (Hovland, Lumsdaine, & Sheffield, 1949). In fact, if a speaker has reason to believe that an audience is unaware of counterarguments, it will probably be best to avoid these arguments deliberately. By mentioning them, the speaker might simply persuade listeners against his or her own claim. The mayor who cites 15 instances of alleged police corruption when the public knows of only 5 is at a disadvantage, no matter how well he disproves the accusations; those additional 10 examples could convince people that there really is widespread police corruption.

On the other hand, if an audience is hostile, if its sympathies are unknown, or if there is any possibility that an audience is aware of opposing arguments, a speaker is best advised to present a two-sided message. Even when people are in agreement with the speaker, the more educated they are (an increasingly common situation in our society), the more likely such an audience will be persuaded by a two-sided argument (Hovland et al., 1949). Educated people are usually capable of thinking of at least a few opposing arguments for themselves and, therefore, might be suspicious of the motives or intelligence of a speaker who does not consider these same arguments.

One also has to realize that great numbers of people are exposed to conflicting arguments on issues through mass media coverage (for a detailed discussion of prior information and message-sidedness, see Weston, 1967). Suppose a mayor claims that there is no corruption in the city's police department. If the public has already listened to television programs highlighting instances of such corruption and read evidence cited in newspaper accounts, the mayor is going to seem foolish and incompetent, or worse. If the public believes the mayor was being dishonest in the message, not only will they fail to be persuaded by the mayor's immediate claim, but they might also doubt the mayor's credibility on other issues.

It would seem, therefore, that in most cases—other than outright propagandizing when speakers are merely recycling shared beliefs for the benefit of their followers—it is usually better to use some form of the two-sided message. The speaker will have to use discretion in deciding how much should be said.

Let us also *stress* that the communicator must make decisions about how discrepant the message is to be from the held beliefs of the receivers. To the extent that at least recognizing opposing arguments makes the receiver seem more informed and logical, it may also work to make the communication and the communicator seem less radical and polarized. When this happens, there is less likelihood of simply rejecting the message because it *appears* to be too discrepant from privately held beliefs.

Structuring Effective Persuasive Messages

We have opted to close this chapter with a discussion of the structuring of messages when the intent is primarily one of producing changes in attitudes and/or behavior. These suggestions are also concerned with persuasion as it occurs across contexts from the interpersonal, small-group, and public-speaking situations to the mass communication situation.

There is little agreement on the effects of logical structure on persuasion. Studies have shown that although severe disorganization does make a message less persuasive, moderately disorganized messages are no less persuasive than very logical ones (McCroskey & Mehrley, 1969). There are several plausible explanations for this result. First, the audience may be capable of organizing information that comes to it in an "illogical" way. Marshall McLuhan, perhaps the most revolutionary communication theorist, claims that the electronic media have created an environment that forces people to rapidly recognize patterns in seemingly random information. Whereas books trained people to think in a logical, "linear" way, electronic media, such as television, ask us to take in vast amounts of disconnected information and do the job of ordering it ourselves. If McLuhan is right, people today are used to dealing with information that is presented in a disorganized way. They could easily understand a speaker who did not present an argument in a logical, step-by-step fashion.

A second explanation is that most of the research about the organization of persuasive messages was done with college students. They may be especially skilled listeners because the college lecture is an especially good example of a disorganized message. Organization might be more important in communicating to a non-college-educated audience.

A third possible explanation of these research findings focuses on the process of feedback. There is more opportunity for immediate feedback in the interpersonal and small-group communication situations than in the public-speaking and mass-communication contexts. People can disrupt the logical pattern of a communicator more easily in those situations in which immediate feedback is present. It would seem, therefore, that adherence to a strict logical structure in these situations is probably neither feasible nor necessarily desirable. There is great emphasis placed on the effective communicator being a person who can adapt to people and situations. That adaptation may preclude use of some of the stricter organizational patterns prescribed in formal public-speaking situations.

In addition to a logical structure, a message also has a psychological structure that should be considered. This means that although the order of the messages may not conform to any set rules of logical structure, there are strategic decisions that can be made to order the different parts of a message so that people will be more or less receptive to persuasive communication. The research and discussion that follow center on the psychological structure of messages and provide some useful generalizations that may be helpful when shaping persuasive messages.

Organizing Supporting Materials

Presenting a two-sided message always involves some decision making because there is more than one way to organize arguments. Suppose a speaker claims that capital punishment should be abolished, he or she might first choose to plow through the opposition's arguments point for point, and only then settle back to a presentation of his or her own claims. There is nothing wrong with this, except that the speaker may lose the argument.

One reason is that an audience very often reacts defensively toward speakers who begin their messages with a strong offensive, especially if the audience happens to agree with some or all of the opposition's claims. William Shakespeare understood this psychological aspect of audience reaction very well. In *Julius Caesar*, Marc

Antony faces a public whose loyalty to Caesar could be severed or reaffirmed by the "right" message. In his speech, Antony gently and unantagonistically describes each of Caesar's virtues while at the same time refraining from obvious attacks against Caesar's opponents. Only later in his oration, when he senses that audience's sympathies have been won, does he dare shift the emphasis of his message from positive claims to an outright attack against Caesar's enemies.

If Shakespeare had been a professor as well as a playwright, he might have warned his students that discussing opposition arguments first may invest them with more importance than one ever intended. In other words, the very fact that a speaker gives opposition statements priority in the message may establish a psychological priority in the minds of audience members—even those who were previously uncommitted. As for those who already support the opposing claims, such a message structure may actually reinforce their attitudes, an unfortunate result for the speaker.

If speakers who are trying to persuade their audience that capital punishment should be abolished pay any attention at all to Antony's speech and to the findings of modern research on the subject, they will decide that a more persuasive method would be to present their own claims first and subsequently discuss, and refute, the opponent's stand (Miller & Campbell, 1959).

The speaker could, for example, emphasize the immorality of taking human life, even in retribution, the unconstitutional nature of capital punishment, and the opinions of highly respected citizens who support his or her claim. Because an audience is often more favorably inclined toward the arguments it hears first, the speaker will already have something of an advantage by the time the discussion of counterarguments begins. These opposition claims might include the notion that capital punishment is the only adequate deterrent for major crimes. In that case, the speaker's refutation could be in the form of third-order data such as statistical figures relating to crime rates. But even if the opposition is not checked on all points, the speaker's arguments will still be more persuasive if they are placed first than they would be if they are placed last.

Identifying the Source of Evidence

When citing an outside source (third-order data, or evidence), a speaker must decide when to state the identity and qualification of the source. This depends on the source's credibility (Greenberg & Miller, 1966). If the receiver believes the source of evidence is highly credible, it can be identified before or after presenting the evidence; it does not matter. When the source's credibility is low, however, it is better to cite the source *after* presenting the evidence. Thus an advertising copywriter preparing a book advertisement for a new novel might proceed this way:

> NORMAN MAILER says: "This is the best novel I have read in 25 years!"

> "A Blockbuster of a novel! Thrilling, incredibly erotic, and possibly the greatest work of fiction ever written in English!"—*The Daily Tribune*

In fact, when the source is cited *after* the evidence, a high-credible source is not more persuasive than a low one. Thus if you do not know how the audience rates a source, you should give the evidence first and then name the source. If, in the preceding example, the copywriter believed Norman Mailer had endorsed so many bad books that his credibility was low, the copywriter might decide to put Mailer's quote first, followed by his name.

Revealing Your Desire to Persuade

The question of whether it is wise to tell someone you want to change an opinion is complex. If the members of the audience are strongly opposed to your claim, warning them in advance that you intend to persuade them is not effective (Allyn & Festinger, 1961). A person speaking to a group of radical feminists would be ill-advised to state that he or she intended to change their minds about job discrimination against women. Let us refer once again to Marc Antony's speech. It will be remembered that he told his audience he was there "to bury Caesar, not to praise him." In reality, he was there to bury Caesar's enemies and enhance his own position. But realizing the ambivalence of the audience (and the fact that Caesar's enemies were scattered among the citizenry), he never even implied his intent to persuade.

However, if a speaker and an audience are known to be in strong mutual sympathy (e.g., if they are friends), the speaker may be more persuasive by openly admitting the intent. If the audience dislikes the speaker, the speaker will probably do better to keep quiet about this intent (Mills & Aronson, 1965). Sometimes an apparent lack of intent to persuade can become a powerful persuasive tool. When someone is led to believe that a message was accidentally overheard, such a person tends to be persuaded by it (Walster & Festinger, 1962). Political gossip columns often work this way. A government official "leaks" information to the columnist, who then pretends it is a secret that has been accidentally uncovered. In such a case, our belief that the official had no intent to persuade us can lead us to accept the claim.

Presenting Problems and Solutions

Suppose that a speaker wants to convince people that the problems of mothers on welfare can be solved by government-funded day-care centers. He or she could structure the message in two ways. The speaker might discuss the problems of welfare mothers and then propose day-care centers as the solution, or could first discuss the merits of day-care centers and then explain the problems of welfare mothers.

Research indicates that the first pattern is much more effective in changing attitudes, both immediately following the message and over a period of time (Cohen, 1957). The problem-to-solution message is more interesting and the solution is more understandable when presented as the answer to a specific problem or need. When the solution is presented first, people may not understand its relevance until they hear about the problem. By that time, they may have lost interest.

Stating Points of Agreement and Disagreement

In most persuasive communication situations, the communicator shares some of the audience's beliefs and disagrees with others. When does the communicator discuss the shared beliefs? When does he or she introduce dispute? Research shows that the best strategy is to discuss points of agreement first, then move to the disagreements (Cohen, 1964). In this way, the speaker captures attention and raises his or her credibility. That credibility then covers the speaker when begining to disagree with the audience.

A politician telling reporters about union negotiations often uses this strategy. The politician points out that he or she also desires a higher standard of living for sanitation workers; that union members certainly deserve higher wages and more benefits for their hard work; and, finally, that he or she and the union leaders merely disagree on a few "minor" points, such as whether the wage increase shall be five cents or five dollars. This sort of strategy is used to persuade the public that the politician is a warm-hearted person. At the actual negotiating table, however, one is often expected to exaggerate disagreements at the outset and then gracefully concede points one by one, as if giving up something. In such cases, however, both sides understand the implied rules of the game. The general public is not likely to be so sophisticated.

Stating Your Conclusions

Research shows that most audiences respond favorably to clearly stated conclusions that call for a specific course of action. A speaker who makes an explicit conclusion creates more attitude change than one who lets the audience deduce which beliefs or actions are favored (Cronkhite, 1969). There are some experts who say that listeners will have more lasting change of attitude if they "participate" in the communication by drawing their own conclusions. But this method is risky, for there is no assurance that the listener will arrive at the conclusion the communicator desires. Thus in persuasive communication situations, it is usually wise for the speaker to state all conclusions clearly and specifically.

Some Concluding Comments

In this chapter, we have considered several issues that are important to the communicator who wishes to structure effective persuasive messages. We have tried to review available research conscientiously and select the research that was carefully executed and appeared to provide valid results. We must end this with a few words of caution. The suggestions we have put forth may not work in every situation. There may be other variables present, or we may simply not know enough to consider all of the persuasive strategies. The mark of any successful communicator is adaptation. It is our hope that you will consider and test the general suggestions we have offered from our understanding of the research; you might truly be surprised about how effective some of them can be in increasing your persuasive ability.

Summary

1. A persuasive message presents an idea or course of action that the source advocates and it suggests reasons why the receiver should agree to it. Most persuasive messages are composed of three parts: claim, warrant, and data. A claim is an explicit or implicit statement that the communicator wants the receiver to accept. A warrant is a general belief stated in support of a claim. Data are specific beliefs stated in support of a claim.

2. Evidence is third-order data from a person outside the communication situation. Evidence seems to have little effect on the persuasiveness of a high-credibility source, but it may increase the persuasiveness of a low-credibility source if the audience was previously unaware of the data. When in doubt, a speaker should use evidence.

3. A fear appeal is a message that says to the listener that harm will befall him or her or someone dear unless the claim is adopted. The credibility of the source can influence the audience's reaction to a fear appeal. A highly credible source is more persuasive when using a strong fear appeal, whereas a less credible source does better with a moderate fear appeal. Strong fear appeals seem very effective when they threaten harm to someone important to the listener. They

are most effective when used with evidence. Receivers who hear fear appeals without evidence tend to return quickly to their original beliefs. A communicator must use caution not to frighten the audience too much because this may lead them to reject the threat as absurd or too unbearable to think about.

4. Messages containing highly intense language are not very persuasive when the audience is quite involved in the topic under discussion. If a topic is less crucial or unimportant to the receivers, highly intense language can be persuasive. Opinionated language may express rejection of those who disagree with the speaker, or it may praise those who agree. Highly credible sources can use opinionated rejections quite effectively, whereas less credible sources do better with non-opinionated language.

5. Message discrepancy refers to the distance between the views of a speaker and those of the audience. Research indicates that speakers who make their beliefs sound close to those of their audiences will be more persuasive. A source with high credibility will be able to depart from an audience's views without much loss of credibility.

6. Experimental research has provided some generalizations that are helpful when structuring a persuasive message: (a) When presenting a two-sided message, speakers should discuss their arguments first. (b) When citing evidence, speakers should consider the credibility of the source of evidence. If the source of evidence has high credibility, it is best to cite the source and then the evidence. If the source of evidence has low credibility, it is best to cite the evidence and then name the source. (c) Speakers should not forewarn the audience of an intent to persuade unless they are friendly with its members. (d) Presenting the problem first and then the solution is more persuasive than beginning with the solution and moving on to the problem. (e) Speakers who make a specific conclusion will be more plausible than those who allow the audience to deduce the beliefs or actions favored.

References

Allyn, J., & Festinger, L. (1961). The effectiveness of unanticipated persuasive communication. *Journal of Abnormal and Social Psychology, 62,* 35-40.

Bettinghaus, E. P. (1968). *Persuasive communication*. New York: Holt, Rinehart & Winston.

Bowers, J. W. (1964). Some correlates of language intensity. *Quarterly Journal of Speech, 50*, 415-420.

Burgoon, M., & Burgoon, J. K. (1990). Compliance-gaining and health care. In J. P. Dillard (Ed.), *Seeking compliance: The production of interpersonal influence messages* (pp. 161-188). Scottsdale, AZ: Gorsuch Scarsbrick.

Burgoon, M., & Stewart, D. (1975). Empirical investigations of language intensity: I. The effects of sex of source, receiver, and language intensity on attitude change. *Human Communication Research, 1*, 244-248.

Cohen, A. R. (1957). Need for cognition and order of communication as determinants of opinion change. In C. I. Hovland (Ed.), *The order of presentation in persuasion* (pp. 102-120). New Haven, CT: Yale University Press.

Cohen, A. R. (1964). *Attitude change and social influence*. New York: Basic Books.

Cronkhite, G. (1969). *Persuasion: Speech and behavioral change*. Indianapolis: Bobbs-Merrill.

Greenberg, B. S., & Miller, G. R. (1966). The effects of low-credible sources on message acceptance. *Speech Monographs, 33*, 127-136.

Hovland, C. A., Lumsdaine, A. A., & Sheffield, F. D. (1949). *Studies in social psychology in World War II* (Vol. 3). Princeton, NJ: Princeton University Press.

Lefford, A. (1946). The influence of emotional subject matter on logical reasoning. *Journal of General Psychology, 34*, 127-151.

McCroskey, J. C. (1968). *An introduction in rhetorical communication*. Englewood Cliffs, NJ: Prentice Hall.

McCroskey, J. C. (1969). A summary of experimental research on the effects of evidence in persuasive communication. *Quarterly Journal of Speech, 55*, 169-176.

McCroskey, J. C. (1970). The effects of evidence as an inhibitor or counterpersuasion. *Speech Monographs, 37*, 188-194.

McCroskey, J. C., & Mehrley, R. S. (1969). The effects of disorganization and nonfluency on attitude change and source credibility. *Speech Monographs, 36*, 13-21.

McEwen, W. J., & Greenberg, B. S. (1970). The effects of message intensity on receiver evaluation of source, message and topic. *Journal of Communication, 20*, 340-350.

Miller, G. R. (1963). Studies in the use of fear appeals: A summary and analysis. *Central States Speech Journal, 14*, 117-125.

Miller, G. R., & Lobe, J. (1967). Opinionated language, open- and closed-mindedness and responses to persuasive communications. *Journal of Communication, 17*, 333-341.

Miller, N., & Campbell, D. T. (1959). Recency and primacy in persuasion as a function of the timing of speeches and measurements. *Journal of Abnormal and Social Psychology, 59*, 1-9.

Mills, J., & Aronson, E. (1965). Opinion change as a function of the communicator's attractiveness and desire to influence. *Journal of Personality and Social Psychology, 1*, 173-177.

O'Keefe, D. J. (1990). *Persuasion: Theory and research*. Newbury Park, CA: Sage.

Reinard, J. C. (1988). The empirical study of persuasive effects of evidence: The status after fifty years of research. *Human Communication Research, 15*, 3-59.

Ruechelle, R. C. (1958). An experimental study of audience recognition of emotional and intellectual appeals in persuasion. *Speech Monographs, 25*, 58.

Toulmin, S. (1959). *The uses of argument.* Cambridge: Cambridge University Press.

Walster, E., & Festinger, L. (1962). The effectiveness of overheard persuasive communications. *Journal of Abnormal and Social Psychology, 65,* 395-402.

Weston, J. R. (1967). *Argumentative message structure and message sidedness and prior familiarity as predictors of source credibility.* Unpublished doctoral dissertation, Michigan State University.

Witte, K. (1992). Putting the fear back into fear appeals: The extended parallel process model. *Communication Monographs, 59,* 329-349.

8

Decision Making

Chapters 6 and 7 introduced key concepts necessary in understanding how people can be persuaded by communication messages, and how sources of persuasion might construct messages to increase the likelihood of gaining compliance from others. The remainder of this book investigates three of the most complicated situations that people face in their everyday communication with others—ones requiring them to make decisions, create and maintain important relationships, and manage significant conflicts. Each one of these topics can be understood only in relationship to information contained in all of the previous chapters. Effective decision making is explained in terms of source and receiver characteristics, as well as the management of perceptions through language use. Establishing and maintaining relationships is discussed in terms of how people share information with each other, and the effect that shared perceptions have on the dynamics of relationships. Managing conflict effectively focuses on understanding the dynamic interplay among structural elements in situations, individual perceptions, and power dynamics.

It is not our intention to provide you with a "magic formula" for dealing with issues as complex as these. There are enough pop-culture cure-all books and programs available in the popular press if you are looking for step-by-step rules for making the right decision, making that special relationship work, and sure-fire ways to resolve conflicts. The advice offered in these types of books works well if your life is simple and you are faced with simple situations that call for simple answers. Rather, we work from the assumption that few of the situations in which we find ourselves are simple enough for any one formula to work. Therefore, it is our intent in the remaining chapters to provide you with research findings that you can use to understand the unique situations in which you will find yourself, and offer communication strategies from which to choose when you must make a decision, deal with relational issues, or manage a conflict situation.

This chapter concerns a fundamental situation that we find ourselves in almost every day—making decisions. Whether we make decisions alone or with other people, there are certain basic procedures that, if addressed, increase the probability of making better decisions. It should be made clear at this point that many of the traditional models of decision making are based on the assumption that people are rational actors. Rational actors make decisions by carefully evaluating the potential outcomes of different courses of action and carefully considering a number of significant, complicated factors. Take for example a situation where, during your second year in college, you need to decide on a major. As a rational actor you would carefully accumulate and organize information on each major suited to your interests, determine the possible effects of choosing a major on a variety of criteria (potential salary, the status of potential jobs in that field, intrinsic satisfaction, stability of the profession, etc.) and on the values you and others assign to each of these criteria. Then, being the rational actor that you are, you would multiply each value by the rating of each criteria, add them together, and, "presto," you will have decided upon the best major for you. If you were to think back on the process by which you decided on your major, few, if any could report going through such a rational process. The main reason given for our lack of ability to process information in a rational manner is explained through the concept of "bounded rationality" (March, 1990; Simon, 1957).

We as humans have a limited capacity to process the information necessary to make the type of predictions that are essential for a rational model to work. While making decisions we become emotionally caught up in the process, which often moves us away from making a well-considered rational decision. Further, it is difficult to remain consistent with the values and preferences we place on certain criteria. As time goes on and as the decision-making process continues, goals change and preferences shift. Even though it is extremely difficult to make rational decisions, we are faced with the fact that we indeed do need to make decisions. Fortunately, communication makes this situation manageable and possible.

We take the position that problem solving and decision making are processes that begin when individuals experience a need and end in the selection of a solution to satisfy that need. Communication functions differently at various points in the problem-solving or decision-making processes. At one point in the process, communication may function to manage a wealth of information; at another point, communication may function to manage conflicts or to regulate the behaviors of others involved in or affected by the decisions made. To grasp the importance of viewing problem solving and decision making as processes, we will first discuss the stages involved in problem solving and decision making and the types of agendas involved in each. Second, we will present the most current information available concerning the ever-changing use of computers and technology in the decision-making process. Third, it is important to examine the methods we use to choose among alternatives and the factors that lead to effective and ineffective decisions. We believe that the most effective way to begin our investigation of decision making is to focus on decisions that result from people working together, that is, in the small-group setting.

Group Problem Solving and Decision Making

Few people in society, if given the choice, would choose to live or work alone. Although there are times when being alone is enjoyable, to survive and grow as human beings we need to associate with others. Often we find ourselves communicating with a group of people. Many times in these situations, communication functions simply to share ideas or to become better acquainted. As will be discussed in detail in Chapter 9, our communication with people in a group carries with it relational implications. Communication also can function to manage conflict among members in a group and often to gain compliance from the entire group, or simply one member. However, it has become increasingly important in our culture, especially in organizational settings, to understand the ways by which people use communication in groups to satisfy the need to solve problems and make decisions.

Groups exist because they serve some function for society, for a group, or for the individual members of a group. Many times a group will serve more than one of these functions and may, at times, simultaneously fulfill all three. For example, an *a cappella* group may contribute to the cultural richness of society, accrue publicity and status for the group itself, and benefit the individual musicians with financial and aesthetic rewards. In most instances, however, one function will predominate. Of course, each function is intended to satisfy particular needs of both the group as a whole and also each of its members. Each function, therefore, has particular effects on the nature of communication within the group. Although there are many specific purposes a group may serve, we will focus on the primary function that small groups normally serve—problem solving and decision making.

Many groups function to identify and solve problems, as well as to make decisions. These functions are really two parts of a single, continuous process. Problem solving involves discovering previously unknown alternatives or solutions, whereas decision making involves choosing between two or more solutions. The problem-solving process generates the substance upon which decisions are based. For example, a community restoration group may study all the possible causes for the problems involved in restoring and maintaining an historic building to identify which problems will create the most difficulty in getting the project completed. This is problem solving. The choice of which problem to address first and how it should be addressed is decision making. Sometimes only the first part of the process is necessary; uncovering the causes of the problem may reveal that the project will be impossible to finish. Generally, identifying problems and making optimal decisions requires that groups alternate between the processes of both problem solving and decision making.

Problem solving and decision making address rather obvious individual, group, and societal needs. People and institutions continually face questions that need answers, problems that need solutions, and conflicts that need resolution. Often a group effort is the most efficient, creative, and satisfying way to meet these needs. For example, upon the invasion of Kuwait by Saddam Hussein's military forces, the heads of member countries of the United Nations gathered to develop the best strategies for mounting an international effort to force Iraqi troops from the small, independent country. The group developed strategies consistent with the needs of the United Nations' policies in a more productive way than any one leader could have accomplished.

This greater productivity of group effort is called the *assembly effect bonus*. If a group's product is greater than the combined product of the same number of people working alone, the extra product is the bonus. Take, for example, the task of listing uses for brown paper bags. One would not expect an immense bonus of creativity to burst forth during this particular challenge. But, in fact, if five people working alone came up with a total of 80 uses, the same five people working in a group might generate a list of 200 uses, and the chances are that their list would not only be longer but also more creative. One member might mention seeing paper bags used as masks by players in a children's theater in San Francisco and that might remind a second member that a paper bag over the head can stop hiccups. This might lead a third member to free-associate to other uses, such as, degreasing chicken stock. The spontaneity, creativity, and diversity of small-group interaction make it an excellent tool for problem solving and decision making.

Stages in Problem Solving and Decision Making. The movement from problem solving to decision making does not occur in one single, swift jump. In his theory of reflective thinking, John Dewey (1910) suggested that rational thinking involves six phases. These stages have traditionally been regarded as the most logical and orderly process for individual or group problem solving and decision making. The first phase is recognition of a difficulty: The individual or group feels or experiences a difficulty or dissatisfaction. In Phase 2, the person or group defines, clarifies, and isolates the exact nature and cause of the problem. Once the problem is identified, in the third phase the individual or group generates possible solutions for the difficulty or dissatisfaction. In Phase 4, possible solutions are suggested and rationally explored vis-à-vis a list of criteria. After adequately studying the possibilities, the individual or group enters Phase 5 in which the optimum solution is decided upon and implemented. In the sixth and final stage, the consequences of the solution are evaluated, and if the solution is rejected, the process is repeated.

Research into group problem solving and decision making has shown that at least three stages, roughly corresponding to those of Dewey, occur (Bales & Strodtbeach, 1951). During the orientation (first) stage, members ask for and exchange information. In the second stage, they then classify, confirm, and repeat the information among themselves. In this evaluation stage, group members seek out and discuss their opinions, analyses, and personal feelings concerning the problem. In the third phase, known as the control stage, members ask for and exchange suggestions, directions, solutions, and possible plans for action.

From Dewey's work and that of his followers, a standard agenda has evolved that is a commonly used order for analyzing problems in groups and can be adapted to any problem-solving situation. The agenda approach requires the group to define at the outset the exact nature of the problem it is confronting. Usually, the group begins by stating the problem as an open-ended, unbiased policy question such as, "Should our student organization attempt to raise funds to help the homeless?" If the question were worded, "How can our student organization raise funds to help the homeless?" the discussion would be biased by the untested assumption that the homeless can be helped with monies raised by the group. Similarly, the question, "Should the homeless be given money?" builds in a bias, allowing an either-or answer with no possibility for exploring other policies, such as helping shelters that house the homeless but not giving money through federal agencies. Either-or questions close off the generation of alternatives rather than encouraging a unconstrained discussion.

Standard Agenda

I. Definition of the problem
   A. Definition of terms
   B. Definition of scope
II. Analysis of the problem
   A. History and causes
   B. Effects and extent
III. Criteria for solutions
   A. Generation of criteria
   B. Ordering of criteria according to priority
IV. Possible solutions
   A. Generation of possible solutions
   B. Evaluation according to criteria
V. Selection of the optimum solution
VI. Plan for action

Once a group has clearly stated its problem, it must define all terms in the question and any other terms likely to turn up in discussion. This step is needed so that group members do not hold widely varying assumptions about what the terms mean. For example, in our helping-the-homeless example, does "fund-raising" mean soliciting money or asking for donations to an event? Does "homeless" refer only to those who stand on street corners begging for money, or does it include those who work at odd jobs but do not have a legal residence? While the group is defining terms, the scope of the problem must be narrowed to manageable proportions. The question, "What should be done to care for the homeless?" would include too many divergent subjects to allow an orderly discussion. We maintain that a more efficient strategy for a group solving of complex problems is to break them down into separate issues that can be discussed one at a time.

Before a group attempts to analyze a problem, it must gather enough relevant information so that it can discuss fully the causes and effects of the problem and its past and present extent. A decision based on inadequate or irrelevant information is not better, and may be even worse, than no decision at all. Furthermore, uninformed people tend to cling to one position instead of being neutral, resulting in conflict and nonconstructive discussion.

Once the problem has been analyzed as completely as possible, the group moves into a stage that is crucial to decision making: the development of criteria, or standards, for evaluating possible solutions. These criteria might be based on such factors as time, money and other resources, ethical and value judgments, and any other considerations that the group feels are important. In developing criteria for the proposed fund-raisers one group might decide that any fund-raising effort must be able to be accomplished during a single weekend, it must not deplete the current funds of the organization, and it must not take place off the campus grounds. Another group might choose different criteria in which the use of current organization funds is not objectionable, any project must take as long as necessary to accumulate sufficient funds to make a significant impact, and the project must be located wherever there is the greatest potential to attract customers. The group must then weigh the importance of each criterion and decide which ones have priority. In this way, alternatives that meet different criteria can be compared according to how they rank in priority.

After the criteria have been chosen and ordered, all the possible alternatives are explored. Each is evaluated according to how well it meets the criteria. Benefits are compared to costs and disadvantages. If no proposed solutions satisfy the criteria, the group must look for more solutions or revise its criteria. The solution or combination of solutions that best meets the criteria is chosen. Thus the first group in the fund-raising example might choose to allow the project to take place off campus. The second group, using different criteria, might decide against an unlimited duration of the project and, instead, call for the project to take place over three consecutive weekends.

In the last stage of decision making, group members must determine the best way to implement the proposal. The group must decide what resources are needed, who will take responsibility for putting the plan into action, when it will begin, and so on. Once the plan has been implemented, its effects must be observed and evaluated. If it is a success, with few undesirable side effects, the process is complete. If the plan is not working, however, the group must revert to earlier stages of the problem-solving process: reanalyzing the problem, generating new criteria or solutions, or finding new ways to implement the original solution. Long-range plans generally require continued observation and revision.

The agenda outlined above has been advocated by many as the most effective, but there are many other strategies for solving problems and making decisions. Certain strategies enable the group to discuss potential solutions to problems in a nonjudgmental environment. One such strategy, generally labeled *brainstorming*, allows group members to communicate their ideas to each other without the fear of public scrutiny. Whichever method is used by a group when attempting to solve problems and when making decisions, the most important goal is to manage the information in such a way that it increases the chances of coming to the best decision. As we will now discuss, technology has greatly increased the chances of meeting this goal of a decision-making group.

Group Support Systems

It would be an understatement to say that technology is changing the way people communicate and exchange information. From personal computers such as those that many of you own to the super-computer networks that can exchange dizzying amounts of information, the ever increasing use of computers has had, and will continue to have, a significant influence on communication behavior. Group Support Systems (GSS) is a newly developing strategy utilized in group decision making. GSS research is conducted under such names as Group Decision Support Systems, Electronic Meeting Systems, Computer-Supported Collaborative Work, Computer-Mediated Communication Systems, and Group Negotiation Support

Systems (Jessup & Valacich, 1993). Whatever the term, GSS-type systems refer to any computer-based information systems used to support intellectual collaborative work (Jessup & Valacich, 1993). It should be stated here that all computer systems designed for decision-making purposes are intended to *assist* people in the process and are extensions of personal computers, word processors, and the like used for individual purposes (Poole & DeSanctis, 1990). Computers are not intended to make the decision for the group, only to help manage ideas and information so that the best decision can be made in the most expedient manner.

GSS are computer-supported group-meeting systems that attempt to make groups more productive by applying information technology. These systems, and others similar to them, are designed to impact and change the behavior of groups directly to increase their productivity. As a pioneering group in this area, the University of Arizona Research Program developed the Electronic Meeting Systems (EMS) framework using a combination of same-time/same-place and different-time/different-place computer networks. For instance, through the use of computers, decision-making groups are able to meet at the same time in the same location, or meet at the same time while members are located in different parts of the country; and now different parts of the world. An amazing new development in same-time/different-place is what is called the "mirror-room," where the visual images of group members are created on mirrors so that not only can a person listen to other group members from anywhere in the world, but can also see their expressions while each in turn are able to see the others in identical environments.

Before we discuss the various impacts that GSS can have on group meetings, it is important for those of you without exposure to these systems to understand the physical nature of most meetings rooms and the common sequence of using GSS-type technology.

Physical Nature of GSS

Most GSS meeting rooms use a network of microcomputer workstations to facilitate communication between group members. The Electronic Meeting System (EMS), for example, uses a two-tiered legislative style semicircle in which group members can work at their own station yet be electronically connected to other members (see Figure 8.1). At the front of the GSS room are large-screen video displays that are visually accessible to all members. These projection screens can be used to display ideas that the group has generated, information on how the group voted on an issue, photographic slides, or a videotape. In addition to the availability of computer terminals and projection screens there are two electronic white boards at the front of the room, and a host of other aids such as gated microphones at each workstation, a videodisc player, and overhead projectors are available to assist in the group meeting process.

Common Sequence of Using EMS

As in most group encounters, the members either choose someone to lead and direct the discussion, or a "leader" emerges. When using EMS, a meeting facilitator generally works with a group leader to develop an agenda and select the support tools to be used during the meeting. An integral aspect of the agenda is the formulation of a question devised to generate ideas and proposals. For example, "How can we reorganize our shipping department to cut down on delays?" or "What areas of the organization can we afford to reduce to remain within our projected budget?" are questions that induce members to start initiating ideas. The question proposed will naturally focus on the type of task the group is engendered to perform.

It is at this point that members begin typing their comments on their individual computer terminal. All individual comments are then integrated and displayed on the projection screens, without the names of the particular individuals associated with the contribution. In this way, participants are able to react and comment on the suggestions without bias and ideas can be evaluated on their own merit. Ideas can be organized by key issues with short clarifying statements included in the display. After the facilitator and the group leader decide that there are enough ideas generated to accomplish the task, the group then prioritizes the list individually and rankings are displayed on the projection screens. These steps can be repeated as many times as necessary.

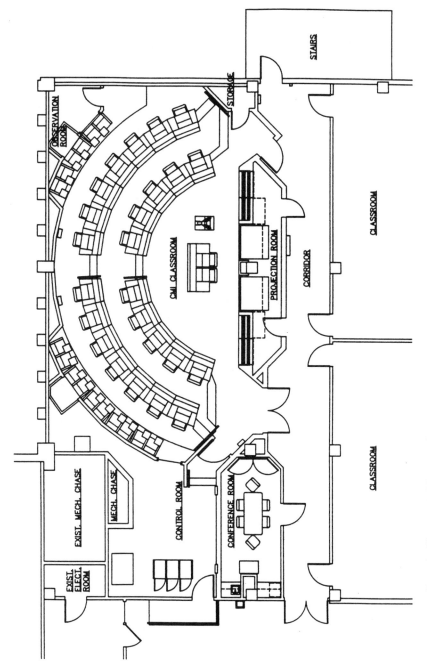

Figure 8.1. Sample Electronic Meeting System Layout

259

Levels of Support

As stated previously, computer systems such as the GSS and EMS are *support* systems. The computer does not (as of yet) come up with the ideal solution to a problem or make decisions for the group. Generally, final decisions are not made at the meeting, but later by the senior members after careful consideration of the information. GSS allows flexibility for the group members as well as the facilitator. Depending upon the needs of the group, three levels of computer support are commonly used. The chauffeured process occurs when one person enters the information that is discussed by the group into a computer terminal. The information is reordered by the computer and the results are projected onto the large screen as a type of group memory. Because the primary mode of communication is face-to-face, the chauffeured process offers the least technological support to members. The supported process increases support through members who use their own computer terminals to enter comments electronically, although face-to-face communication is still allowed at this level of support. The level at which the most electronic support is furnished is through the interactive process. Similar to the support level in which individuals have their own computer terminals, group memory is accessible through individual workstations. This level differs markedly from the previous two because only electronic communication is permitted. As will be discussed later in this chapter, the anonymity at this level can have a significant impact on the group decision-making process.

Group Characteristics

Of course, computer-based systems are not a "techno-cure" for all the ills of group meetings. To estimate how effective GSS will be in group decision making, it is important to view the interaction between group processes and characteristics of groups that effect those processes. There are four primary factors that not only affect group processes but also vary from situation to situation: group, task, context, and technology (Nunamaker, Dennis, Valacich, Vogel, & George, 1993). *Group characteristics* include the size of the group, how physically close the group members are to each other, who is in the group (i.e., peers or "power players"), and the cohesiveness of the members. *Task characteristics* include the type of activity the group needs to perform. As we stated earlier in this chapter, group tasks can vary from making decisions to simply gathering information. Each type of task will, in some way, influence the dynamics of group processes. *Context characteristics*, such as the culture of the group, the time pressures the members are under to finish their task, and who will receive rewards or punishments depending upon the outcome, can influence group processes. *Technology characteristics* refer to the type of GSS components the group uses. If the outcome of the meeting is member satisfaction, certain GSS components will be more useful than if the outcome is efficiency. Each of these characteristics interacts with group processes to impact the effectiveness of GSS.

Group Processes and GSS

All of us have, at some time, been a member of a group involved in either making a decision, accumulating information, or generating plans. As we can attest, certain aspects of what happens in the group process improve the outcomes: We can consider these factors the "gains" of a group process. Members are able to supply more information than any one member could alone. Groups can catch bad ideas and evaluate them more objectively than the individual proposing the idea. Working in groups is generally stimulating and people can potentially learn from skilled members of a group. However, the list of group process "losses" (aspects that impair outcomes) is a bit longer than the list of "gains." Some group process losses include the trouble of allocating time to all members, and only having one member speaking at a time. In the latter example, people waiting to talk may lose their ideas. For a number of reasons, some group members forget the information discussed, while others are more interested in socializing than focusing on the task. Especially powerful members can unduly influence other members and dominate the group's time. And there is always the problem of "slackers" or "free-riders"—those people who rely on others to accomplish the group's goals. This is definitely not an exhaustive list of the gains and losses of group processes; however, the balance of these factors can be affected by GSS.

GSS is a means to deliver support to the task and process of decision making, as well as promoting effective task and process structure. GSS provides task structure by improving the performance of individual decision makers through improving group performance and reducing the losses of inadequate information analysis. Because GSS has the capacity to generate ideas anonymously, it can increase the gains of learning from other members and increase the potential for objective evaluation of ideas, while diminishing losses due to conformance pressure and evaluation apprehension. Unfortunately, anonymity can also lead to an increase in free-riding, as well as the airing of ad hominem attacks on others (Brashers, Adkins, & Meyers, in press).

GSS produces support for the task by reducing process losses from the incomplete use of information and deficient task analysis. GSS allows members to retrieve information from previous meetings that is already computed and make it accessible to all members. Synergy (members using information in ways that are different from each other) is promoted by providing information to the group without adding additional structure. Losses due to memory failure, information overload, and inattentiveness can be decreased by using GSS.

Process structure (rules that direct the patterns or content of communication) is enhanced through the use of GSS. Agendas can be followed more easily by reducing the chance of incoordination problems. The group losses associated with talk-time are eliminated by producing all messages to the group when they are recorded. Certain GSS require individuals to produce ideas separately before sharing ideas, decreasing incidences of free-riding and blocking. The impact of GSS on process structure has been shown to be specific to the type of system incorporated into the group process (Hirokawa & Pace, 1983).

Finally, an important means by which GSS provides process support is through parallel communication. Because each member has her or his own workstation connected to all other workstations, members can communicate simultaneously without a loss of "air time." Talkative members cannot monopolize the meeting and those

more interested in socializing have no avenue to engage in that behavior. Because GSS allows for parallel communication, increases in
information overload may occur in which members have a difficult
time synthesizing the potential multitude of information presented.

In sum, computer-supported group decision making has many
potential benefits for increasing effective communication. The ability
to participate simultaneously overcomes the pressure of talking in
a group or becoming lost in conversations. GSS also provides an
equal opportunity for participants to contribute to discussions due
to anonymity. Anonymity all but eliminates evaluation apprehension and helps overcome the constraints of social context cues (i.e.,
normative history, status cues, intimacy levels). Anonymity also distri-
butes influence more evenly than face-to-face encounters and regu-
lates the influence of power. Finally, GSS provides various avenues
to reach a decision, from idea generation to prioritizing ideas and
voting procedures (Brashers et al., in press). Given the attractiveness and diversity of computer technology designed to assist individuals and groups in a variety of tasks, GSS technologies will
continue to modify significantly the productivity of meetings as
well as transform the communication processes of group work
(Dennis & Gallupe, 1993).

Choosing Among Alternatives

As we stated earlier in this chapter, seldom are any of us given
the opportunity to make decisions, whether alone or in a group, in the
most rational way possible. We may know the "standard agenda"
and be familiar with the latest in technological advances to support
our decision-making process. We may know the most efficient
communication strategies to use in influencing others and have
gathered all the relevant information available. But in the end, the
"best" choice must be made. The question then remains, "How do
people go about choosing among various alternatives?" Janis and
Mann (1977) shed light on finding an answer to this question by examining the ways in which people, groups, organizations, and countries
typically choose among alternatives. By understanding the ways we
choose among alternatives, it will be possible to then choose the

most appropriate communication strategies that correspond to the factors that influence our decision making.

Optimizing Strategies

Janis (1972) frames the methods by which we decide among alternatives as "strategies." A strategy can be considered a plan of action or a method devised through practice. There are two major strategies that people employ when choosing among alternatives. The first is called an *optimizing strategy*, whereby a choice is made, or a course of action is taken, that will result in the "highest" outcome. When employing an optimizing strategy an actor (person, country, group, etc.) goes through a system of weighing alternatives based on a cost/reward ratio. Our earlier example of choosing among alternative majors for your college career is typical of an optimizing strategy. This strategy assumes that we have the capacity to be rational actors. Needless to say, rarely are optimizing strategies used by individuals when making decisions. Return to our discussion of Simon's (1957) concept of bounded rationality. We have a limited capacity to process information. Making the "optimal" choice would entail processing vast amounts of information in order to maximize our decisions. Compounding this problem is the tremendous amount of time involved in accumulating and then synthesizing the information necessary to make the decision. Information overload is likely to occur by looking at all possible alternatives. According to Miller (1952) humans are capable of processing only seven pieces of information simultaneously, plus or minus two. This limit in our capacity to process information forces us to "chunk" information into manageable groups. Optimizing strategies also present high costs in terms of effort and money.

Suboptimizing Strategies

It is reasonable to conclude that most of us do not use optimizing strategies when making decisions. Janis and Mann (1977) argue that actors usually use a *suboptimizing strategy* that maximizes some aspect of the gains involved at the expense of others. This type of "give and take" is common in organizations in which most decisions are suboptimal. It is important to point out that suboptimal strategies are not unsatisfactory methods of choosing among alternatives, nor will these types of strategies always result in poor decisions. Given the costs involved in optimal strategies, suboptimal strategies are useful and productive means by which to choose among alternatives.

There are five general types of suboptimizing strategies that actors employ. The first is termed *satisficing strategies* (Simon, 1976). When using a satisficing strategy, an actor seeks a course of action (i.e., chooses an alternative solution) that is "good enough" or at least meets a minimal set of requirements. Confronted with a situation in which a choice must be made, people often work under a loose set of criteria whereby the choice can be deemed workable. For example, when looking for an apartment, potential roommates may simply want to live close to school in a place that they can afford. In choosing among all the available housing, the first apartment that meets these requirements is the chosen alternative: It is "good enough." If the minimal set of criteria used to make the decision is equal to the choice being made (i.e., just a place to sleep) then this type of strategy is in its own way effective. However, choosing the first alternative that comes along can have devastating effects if the stakes are choosing a new product line or even choosing a college.

The second type of suboptimizing strategy is called *quasi-satisficing*. Making decisions using this strategy entails deciding on a course of action based on a single moral precept. Occasionally there will be reports in the media of someone acting in an heroic manner by racing into a burning building to rescue someone, or diving into icy water to save someone who is drowning. Indeed, entire prime-time television programs are now devoted entirely to these types of behaviors. These people, and many like them, probably used a quasi-satisficing strategy when they acted this way. In times of trouble, people tend to act on instinct without weighing alternative courses of action. No assumption of satisfying a minimal set of criteria is used; the decision is the "best" or the "only appropriate" decision that could be made. The greater the felt responsibility, the more apt an actor is to use a single moral imperative when taking a course of action. Often, the choice involved really is not a "choice," but the only moral action to take. Considering alternatives would be immoral. This type of suboptimal strategy, although at times immediately beneficial, can result in socially inappropriate actions. If an actor is guided by a set of socially unsuitable mores, actions taken can be evaluated as morally objectionable by certain segments of society.

Elimination of aspects is a strategy that uses a combination of decision rules and applies them to a problem in order to select easily from alternatives that meet the criteria (Tversky, 1972). The elimination usually begins with the most valued requirement. Each alternative is compared against this criterion, until one is left. This type of sub-optimizing strategy was used by one of the authors when deciding on what new car to buy. The most valued requirement for this decision was sporty looks, followed by cost (affordable), immediate acquisition, and, finally, fuel economy. After obtaining information on a group of cars that met the first requirement (sporty looks), the process of elimination began. As most of you know, the criteria of sporty looks and affordability are generally at odds. All alternatives were eliminated by the second requirement, forcing the reordering of requirements and the addition of others. This is a common drawback when using this strategy. The opposite predicament also occurs—depleting aspects before finding one alternative. In this case, it is necessary to introduce another aspect to narrow the alternatives. This assumes that alternatives that are retained are better in all ways than the ones eliminated. For instance, if one alternative is eliminated on the basis of the second aspect, it is not available to be evaluated on the other aspects. This strategy of rank ordering requirements can have its downfalls, but this is perhaps the most psychologically realistic of the suboptimizing strategies. Actors can usually come up with realistic criteria by which to evaluate given alternatives, and actors are generally cognitively able to separate the value of the requirements.

Incrementalism or "muddling through" is a type of decision-making strategy wherein a succession of small satisficing strategies lead to the chosen alternative. Muddling through usually occurs in large companies and in government (Lindblom, 1980). Decisions that need to be made in these organizations are often made to assure or retain the status quo. In this way, no major changes or decisions are made that might disrupt the flow of the organization. Incrementalism is geared toward "putting out fires," not changing the entire situation.

Usually this strategy is based on a consensus or agreement upon ideas, rather than on the values of the issue.

Let us return to our example of choosing a major while attending college. If you did not use an optimizing strategy to decide on your major area of study, perhaps this scenario is more familiar. You start your college career as either an "undecided" or in an area that sounded interesting at the time. You "decide" to enroll in courses that fit the general requirements of the college or university. After a semester or two (or three) you accumulate so many hours that you need to choose a major. You assess the courses that you have taken (and passed) and find a major that "fits best" with what you have already chosen. You continue taking classes in this major. On the off chance that you are one of the few students who becomes disenchanted with this choice and change your major more than once, the process of finding another one that "fits" the courses you have already taken begins again. If you were lucky enough to be at this juncture early in the process, you have one or two more opportunities to change and "decide" on a different major. Those who change late in their academic career find themselves majoring in an area that seems to fit what they did during college. This is an example of choosing a major through incrementalism. Each small satisficing action did not deviate very far from the previous decision and the accumulation of a series of "muddling through" strategies results in the situation you are now in. Let us be quick to point out that this is not an indication that choosing a major in this way is bad or ineffective. On the contrary, many great careers, relationships, and companies began in just this fashion. The point is that incrementalism is another means by which we choose among alternatives, the worth of which rests in the type of decisions that must be made, and often the reflection upon the consequences of the decision.

Finally, *mixed scanning* is a combination of both optimizing and suboptimizing strategies making use of the benefits of incrementalism (Etzioni, 1986). In mixed scanning, the major choices are made through some type of conscious weighing of alternatives (e.g., optimizing, elimination of aspects) to set the direction of change. After the primary course is set, the smaller decisions and problems are worked out through an incremental process. You may have heard two people in an intimate relationship say to each other, "Let's just get married. We can always work out the little problems later." Although at least one of the authors of this text wonders whether any marital problem can be termed "little," choosing among alternatives in this manner is an example of mixed scanning. Organizations may find this a reasonable method of making decisions, relying upon the members to "put out fires" as they come along.

The Process of Decision Making

It should be evident by now that the process of decision making is complicated by a number of factors, many of which are difficult for one individual to manage. The final portion of this chapter will address the factors that require close attention if the decision-making process is to be as effective as possible. As stated previously, attending to these factors does not guarantee that optimal decisions will be made, but in light of all the problems that can (and do) arise when attempting to make a decision, not confronting these issues will decrease the likelihood of making the best choice.

Factors That Influence Effective Decision Making

Effective decision making requires close attention to several factors. Individuals engaged in a group decision-making process must realize that they now constitute a distinct entity and no longer have the luxury of trying to satisfy their own needs. Primary among these factors is recognition by all members of the *exact purpose* or goals of the group. Although a group may meet regularly to solve some problem, many of the individual members may have differing interpretations as to the goals of the group or how a decision should be made. A group concerned with increasing an awareness of the threat of contracting the HIV virus might attempt to educate the public regarding sex-role behavior. This purpose will not be accomplished if some of the members interpret the goal as simply placating members of the gay faction, whereas other members focus on establishing concern by the larger heterosexual community. Recognition of common goals not only increases the chances of meeting the goal, but it also generates *group identity,* another factor for effective group participation. A sense of group identity helps insure relevant and pertinent discussion regarding any goal the group chooses. Relevant discussion is also closely related to *well-defined roles* for individual group members. Of particular importance is the leadership role because this role exerts influence on the communication transactions in such a way as to promote pertinent discussion. Lack of effective leadership can significantly impede discussion attempts. A final consideration of effective group decision making is that every member must have an accurate understanding of the *specific communication situation.* For group discussions of ideas and positions to be effective, each member must know when to speak and when to listen. In addition, each member must accept the communications of others as discussion, not as final opinions or solutions.

Individual members must subordinate their goals for the accomplishment of the *group goal.* First, the importance of having every member of the group recognize and accept the group goal or purpose cannot be overemphasized. Second, the group must be in possession of all available *facts and evidence* relating to a specific topic if they are to solve a problem in that content area. Moreover, inputs from various group members must be weighed against the relative credibility and expertise attributed to a particular group member. In other words, group members must defer to superior knowledge or experience of another member when appropriate. Third, the group must employ a *systematic thought process* for any joint discussion. Some individuals seem to display a marked absence of cognitive structure or common sense. Decision making and problem solving, in particular, must be approached in a logical and systematic fashion. Systematic thinking will prevent a social group from gathering at the park on Sunday afternoon with no provisions for softball equipment or a business meeting from taking place with portfolios missing for half the members. The fourth component is *group structure.* Group structure (e.g., size, communication networks, and group interaction) will mediate the nature and quality of discussion within decision-making groups. Fifth, individuals attempting to make an effective decision must adhere to a common *perceptual framework.* This means that communications between members must have a common frame of reference in that each member must ascribe the same meanings to the communication. *Leadership,* the sixth component, is vital to insuring equality of participation, quality outcomes, and group harmony. We will discuss this dimension in more detail in a later section of this chapter.

Obstacles to Effective Group Decision Making

In Chapter 4 we discussed some common obstacles to effective communication. In so doing, we defined the selectivity processes as selective exposure, attention, perception, and retention of communication stimuli. As in other communication contexts, the *selectivity processes* are a source of frustration to effective decision-making processes. These processes prohibit individuals from acquiring the necessary communication to relate to others, to approach problems in an organized and systematic fashion, and to recognize the exact nature of the group's purpose. On the basis of selective exposure, individuals may support other members and their proposals simply because their attitudes or values are consonant rather than evaluating their ideas on their own merits. Similarly, less attention may be paid to information that is inconsistent with an individual's views on a particular matter. Although these two processes may or may not be conscious, selectivity of perceptions and retention are out of the control of the individual. Effective discussion or problem solving rarely takes place when group members perceive fundamental issues differently or have forgotten crucial bits of information. These selectivity processes are unavoidable in all forms of face-to-face interaction. As we have noted previously in this chapter, they can be compensated for by a climate of openness, honesty, and tolerance, or the adoption of the appropriate Group Support System.

Another obstacle to effective group discussion is provided by *blockers,* or individuals who talk too much, talk too little, or engage in defensive behavior. Individuals who talk too much and too frequently not only block group goals, but also provide a source of frustration and exasperation for the other members who are attempting to formulate a decision. The individual who talks too little can deprive the group of a valuable source of potential information, as well as take up space that could be used by a more active contributor. If the group members continue to ignore such a recalcitrant participant, he or she surely will persist in withdrawing from the group and become a free-rider. In addition, such an individual might discourage other members from participating by generating a climate of nonparticipation. A supportive climate within the group, gentle coaxing, or posing direct questions at this individual could provide the necessary catalyst for involvement.

Group participants may engage in defensive behavior under certain circumstances. The presence of an extremely aggressive and dynamic individual can threaten the rest of the members in such a way that they will defend every contribution or idea to gain comparable prestige. Directly attacking the ideas or opinions of another in a sarcastic or insulting manner, even when these opinions have marginal utility, will surely create a defensive air. In a similar vein, defensive behavior usually results when personalities enter into a discussion. Care must be taken to acknowledge the logic of an individual's contribution without projecting the ideas as part of their personality.

The *hidden agenda* is another source of frustration to effective group decision making. A hidden agenda exists when the group goal or the goals of one or more of the individual members differs from the stated purpose of the group. It is not uncommon for individuals to join certain groups solely to meet other people. These individuals will direct more energy toward cultivating social relationships than to accomplishing group goals or tasks. Hidden agendas often lead to behaviors and patterns of interaction that are detrimental to the group's purpose.

Another obstacle involves the distinction between *ideal* and *practical solutions*. Group problem solving and decision making may focus on the "ideal" resolution to a problem that is far too complex and difficult for solution. Instead of concentrating on discussions that may result in some practical outcomes, individuals attempt to do the impossible. These efforts can waste time, create tension and conflict, and result in nonproductive consequences. Group interaction is characterized by a *tendency toward conformity*, which has an obvious impact on the effectiveness of discussion. People have been shown to conform in judgments about the lengths of lines even when individual perceptions differed significantly from the consensus opinion (Asch, 1951). This tendency toward conformity also operates in other areas, such as stated opinions or discussions. Many people will agree to anything if they become tired, bored, or frustrated enough. It is also not uncommon for individuals to conform when they are disinterested in the agenda or feel inadequate concerning their abilities to contribute to the group.

Effective discussion will also be impeded when individuals react to others using *stereotypes and traditions.* Forming impressions of others using stereotypes may be a useful cognitive misering devise; however, if individuals rely solely on stereotypical indices of others, a distorted view of ideas (either positively or negatively) may result. Methods, procedures, and ideas that were relevant and cogent in the past may not be operable any longer. Utilizing these outmoded concepts may create undue conflict and render group decision making ineffective.

These are the obstacles most common to the disruption of effective decision-making processes. Of course, there are many potential obstacles that might impede group discussion and decision making in any given situation. Recognition of these obstacles is a necessary first step in evaluating the effectiveness of group discussions. Unfortunately, group discussion does not always have positive consequences, and as most of us can attest, there are both advantages and disadvantages to the small-group discussion context when making decisions.

Costs and Benefits of Group Decision Making

Research has shown that discussion techniques have a number of advantages and disadvantages that accrue from using a group to make decisions. These considerations will not apply in situations in which the ultimate authority of the group lies with one individual and the rest of the group members are excluded from discussions where group policy or action is decided.

One of the advantages of group decision making is that *quality outcomes* are likely to result. Research has demonstrated that group decisions through discussion are frequently superior to those of individuals working alone because of the interaction and corrective feedback among members working conjointly (Thompson, 1967). The assumption here is that the group members possess sufficient expertise to render a viable solution and produce informative and constructive communication. Another advantage is that *acceptance* of ideas and procedures is more likely when group discussion precedes some outcome. Again, research has demonstrated that decisions made by subordinate group members will experience greater acceptance simply because they played an integral part in the decision-making process (Martin, 1968). Group members will also be *more committed* to the group task and to the implementation of some negotiated decision when they have been directly involved in analyzing problems and selecting solutions through discussion. Another positive aspect of group discussion techniques is the potential for *increased status*. Some scholars maintain that the responsibility and interaction involved in group decision making engenders a sense of status and recognition for the participants (Martin, 1968). This is roughly akin to the pride and accomplishment one feels when one has contributed something to the accomplishment of a goal. These positive consequences of group discussion may be offset by the structure of the specific group under consideration, however.

As we discussed previously, one of the most basic costs involved with group discussion is *time expenditure*. The voicing of many opinions or recommendations for action can take a great deal of time. If the purpose of the group is vocational or recreational in nature, this is no problem. If a problem is to be solved or a decision to be made, however, an inordinate amount of time can be spent on matters that might just as easily be handled by one individual, especially if this individual is in a power position. Group discussion will also require advance preparation in some cases. This is additional time expended. The time factor must be evaluated in terms of group outcome or the quality of a decision. Monetary expenditure is another potential factor closely related to time expenditures. If the discussion is scheduled during school or working hours, participants will have to leave their classroom or jobs, representing a monetary loss of some sort. Decision making by groups also frequently necessitates having various materials readily available for the group. *Conformity* is an additional cost to group decision making.

A final cost of group discussion is *groupthink*. Irving Janis (1972) analyzed a set of important government decisions on foreign policy and found that long-standing, cohesive groups tend to arrive at decisions in a characteristic way, which he termed *groupthink*. This small-group phenomenon will affect the communication patterns of the group, and any group discussion that meets the criteria set forth by Janis is likely to be affected by groupthink. Janis has compiled a list of symptoms of the groupthink syndrome:

1. An illusion of invulnerability, shared by most or all members, that creates excessive optimism and encourages taking extreme risks.
2. Collective efforts to rationalize to discount warnings that lead other members to reconsider their assumptions before they recommit themselves to their last policy decisions.
3. An unquestioned belief in the group's inherent morality, inclining the members to ignore the ethical or moral consequences of their decisions.
4. Stereotyped views of enemy leaders as too evil to warrant genuine attempts to negotiate or as too weak or stupid to counter whatever risky attempts are made to defeat their purposes.
5. Direct pressure on any member who expresses strong arguments against any of the group's stereotypes, illusions, or commitments, making clear that this type of dissent is contrary to what is expected of all loyal members.
6. Self-censorship of deviations from apparent group consensus, reflecting each member's inclination to minimize to him- or herself the importance of personal doubts and counterarguments.
7. A shared illusion of unanimity concerning judgments conforming to the majority view (partly resulting from self-censorship of deviations, augmented by the false assumption that silence means consent).
8. The emergence of self-appointed mindguards—members who protect the group from adverse information that might shatter their complacency about the effectiveness and the morality of their decisions.

Summary

1. Due to a limit capacity to process large amounts of information, we run the risk of making less than optimal decisions. Communication strategies can be evoked that facilitate more effective decision making.

2. Small groups are particularly adept at problem solving and decision making. Small-group interaction seems to produce an assembly effect bonus; that is, the group's product is greater than the

combined product of the same number of individuals working individually. The reflective thinking theory suggests that there are six steps in problem solving and decision making: recognizing the difficulty, defining and clarifying the problem, developing criteria for resolution, suggesting solutions, selecting the optimum solution, and implementing the plan.

3. Effective decision making in small groups requires that all members recognize the exact purpose of the group, all have well-defined roles, there is a group identity, and there is a common knowledge of the specific communication situation. In addition, members must subordinate personal goals for the group goal, have all the facts and evidence available and employ systematic thought processes, work from a common perceptual framework, and have effective leadership.

4. Rapidly evolving technologies have created new methods for facilitating group decision-making processes. A variety of electronically mediated group support systems have been developed to impact and change directly the behavior of groups to increase their productivity. This is accomplished by utilizing an electronic meeting systems framework, combining same-time/same-place and different-time/different-place computer networks.

5. Due to information processing limitations, most individuals must rely on suboptimizing, rather than optimizing, strategies (which utilize all available information) when choosing among outcome alternatives. Suboptimizing strategies maximize some aspects of the gains involved at the expense of others. These strategies include: satisficing, quasi-satisficing, elimination of aspects, incrementalism, and mixed scanning strategies.

6. Selectivity, hidden agendas, conformity, interpersonal conflict, and the use of ideal solutions, stereotypes and traditions, and improper logic are all factors that impede effective decision making.

7. Group discussion may result in positive outcomes such as quality output, more acceptance of ideas or procedures, more commitment by group members, or increased status for individual members. Negative consequences, however, such as time and monetary expenditures, risky decisions, and groupthink (the tendency for long-standing, cohesive groups to arrive at decisions in a characteristic way) may result from small-group decision making.

References

Asch, S. E. (1951). Effects of group pressure upon the modification and distortion of judgements. In H. Guetzkow (Ed.), *Groups, leadership, and men* (pp. 171-190). Pittsburgh, PA: Carnegie Press.

Bales, R., & Strodtbeach, F. (1951). Phases in group problem solving. *The Journal of Abnormal and Social Psychology, 46*, 485-495.

Brashers, D., Adkins, M., & Meyers, R. A. (in press). Argumentation in computer-mediated decision-making. In L. Frey (Ed.), *Communication in context: Studies of naturalistic groups.* Hillsdale, NJ: Lawrence Erlbaum.

Dennis, A. R., & Gallupe, R. B. (1993). A history of group support systems empirical research: Lessons learned and future directions. In L. M. Jessup & J. S. Valacich (Eds.), *Group support systems* (pp. 59-76). New York: Macmillan.

Dewey, J. (1910). *How we think.* New York: Basic Books.

Etzioni, A. (1986). Mixed scanning revisited. *Public Administration Review, 46,* 8-14.

Hirokawa, R. Y., & Pace, R. C. (1983). A descriptive investigation of the possible communication-based reasons for effective and ineffective group decision-making. *Communication Monographs, 50,* 363-379.

Janis, I. L. (1972). *Victims of groupthink.* Boston: Houghton-Mifflin.

Janis, I. L., & Mann, L. (1977). *Decision-making.* New York: Free Press.

Jessup, L. M., & Valacich, J. S. (1993). On the study of group support systems: An introduction to group support system research and development. In L. M. Jessup & J. S. Valacich (Eds.), *Group support systems* (pp. 3-7). New York: Macmillan.

Lindblom, C. E. (1980). *The policy-making process* (2nd ed.). Englewood Cliffs, NJ: Prentice Hall.

March, J. G. (1990). Bounded rationality, ambiguity, and the engineering of choice. In J. G. March (Ed.), *Decisions and organizations* (pp. 266-293). Cambridge, MA: Basil Blackwell.

Martin, H. (1968). Communication settings. In H. Martin & K. Anderson (Eds.), *Speech communication: Analysis and readings* (pp. 70-74). Boston: Allyn & Bacon.

Miller, G. A. (1952) The magical number seven plus or minus two: Some limits on our capacity for information processing. *Psychological Review, 63,* 81-97.

Nunamaker, J. F., Dennis, A. R., Valacich, J. S., Vogel, D. R., & George, J. F. (1993). Group support systems research: Experience from the lab and field. In L. M. Jessup & J. S. Valacich (Eds.), *Group support systems* (pp. 123-145). New York: Macmillan.

Poole, M. S., & DeSanctis, G. (1990). Understanding the use of group decision support systems: Adaptive structuration theory. In J. Fulk & C. Steinfield (Eds.), *Organizational communication technology* (pp. 173-193). Newbury Park, CA: Sage.

Simon, H. A. (1957). *Models of man.* New York: John Wiley.

Simon, H. A. (1976). *Administrative behavior: A study of decision-making processes in administrative organizations* (3rd ed.). New York: Free Press.

Thompson, W. (1967). *Quantitative research in public address and communication.* New York: Random House.

Tversky, A. (1972). Elimination by aspects: A theory of choice. *Psychological Review, 79,* 281-299.

9

Relational Communication

In previous chapters we have been concerned with how people communicate to influence others and bring about changes in attitudes and/or behaviors. In Chapter 8, we focused primarily on how actors structure the decision-making process, on factors that facilitate that process, and on factors that may inhibit effective decision making. Also, we focused our concerns on how the content of communication can be structured and manipulated to insure that the outcome of a communication transaction has increased compliance on the part of the receiver, or how the content of communication can increase the possibility of arriving at an "optimal" decision. The focus of this chapter is somewhat different. We will turn our attention now to how communication is used to establish, maintain, and dissolve relationships. People communicate their feelings about other people and about the communication that is occurring through many methods. Earlier we discussed the use of nonverbal communication as a system of meta-messages about what was going on in the verbal channels and as relational communication expressing feelings about the other people involved in the communication transaction. This chapter is an attempt to systematically investigate the reasons why people communicate on relational levels and how people go about managing social relationships, and also to discuss the possible positive outcomes of communication that are effective in establishing and maintaining satisfactory relationships with others.

It is probably wise to begin this chapter by explicitly outlining some of our assumptions about the relational communication process. First, we do not believe that a true dichotomy exists between relational communication and content communication. It is inconceivable to us that any message can be either content or relational in nature. When your roommate reminds you of your household duties by saying, "You forgot to do the dishes last night!" it is clear to you that not only does your roommate want you to do the dishes, but that he or she is angry at you. What aspects of the message carry the most importance for your relationship with your roommate? Doing the dishes because they need to be done, or the feeling that your roommate thinks you are irresponsible? Although some portions of our communication are more content oriented than others in that we are trying simply to transmit information or to convince people of the validity of our position, we still include a great deal of relational cues as to how we feel about our intended receivers and about the messages we are producing.

A second assumption that others make that we do not accept is that relational communication typically occurs in dyadic communication, but rarely in any other context. Whether in the interpersonal context or in front of a television camera, we are providing relational information that others will put to use. Although it is true that we spend a great deal of time and exert much energy in our efforts to establish and maintain effective interpersonal relationships, the use of communication to develop social relationships is not limited to this context. In small-group communication, in public-speaking situations, as well as through mediated channels, the relational aspects of our communication efforts are as critical to our success at communicating effectively as the content of the messages themselves.

We also believe that people have a need to affiliate with others and that they desire to communicate with others in such a way as to express their feelings toward them appropriately. Later in this chapter we will discuss in greater detail several different reasons that have been advanced as to why people possess this need to affiliate. We further assume that much relational communication is done so that others will see us as we see ourselves or as we would like ourselves to be seen. We also believe that people desire to be liked by other people. Communication that promotes these types of feelings is gratifying and most people desire to understand more fully the process that leads to effective relational communication.

Our last assumption is consistent with the general thrust of this book. Just as people employ strategies to produce change, make effective decisions, or manage conflict, they also strategically communicate to promote more effective social relationships with others. In the next section we will discuss some of the ways communication can be used to define relationships between people.

Interpersonal Orientations

It is useful to analyze communication within relationships from several different perspectives. As we mentioned earlier, content is always being communicated. We express our feelings about ideas, objects, and issues. We desire people to believe as we believe, and we attempt to share information. We also communicate in ways designed to determine the beliefs of the other person in the relationship. We also tend to seek information about the other person's perceptions and beliefs about ourselves and our ideas (Laing, Phillipson, & Lee, 1966).

The content approach can be used to determine if people in a relationship agree or disagree on the topic being discussed. Many times communication is designed to share with the other person what our beliefs and attitudes are on a range of issues. People evaluate issues and ideas differently, and this difference can range from very slight to very great. For example, two people might want to determine how the other feels about recently proposed environmental laws. Their first task is assessment of agreement (see Figure 9.1).

The feelings that each person has about the topic of communication is called the *direct perspective*. Much communication, especially

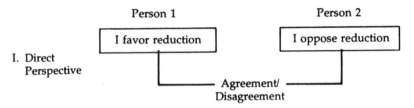

Figure 9.1. Assessing Agreement in a Dyad

in initial stages of interaction, is aimed at determining what direct perspective each participant holds on a range of issues. People assess the degree to which agreement and disagreement are present and often plan communication strategies aimed at changing the other person's perspective.

The belief approach is aimed at assessing understanding and misunderstanding in the relationship. It adds the metaperspective, which is our perception of what the other person feels or believes about the content of communication (see Figure 9.2).

In this example we have disagreement on the direct perspective: Persons 1 and 2 do not have similar beliefs. However, this is a case of both understanding and misunderstanding being present in the dyad. He misunderstands her position on the need for stricter environmental laws. His metaperspective is not at all consistent with her direct perspective; but, her metaperspective is consistent with his direct perspective. In other words, she understands him on this issue. As you can see, there can either be understanding or misunderstanding regardless of whether people agree or disagree on issues. It could be ruinous to the relationship to ignore this important level of analysis in relational communication. If Person 1 assumes he is correct about the attitudes of the second person, he will, of course, commit errors. One common error is to assume that we know a great deal about other people's attitudes, opinions, and beliefs. There is also a tendency for us to believe that people we know are more similar to us than they really are (Byrne & Blaylock, 1963; Sunnafrank, 1985). The person wishing to be more effective in relational communication will strive to assess just what the other person thinks and feels. Moreover, one should remember that it is important to attempt to gain understanding, even if one is not in agreement with the direct

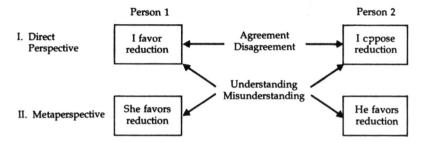

Figure 9.2. Assessment of Agreement/Disagreement

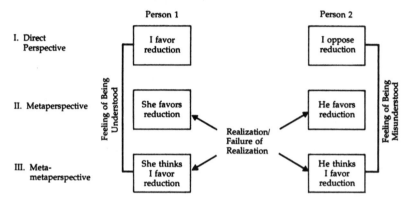

Figure 9.3. Assessing Realization or Failure of Realization

perspective of the other person. Misunderstanding of the other's position may lead to problems.

The third approach, perceptions and beliefs about ourselves and our ideas, is concerned with realization or failure of realization. This approach is concerned with an analysis of what you think the other person thinks you think.

In Figure 9.3, there is both a realization and a failure of realization depicted. In this case, Person 1 should have a feeling of being understood (realization). Person 2's situation is different in that she has evidence that Person 1 does not understand her direct perspective (failure of realization). Person 1 opposes stricter environmental laws, and it is his belief that Person 2 thinks he favors stricter laws. Therefore, his meta-metaperspective is consistent with his direct perspective. It is likely that he feels satisfied that at least he has communicated effectively enough so that she understands what he believes.

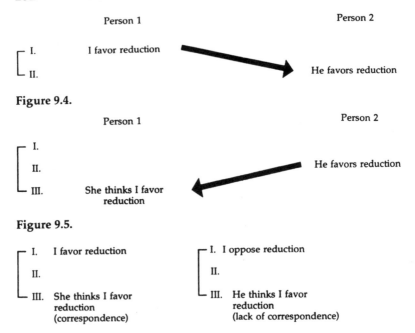

Figure 9.4.

Figure 9.5.

Figure 9.6.

Person 2 cannot help but feel misunderstood, and she is likely to be frustrated with this communication transaction. She actually favors stricter environmental laws, but he thinks she is opposed to stricter environmental laws. If they have spent time communicating and this occurs, she is likely to be dissatisfied with this communication outcome. Perhaps it would help to summarize what happens in terms of understanding at each level.

- *Understanding.* Understanding happens when the metaperspective of one person corresponds to the direct perspective of the other individual. This happens when a person correctly identifies your beliefs (see Figure 9.4).
- *Being Understood.* Being understood occurs when the meta-metaperspective of one individual is the same as the metaperspective of the other person. Person 1 understands what Person 2 thinks (see Figure 9.5).
- *The Feeling of Being Understood.* One has the feeling of being understood when one's own meta-metaperspective corresponds to his or her own metaperspective (see Figure 9.6).

There is some satisfaction involved in feeling that one understands another person and in feeling that one has been understood (Laing et al., 1966; Sunnafrank, 1985). When there is a lack of correspondence between perspectives within a relationship, communication strategies are likely to be used to gain understanding. As we have said, people will make great efforts to assure agreements at the first level. There are times, however, when people just agree to disagree. This probably occurs when we clearly understand the position of other people and accept that it is not likely that we will be able to change their position.

It is interesting to pose the question of whether people prefer to understand or be understood. As we have pointed out, there are two very separate outcomes of dyadic communication. People who are constantly trying to make themselves understood often come away from a communication transaction with little understanding of the other person. Often we also assume that people do not understand us, when in fact they disagree with us. We have had students who were unhappy with their grades come and argue forcefully for a change in our evaluation. After listening to their appeal, we have often felt that we just could not agree with their position. More than once, students have responded that we just did not understand. Actually, we did understand rather clearly the case that was being advanced. However, students can be so involved with being understood that they fail to understand what we were saying in response. There is a difference between agreeing and disagreeing, understanding and being understood.

Clearly, some people may not understand each other or care enough to expend much effort in reaching understanding. People also have more understanding concerning some issues than others. It is possible, as in the example we used, for one person to have a great deal of understanding whereas the other one completely misunderstands everything that is happening.

This model of analysis can be valuable for locating communication problems between two people. It can suggest the proper level of perspective on which to center attention, and it can locate sources of understanding. Perhaps it would be useful to suggest some questions that can be asked about relational communication.

1. Do we agree or disagree on the content of what we are talking about?
2. Are we going to adopt a communication strategy that attempts to produce agreement, or are we going to agree to disagree?
3. Do I understand your position? How sure am I that I understand? What am I basing this on?
4. Do you understand how I feel about the issue? What have you done to indicate understanding or misunderstanding?
5. Is my communication strategy designed to make sure that I am being understood, or am I investing as much energy in understanding?
6. Do you believe that I understand you?

The answers to these questions must dictate communication strategy. There is little use in stressing agreement/disagreement if lack of understanding is the problem. You can use feedback to indicate that you do not understand the other person, or you can come right to the point and suggest to the other person that you do not believe that you are being understood. Directing the communication to the proper level can lead to correspondence between levels of understanding.

Fundamental Dimensions of Relational Communication

Interpersonal Control in Relationships

Control of the situation in relational communication is always an issue. Communication will be developed to establish rules of control, and this will affect all the behavior of the participants in relational communication. In any situation, there should be no question of whether control exists or not. The appropriate questions are, Who is in control? Under what conditions? In most relationships, people develop patterns of interaction that help answer those questions. We will discuss three such types of relationships: complementary, symmetrical, and parallel.

Complementary Relationships. The earliest work in relational communication can be traced to Gregory Bateson's (1935) research among Iatmul tribesmen in New Guinea. Bateson focused on the degree of equality between people involved in relationships. Those relationships in which partners emphasized differences between themselves were termed *complementary*. Typically, complementary relationships are characterized as those in which one partner dominates or attempts to gain control of the relationship and the other submits or accepts a submissive role. The behavior of one must be mutually complementary to the other. When one partner attempts to initiate plans, the other person is accepting. Many, if not most, superior/subordinate relationships are complementary. For example, the parent/child relationship is complementary in that to be a parent, a person needs a child. The parent and the child are mutually complementary, and one usually initiates action and is in charge. This is also the case in some marital relationships, with one spouse in charge and the other willing to follow. The partner in the dominant role assumes the superior, primary, or "one-up" position. The other spouse, then, is in a subordinate, secondary, or "one-down" position. In this type of relationship messages differ and are often in opposition. Those individuals who find this type of relational arrangement satisfactory give some measure of credence to the adage that "opposites attract."

Complementary relationships may sound very undesirable and may lead us to reject this kind of communication pattern prematurely. However, complementary relationships are not necessarily dysfunctional. Individuals whose relationship exhibits this type of arrangement often experience harmony, and coordination of activities is often easier. The person in the submissive position often learns a great deal by listening to the dominant person and doing what that person says. This is especially true if the dominant person has control based upon expert power. In these types of relationships, we would probably not desire to be on an equal basis with the person possessing expertise. For example, it is usually the case that our relationships with our doctors are complementary. It would be inappropriate, and potentially risky to our health, to assert our equality to our physician. For obvious reasons we (usually) willingly follow orders and do what the doctor prescribes. The bases of power that we discussed earlier in the book all provide ample reasons why people accept complementary relationships. The power to reward or punish, expertise, and many other factors combine in ways that make us willing followers at times. We also accept complementary relationships because they can be efficient. Often times it just is not worth hassling about the power to control; it is easier to do what is expected.

The marriage situation is an interesting arena to investigate complementary relationships. Some would suggest that traditional values would hold that the man is the master of the house, sets agendas, makes important decisions, and controls activities. The woman is seen as submissive, and she reacts rather than makes suggestions. However, some very interesting research has turned up intriguing findings. In one study (Millar, 1973), only about 25% of the couples reported complementary relationships with the man being dominant. More than 50% of the couples reported reversing the traditional concept, with the woman being dominant. The women in these relationships controlled most conversations, whereas the men tended to smooth over rough spots. Millar's findings suggest that dominating husband/submissive wife relationships may be a myth that needs to be dispelled. During the 1990s, the traditional values may be changing even more dramatically. As ever-increasing numbers of women occupy positions of authority and high status in the work place it stands to reason that women's roles within relationships will continue to change. Conversely, with more men taking on the roles traditionally held by women, relational expectations based on "traditional values" will no doubt be continually reevaluated. How these role expectations will be manifested is unclear. Suffice it to say that we anticipate that the roles of men and women in relationships will continue to evolve in new and dramatic ways.

Although complementary relationships are appealing to many men and women in relationships because they are efficient and free from the hassles associated with each of the partners jockeying for control in any given situation, they are not without their problems. When the same person is always in control, there is a real danger that the relationship will become stagnant. When one person is always dominant, the other does not grow and develop new competencies. Also, the dominant person usually feels that he or she must provide protection in exchange for compliance (Mills, 1967). People tend to become resentful of doing things when they perceive they have no choice. Actually, both people can get trapped into roles that they do not want to occupy. If anything happens to the relationship, the people involved may be unable to function independently. A person used to being dominated totally may have little ability to make decisions.

Symmetrical Relationships. Symmetrical relationships are based upon the notion of equality. In symmetrical relationships, both partners believe that they have an equal right to define the relationship. Both individuals assume that they are free to exercise control, and that the options available to one are also available to the other. In a symmetrical relationship, the differences between the participants are minimized (Watzlawick, Beavin-Bavelas, & Jackson, 1967).

Most of us would probably assert that symmetrical relationships are very desirable. In our culture we often pay homage to the notion of equality, and many of us prefer not to think of our relationships in terms of control, dominance, and submission. The question of dominance, however, is not necessarily settled even when both people agree that their relationship is symmetrical. In this case, the communication between the two relational partners might become very competitive. Therefore, dominance does not become an ignored issue; the relational partners are simply competing for it. We have all been involved in conversations in which one participant will mention something that he or she has done only to have the other person immediately come back with a report of an equally (or more) impressive accomplishment. These kinds of communication patterns rigidly attempting to maintain equality and to resist dominance by one person can easily escalate into real conflict in the relationship.

Although one might think that symmetrical relationships in which both people agree on the right of equal control would be stable and enduring, the opposite is often the case. These types of relationships are frequently unstable because every issue and decision has to be negotiated. Problems are likely to erupt if one person cannot take an action without negotiating the right to take that action. In a marriage, problems that threaten the relationship often occur over each spouse's demand for equality. To negotiate who has the right to do what, to whom, and how often in every instance is tedious and demands great amounts of patience.

As you can see, symmetrical relationships are just not workable in many contexts. The inefficiency associated with negotiating every action could easily cripple co-workers. One probably would not want to discuss every action with a partner. When the objective of the pair is some sort of efficient productivity, a completely symmetrical relationship will probably prove unsatisfactory.

In an earlier section of this chapter, we discussed the seeking of understanding and attempts to be understood. The symmetrical relationship is one in which understanding may be inhibited. Much of the communication activity is not centered on the understanding process. Neither person is really concerned with interpreting what the other is saying. Little effort is directed either at understanding the direct perspective or in assessing metaperspectives. We tend to look at how the other person is viewing our equality and not what is being understood. Communication is persistently aimed at defining status, and hostility is frequent. When two people with large egos communicate, attempts to maintain symmetry are assured. When Mark Twain first met the painter James Whistler, Twain approached one of Whistler's paintings in progress and nearly touched it with his gloved hand. Whistler exclaimed, "For the love of God, be careful! You don't seem to realize that the paint is fresh." "That's all right," responded Twain, "I have my gloves on." Symmetry was maintained.

We have now addressed some of the difficulties associated with both complementary and symmetrical relationships. Perhaps one solution to these problems would be to consider roles that are neither rigidly symmetrical nor complementary.

Parallel Relationships. A pattern of communication that might prove satisfactory in a variety of encounters has been labeled parallelism (Lederer & Jackson, 1968). Instead of holding to rigidly symmetrical roles that can promote competition and/or hostility, or instead of relying solely on complementary relationships that produce stagnation and inhibit growth, people can develop a more flexible style.

A parallel relationship allows each participant to have some areas of control, and each person plays the dominant or one-up role at times and then plays the submissive or one-down role at other times. In certain kinds of decisions, they can agree to equality and concede that each has the right to control, suggest, and direct. There is actually a cross-over of complementary and symmetrical roles. This kind of relationship often occurs in informal relationships in which frequent topic shifts lead to different people taking control. In many cases, the nature of the topic and the degree of agreement or disagreement will determine who controls the communication at any given time. Even though there is a pattern of interchangeable relationships, there can be areas in which people concede the right to determine direction mutually, and the communication can instantly become symmetrical.

In more enduring relationships such as marriage, friendship, and family dyads, this pattern can be very workable. A husband and wife may concede different areas of control based on different areas of competence. They may also agree to rotate tasks that neither particularly enjoys. They then form a series of complementary decision-making units. They can still agree that they must be symmetrical when it comes to major decisions, however, such as taking a new job or moving to a new location. Communication is not based upon the need to do things in the same way "because we have always done it way." The flexible pattern allows change and can prevent some of the problems we discussed earlier with rigidly complementary relationships.

The parallel structure also allows relational partners to avoid the constant competition associated with rigidly symmetrical roles. Free from the need to "win" on every issue, partners can accept that understanding and negotiation can be as important to the long-run health of the relationship as anything else. There is a tendency in parallel relationships for partners to avoid all-or-nothing statements or absolute demands. However, this does not mean that each person must be totally flexible. Each person must still define limits of what is tolerable but do so in a way that is not threatening to the other. There is usually a great deal of emphasis placed on meta-perspectives. It is incumbent on each person to understand the feelings of the other person because those feelings become the basis for negotiating appropriate behaviors. When the power structure of each individual is equivalent and when the association is voluntary, a parallel relationship is likely to be beneficial.

Relational "Topoi"

After reading the last section on different patterns of interaction within relationships, you might argue that this three-dimensional model is overly simplistic and fails to capture the variety of communication exchanges that occur over time within a given relationship, especially the ones in which you are involved. In response to traditional models that conceptualize relational communication as operating along two or three dimensions, Judee K. Burgoon and Jerald L. Hale (1987) offer an elaborated view of relational message "themes" based on an analysis of a variety of literature from anthropological and psychotherapeutic studies, nonverbal biological or intraspecific displays to investigations of semantic meaning and research on interpersonal evaluations. The authors offer a fundamental *topoi*, or source of information, about seven general themes with which relational communication can be evaluated.

Although these relational themes are interrelated to some extent, each is a distinct indicator of the status of a relationship. Along a *dominance-submission*, or *control*, continuum, communication signals the degree to which a relational partner is dominant, persuasive, aggressive, controlling, and ingratiating and reflects the degree of equality or inequality within the relationship. Obviously, both the things we say and how we say them communicate to others our desire to either control or yield control of an interaction. Our ability to select message strategies that clearly and unambiguously signal our intentions maximizes the likelihood of achieving a desired outcome.

Within the emotional *arousal*, or *activation*, dimension, verbal and nonverbal messages indicate the extent to which another's presence is stimulating and arousing. Although it is usually not difficult to communicate how much we enjoy and are stimulated by the presence of another person and that we desire an interaction to continue, it is often the case that we suffer severe relational consequences by our failure to control or at least mask our disinterest in what another feels, thinks, or says. From our perspective, effective communicators are aware that a variety of cues signal others that what they are communicating is important and interesting and is being attended to carefully.

Messages also signify how much *composure,* or *self-control,* an individual manifests while engaged in relational interactions. One's rate of speech, number of nonfluencies, and amount of gaze aversion are all measures of how poised, relaxed, calm, tense, or nervous one is while communicating with another and, for obvious reasons, will have a profound affect on how a relationship develops and is maintained. This is not to suggest that signaling that one has total control over one's behavior is always the preferred state of affairs. It is often the case that a lack of composure indicates that the outcome of an interaction is important to us! This seems to be especially true in our initial interactions with people to whom we are attracted. For example, when we first ask someone on a date, it is considered appropriate to display nervousness and uncertainty in our communication efforts. To do otherwise might indicate that we care little about the outcome of our request or that we are not all that interested in the other person. Displaying a modicum of anxiety, apprehension, or excitement will likely communicate to the target of our message that our desire for further interaction is genuine and important to us.

Relational communication can also be analyzed in terms of *formality or informality*—the extent to which interactants make their exchanges casual and informal or proper and formal. This aspect of relational communication is, perhaps, the most important in the initial stages of relational development. It is often the case that relationships begin on a "sour note" when the expected degree of formality is violated by one individual or another. The impact of this violation of normative expectations is especially true in settings in which formal roles are prescribed. For example, in many academic institutions it is expected that new graduate students will address professors formally—"Good morning, Professor (Doctor) Smith" rather than with the informal "Good morning, Debbie." The relational consequences of this type of violation of an implicit academic "courtesy" could range from mild to severe. In either case, failure to consider this dimension of relational communication will impact initial and subsequent interaction with others. Obviously, in this type of scenario, it is wise to err on the side of formality, allowing the other to define the relationship in more informal terms as the relationship develops.

Relationships differ in the degree to which they exhibit a *task* versus *social orientation*. Within this dimension, the things we communicate signify the degree to which each of the interactants is task oriented or interested in the social aspect of the relationship. Extending the issue of formality/informality, more formalized communication patterns strongly indicate that the purpose of the relationship is tied to specific goals or tasks to which individuals may or may not be committed. Conversely, as communication patterns develop along more informal lines, interactants may be attempting to express that the social aspect of the relationship is weighted more heavily than the task component. Managing this aspect of communication can be extremely problematic for individuals committed to both task and social dimensions of a relationship. We often engage in a careful balancing act trying to facilitate goal attainment while simultaneously managing important personal ties.

Along with control and trust, the final dimension of relational communication has long been considered one of three primary components to any relationship: *level of intimacy* (Millar & Rogers, 1987). In Burgoon and Hale's (1987) relational topoi, intimacy is composed of the following sub-themes, each of which independently affects the overall degree of intimacy experienced within a relationship. First, our communication with others differs in the amount of *affection or hostility* it conveys. Second, the degree to which we signal *inclusion or exclusion* is a function of relational intimacy. The *intensity of involvement* in a relationship is a third variable that influences how intimate our relationship is with another person. A fourth component of intimacy, which is clearly tied to communication, is the aspect of *depth versus superficiality*. The topics we discuss and the degree of disclosure about those topics is a clear indication of how intimate we intend to allow a relationship to become. The last relational sub-theme is *trust*. Of all the dimensions of intimacy, none has received more attention than trust. Slow to evolve and easily violated, the trust we have of another with whom we have an intimate relationship may be the most reliable indicator of whether or not that relationship will develop and be maintained over time. Generally speaking, trust is a measure of the degree to which individuals communicate about aspects of themselves that are not intended to be revealed to others. In addition to individuals sharing their hopes, dreams, and desires, trusting relationships are typically those in which we share our fears, guilt, shame, and anxieties. Clearly, most of us do not engage in this type of intimate communication unless we believe that this information about ourselves will be treated as private and exclusive and, perhaps most important, will never be used against us by the other person.

Burgoon and Hale's (1987) typology of relational communication themes has provided communication scholars with an expanded model with which to explore a wide variety of communication phenomena. Although space limitations preclude a fully expanded review of research spawned by the topoi, suffice it to say that studies of relationship development, communication competence, and relational communication within the therapeutic setting are a few of the areas that have been enriched by application of this more comprehensive approach to fundamental dimensions of relational communication.

In the next section, we discuss some of the important variables that are known to affect both how people relate to each other and what kinds of communication will occur between them. When some of these important variables are present in any communication transaction, the probability of developing effective social relationships is markedly increased.

Factors That Promote the Establishment of Social Relationships

Liking and disliking are among the most basic factors in determining whether people will even communicate with each other, and if they do communicate, what the outcomes of that interaction will be. People associate with others on the basis of these feelings, and although there is no doubt that these feelings affect communication patterns, it has been widely believed that such feelings are fundamentally irrational. Indeed, they often seem that way, as in the case of two friends who seem to have nothing in common except for the fact that they "feel good" around each other.

People have developed methods, however, to measure interpersonal attraction, and it is more patterned than one might first suppose. The sociometric test is one such way to test interpersonal attraction. It was devised to determine the preferences of group members for other people in the group by establishing procedures for indicating amount of liking for others. Moreover, this method allows criteria for choices of "most liked" people to be established. For example, in a company, each worker might be asked to choose people with whom he or she might like to work on a project. These choices might be unlimited in number, or the worker might be asked to pick the first three choices in order of preference, or the entire work group might be ranked from most desired to least acceptable. The criterion of preference might vary; the worker may be told to make a selection on the basis of workability, which is called *task attraction*, simple *social attraction, physical attraction*, or any other basis. When the data are analyzed, one gains information about the individuals most frequently chosen and those not chosen at all, and one also gets a picture of patterns of attraction in the organization. If everyone picks the same person as a first choice, it obviously indicates that this person is a key member of the group and is attractive to the others for some reason. Likewise, four or five people may all choose each other, indicating that they belong to a mutually attractive subgroup or clique.

There are other available means for the measurement of interpersonal attraction. For example, nonverbal researchers have found that eye contact, changes in the size of the eye's pupil, and the distance between two standing persons have all been used to measure interpersonal attraction. These attempts to measure attraction have provided valuable evidence that we are attracted to people in some understandable and systematic way; liking is not *just* an irrational, affective response. However, our concern is broader than just assessing attraction when it occurs. We want to understand why people find some people attractive and, therefore, desire to continue to communicate with them and yet find other people not worth the effort communication requires. With that goal in mind, we turn our attention to some of the variables involved in the interpersonal attraction process.

Rewards as a Determinant of Attraction

As we suggested in an earlier chapter, traditional learning theory suggests that proper applications of rewards can produce many kinds of behavioral change. It would not be too presumptuous to claim that persons generally like others who provide rewards and dislike people who provide punishment and/or withhold desired rewards. These rewards can range from material inducements to social approval, but we are likely to continue communication with those people who provide some reward for us. However, there is much more to the relationship between reward and attraction than the commonsense notions just discussed might suggest.

To be the recipient of increased liking *or* disliking, a person need not be the one who is giving the rewards to other people. There is evidence to suggest that merely being present when a reward is provided to another person is sufficient to prompt the receiver of the reward to be more favorable toward you (Lott & Lott, 1960). Your mere presence when someone is being punished or having rewards withheld, however, may be enough to trigger a dislike for you by the person being punished. In a study that tested the above assumptions, three children were placed in a situation in which they were asked to play a board game independently of others in the room. If a child safely landed a rocket ship in the game, a reward was given to that child. The other children had nothing to do with the success or failure of the player, and they were not involved in providing the reward. Children who succeeded liked the other two children more than did children who failed. Many of us have been in situations in which we generally liked people who were present in a rewarding situation, even though they had nothing to do with making the situation more rewarding. There is something that is probably more important to this discussion of interpersonal attraction. We have likely had people respond in a liking or disliking manner to us simply because they were receiving rewards or punishments at the time. The point is that although we can reward people and increase their liking for us or punish them and diminish their positive regard, we also will find ourselves in situations in which our attractiveness to other people will be determined by the rewarding and/or coercive power of others who are in control of the situation.

There may be other situational factors not associated with other people directly rewarding people with whom we would desire to develop a sensing of liking. For example, variables such as people's personal comfort can lead them to *judgments about us even if we have absolutely nothing to do with their levels of comfort.* People placed in an uncomfortably hot room rated strangers in a much more negative way than did people who were placed in a comfortably cool room (Griffitt & Veitch, 1971). Furthermore, people who perceive their discomfort to be the greatest are the most likely to rate people as unattractive.

Related to these kinds of judgments is the fact that moods can be induced that alter people's perceptions of other people's attractiveness. In an interesting study, subjects were asked to watch either a movie that was funny and meant to produce positive feelings or a movie that was sad and meant to produce depression. Following the movie, each subject was asked to rate a person on attractiveness. As expected, those people who watched the movie that produced positive feelings rated the individual as more attractive (Gouaux, 1971). Not only can positive mood states increase the perceived attractiveness of another person, they may also lessen an individual's initial negative impression toward a person. In other words, changes in moods can make unattractive people appear more attractive. In one study, people either witnessed a person deliver an insult to others or else were themselves insulted by this person. After this insult was delivered, half of the people looked at some humorous cartoons, but the other half did not. Those people who had been induced to change their moods by use of humor rated the initially unattractive source as more attractive than did people who had not received the humorous intervention (Landy & Mettee, 1971). A hostile encounter had been altered by humor. We have witnessed many people who play this role of tension reliever through humor very well in communication transactions.

Social Exchange Perspectives

Underlying much of the relationship between rewards and attraction is the concept of equity. Relationships that are perceived as equitable are more attractive than those that are unfair. *Equity* is defined as an individual's ratio of costs to rewards compared to the partner's ratio. This "economic" view of relationships may appear cold or calculating, but most of us can remember being in a relationship in which one person was giving up time, money, gifts, emotions (inputs) and not receiving comparable rewards (outcomes) in return. If the ratio of costs to rewards is equivalent to the partner's cost/reward ratio, equity exists. The greater the discrepancies between ratios, the more perceived inequity in the relationship. Equity Theory (Walster, Walster, & Berscheid, 1978) argues that people in relationships try to maximize their outcomes and minimize their costs. Equitable relationships result in increased attraction. The more equitable the relationship, the greater the propensity for both partners to work to maintain the relationship and the less the distress that will be experienced. Conversely, the greater the perceived inequity, the more likely the disadvantaged partner will look for alternatives, such as other people with whom to exchange resources (Thibaut & Kelly, 1959). As inequity increases, perceived attractive decreases and the less likely it is for the disadvantaged partner to remain in the relationship. Just as distress decreases within equitable relationships, it will increase in inequitable ones, leading the disadvantaged partner to reduce the distress. This can generally be accomplished by an actual change in the input to the relationship (i.e., give less to the partner) or by a psychological change (i.e., reevaluate the cost/reward ratio to regain equity). Most of us find our partner attractive if he or she make attempts to assure that the relationship is equitable. Over time, equitable relationships lead to deepening degrees of intimacy and liking.

Similarity and Attraction

Although it may be true in the world of physics that opposites attract, it is generally not the case when it comes to people in social relationships. Aristotle long ago suggested that we choose those people as friends "who have come to regard the same things as good and the same things as evil" (McKeon, 1947, p. 103). There is contemporary research that clearly supports this conception of the role of similarity and attraction.

Byrne (1971) attempted to discover why people like or dislike each other. He concluded that the principle of reinforcement explained most of the variation in interpersonal attraction. Using Reinforcement Theory, Byrne focused on the component of similarity in attitudes as being the greatest predictor of whether people would like each other. A great amount of research supports the concept that people who believe that others are similar to themselves are attracted to them (Byrne, 1971; Sunnafrank, 1985), are more likely to be persuaded by them (Berscheid, 1966), and communicate more with them (Rogers & Bhowmik, 1970). Although this may sound like common sense, the implication is that people only have to believe that they share similar characteristics to be attracted to someone. People can find similarity on a number of dimensions. Berscheid and Walster (1978) identify the six dimensions of similarity: attitude, personality, social characteristics, physical characteristics, intelligence, and education. Similarity also relates to the concept of comfort discussed earlier. The more similarity one perceives with another, the more comfortable and, hence, the more attractive.

There are some other findings that are interesting in terms of how people perceive similarity in others whom they find attractive. Although we have said that people become more accurate at judging others the more they communicate with them, we did not say that they become completely accurate. In fact, when someone is attracted to another person, there is a common perceptual distortion that occurs. People regularly judge people whom they find attractive to be more similar in attitudes and values than they actually are. In other words, we tend to judge our friends as more like us than they really are. This same tendency to overestimate the similarity of attitudes and values exists among married couples. In an interesting study of married couples, it was found that the greater the satisfaction with the marriage, the greater the perceived similarity by the partners (Levinger & Breedlove, 1966).

What all of this says is that similarity can be a potent predictor of who forms satisfactory social relationships with whom. Obviously, we have more to communicate about with people who are similar to us, and as the theories discussed in Chapter 6 suggest, we tend to like people who share our attitudes, or we are in a state of inconsistency that motivates us to change attitudes and/or liking of the person. Moreover, as a result of communicating with people, we tend to become more accurate across a number of issues in judging whether they are similar or dissimilar. When we do become more and more attracted to someone, however, we judge them to be similar to us even though they may not be. In line with this, the more attractive we perceive someone to be, the more similar we also assume that person is to us. It is also probably true that we tend to exaggerate differences between ourselves and those people whom we find unattractive for whatever reason. Once again we have identified a spiral effect for attraction. The more similar I perceive you to be, the more likely that I will also find you attractive; the more attractive I find you, the more similar I will perceive you to be.

Propinquity and Attraction

One obvious, though easily overlooked, variable that determines attraction is propinquity, or nearness. Clearly, it is difficult to like someone unless you know of him or her, and it is difficult to know a person with whom you do not have contact. It follows, then, that the more contact you have with a person, the more opportunity you have to develop liking, and there are good reasons to believe the greater the probability that you will actually grow to like the person. In the first edition of this book, we said that proximity had been called "the almost sufficient condition" for attraction. We also, at least implicitly, indicated agreement with that statement. Well, we have learned something in the past several years and would say at this time that although proximity is an important determinant of liking, it can also be an important agent in promoting dislike. It is obviously important in the formation of attraction.

There is a multitude of research studies to support the notion that people who are close to each other in geographical distance are more likely to become friends or enemies. Reinforcement theory would suggest that people who are in close proximity to each other communicate more with one another and, therefore, have more opportunity to reward or punish each other. Thus we would expect people who communicate more to develop more intense friendships or hatreds. Another perspective predicts more positive outcomes of increased communication. Given the assumption that people are more comfortable with people who are more predictable, we can assume that the more we communicate with people, the more predictable they become to us, and, therefore, we find them more attractive because of that feeling of comfort. We shall first look at the positive effects of proximity on attraction.

Several studies have suggested that there is indeed a direct relationship between proximity and attraction. For example, students who lived together in the same residence halls or apartment buildings or who sat next to each other in classrooms tended to develop stronger friendships than with students from whom they were separated by even small distances (Byrne, 1961; Festinger, 1952). Clerks in a department store reported being more friendly toward people who happened to work next to them than toward others who worked only several feet away (Gullahorn, 1952). There is also evidence to suggest that physical proximity is an important determinant of mate selection (Katz & Hill, 1958).

In line with these findings were the results of studies of married couples living in apartment buildings in a new housing project. Friendships were found to increase in proportion to the degree of geographical proximity: Couples who were next-door neighbors developed friendships with much greater frequency than did people who were separated by one or more apartments.

Even more interesting, in our opinion, was the effect of architectural design. For example, those couples who inhabited the few apartments that faced the street reported half as many friends in the apartment complex as those people residing in apartments that faced the courtyard (Festinger, Schacter, & Busk, 1950). Less prominent architectural features such as the position of stairways and mailboxes also had an effect on friendship formation; if residents lived near the stairways—and thus the major flow of traffic through the apartment complex—or if their mailboxes were clustered with those of other residents, they generally developed a greater number of friendships. It is both a bit frightening and surprising to note how the interaction patterns of people can be virtually planned by such decisions.

People who are in close proximity have more opportunities to interact and more opportunity to reward others. We continue to interact with the people who reward us and avoid the people who punish us *if we can*. Sometimes people continue to interact with others who frequently punish them, however, only because the alternative is to associate with people who punish them even more.

There are many situations, such as in work and living arrangements, in which people have no choice but to interact with people who are in close proximity.

It is usually the case that when people are forced to be in close proximity to others, ways are found to work out amicable relationships; it is certainly in the best interest of everyone concerned. Even when there are important racial, religious, or value differences among people, overcoming of prejudices can be accomplished when proximity makes it clear that it is desirable for all involved to have satisfactory social relationships. For example, people showed less prejudice toward people of different races when they lived in integrated housing, worked together, studied together, or had been forced to interact in a variety of ways. The implications of these findings are apparent and important. Prejudice, a totally unsatisfactory social relationship, is maintained when there is no opportunity for people to share rewards and/or punishments. One way to overcome such maladaptive responses is to provide more possibilities for communication.

In addition to our general preference to be optimistic about the nature of the human being, there are also good reasons to suggest that familiarity is more likely to promote affinity rather than hatred. If an individual is optimistic about the possibility of other people providing rewards, there is more likelihood that the people will also respond in a positive manner. It probably serves no purpose to assume that other people will respond negatively, for there is the danger of that negativity promoting a self-fulfilling prophecy.

There is evidence of a direct relationship between familiarity and liking. People who had interacted several times with other members in a group showed more liking for the other members than did people who had communicated only a few times. It seems that mere exposure to other people can produce more positive feelings of liking. At times, even though the encounters were not totally rewarding, people still tended to like other people when they had the opportunity to communicate more with them. This is best explained by the predictability notion that we advanced in the beginning of this section. As we communicate more with others, they become predictable to us. Even though we may not like the fact that some of their communication behavior is unrewarding or even punishing, if we know more about them, we can probably explain more of their behaviors. When we have had a long history of interaction, we can probably more easily explain negative reactions by saying, "He was just in a bad mood" or "She always reacts to me that way when I am too talkative." In other words, the more we know about a person, the more we can explain their behavior by our understanding of them and of how we affect them.

There are apparent contradictions to the direct relationship among proximity, familiarity, and liking that we must discuss. There are reasons to believe that in many cases, as the distance and/or unfamiliarity between people decreases, attraction decreases. There is considerable evidence to support this hypothesis, implausible as it might seem upon first consideration. For example, police records of a major city in this country reveal that victims in a majority of robbery cases were either related to or acquainted with the thief. It was similarly found that victims of aggravated assault and homicide have lived in close proximity to the perpetrators of the crimes. In fact, almost one third of all murders occurred within the family unit (Berscheid & Walster, 1978). Reconciling these contrary groups of research findings based on proximity may not be an impossible task if we understand the underlying factors involved in them. The closer people live or work together, the greater the opportunity for sharing experiences and gathering information about one another; and it is primarily through interpersonal knowledge that we develop strong sentiments. Also if people are inclined to use coercive power (see Chapter 2), they are most likely to use it on people who are close. We assume that because people will generally recognize that people need each other for a variety of personal reasons, they will utilize their knowledge of one another to promote mutually rewarding communication transactions. But we do not preclude the fact that exploitative needs can be easily satisfied through close proximity with others.

We would like to end this section by discussing some notions that underscore the process of orientation to communication. In any given relationship, people receive a variety of evaluations from a single person over time. Although we have continually pointed out that reinforcement theory would suggest that a recipient of totally positive communication would like the communicator more than would a recipient of uniformly negative communication, there are reasons at least to consider this conclusion. It has been argued that social approval is more valuable when given sparingly and maybe even reluctantly (Homans, 1961). Praise from someone who rarely gives positive feedback should result in more positive notions of self-worth than praise from one who continually hands out flattering comments. A good grade from a tough professor should mean more than one from a known easy grader. Though these things may be true, it does not necessarily increase our attraction toward the person. Although the good grade might be very meaningful from a given professor, it might not raise our self-esteem or in any other way change our attitude that he or she was an irascible individual devoid of reasons to be liked. We believe that the research is not very supportive of the alternative spare-the-praise approach.

Physical Attraction

Textbook writers being ever vigilant of the need not to offend any segment of their potential market have given less attention to physical considerations as a determinant of attraction and, therefore, continued social interaction than this variable probably deserves. Many people resist the notion that we in this culture rely so heavily on physical attributes as the basis of our judgments of people. Simply stated, however, our perceptions of the physical attractiveness of other people are especially important predictors of subsequent communication patterns. This is especially true in the early stages of a relationship when people are making judgments on cultural- or sociological-level data. It is also probably more true in non-interpersonal situations, such as the public-speaking and mass media contexts, in which we have less opportunity to collect psychological-level data. Whatever the context or nature of the relationship, there is ample evidence that perceptions of physical attraction are extremely important.

Physical attraction naturally varies from person to person; one person's Madonna is another's Medusa. Certain cultural-level stereotypes do exist, however, and there is much research that indicates that within a society there are high levels of agreement about those characteristics that constitute physical beauty. From childhood on, one is bombarded with photographs of movie stars, fashion models, brilliant young men and women stepping out of limousines, and other standards of attractiveness. It is difficult to escape this conditioning, especially because it plays such an important role in determining attraction between people. Agreements on physical attraction among people is surprisingly high and reliable. Adult men and women demonstrated great agreement in judging the physical attractiveness of 84 women from photographs (Kopera, Maier, & Johnson, 1971). This agreement on what constitutes beauty has been shown to exist also among different age groups. Although standards of beauty vary from culture to culture, there seems to be adequate cultural-level agreement on the nature of beauty and plainness.

Assuming that we can agree on what constitutes physical attractiveness, the question of how it affects our communication behaviors is of primary concern to us. Although many of us would like to believe that we are above making judgments about the way people look, there is much evidence to suggest that we do just that. As we said, in the early stages of a communication transaction, there is limited information about the new acquaintance. There is a tendency to treat the person as "object" and make an evaluation on the basis of looks. In study after study, people have indicated they were more attracted to physically attractive people than they were to physically unattractive people. We also tend to attribute certain personality and social characteristics to people we find physically attractive. Physically attractive people of both sexes have been judged to be more sexually responsive, kinder, stronger, more sociable, higher in character, and more exciting to be around. We also perceive them as having better job prospects and as more likely to have happy marriages (Dion, Berscheid, & Walster, 1972). Obviously, a lot of inferences are made from limited knowledge.

There may be sex differences that affect how important physical attraction is in developing social relationships. Surveys indicate that men consistently place more importance on physical attractiveness in making dating choices than do women; intelligence is most often mentioned by women as the most important characteristic for dates. Moreover, attractive women report having more dates than do unattractive women whereas there tends to be no difference between the number of dates reported by attractive and unattractive men (Dion et al., 1972). Many explanations might be offered for the preceding data. For one thing, it might be more socially appropriate for men to report that they desire to date only physically attractive women; it supports the image of the "macho" man. It also might be socially appropriate for women not to report that they put a great deal of stock in physical attributes. They might well be responding to decades of conditioning that suggest that such statements are not appropriate in this culture for women. Whatever the reasons, there do seem to be differences between men and women in what *they will admit to as being important* in their judgments of other people.

The possession of culturally defined physical attractiveness obviously has value in interpersonal relations. The physical attributes of those with whom we associate also can affect judgments of our attractiveness and social desirability. In one study a man was seated first next to an attractive woman and then next to an unattractive woman. People were told in one case that the two were romantically linked; in the other instance, people were told that they were not associated with each other. When people believed there was no interpersonal linkage, people's impressions of the man did not change. When the man was romantically linked to the attractive woman, however, he was seen as more socially desirable and more likable. The exact opposite was found when he was linked with the unattractive woman (Sigall & Landy, 1973).

There is no doubt that physical attractiveness can be used as a source of power in social relationships. An attractive person may be the target of ingratiating communication by people who hope to gain a more intimate relationship with the beautiful person. In one instance, men were asked to rate two written essays—one by an unattractive woman, the other by an attractive woman. Half of the subjects in this experiment were given a poorly written piece whereas the other half were given a paper that was high in quality. Estimates of the quality of the essay were the highest when the woman was attractive and lowest when she was unattractive regardless of the actual quality of the writing (Landy & Sigall, 1974). Evidence also suggests that physically attractive people are more influential, especially when the audience is aware of the intent to persuade. People desire to give attractive people what they want, we presume.

Employers are not unaware that physical attraction leads to more positive encounters with strangers, and it is not hard to understand why many employers hire the way they do to fill jobs that require dealing with the public.

It is important to remember that this reliance on physical attributes diminishes as people gather more psychological-level data about people. Although these qualities are extremely important in initial encounters, we personally take some comfort in the fact that they become less important over time. We do not want to diminish their importance too much, however, because the initial phases of any communication transaction are important determinants of whether communication will even continue. Let us conclude by stating that an awareness of the fact that these kinds of judgments are made and that the inferences we draw from them are often error laden might assist us in refusing to be satisfied with just cultural-level data. Even though beauty is only skin deep, there is no reason that our communication relations must remain at that shallow depth.

Phases of Attraction. Interpersonal attraction tends to develop along three identifiable phases (Burgoon, Heston, & McCroskey, 1974). In these phases of attraction, different kinds of data are used to make inferences, and the role of communication is markedly different. In the *phase of initial attraction*, we rely on cultural-level data and often tend to treat people as objects. The physical attributes of other people are often the most important variables in determining attraction. Sociological data are also used, for they are obtained as we make judgments based upon what we know about group memberships. Many of the feelings of interpersonal attraction in this phase precede communication with the others involved. Object properties, such as dress, appearance, personal mannerisms, and known group affiliations, shape our perceptions. As communication occurs over time, we pass from this initial phase of attraction.

In the *intermediate attraction phase*, more data are available to make sociological- and, probably more important, psychological-level data judgments. The initial attraction phase is often transitory, and there are few of us who have not experienced the feelings of strong initial attraction toward another person only to discover later that we really could not tolerate him or her. Although the initial phase of attraction is based upon object properties, the second phase is based primarily on human communication. Greater emphasis is placed upon the social rewards available from the communication relationship. If other people reciprocate our attraction, we derive pleasure from the relationship. We communicate to determine similarities, and we seek to establish mutually beneficial reasons for continuing the relationships. When we do derive these satisfactions and find bases of similarity, we find more to communicate about and can become very dependent on people in the transaction. These kinds of communication encounters are dependent on continued social reinforcement and mandate considerable amounts of positive feedback. We are constantly seeking information about other people and also desire to know just how well we are doing with them.

In *long-term attraction phases,* we develop more stable perceptions of people, and most of our inferences are based on psychological-level data. We react to people because we know them. We know that, as we discover new bases of similarity, we feel more comfortable in the presence of those people. Our communication is less concerned with deriving social reinforcement, we are probably more willing to tolerate negative feedback and idiosyncratic behavior, and we are less uncomfortable during periods of silence or stress. We have more understanding of both how the other people communicate and why they react in certain ways. We also probably have more understanding of our own communication behavior and are less concerned with creating certain images. However, we do not mean to indicate that in this phase attraction will always remain regardless of how we communicate. Even in this phase of a relationship, the communicator must be willing to adapt to changes in the other and be sensitive to the kinds of properties that led to the present social relationship. One must also remember our discussion of level of expectation. A great deal is probably expected of the participants who achieve this level of attraction. There is always the danger that expected levels of caring will not match actual behavior, and attraction, even among close friends, can be diminished. Understanding the variables that determine attraction is a prerequisite for maintaining satisfactory social relationships.

Reduction of Uncertainty

Another factor that leads to the formation of satisfactory social relationships is reduction in the uncertainty level between the participants. Theorists have generally taken the view that we strive to make our behavior and the behavior of others predictable, and we try to develop causal structures that provide some explanation for our behavior and the behavior of others. Berger and Calabrese (1975) have developed an interesting theory concerning initial interactions between people. The central assumption of their theory is that when strangers meet, their primary concern is one of uncertainty reduction or increasing predictability about the behavior of both themselves and others in the interaction. Individuals may be attracted to each other for reasons we discussed earlier in the chapter, and yet be hesitant to initiate preliminary contact because they are uncertain as to how the other person will respond to their advances. Uncertainty as to the outcomes of initial encounters has probably contributed more to chronic loneliness in people than we care to think about.

It is certain that all of us can define specific types of uncertainty that are bothersome to us. Berger and Calabrese's (1975) concept of uncertainty might be useful for identifying this dimension of initial interactions. They discuss uncertainty at two distinct levels. First, at the beginning phase of an interaction, there are a number of alternative ways in which each communicator might behave. Thus one of the chores for each person is to predict the most likely alternative actions the other might employ. For example, after talking to an attractive woman for some time at a cocktail party, a man might wish to extend a dinner invitation for the coming weekend. Any normally prudent man would at least speculate as to the possible reactions of the woman. Moreover, he might attempt to predict all possible reactions and prepare satisfactory rebuttals to increase further the likelihood that she will join him for dinner. It has been suggested that this element of uncertainty in initial encounters offers the most exciting moments of social relationships. People become excited over the prospect of anticipating the outcomes of initial encounters, whereas they settle into a routine when they are certain as to the outcome.

The second sense of uncertainty involves the problem of retroactively explaining the other person's behavior. Many times we are confused or uncertain about a particular behavior of another and wonder why that person behaved the way he or she did. We are aware that in each situation there are many possible explanations for a particular behavior. The problem here is for the individual to reduce the possible number of alternative explanations for the other person's behavior. As long as there is some element of uncertainty as to the motives of another, it is a wise strategy to remain open to plausible alternatives. Rejection of your dinner invitation might mean the other person is just not feeling well, has a previous engagement for that evening, or has pressing problems at the moment. Similarly, reluctance on the part of another to talk to us might indicate shyness or nervousness or simply the inability to think of anything else to say.

Uncertainty, then, involves both prediction and explanation. Satisfactory social relationships afford the opportunity of reducing this uncertainty through communication. Although reduction of uncertainty can alleviate tension and create a warm climate, it can also take some of the excitement and anticipation out of a relationship. Social theorists have suggested that we engage in close, personal relationships because we desire to be certain as to where and when we will have basic needs such as love, affection, sex, and affiliation satisfied. Although this may become tedious to some, this element of certainty provides us with the stability and contentment to turn our attention to other matters such as goal and career patterns.

Communicating Involvement in Relationships

Basically, the research into involvement has looked at how change in one person's expressed involvement can produce affective, physiological, and cognitive changes in another person. A number of theories have been advanced that attempt to explain how people respond to involvement behaviors by either engaging in or avoiding further interaction.

Patterson's Arousal Labeling Model

The basic tenet to Patterson's (1976) Arousal Labeling Model is that changes in involvement have an arousal potential; that is, communicating interest in another person causes a physiological response. These responses vary in degree and cause fluctuations in heart rate, respiration, and other physiological indicators. Depending upon whether these responses are labeled as either positive or negative, individuals engage in either approach or avoidance behaviors. If during the course of an interaction we experience arousal cues that we label as good, positive, rewarding, and so on, we will likely *reciprocate* the behaviors that lead to the arousal. For example, if you are sitting in class and one of your classmates, whom you think is especially attractive, smiles at you and waves, the arousal you experience due to the increase in involvement will be labeled as a positive experience and you will likely reciprocate with a smile and a wave. Arousal cues that are labeled as negative, bad, punishing, and so on, will lead to *compensatory* behaviors. To extend our classroom example, if an unseemly or otherwise unattractive classmate engages in the same type of affiliative behavior (i.e., smiles and waves), and you label the arousal the behaviors produce as negative, you will compensate by averting your gaze, moving away from the person, or otherwise failing to acknowledge the greeting. Also, the context in which we make judgments about other's communication of involvement has a significant effect on whether or not a behavior is labeled negatively or positively. For example, if the attractive person in our example waved and smiled at you as you walked across campus with your fiancé on your arm, the same physiological responses would occur. For the sake of your long-term relationship, however, you would likely label the arousal negatively and engage in compensatory behaviors. Likewise, if you were alone in a room with the unattractive person and he or she waved and smiled at you, the arousal would still occur, yet you might label the behavior as positive and reciprocate the salutation.

A number of important ideas can be gleaned from Patterson's Arousal Labeling Model that relate directly to how we form relationships and communicate involvement with each other. First, physiological responses to changes in a person's level of involvement are often a powerful mediating influence on how we will respond. Second, contextual cues often moderate the labeling of these responses as either positive or negative. The major criticism that this model has drawn is that it assumes people respond rationally and thoughtfully to other's behavior. Can we assume that when a person communicates a change in involvement, we are consciously aware of the physiological responses, we purposefully assess the contextual cues, and subsequently decide on reciprocating or compensating the behavior? One thing we can state with a certain degree of confidence is that the state of arousal we are in when we experience changes in others' involvement does affect our behavioral response to their communication, and it is an ongoing influence on how a relationship will progress.

Cappella and Green's Discrepancy-Arousal Model

An attempt to account for the criticism in Patterson's Arousal Labeling Model—that is, that individuals devote time-consuming cognitive energies in identifying and labeling the arousal caused by others' involvement behaviors—is provided by Cappella and Green (1982) in their Discrepancy-Arousal Model. This model attempts to explain how we are able to respond quickly, appropriately, and with little reflection to other's involvement behaviors. In ongoing interactions, involvement levels wax and wane quickly. These *rapid-action sequences* leave little or no time to ponder cognitively an appropriate response to each involvement behavior. Cappella and Green suggest that our compensatory and reciprocal behaviors are responses to the degree to which involvement behaviors deviate from expected levels. *Expected levels* are a function of situational, relational, and individual factors. Involvement behaviors that deviate from these expected levels create arousal. Generally speaking, if the deviation from the expected behaviors is small, the involvement gesture will be labeled positively and reciprocated.

Returning to our classroom example, given the situation of a classroom where most students talk to each other and assuming you view yourself as an attractive individual, a smile from an attractive student is a small deviation from what is normally expected. According to the model, the involvement gesture in this case would be labeled positively and reciprocated. By the same token, if there is a large discrepancy between the expected level and the involvement behavior, it will be labeled negatively and compensated. In the same situation, if the attractive student sat on your lap and began pawing you in front of your classmates and teacher, arousal occurring from this large level of discrepancy involvement might be labeled negatively (i.e., embarrassing) and the behavior compensated (i.e., remove the person from your lap, slap his or her face, etc.).

The strength of this model lies in its ability to explain how reciprocal and compensatory behaviors in reaction to involvement gestures are automatically and spontaneously enacted. As individuals become socialized and gain experience through a variety of interactions, expectations for appropriate behavior can be easily accessed and appropriate responses can be triggered with ease and little cognitive effort. The Discrepancy-Arousal Model differs from Patterson's Arousal Labeling Model in that it attempts to address "quick" responses to involvement behaviors as being a direct result of changes in arousal mediated by *affective* reactions and *not* the result of a cognitive search after the arousal has been labeled.

J. Burgoon's Expectancy Violations Model

Implicit in Patterson's Arousal Labeling Model and explicit in Capella and Green's Discrepancy Arousal Model is the pivotal notion of expectations of communication behavior. J. Burgoon (1978) developed an explanatory framework of involvement that focuses on nonverbal behaviors and expectations, how these expectations are determined, and what behaviors will occur when these expectations are violated. The Expectancy Violations Model assumes that over time people develop expectations and preferences about how others should behave. Societal norms play a large part in how our expectations of appropriate behaviors develop. Over time, as these expectations are confirmed through our interactions with others, they serve as a standard against which we judge the appropriateness of others' actions. These expectations allow us to anticipate, to a large degree, what nonverbal behaviors are deemed appropriate in a given circumstance. Further, these expectations provide us with the ability to assign positive or negative evaluations to the behaviors others enact. If our expectations are not violated in any significant way, a given interaction will unfold in a stable and predictable manner and our responses will continue to operate without our conscious awareness of them (i.e., automatically and spontaneously).

Any noticeable or sustained violations of our expectations of another's behavior produces an arousal effect and prompts an alertness or orienting response. By this we mean that our attention will be diverted away from the content of the conversation and focus on the violation in an attempt to assess its meaning. All subsequent communication will be evaluated in terms of the meanings we assign to the violation. Two key factors influence how individuals evaluate violations of expectations. First, an evaluation of the reward power of the violator is made based on communicator characteristics, such as reputation, status, attractiveness, personality, gender, degree of familiarity, communication style, and use of affiliative feedback. These characteristics combine to create a general measure of "rewardingness." A nonverbal act can be evaluated very differently depending on the reward value of the person committing the violation. Second, relational messages must be interpreted in light of their specificity and clarity. That is to say, when messages are ambiguous or are amenable to multiple interpretations, the reward power of the violator will have a strong impact on how the violation is interpreted. On the other hand, if the meaning of the act is interpreted as unequivocal, personal preferences dictate evaluation of the behavior. Thus violating norms or expectations with unequivocal behaviors such as sneering, communicating in a monotone voice, and so on, will likely produce negative consequences. If, for instance, a culture disapproves of touch initiated by subordinates, subordinates who engage in this type of behavior will likely suffer negative consequences. Conversely, if a culture values high levels of interaction involvement, but it is normative for people to display only moderate levels, a display of extreme interest may serve as a positive violation and prompt more favorable communication outcomes than conforming to the social norm.

Privacy Regulation

At the other end of the involvement continuum is privacy. It goes without saying that involvement in relationships, satisfying and necessary though they may be, reduces the amount of privacy experienced. Although most, if not all, of us have a clear need to be included in relationships and to have a variety of social experiences, we also have the need for privacy. We want to be able to communicate with others, as well as to refrain from interacting. For most relationships to become intimate, a certain level of self-disclosure is necessary. In that same relationship, however, we also need to keep some thoughts, feelings, and ideas private. Most of us would be uncomfortable if we had the perception that everything we thought or felt was known by another person regardless of the depth of our feelings or the amount of trust we had in him or her.

There are four general types of privacy that we often try to protect in any relationship. *Physical* privacy includes the freedom from others invading our "space." For example, dormitory living affords less privacy than sharing an apartment with one or two people and is, in turn, less private than living in a house or alone. Think for a moment about other ways in which your physical privacy is invaded. The more communication channels you have accessible to others, the less privacy you have. Telephone companies are making fortunes devising more intricate and sophisticated technologies, the sole purpose of which is to make us more accessible to others, thus reducing our physical privacy. In one single area, you can be contacted by phone, by fax, over an intercom, by memos, and, of course, by someone coming to your door. In all of these instances, people have access to your physical space, many times invading your privacy.

Social privacy is the ability to control the degree or amount of social contacts you have. We generally want to be able to control whom we interact with, when we interact, and where the interaction takes place. Professors' offices are in many instances "sacred places" in which only certain people can visit at certain hours of the day. This may be a reaction to graduate student offices where four to ten students share office space. In the latter situation there is a constant flow of people, some with whom you may not wish to interact. The inability to choose and control the amount of contacts you have, or at the very least to limit others' access to you, decreases our social privacy and strains relationships by forcing interaction.

Perhaps the most closely guarded privacy is *psychological* privacy—our ability to control affective and cognitive inputs. In other words, we need a level of freedom to think what we want (inputs) and to choose under what circumstances (and with whom) we will express it (outputs). Certain situations may force us to suppress ideas or emotions and express others that may not be in keeping with our ideologies or how we feel. An organization's culture may be fashioned in such a way that supervisors are not allowed to communicate sociably or affectionately toward a subordinate. It is not uncommon for organizations to frown upon employees dating each other, or at the very least, taking up company time in intimate socializing. This is not to say that an employee cannot "think" the thought, but as an old proverb maintains, "No thought is complete until it is voiced." In the same way, psychological privacy allows us to evaluate our own thoughts *and actions*, conceal our weaknesses, and maintain secrets that protect us from embarrassment or shame. Few social situations are as uncomfortable as when you are forced into disclosing a sensitive issue, especially if it occurs in front of people you do not know very well. We want to protect our innermost feelings, but when we disclose them we want to be able to choose with whom we share them.

The final type of privacy goes beyond personal interaction with others to a more global concept of privacy. *Informational* privacy is the right to determine how, when, and to what extent personal data are released to others. In an age of rapidly evolving communication technologies, this type of privacy has become extremely salient. At the push of a button, information concerning your medical background, credit ratings, educational background, telephone records, and a variety of more personal information can be acquired immediately by anyone with access to these data sources, often without your knowledge or consent. Although legislation is enacted to protect our informational privacy, our degree of control over how this information is regulated is far less than over the previous three types of privacy and is almost completely beyond our control.

The amount and ways in which we disclose information in relationships is, in one sense, a measure of the depth and commitment of the relationship. Generally speaking, in many relationships we want to be able to reveal aspects of ourselves that cast us in a positive light, while maintaining the ability to conceal our weaknesses. In intimate relationships we are willing to relinquish aspects of our privacy, such as disclosing information, socializing with people with whom we may not care to interact, or giving up portions of our physical space, in order to maintain and promote relational development.

Power and Status as Determinants of Social Relationships

Earlier we discussed the components of power that people can exert over other individuals. When people have the means of power, they assume different status relationships with the people with whom they communicate. Status itself is a source of power, and because power confers status, the two concepts are treated synonymously.

The status that we ascribe to people can be an important determinant of the kinds of communication behavior in which we will engage with them. That status can be derived externally or internally, from outside or within the particular relationship we have with others. Sources of external power include such factors as previous success and reputation, age, socioeconomic status, education, position, and so on. A person might also gain power in a relationship with you by being highly credible, by developing your attraction toward him or her, by controlling resources, or by somehow controlling rewards and punishment. Power developed within the relationship usually is perceived as more legitimate than externally bestowed power and, therefore, is more likely to influence your relationship with the source of power. The fact that people have high status or are powerful may also be a source of attraction that might motivate a person to establish some sort of social relationship with them. It is always amusing to read about how the powerful people in politics are so sought after as social companions; it is probably less amusing to realize that many of us are also attracted to the powerful in the same way.

Power is in many ways a determinant of the kind of social relationship we will have; it influences not only how we will communicate with those we perceive to be powerful, but it also is a potent predictor of how the people with power and high status will communicate with us. One form of dealing with the powerful is the adoption of the communication strategy of ingratiation. *Ingratiation* is the willing adoption of communication strategies by people to increase their attractiveness in the eyes of those who have power. This is one of the modes of influence available to those who otherwise have no power to influence or control the nature of a given relationship. A student who attempts to use ingratiating communication to gain the favor of a professor, or the person who shuffles and bows on the way up in a company is more acceptable if one understands that this is the only way some people perceive they can gain liking or be influential. However, ingratiation is rarely successful if it is perceived as ingratiation. People often are turned off by others who are openly seeking favor by such manipulative communication strategies. A certain amount of cleverness is mandated in concealing the intent of this form of communication from the powerful source.

Ingratiation can be accomplished in several ways to better a relationship with a powerful and significant other. You can indicate your conformity with the attitudes, beliefs, and values of the high-status person. You can compliment the other, or you can spend a considerable amount of effort trying to communicate to the other person how really worthwhile you are. All of these communication strategies are accomplished to make you more likable to the powerful person because this person is somehow able to provide rewards that you consider important. We all engage in ingratiating communication to some degree—in praising a boss, attempting to develop a relationship with a friend, or complimenting a person for doing something that we might really believe manifests extremely bad taste. It is probably true, though, that at some point we have to wonder if it is really worth having a person like us or if we want to continue trying so hard to please. Relationships that do not move beyond the level of ingratiation will in some way probably not be seen as satisfactory over time.

We also know that people who have high status—which can include ourselves (when we find ourselves possessing this kind of power)—communicate differently with those people with whom we are involved. On the basis of an abundance of research, we can suggest ways in which status affects interaction patterns (Collins & Guetzkow, 1964):

1. High-status people have an ability to influence other people without making overt behavioral attempts to gain influence.
2. High-status people initiate more communication transactions with others than do low-status people.
3. High-status people initiate more attempts at influence and are more successful at influence. They are also more resistant to influence attempts than are low-status people.
4. People with high status tend to spend more time communicating with other people of similarly high status.
5. Low-status people tend to behave deferentially toward high-status people and are upset if ambiguity exists in how the high-status people are reacting to them.
6. There is a low level of trust exhibited by low-status people toward people of higher status.
7. When low-status people are supported by their peers, they tend to be less deferential and less threatened by people with more status.

All of this suggests that we must recognize status differences as critically important in our attempts to establish satisfactory social relationships. If we are low in status, even sincere attempts to develop a relationship with someone of higher status might be perceived as ingratiation behavior. Moreover, the preceding discussion suggests that we ought to be aware of how our communication with others changes as differences in status among participants become apparent. It is through such an awareness of our communication behaviors that we can adapt to those differences and attempt to develop what we consider to be satisfactory relationships with other people, even though status differences do exist.

There are also reasons to believe that as relationships develop and the patterns of interaction become based less on externally imposed status relationships and develop their own rules of conduct within that relationship, externally imposed status demands take on less import. Because the internally imposed status differentials are subject to negotiation by the parties involved, they are less likely to be looked upon as a constraint prohibiting effective communication; they are more likely to be seen as a legitimate form of behavior.

We are not suggesting that violations of status-imposed rules of communication conduct always end in negative outcomes. One of our respected colleagues once described an author of this book as a person always willing to tell someone to go straight to hell if the person deserved it, without regard to whether that person was of higher status or, in fact, had a means of control. He further stated that this behavioral pattern was something that he found desirable and was a primary reason why a close friendship between the author and himself had developed. Obviously, the violation of rule-governed behavior paid off in this relationship. However, since we have become a bit older, the thought has crossed our minds more than once about how many people we may have denied ourselves a satisfactory relationship with simply because we did not understand or refused to comply with expected communication behaviors. There is an obvious risk involved in such behavior, and the negative outcomes associated with rule violations should be carefully considered if it is important to develop a satisfactory relationship with a significant other. There are probably some costs involved in not being your own person, too. In any case, these are the kinds of things to think about in considering this important determinant of developing social relationships.

We have discussed the factors that promote satisfactory social relationships and we hope that you can put this information to use in deciding *when* it is likely that you and another can establish close interpersonal bonds and *what* types of costs and rewards are possible for all concerned. Without being unduly pretentious, we will suggest *how* to establish satisfactory social relationships in the final section of this chapter.

Toward Developing Social Relationships, or, What Follows "Hello"?

Although the relational communication context, as we have defined it, is a prime arena for the development of social relationships, satisfaction of social needs and positive outcomes are obtained in a variety of communication situations. The groups we belong to can satisfy important social needs even though we are not in an interpersonal relationship with every member. Positive rapport and rein-forcement by an audience, a class, or a large group can satisfy some of our basic needs to communicate effectively with others and to share our feelings even though we could hardly claim to be on an interpersonal basis with anyone present. The organizations in which we work help us satisfy social needs. In most communication situa-tions, we will be attempting to communicate in a relational manner. The following suggestions might be useful in a variety of com-munication situations in which something must follow "Hello." The inclusion of the word *toward* in the section heading indicates that the development of social relationships is no easy matter. In sug-gesting some possible approaches to developing satisfactory social relationships, we do not mean to imply that we are necessarily good at it. Our intent is to provide some approaches that have worked for others in the hope that they might also work for you. We do recognize, however, that the way we communicate plays a vital role in this process. Communication, in one form or another, will determine whether a relationship will progress past the initial encounter stage.

Many people are misunderstood in social relationships because their communication attempts are either lacking or inappropriate. Woody Allen (1976) characterized this situation aptly through his fictitious college professor, Sandor Needleman:

> Needleman was not an easily understood man. His reticence was mistaken for coldness, but he was capable of great compassion, and after witnessing a particularly horrible mine disaster once, he could not finish a second helping of waffles. His silence, too, put people off, but he felt speech was a flawed method of communication and he preferred to hold even his most intimate conversations with signal flags. (p. 46)

Most of us have probably felt at one time or another that we might as well be communicating with signal flags. Although we do not recommend the use of signal flags for intimate conversations, we do agree with Needleman up to a point. Speech *can be* a flawed method of communication. It is hoped that after reading this book your speech will not be considered a flawed method of communica-tion. In addition, we hope that you will appreciate our insistence that effective communication *must* go hand in hand with satisfactory social relationships.

Similarity and Attraction

We strongly urge that you resist the tendency to seek out social relationships solely on the basis of physical attraction. Although we agree that physical attraction is a necessary prerequisite for many, attention to other factors is more likely to increase your chances for satisfactory social encounters. Much of the success in establishing social contacts depends greatly upon your initial *choice* of patterns. A thorough analysis of the degree of similarity and attraction between you and another can be invaluable in making this choice. Why do you suppose that some people always manage to succeed in striking up acquaintances with others? The most probable explanation is that they are very careful in deciding to whom they will extend their friendship. In addition, one can notice that their self-concept is positive, probably because their rejection or failure rate is low. Choosing the "wrong" people to interact with can be disastrous because not only do you fail in your friendship overtures, but your self-concept is also weakened from repeated failure. In time your self-concept can become so negative that you communicate this negativity to others.

Rather than reiterate the dimensions of similarity and attraction, we suggest that you review the information in the beginning of this chapter and determine the types of individuals who are most likely to respond to you and to make some sort of contribution to your needs. Two approaches are possible for achieving desirable results. First, you could assess mutual interpersonal attractions and select individuals who are similar in important attributes to you. Similarity can provide mutual interests and ensure harmony. A second approach is to assess interpersonal attraction but select dissimilar attributes. This is the "variety is the spice of life" approach. At any rate, you should analyze interpersonal similarity and attraction carefully and choose the approach that works for you.

One final comment regarding selection of potential social partners is in order. Effective social relationships is a percentage game that *usually* begins slowly and progresses gradually. The individual who goes out with the express purpose of striking up a relationship in one night is usually ripe for much disappointment and rejection. Many of our students come to us lamenting the fact that they have scoured most of the bars and entertainment centers in town and just cannot meet anyone. Some individuals are good at meeting others and at quickly establishing relationships. Most of us are not. We have to proceed wisely and slowly. We could all rest easier if we accepted the fact that many desirable people will cross our paths in life, but we will never meet them or have the opportunity of establishing a social relationship with them. The one thing we can all do, however, is recognize the nature of initial encounters and be prepared whenever the situation is right for us to interact with another.

Initial Interactions

Many people in social settings find themselves at a loss for words after they say "Hello" to someone. Although this could mean that they are shy, uncomfortable, or not feeling well, it could also mean that they do not understand the highly structured context of initial encounters. One explication of initial interactions suggests that there are three distinct phases to this process (Berger & Calabrese, 1975). The first stage of interaction is the *entry phase.* During this phase, communication content is highly structured, with message content focusing on demographic kinds of information. This is the stage in which you alternately ask each other's name, occupation, major, hometown, and so on ad nauseam. Initially, the amount of information asked for by each interactant tends to be symmetric. If the amount of information is not symmetric, a hasty reevaluation is in order. Attention to some of the nonverbal factors discussed earlier in the book may provide some clues as to whether the other person is bored with these trite exchanges or is not unduly impressed with your routine. If their nonverbal cues indicate that they are attracted to you, it probably does not matter what you talk about. At this point, you could move into the latter part of the entry phase, where people begin to explore each other's attitudes and opinions.

The second phase of the interaction is the *personal phase,* when the interactants engage in communication about central attitudinal issues, personal problems, and basic values. This phase could begin after several minutes of interaction, but it normally does not occur until the individuals involved have interacted on several occasions. Keep in mind that when personal or intimate information is revealed too soon in a relationship, information exchange is not symmetric, and the other person might be tempted to "get up and walk to his or her destination."

The final phase of interaction is the *exit phase*. During this phase, decisions are made concerning the desirability of future interaction. Usually, these decisions are discussed, and plans for future interaction are made. It is usually wise to determine if the other person is willing to interact with you *generally* at some future time rather than restricting future meetings to a specific activity on a given day. With a firm commitment to interact in the future, both parties can work out the details later. Most of us at one time or another have interpreted a refusal to interact with us in a specific setting as a rejection rather than considering other possible explanations, such as a prior engagement, busy work schedule, or an aversion to a suggested activity. Prior to suggesting future interaction, the prudent individual also will determine if the other interactant has some close, interpersonal ties, such as being married.

Initial encounters are obviously very important in social relationships because they will determine whether you will interact with another on a regular basis. Unfortunately, we do not have any pat formulas that, when applied, will instantly make social contacts for you. The best we can do is suggest that you employ effective communication strategies and learn what to *expect* at each state of the initial encounter. One thing is certain, however: People who expect the least are rarely disappointed.

Some communication theorists suggest that if a person is willing to exchange demographic information during the entry phase for at least four minutes, he or she is highly likely to maintain the conversation even longer (Zunin & Zunin, 1972). This would indicate that if we can get past the first four minutes of initial encounters, we stand a good chance of developing *some type* of relationship with that person. There is also some evidence suggesting that the amount of verbal communication is directly proportional to the degree of interpersonal similarity (Shaw, 1976). Thus we can make an estimate of interpersonal similarity based on the amount of information exchanged during the entry and personal stages, and we can expect others who produce a lot of communication with us to be similar in important attributes. Finally, nonverbal affiliative expressiveness has been shown to be positively related to interpersonal similarity (Mehrabian, 1971). When initial encounters are marked by high levels of eye contact, large numbers of head nods and hand gestures per unit of time, and frequent displays of pleasant facial expressions, we can expect that the other person likes us at an interpersonal level.

We hope we have provided some insights into wisely choosing your social partners and evaluating your initial encounters for possible future interactions. Satisfactory social relationships, however, require more than this. After deciding with whom you wish to interact and evaluating the potential for future interaction, the task still remains of establishing a compatible relationship with that person. In a word, you have to develop *affinity* with that person.

Developing Affinity

By *developing affinity*, we mean that individuals should manipulate their verbal and nonverbal communications so that others will "like" them. We will not belabor the points we raised earlier concerning nonverbal cues and interpersonal similarity and attraction. Suffice it to say that others will be attracted to you on the basis of the verbal and nonverbal gestures you provide them. Your job is to provide the proper cues for the right people at the correct time.

As we stated earlier, *physical appearance* is a prime motivator in social relationships. Because social relationships often begin on the basis of first impressions, the physical image you convey to others is highly important. There is very little we can do about our physical stature, but we can control much of our physical appearance by insuring that we are dressed appropriately for the occasion, that we are clean and well groomed, and that we have maintained some semblance of fitness. Of course, it would be ridiculous to recommend a particular manner of dress or hairstyle. The important point is that your physical appearance should appeal to the object of your social interests. It is possible that two individuals who are completely polar as to physical appearance and adornment might develop a close relationship, but the chances that either will get by the first encounter are highly unlikely. Some individuals display marked preferences for a particular type of body build. For example, many men in our society seem to be fixated on copious female bustlines, whereas many women are infatuated with male brawn and muscle. Very little can be done, short of instrumental conditioning, to compensate for preferences such as the "boob" and "muscle" syndromes. When dieting and exercise are inadequate in altering our body type, we simply must resign ourselves to the fact that some people just will not like the way we look.

By stressing relevant similarities, we can overcome many of the potential sources of conflict in a relationship while creating a mutually stimulating environment. As we have stated frequently in this text, people feel warmly disposed toward others who have similar values, interests, and goals. For those who are bored with the demographic exchanges that take place during the entry phase of initial encounters, try probing the other person's attitudes and interests for possible topics of conversation during the latter phases of the encounter. In addition, by stressing relevant similarities, you are also denying the possibility of discovering strong areas of disagreement that could be fatal at the initial stage of social interaction. Very few people become attracted to others for their ability to start fierce and spirited discussions.

At some point in a relationship, people will make decisions concerning whether their needs will be met. One of the most effective ways of ensuring a satisfactory social relationship is to *satisfy the needs* of the other person. It makes precious little difference what these needs are because if you do not satisfy them, it is a safe bet that the person will find someone who will. During the exit phase of initial encounters, people often consider future interactions on the basis of whether certain needs will be fulfilled. Part of the rational approach to developing social relationships is to determine whether you are capable of meeting, or care to meet, the needs of the other person. If not, the relationship probably would not work out anyway, and the best interests of all concerned would be better served by either restricting or severing the relationship.

A spirit of *cooperation and trust* can greatly aid the development of social relationships. Affinity grows out of a climate of mutual trust and cooperation in working toward joint goals. It is difficult to conceive of a person liking another who will not cooperate in the relationship, much less liking a person who is not trusted. When we are willing to forgo some of our independence by cooperating with another, we are showing our regard or affinity for that person. Likewise, we show our regard for another when we entrust him or her with many of our fragile emotions and feelings. Mutual cooperation and trust do not have to result in positive outcomes. Sometimes it is simply enough that people *engage* in a cooperative effort. People will keep coming back for more as long as they believe both parties are trying. It is a case of "if at first you don't succeed, try, try again."

A final consideration in developing affinity is to engage in *self-disclosing behavior*. As we noted earlier, self-disclosure usually leads to reciprocal self-disclosure. People who are somewhat reticent to divulge personal information about themselves will usually open up more when someone reveals personal information to them. Obviously, we must be careful about the type of information we divulge. During the initial phases of a relationship, it is risky to reveal some disgusting facet of your personality. Though a person might accept the fact that you frequently pick your nose when this is disclosed later in the relationship, he or she might not be able to handle this quirk if informed of it immediately after you say, "Hello."

Relationships in Decay

Sometimes, no matter how much effort people put into making a relationship work, a relationship breaks down. Relationships generally break down when (a) one person is generally dissatisfied with the other, (b) the relationship has served its purpose, and/or (c) there are some faulty relational properties. These faulty properties could be that the communication patterns of both people do not match, or the communication patterns and the implied roles do not work within the interaction. For example, one or both partners may have poor social skills or lack of a satisfactory level of communication competence. If one partner falls into a communication pattern of constantly complaining, while the other is not willing to give in to his or her demands, the relationship may decay. Relationships in decay generally dissolve either through "passing away" or through "sudden death." Passing away is a slow process marked by stages of reconciliation attempts. For those of us who have gone through this type of relationship dissolution, we know it is a painful process. Sudden death is a quick (albeit still painful) removal from the relationship. The majority of this chapter has been dedicated to relationship development and maintenance, processes that involve at least two people. Our current area of relationship deterioration differs markedly because breaking up can be done unilaterally. We wish to emphasize that relationship deterioration is not the reverse of relationship formation. When dissolving a relationship, histories already have been created; self-concepts and images have been formed, and this "muddies" the issue. It is important for any chapter on relational communication not only to address the formation of relationships, but also the role communication serves when relationships are in decay.

Stages of "Coming Apart"

We have provided some insights into how communication functions in relationships that are "coming together" and being maintained. Knapp's (1984) model of interaction stages provides a useful framework from which to address the role of communication in relationships that are "coming apart." Knapp suggests that most intimate relationships are characterized by as many as 10 different stages, each identified by their own particular communication behaviors. Initiating, experimenting, intensifying, integrating, and bonding are five stages characteristic of relationships in development and commitment. Relationships in deterioration are also characterized by five stages, each with its own unique interaction properties.

Differentiating refers to relationships in the early stages of disengaging or uncoupling. As opposed to relationships in which couples are fusing, or integrating, couples in the differentiating stage begin to exhibit communication that stresses how different they are (or have become) in attitudes, interests, sexual needs, and the like. Arguments and conflicts may manifest, often as a test of the other's willingness to tolerate some attitude, belief, or behavior that poses a threat to the relationship. Communication about the relationship changes from an emphasis on how "we" might resolve issues to how "I" want things settled.

Failure to resolve the tensions associated with differentiating will likely lead to the next phase of dissolution: *circumscribing*. Unresolved tensions and conflicts have now become extremely sensitive topics that relational partners will avoid communicating about. An unwillingness to communicate is typical at this stage of the relationship. Usually, these forbidden topics become especially sensitive because bringing them up risks confronting any number of other issues that also remain unresolved. Of the restricted interaction that does occur, little communication stresses commitment to the relationship. Communication typical of this stage of decline might be characterized by phrases such as, "It's none of your business" or "Let's not talk about that anymore" (Knapp, 1984). These messages strongly suggest that a new set of relational rules have supplanted an earlier, more open approach to resolving conflicts.

Almost certainly circumscribing will lead to further restrictions on communication. As more unresolved conflicts accrue, efforts to communicate may, for all intents and purposes, cease. Each relational partner can pretty well predict how any attempt to communicate will end—in frustration and anger. This leads to the next phase of dissolution: *stagnating*. Verbal communication is now at a stalemate; previous failures have so contaminated each partner's expectations that little, if any, effort is made to even try to communicate with each other. Nonverbally, participants may be communicating their anger, mistrust, and other unpleasant emotions. Verbal exchanges, when they occur, are typically very formal, well thought out, and carefully chosen, very similar to communication between strangers. In this stage, unless the participants have a particular need to punish each other (and, oddly, many do!), this stage of decay is short lived. For most people it is simply too painful a situation to endure and most relationships quickly progress to the next stage: *avoiding*.

Because most participants in intimate relationships share the same physical environment, avoidance allows them an escape from the mental torture associated with circumscribing and stagnating. In this stage, the purpose of most communication is to preclude any likelihood of face-to-face interaction. Messages that are exchanged are intended to convey to the other person that communication channels are now closed. Avoiding typically entails a wide range of behaviors from avoiding each other at times that are usually shared, such as meals, to actual physical withdrawal from shared living arrangements. For most relationships in this stage, little hope remains for salvaging and restoring relational bonds and only one stage remains: *terminating*.

It is difficult to predict the type of communication that relational partners will engage in when a relationship is terminated. A great many factors will influence how a relationship is viewed in this stage. On one hand, it seems reasonable to attempt to hold on to the positive aspects of a failed relationship, perhaps characterized by a final statement of "I'll always cherish the time we spent together." After all, there must have been some reasonable basis for having made the commitment to begin with, otherwise the relationship would never have developed! On the other hand, most of us have known (or been involved in) relationships that have ended abruptly and in great anger with a final, "And I hope you drop dead, too." One thing we can predict is that some attempt will probably be made to communicate about why the relationship ended. This communication may be solely between the participants in the relationship or include others who have witnessed the termination, such as close friends or family members. This communication has been characterized as "grave dressing" or attempting to put to final rest the relationship and its meaning to those affected by the termination. In this final, or end-game, stage, Knapp suggests that communication serves three functions and that "termination dialogue" will exhibit (a) a summary statement, (b) behaviors signaling the impending termination, and (c) messages that indicate what, if anything, the future relationship will be.

Of course, in this stage (or any of the other stages for that matter), communication may be affected greatly if one of the partners does not want the relationship to end. In this situation, the most likely effect will be to prolong the time spent within a given stage.

In this chapter we have attempted to address a variety of issues associated with communication and relationships with other people. Although there is great variety in why and how relationships form, develop, and sometimes dissolve, all of them seem to share certain characteristics. Our goal has been to explicate certain aspects of relational communication that are within our capacity to develop and control to some degree. Obviously, there is no magic formula that we can share with you that will guarantee that your relationships will be satisfactory and long-lasting. We will suggest, however, that increased awareness of the functions that communication serves in relationships may increase your ability to form and maintain closer ties with those people who are important in your life.

Summary

1. People develop patterns of interaction that exert control in relationships. In symmetrical relationships the differences between people are minimized. Both individuals believe that they have an equal right to exercise control and that the options available to one are available to both. Such a relationship can be very competitive, and hostility is frequent. People are constantly trying to determine how the other person views his or her equality. Almost every situation requires negotiation prior to taking any action. Complementary relationships maximize the differences between people. One person is one-up (superior), and the other is one-down (subordinate). One initiates and plans activities, and the other agrees. These relationships are often harmonious, and the coordination of activities is relatively easy. Complementary relationships often can stagnate, however, and people fail to grow and develop as individuals. The dominant person tends to provide protection in exchange for compliance. Parallel relationships allow each person to have areas of control while still allowing for equal participation in some areas. This flexible pattern allows changes in roles and can prevent some of the problems associated with rigidly complementary or rigidly symmetrical relationships.

2. A more fully expanded model of relational message themes derived from a variety of research indicates that relational communication can be viewed in terms of seven separate variables: dominance-submission (control); emotional arousal (activation); composure (self-control); similarity (identification); formality-informality; task-social orientation; and intimacy, which is subdivided into affection-

hostility, inclusion-exclusion, intensity of involvement, depth-superficiality, and trust.

3. People communicate with other people because they perceive communication to be rewarding. People who provide positive reinforcements are more likely to be found attractive than those who provide negative reinforcement or punishment.

4. Similarity is a potent predictor of interpersonal attraction. We are more attracted to those who share our attitudes and values and tend to communicate more with them. Over time we also tend to see those people to whom we are attracted as more similar than they really are. Moreover, the more satisfied we are with a relationship, the more likely we are to see the other person as similar to us.

5. It is usually the case that when people are in close proximity, they develop more intense liking or disliking relationships. Because they interact more and have more opportunity to exchange rewards, an optimistic view would hold that increased attraction results. The closer people are to us, however, the more opportunity they have to use exploitative techniques and/or coercive power. Thus proximity can lead to either positive or negative outcomes.

6. Physical attraction is a very important variable, especially in the early phases of interaction. We do have culturally defined standards of physical attractiveness and tend to attribute all kinds of positive psychological and sociological characteristics to those whom we find physically attractive.

7. Physical attractiveness is a source of power in a relationship, and we may communicate very differently with those who possess a high degree of physical attractiveness.

8. There are three identifiable phases of attraction: initial, intermediate, and long-term. The kinds and quality of communication vary markedly across these phases.

9. Central to some theories is the belief that when strangers meet, their primary concern is one of reducing uncertainties about the other, or increasing predictability about the behaviors of both themselves and others in the interaction. Uncertainty involves both prediction and explanation. One of the reasons people engage in close, personal relationships is a desire to be certain that basic needs, such as love, affection, sex, and affiliation, will be satisfied.

10. Three models of relational involvement offer an explanatory framework through which to understand more fully individual's reactions to communication that signify others' involvement cues. Patterson's Arousal Labeling Model (ALM) suggests that involvement cues create arousal that is labeled either negatively or positively. Positive labeling results in reciprocation, while negative labeling generates compensatory behaviors. Cappella and Green's Discrepancy Arousal Model (DAM) assumes that individuals' reactions to involvement cues are spontaneous and automatic. Involvement cues that vary little from expected behavior will be labeled positively and reciprocated. Large deviations from expected behaviors generate negative reactions that lead to compensation. J. Burgoon's Expectancy Violations Model (EVM) assumes that over time people build up expectations and preferences for others' nonverbal behavior. Reactions to violations of expectations are contingent upon (a) the "rewardingness" of the violator and (b) individual interpretation of the message. As in DAM, positively labeled violations are reciprocated while negative violations are compensated.

11. Privacy is an issue in all relationships. Physical, relational, social, psychological, and informational privacy provide individuals with both control and ability for self-determination.

12. Status and power differences are important determinants of whether we will find others attractive. As status differentials become apparent, communication patterns change. People with high status tend to interact very differently in a variety of communication contexts from the way people low in status do.

13. Possible outcomes of satisfactory social relationships include satisfaction of needs for affiliation, affection, and affinity and an opportunity to develop the self-concept, to confirm self-image, to reduce uncertainty, and to conduct impression management.

14. People have a strong need to be with others that can only be satisfied through social relationships. People will normally seek out others for companionship. At other times, people have shown greater needs to affiliate with others when they are in stressful situations, when they are bored, or when they are lonely or are experiencing social isolation.

15. Affection can be achieved only through social contacts with others. The human organism is incapable of providing affection and warmth for itself. Affection gained from a social relationship can

take one of two forms. It can be the concern that indicates another person cares about us and is concerned with our welfare, or it can be the deep feelings that result from loving relationships.

16. Individuals who do not wish to be liked and respected by others are rare. Affinity, or mutual liking, results from social relationships based on perceptions people form about us regarding our objective properties, our social behaviors, and our individual mannerisms. Individuals vary in their need for affinity. Traditionally, leaders have lower needs for affinity and must make decisions that may cause people not to like them.

17. Developing satisfactory social relationships is a difficult task that requires the use of effective communication strategies. The initial choice of social partners, based on degrees of similarity and attraction, can be a potent factor in determining favorable social outcomes. Similarity and attraction should not be based solely on physical attraction.

18. The initial interaction is very important to the development of social relationships because if a favorable impression is not created at the outset, nothing much is likely to follow. The initial interaction is characterized by three highly structured stages: the entry phase, the personal phase, and the exit phase. Demographic information is usually exchanged during the entry phase, which usually terminates after approximately four minutes if one of the parties becomes disinterested. The exchange of central issues and attitudes takes place during the personal phase. Increased nonverbal, affiliative behavior occurs at this stage when one or more of the parties has some interest for the other. During the exit phase future interactions are discussed, or the relationship is terminated.

19. Active roles in developing increased affinity are among the most effective ways to insure a satisfactory social relationship. Affinity is best achieved by stressing relevant similarities, satisfying the needs of others, mutual cooperation and trust, and self-disclosing behavior.

20. Sometimes, even with the best intentions, relationships fail. General dissatisfaction, relationships that have served their purpose, or some faulty relational properties (e.g., mismatched communication properties) can lead to relational decay. Relationships in dissolution are characterized by specific types of communication behaviors

associated with five separate stages of disengagement: differentiating, circumscribing, stagnating, avoiding, and terminating.

References

Allen, W. (1976, July 24). Remembering Needleman. *The New Republic*, p. 46.

Bateson, G. (1935). Culture, contact, and schismogenesis. *Man, 35*, 178-183.

Berger, C., & Calabrese, R. (1975). Some explorations in initial interaction and beyond: Toward a developmental theory of interpersonal communication. *Human Communication Research, 1*, 99-112.

Berscheid, E. (1966). Opinion change and communicator-communicatee similarity and dissimilarity. *Journal of Personality and Social Psychology, 4*, 670-680.

Berscheid, E., & Walster, E. H. (1978). *Interpersonal attraction*. Reading, MA: Addison-Wesley.

Burgoon, J. K. (1978). A model of personal space violations. *Human Communication Research, 4*, 129-142.

Burgoon, J. K., & Hale, J. L. (1987). Validation and measurement of the fundamental themes of relational communication. *Communication Monographs, 55*, 58-79.

Burgoon, M., Heston, J. K., & McCroskey, J. C. (1974). *Small group communication: A functional approach*. New York: Holt, Rinehart & Winston.

Byrne, D. (1961). The influence of propinquity and opportunities for interaction on classroom relationships. *Human Relations, 14*, 63-70.

Byrne, D. (1971). *The attraction paradigm*. New York: Academic Press.

Byrne, D., & Blalock, B. (1963). Similarity and assumed similarity between husbands and wives. *Journal of Abnormal and Social Psychology, 67*, 636-640.

Cappella, J. N., & Green, J. O. (1982). A discrepancy-arousal explanation of mutual influence in expressive behavior for adult and infant-adult interaction. *Communication Monographs, 49*, 89-114.

Collins, B. E., & Guetzkow, H. (1964). *A social psychology of group processes for decision making*. New York: John Wiley.

Dion, K., Berscheid, E., & Walster, E. (1972). What is beautiful is good. *Journal of Personality and Social Psychology, 24*, 285-290.

Festinger, L. (1952). Group attraction and membership. In D. Cartwright & A. Zander (Eds.), *Group dynamics: Research and theory* (pp. 63-70). Evanston, IL: Row, Peterson.

Festinger, L., Schacter, S., & Busk, K. (1950). *Social pressure in informal groups: A study of human factors in housing*. New York: Harper.

Gouaux, C. (1971). Induced affective states and interpersonal attraction. *Journal of Personality and Social Psychology, 20*, 37-43.

Griffitt, W., & Veitch, R. (1971). Hot and crowded: Influence of population density and temperature on interpersonal affective behavior. *Journal of Personality and Social Psychology, 17*, 92-98.

Gullahorn, J. T. (1952). Distance and friendship as factors in the gross interaction matrix. *Sociometry, 15*, 123-134.

Homans, G. C. (1961). *Social behavior: Its elementary forms.* New York: Harcourt Brace & Jovanovich.

Katz, A. M., & Hill, R. (1958). Residential propinquity and marital selection: A review of theory, method, and fact. *Marriage and Family Living, 20,* 27-35.

Knapp, M. L. (1984). *Interpersonal communication and human relationships.* Newton, MA: Allyn & Bacon.

Kopera, A. A., Maier, R. A., & Johnson, J. E. (1971). *Perception of physical attraction: The influence of group interaction and group coaction on ratings of the attractiveness of photographs of women.* Proceedings of the 79th Annual Convention of the American Psychological Association, Miami.

Laing, R. D., Phillipson, H., & Lee, A. R. (1966). *Interpersonal perception.* Baltimore, MD: Perennial Library.

Landy, D., & Mettee, D. (1971). Evaluation of an aggressor as a function of exposure to cartoon humor. *Journal of Personality and Social Psychology, 12,* 66-71.

Landy, D., & Sigall, H. (1974). Beauty is talent: Task evaluation as a function of the performer's physical attractiveness. *Journal of Personality and Social Psychology, 29,* 299-304.

Lederer, W. J., & Jackson, D. D. (1968). *The mirages of marriage.* New York: Norton.

Levinger, G., & Breedlove, J. (1966). Interpersonal attraction and agreement: A study of marriage partners. *Journal of Personality and Social Psychology, 3,* 367-372.

Lott, B. E., & Lott, A. J. (1960). The formation of positive attitudes toward group members. *Journal of Abnormal and Social Psychology, 61,* 297-300.

McKeon, R. (1947). *Introduction to Aristotle.* New York: The Modern Library.

Mehrabian, A. (1971). Verbal and nonverbal interaction of strangers in a waiting situation. *Journal of Experimental Research in Personality, 5,* 127-138.

Millar, F. E. (1973). *A transactional analysis of marital communication.* Unpublished doctoral dissertation, Michigan State University.

Millar, F. E., & Rogers, L. E. (1987). Relational dimensions of interpersonal dynamics. In M. E. Roloff & G. R. Miller (Eds.), *Interpersonal processes: New directions in communication research* (pp. 117-139). Newbury Park, CA: Sage.

Mills, T. E. (1967). *The sociology of small groups.* Englewood Cliffs, NJ: Prentice Hall.

Patterson, M. L. (1976). An arousal model of interpersonal intimacy. *Psychological Review, 83,* 235-245.

Rogers, E. M., & Bhowmik, D. K. (1970). Homophily-heterophily: Relational concepts for communication research. *Public Opinion Quarterly, 34,* 523-538.

Rosen, S., & Tesser, A. (1970). On reluctance to communicate undesirable information: The MUM effect. *Sociometry, 33,* 253-263.

Shaw, M. (1976). *Group dynamics: The psychology of small group behavior* (2nd ed.). New York: McGraw-Hill.

Sigall, H., & Landy, D. (1973). Radiating beauty: Effects of having a physically attractive partner on person perception. *Journal of Personality and Social Psychology, 28,* 218-225.

Sunnafrank, M. (1986). Predicted outcome value during initial interactions: A reformulation of uncertainty reduction theory. *Human Communication Research, 13,* 3-33.

Thibaut, J. W., & Kelly, H. H. (1959). *The social psychology of groups.* New York: John Wiley.

Walster, E., Walster, G. W., & Berscheid, E. (1978). *Equity: Theory and research.* Boston: Allyn & Bacon.

Watzlawick, P., Beavin-Bavelas, J., & Jackson, D. D. (1967). *Pragmatics of human communication: A study of interactional patterns, pathologies, and paradoxes.* New York: Norton.

Zunin, L., & Zunin, N. (1972). *Contact: The first four minutes.* Los Angeles: Nash.

10

Communication and Conflict

Conflict in one form or another seems to be an inescapable part of the human condition. We will argue, with substantial support, that individuals, groups, and whole societies advance most when conflict is recognized as an inevitable and even healthy aspect of human interaction and when communication is valued as a means of managing conflict. Ancient Greek and Roman civilizations recognized and valued dissent as an integral part of their societies. Our present-day legislative and judicial systems have as their origin this recognition of the inevitablity of conflict.

We also work under the assumption that conflict is manifested only through some type of communication behavior. Although it is possible to communicate without conflict, conflict without some type of communication is impossible. At times, conflict is readily discernible through communication, as the following anecdote shows.

British parliamentarians Benjamin Disraeli and William Gladstone were arch political enemies who frequently bumped heads in the public arena. After a particularly heated debate on the floor of the

House of Commons, Gladstone, addressing Disraeli, shouted, "Sir, you will come to your end either upon the gallows or of venereal disease." Disraeli replied rather calmly, "I should say, Mr. Gladstone, that depends on whether I embrace your principles or your mistress." Disraeli was called upon to define the difference between calamity and misfortune, he replied, "If Gladstone were to fall into the Thames, if would be a misfortune; but if someone dragged him out, *that* would be a calamity.

Unfortunately, some types of conflict revealed in communicative behaviors are not as easily recognized and understood as in our example. In addition, one can readily observe that there are many different kinds and intensities of conflict. The type of conflict you experience when deciding which outfit to wear to a party is hardly the same sort of conflict you experience in deciding to give up the single life for marriage. Although scholars have difficulty deciding upon the elements that are necessary to define conflict, we take the position that conflict is an *expressed* struggle between *at least* two parties either of whom perceives incompatible goals and interference from the other, which precludes the attainment of a goal (Hocker & Wilmot, 1985).

In the first part of this chapter we will discuss conflict from a more traditional communication perspective, differentiating types and levels of conflict, both at the interpersonal and the intergroup level. Next we will focus on five different communication styles or approaches to conflict. Once conflict has been discussed in this manner, we will address general conflict patterns that occur during intergroup interaction. The following section will present different types of decisions that may increase the likelihood that conflict will occur. Finally, we will attempt to address both the costs and the benefits that are possible when individuals and groups find themselves in conflict situations.

Types of Conflict

Real Conflict

The first type of conflict that can occur at any of the previously mentioned levels of interpersonal interaction is *real* conflict. Real conflict results when goals or behaviors are incompatible owing to a struggle for resources *when* a zero-sum situation exists. In a zero-sum situation the gains by one person must result in losses to another, such that the gains of all persons involved equals zero. For example, if each of five people brings $10 to a poker game, the combined winnings and losses of all five players at the end of the game will equal zero. This poker game is a zero-sum situation because in order for one person to win a particular amount, others playing the game must collectively lose that same amount. Real conflict in an inter-personal situation exists when one person "winning" or satisfying personal goals, results in another person "losing" or failing to gratify needs. It is probably not difficult for any of us to remember situations where we have spent time with one person, while someone else wanted to spend time with us. Because there are only 24 hours in a day (zero-sum situation), real conflict would occur between our two companions because time spent with one will have to result in the rejection of the other.

Artificial Conflict

The second type of conflict, *artificial* conflict, resembles real conflict except it occurs in a non-zero-sum condition. In this situation, gains by one party do not necessarily have to result in losses by another party. Compromise or cooperation can result in gains for all concerned parties. To extend our example above, both of your companions do not have to be in conflict if you are able to pay attention to both and spend sufficient time with both to satisfy their needs, and your needs as well. This artificial conflict will turn to real conflict only if you, or one of your companions, feels that three is a crowd and one has to leave.

Induced Conflict

When an individual or group creates some conflict for purposes other than the apparent ones, it is *induced* conflict. Group leaders often will attempt to strengthen their hold on their followers by creating an "enemy" or external threat so that the group will band together in a submissive and cohesive unit to defeat this conflict or threat. While trying to build a debate team in a small-town high school, one of the authors arbitrarily chose another school "down the road a piece," as the "enemy." The induced conflict helped the newly forming team to become cohesive, and the common enemy increased team solidarity for the coach. Most of you are probably familiar with the person who always seems to be in a state of crisis. If no crisis is available, he or she will create one for purposes of sympathy, attention, or the pure joy of misery.

Violent Versus Nonviolent Conflict

The fourth type of conflict involves *violent versus nonviolent* conflict. The difference between violent and nonviolent conflict is the distinction between the use of force and the use of rhetoric. Whenever some conflict progresses from a verbal exchange to physical aggression, the conflict becomes violent. Both nonviolent and violent conflict can be effective methods of bringing about change and managing conflicts. As we will discuss in the second part of this chapter, displaying force is an effective means of managing grievances given certain situational factors. With a few exceptions, most societies strongly recommend nonviolent conflict, even though many societies can trace their beginnings, as well as their growth, to violent conflict.

Face-to-Face Versus Mediated Conflict

The fifth type of conflict is *face-to-face versus mediated* conflict. Most conflict arising between individuals and within small groups is face-to-face as opposed to mediated conflict. Members of larger organizations have management, labor unions, and professional groups to resolve their conflicts. Individuals and members of small groups often have conflicts that have to be dealt with immediately through interpersonal communication. Therefore, the conflict is generally much more subjective and personal. Large organizations and institutions can retain legal counsel to settle their disputes in the impersonal and objective atmosphere of the courtroom, whereas individuals and group members can rarely be that detached from their conflict. Mediated conflict situations also will employ mass communication processes for resolution whenever appropriate. Interest groups will frequently take their case directly to the public through the mass media in hopes that public opinion will successfully mediate the conflict in their favor. Neighborhood mediation programs have been established to allow individuals to manage conflicts by coming to some type of mutual agreement in the most equitable way. We will discuss third-party intervention in some detail later in this chapter.

Principles and Pragmatics in Conflict

The final type of conflict involves *principles and pragmatics*. Every individual brings into each interpersonal and group relationship a set of values and principles. Conflict often arises when choosing the principles and values with which to operate in specific situations. For example, members of a group may experience considerable conflict over the principle of aiding a foreign country that is beset with internal problems. Such a situation occurred when the United Nations debated the merits of giving aid to starving people in Bosnia and Hertzegovina. There was conflict about the role of the United Nations interceding in the problems of a sovereign land, but adherence to the principles of protecting the lives of people under duress from an unsupported aggressor lead to several types of pragmatic conflict. First, in acting on this principle, some factions opposed the use of force, while others maintained that force should be a viable option to protect U.N. forces and insure that food and supplies reached those in need. Second, acceptance of an adherence to certain principles generated conflict with other previously accepted principles or values; the rights of conflicting factions to manage their conflict in their own way without outside interference. Clearly, conflict over principle and pragmatism indicates a need to recognize the overlapping nature of conflict that results from competing sets of values. Another source of potential conflict in this area involves differing orientations. Two individuals experiencing marital discord may adopt differing orientations regarding the source of conflict. The husband may feel that the conflict does not merit becoming upset and, furthermore, says, "She will forget all about it tomorrow." The wife, however, may feel that no problem is too trivial to discuss and that candid and immediate discussion is the only path to marital harmony. With these two types of orientations, the probability for conflict is high.

Conflict Styles

In much the same way that conflict can manifest itself in a variety of forms and types, there is also a variety of styles that individuals and groups typically employ in conflict situations. Communication researchers interested in investigating the advantages and disadvantages of individual conflict styles generally adhere to four basic assumptions (Hocker & Wilmot, 1985). First, throughout the course of interacting with others in conflict situations, individuals develop a patterned response to conflict. This generally occurs when someone asserts that there are only one or two "choices" in most situations. We have probably all met the type of person who attempts to deal with conflict by retreating, no matter what the situation. Continual use of this avoidance style of conflict management creates a pattern whereby the individual becomes "stuck" in that style.

A second assumption is that people generally form a conflict management style because it makes sense to them. People who have grown up in households where the adults always managed their conflicts by confrontation or competition may prefer to avoid conflicts at all costs. However, if they learned that this type of conflict management style was functional and worked well to deal with the conflict, then adoption of this style is reasonable. Someone's conflict style only makes sense if you understand what that person has learned and experienced. What may appear as an ineffective conflict style to us, may make perfect sense to that person for a variety of valid reasons.

The third assumption maintains that no one style is better or worse than any other style. Because people develop styles that make sense to them, any evaluation of the rationality or reasonableness of the conflict style is based on how well the choice works in obtaining the desired goals. For example, compromise might be reasonable in an academic situation because professors and graduate students have to maintain a creative atmosphere and share scarce resources, but if the same people were in conflict with an outside source concerning the elimination of a course that may damage the department, compromise may be disastrous for the department's goals.

Finally, it is important to note that the conflict style people use undergoes changes in light of various situations. When people find that a particular style of conflict management results in, for instance, punishment, they may be more inclined to reassess this style and perhaps adopt a style that may result in rewards. People attempting to manage their marital conflicts by always competing may find that a certain level of compromise may result in more pleasurable rewards.

Particular Conflict Styles

Although there are many ways to classify conflict styles, the following five categories will allow you to identify general styles of conflict and how they compare to each other.

Avoidance. Avoidance is a conflict management style in which communication and behavior is unassertive. People who use avoidance typically ignore conflict situations, perhaps pretending that they do not exist. If they acknowledge the conflict, they may simply refuse to openly engage in any communication to resolve it. Adopting this style certainly does not mean that people using an avoidance strategy will not get what they want or that avoidance is ineffective. On the contrary, many intimate couples avoid discussing certain delicate topics and thus avoid overt conflict and potential hurt feelings. Avoiding conflict also does not mean that conflict does not exist. As we have stated earlier, from this perspective, conflict is the *perception* of incompatible goals. If the couple in our example perceives that their goals are incompatible on a delicate issue, the conflict is essentially not expressed by using an avoidance style of management. Adopting an avoidance style has the advantage of giving a person time to think over the situation and not act in haste. Reliance on this style, however, could result in a "backwash" of poorly-managed conflicts that have been allowed to fester over time.

Accommodation. The accommodating style is one in which people in conflict do not assert themselves, but try to cooperate with others. People using this style will generally view the other person's needs and goals as superordinant to their own. This does not always mean that relinquishing personal goals is preferred. In some cases an individual may accommodate the goals of another while still holding his or her own personal goals in high regard. For example, if your supervisor wants you to come in to work earlier than normal to finish a job, you may accommodate or obey his or her wishes, even though your desire to stay at home is still present. There may be times when the relinquishing of goals may be done gladly, especially when the other's point of view is superior to your own. This style has the advantage of creating harmony and maintaining a relationship. Continuous accommodation can reduce options for creativity in managing conflict situations, however, and further the person's lack of power.

Competition. A competitive style is one in which individuals seek to dominate the situation. This style is characterized by aggressive, assertive, and uncooperative behavior. A person with a competitive style wants to engage others in direct confrontation, trying to "win" at the others' expense. Earlier scholars and theorists have criticized competition because of the undue strain it places on interpersonal relationships. Horney insisted that, at times, competition is a problem for everyone in our society—an "unfailing center of neurotic conflicts" (1937, p. 188). A more recent distinction by Deutsch (1969) suggests that the term *competition* refers to an opposition in the goals of the interdependent parties such that the probability of goal attainment for one decreases as the probability for the other increases—I win, you lose. One obvious advantage to a competitive style is the ability for quick management to take place. In times of emergency, managing competing goals through immediate confrontation may be the most efficient. As stated above, however, competition has the potential to harm relationships, forcing one party to either "fight" or "flee"; win or lose.

Compromise. A compromise style is characterized by a "give and take" philosophy. People using a compromise style attempt to manage conflict by an equal exchange of concessions and "splitting the difference." The spouse of one of the authors enjoys shopping in a nearby Mexican border town. The price offered by the salesperson is generally not the price she is willing to pay. After a few rounds of bantering and bargaining, both people finally agree on a price somewhere in the middle ground. The seller is willing to make a little profit and the buyer is willing to pay a little cash. Each wins, each gives something up. This style allows conflict to be managed expediently in a seemingly rational manner. A problem with the compromise style of conflict management is that one party may give up too quickly and not work for a mutually beneficial arrangement. Also, this style may result in situations in which everybody loses and no one wins.

Collaboration. At first blush, collaboration appears to be very similar to cooperating or compromising. However, a person using a collaborative style attempts to manage incompatible goals by working toward the goals of the other. In this way, both people (ideally) end up winning. Conflict management that only focuses on the other would be accommodation; a focus on me against you is a competitive style; whereas a collaborative style attempts to manage conflict with a "we" focus on the goals. Needless to say, this type of style demands high involvement and can be extremely time consuming, making it unrealistic in situations in which your investment in the situation is low. With its emphasis on the "we" of conflict management, collaboration has the potential to affirm both parties' importance in the relationship and it deters the use of aggression when managing conflicts.

Intergroup Conflict Patterns

The direction that conflicts can take vary from situation to situation. Some conflicts play out quickly, many times depending upon the power and personality of those involved. Other conflict episodes can continue for decades, evidenced by long-standing feuds between rival factions. We argue that conflict itself is inherently neither good nor bad, productive nor unproductive. Although conflict may be productive for some, it can be unproductive and even damaging for others. Generally, conflicts between groups of actors develop in similar ways. These patterns or phases of conflict can be described in terms of which communication patterns are employed when people attempt to manage their differences. Before we discuss these five phases, it is important to point out that groups involved in conflict can fluctuate back and forth between phases. In other words, these phases are generally present in most conflict situations; however, in the case of complex conflicts, de-escalation and resolution may not occur and interactants may be caught in spirals of escalation for extended periods of time.

Disagreement

During the exploration of interpersonal and task situations, groups frequently discover that disagreement exists between two or more members. During the disagreement stage, group members must decide if a real disagreement exists or if the disparity is actually a simple misunderstanding. For example, a group of students at our university was given the task of designing activities for their sororities' traditional Parents' Weekend. Because this festivity was to follow the university-wide Parents' Weekend, one member suggested that they change their weekend to a Mother's Weekend, taking into consideration the number of students whose parents were divorced. Another member suggested that it should be a Father's Weekend extending the reasoning that mostly mothers came to the earlier Parents' Weekend. Obviously, it did not take long to discern that an actual disagreement existed, and it was not simply a misunderstanding.

During the disagreement phase, group members must find out whether the issue is of immediate concern to the group's goals, or whether the disagreement can be passed over for the time being. Also, group members must decide whether the conflict can be resolved by changing some minor situational factors. For this conflict episode, each member's goals was in direct opposition to the other's, and through discussion of the proposals, previously unnoticed issues of disagreement began to arise. Issues of which parent is more important, which parent enjoys these types of events more, which member's parents should take precedent over other members' based on seniority were brought into the situation.

Confrontation

Once it is realized by the group that the actions and/or beliefs of one or more members are incompatible with and hence are resisted by one or more of the other group members, the confrontation phase begins. Individuals begin to communicate their positions, both emotionally and rationally. During this phase three things are likely to happen that heighten the conflict between members. First, as people argue their position, they become more convinced that their position is the most reasonable and rational. This *commitment inten-sification* can function to move the conflicting parties further away from each other, successfully heightening the dissimilarity between their positions. In our example, the member advocating a special day for mothers vehemently maintained that mothers appreciated these events more than fathers, and fathers were more likely to come to the university's ritual than to a sorority gathering. As the other member argued her position, both became steadfast in their positions, becoming more committed as they presented their arguments. Another outcome of this phase is *tension building*. As commitment increases, anxiety and tension become more dominant. Emotional expressions begin to replace logical discussions. Perhaps the most telling situation that occurs during this phase is the formation of *coalitions*. Subgroups form within a larger group during this phase, often because the conflicting members are attempting to gain support for their position. In our example, the conflicting parties were successful in dividing the entire body of sorority members into two coalitions.

Escalation

According to researchers, during the escalation phase the number of issues can expand, people become more ego involved, and the conflict itself becomes the issue; that is, it takes on a symbolic importance of its own (for an excellent discussion of communication and conflict escalation, see Folger & Poole, 1983). As members become more committed to their position, tension builds and coalitions form; conflict escalates as new issues are raised, many of which have little to do with the issue at hand. In our example, members began referring to duties that some members failed to perform at a social gathering in a previous year, other members referred to the sexual improprieties of certain people in the opposing coalition, while still others brought up unpaid debts. It is important to note that during conflict escalation misunderstanding and distrust occur, moving members away from cooperative responses until they become opponents locked in an escalating cycle of competition that generally leads to frustration. Escalating patterns of conflict are, in part, the products of the norms of reciprocity and self-defense. When someone's "face" is attacked, they generally respond with a similar communication strategy and attack the other. This personalization causes conflict to escalate into a symbolic activity in which "winning," not the resolution of the issue at hand, becomes the driving force.

De-Escalation

If group members can get beyond the escalation phase, they will enter the stage of conflict de-escalation. There are many reasons why people move to de-escalate conflicts. As mentioned previously, conflict escalation can be frustrating and emotionally taxing for all concerned. People may reach a point where they are "too tired to argue anymore" and just want to decide on how to resolve the conflict. This refocusing on the issue at hand moves the communication to a more cooperative and seemingly rational level. People begin attempts to negotiate, or seek an equitable resolution for all concerned. During this phase, rebuilding trust occurs slowly. For any group that has experienced disagreement, confrontation, and escalating conflict, regaining mutual trust can be very problematic. As discussed in Chapter 9, trust is difficult to foster and, once lost, is difficult to regain. Trust may be regained if individuals communicate their intentions carefully and exhibit consistency between their purpose and their behaviors. In our situation, a senior member took charge of the situation, reprimanding those who were "losing their heads" and calling for apologies from the "warring" members. Slowly, members began to realize that they had lost sight of the issue, dragging up a lot of irrelevant "garbage" that was not going to help resolve the problem.

Conflict Resolution

It can be argued that conflict never can be truly "resolved" in the sense that all the issues that surrounded the conflict episode disappear. We will discuss the aftermath of conflicts in a moment. Suffice it to say that all conflicts reach a phase of resolution through a variety of forms. Resolution may occur by one member withdrawing demands or relinquishing goals, or, through a display of power, one side may impose its views on the other. In a more cooperative manner, members may concede points until agreement is reached, or arguments and positions may be communicated in such a way that one side is converted to the other's point of view. Of course, conflicts can also be resolved through dissolution of the group. The sorority members in our example did not dissolve, nor did one party withdraw, but, like intelligent college students, they began weighing the merits of each alternative until a decision was reached to combine both festivities and have a sorority-specific Parents' Weekend. In this way those who already had one parent attend the university function could invite the other, and those who wanted to could have both parents attend.

Conflict Aftermath

Conflict aftermath is the "residue" that is left over from all of the other stages. Two important repercussions occur from any conflict episode: short-term effects and long-term effects. The short-term effects can be as simple as the quality of the decision made and the impact on the working relationships of the members (if the group continues to function as a group). However, if the resolution occurred from a "power play" or one subgroup acquiescing to the goals of the other, frustrations may result, leading to the potential of more conflicts and commitments for revenge. In either case, the dynamics of conflict episodes alter the perceptions that people have of each other, for better or worse. Some conflict episodes may result in the redefining of relationships as competitive or cooperative and also result in the formation of new rules and regulations regarding protocol. It is inevitable that conflict episodes will become a part of the history and, therefore, part of the relationship for all individuals involved.

Decisions That Promote Conflict

Involvement in society necessitates making all sorts of decisions. As participants in the human experience, we must choose between different types of consumer products, ethical standards, moral philosophies, career opportunities, leisure activities, companions, and lifestyles. Although many different kinds of choices present themselves, we find it helpful to discuss the three major categories of choices that confront people in our society and ultimately cause conflict (Brown, 1965).

Approach-Approach

Approach-approach decisions involve a choice between two conflicting alternatives, both of which have different but favorable consequences. Only one of the two may be chosen. For example, approach-approach conflict would occur if a voter has only two candidates to vote for on a ballot and the voter likes them both. Similarly, when members of a social fraternity vote on whether to take prospective members on a skiing trip or to a professional football game they have placed themselves in an approach-approach situation.

Three major variables determine the amount of conflict present in approach-approach situations. The first is the *value* of the alternatives. More conflict is likely to occur when the relative value of two or more alternatives is approximately equal. Moreover, conflict will be greater if the absolute values are high than if they are low. For example, given the choice between buying a new car or vacationing in Europe for the summer, conflict will be great owing to the absolute value, or desirability, of both alternatives. However, the conflict involved in deciding between a vacation in Europe and replacing the still-servicable roof on your house might be less, owing to the perceived lower absolute value of replacing a roof that looks shabby but still works. Relative values are determined by comparing available alternatives. A comparison between a new car and a vacation in Europe would yield relatively equal value because both are attractive. The *probability* of occurrence of a desired outcome is the second factor affecting the amount of conflict. Conflict is greatest when the desired outcomes have an equal chance of occurring. A typical situation might involve a student who has an English paper due at the end of the week and a history exam on the same day. The student recognizes the worth of both courses for professional development and wishes to receive a good grade in both classes. If the student has a high probability of achieving excellence in both courses, conflict will be greater when deciding whether to spend more time on the paper or on preparing for the examination than if the decision were made with an unequal chance of receiving a good grade in both courses. The third factor concerns the *number* of different alternatives available. Generally, potential for conflict increases as the number of alternatives increase. This is especially true in group settings. Two individuals can many times reconcile differences when several choices are available more readily than can a group of individuals because the number of available alternatives can be more expediently reduced. For instance, a husband and wife can narrow the field of all available cars to one choice each, but five people who want to lease a car might only be able to narrow the field to five different choices.

Of the types of decisions affecting the amount of conflict involved in choice, the approach-approach conflict is probably the easiest to resolve. If two or more alternatives are equally desirable, the very least that can happen in choosing one over another is selection of a desirable consequence. In addition, choosing between attractive alternatives involves less potential for hostility, and a method of compromise is easier to reach.

Approach-Avoidance

When a group of individuals is faced with making one decision that carries intrinsically unpleasant consequences and a desirable outcome simultaneously, it is involved in an approach-avoidance conflict. The decision to take a job with a prestigious company at an attractive salary may entail the responsibility of spending evenings and weekends away from home. Conflict will be present to the extent that the positive and negative aspects of the decision are equal. There are instances in which refusing to play the game, or simply making no decision, is an effective response. However, this is not the case in this situation. Failure to make a decision in an approach-avoidance situation actually makes a decision because failure to make a decision relinquishes all positive aspects that might have been possible. Decisions concerning principles and pragmatics often involve approach-avoidance conflicts. When positive aspects of adhering to positive principles are offset by the specific problems of making this type of decision, conflict must result. Our earlier example concerning the engineers from Morton Thiokol who attempted to postpone the launch of the Space Shuttle *Challenger* serves as a prime example of an approach-avoidance situation. Faced with a decision to maintain their principles or succumb to group pressures, these engineers "stuck to their guns." In the investigations that followed the explosion, their testimony was instrumental in specifying the true cause of the disaster. However, they did lose their positions at Morton Thiokol. Much of the internal torment they no doubt experienced resulted from the fact that neither the positive nor negative aspects of their decision outweighed each other. When an individual or group cannot reconcile the lack of equality in terms of the positive and negative consequences of a decision, *ambivalence* is likely to occur. When ambivalence is present and persists over a period of time, withdrawal from the situation is probable.

Avoidance-Avoidance

When an individual or group faces the task of deciding between two alternatives, both of which carry undesirable consequences, an avoidance-avoidance situation will result. Simply stated, in this situation it is a matter of choosing the "lesser of two evils." As we pointed out in the preceding section, there are certain times when it is acceptable to agree to none of the available alternatives. Avoidance-avoidance conflicts may or may not fit these occasions. For example, a prisoner of war who must talk or be tortured faces an avoidance-avoidance conflict from which he or she cannot withdraw; one of the undesirable alternatives must be chosen. It is sometimes possible to reject both choices and withdraw from the situation, however, as when a person cannot decide which car to purchase and resolves the conflict by not buying any car. The nature of avoidance-avoidance conflicts is such that people are rarely satisfied with any decision. When individuals are continuously forced to make avoidance-avoidance decisions, they usually seek new jobs, replace old friends, and make drastic changes in their lifestyles. Obviously, in conflict situations people should strive to ensure that one of the available options is favorable. This is often easier said than done.

Many psychiatrists believe the ability to handle conflict effectively and to make rational decisions is the mark of a well-adjusted personality. Neurotics, however, may be too rigid to alter their goals or too lacking in self-confidence to make a decision in the first place. We are all too familiar with the nagging friend who never seems to have a handle on life and always seems to make the wrong decision. Individuals who change goals or directions at every turn may have no solid core of character or values; they are shaped by events instead of shaping their lives. People shape their own lives by understanding their options and choosing the alternatives best for them.

Costs and Benefits of Conflict

In order to analyze the costs and benefits of conflict for individuals and for society, some general assumptions must first be made concerning the nature of conflict. Our first assumption is that individuals in society are not naturally in a state of harmony, and, therefore, conflict is a natural and inevitable occurrence of the human condition. Second, an equitable solution is not always possible for resolving conflict. Some conflicts are so severe that resolution will never be possible. Third, not all conflict is detrimental to the individual and society. Fourth, conflict does not represent a breakdown in communication (see Chapter 1). Rather, it represents a distinct type of communication, and it may be the only manner in which certain values and ideals can be expressed. With these four assumptions in mind, we can now discuss the positive and negative consequences of conflict.

The Costs of Conflict

We are all familiar with the negative consequences of conflict in interpersonal relationships. Conflict often motivates people to become *less communicative* owing to real or imagined differences. When this happens, we often withhold information, and we may even supply distorted or false information to those with whom we are in conflict. Marriage counselors are frequently called upon to arbitrate conflicts stemming from severe differences between sexual desires. When conflicts arise between husband and wife on the basis of an unsatisfactory sexual relationship, reticence to discuss the matter often develops on the part of one or both of the partners. When the problem becomes sufficiently magnified, the end result usually lies somewhere between the divorce court and a marriage counselor. Thus conflict may *intensify* real or imagined differences and create the familiar case of making mountains out of molehills.

Conflict may also impede *efficiency* of operation between individuals or groups. Individuals may no longer function smoothly with each other on a day-to-day basis because "something seems to be wrong with us lately." Friction also creates a climate of dissension and incompatibility in groups and often results in group goals and individual needs (the reason individuals belong to groups) being thwarted. In addition, when relationships become inefficient and less facilitating, considerable energy must be spent in resolving the conflict rather than working toward group goals or satisfying individual needs.

One of the most serious consequences of conflict is the potential affect it has on a person's *self-image* or *concept*. Individuals who constantly wrestle with conflict have little time left to develop skills and satisfy desires. They may develop a distorted sense of self-worth and feel inadequate before the pressures and demands of society. Moreover, when conflict becomes severe with no solution in sight, people often assault the self-concept of others. A competing position becomes "stupid and untenable," and failure to agree in kind and in principle becomes "intolerant and pigheaded." A final drawback to conflict is that it breeds *distrust and suspicion*. Individuals cannot relate to one another interpersonally if they distrust each other, and groups cannot function cohesively if the motives of others in the group are suspect. In addition, the distrust and suspicion bred by conflict may lead to open hostilities. We need not dwell on the armed conflicts that have occurred in recent years over religious, racial, economic, and political disagreements. We can strive toward more effective management of conflict after we understand the potentially positive aspects of this phenomenon.

The Benefits of Conflict

Until several years ago, scholars were in almost uniform agreement concerning the disruptive influence of conflict on society. Lewis Coser (1956), a noted sociologist, was one of the first to support the positive value of conflict. Coser argued that conflict has socially desirable qualities because it creates associations and coalitions that bring members of society together who might otherwise have nothing to do with each other. It binds a group together and provides a safety valve that allows a release of pressure and thus promotes group autonomy. According to Coser, conflict and contradiction not only precede unity but also are operative in it at every moment of its existence. He also warns that conflict is truly nonfunctional in those social structures in which there is insufficient or no toleration for handling conflict. He suggests that the intensity of struggles that tend to tear apart a social system may result from the *rigidity* of the structures, not from the conflict. This point was clearly demonstrated during the student/police confrontations of the 1960s. The rigid structure of many police forces was unable to tolerate many of the minor disturbances in student-initiated anti-war protests, and the comparable rigidity of some militant activists was unable to accommodate any compromise offered by the establishment. More recently we have begun to see an escalation of tensions and conflict over the issue of abortion. Those on both sides of this highly controversial topic have been unable to reach any satisfactory compromise and once peaceful demonstrations have frequently escalated to violent confrontations. Mutual rigidities such as these prevent the development of equilibrium, evidenced by the resulting violence.

Thus in explicating the positive aspects of conflict, we do not believe that all conflict should be (or can be) resolved or that conflict is never warranted. Conflict is beneficial when it prompts necessary *social change*. Social change is often desirable and necessary in interpersonal relationships and among groups in society. For example, competing opinions concerning minority groups in our society may result in a more equitable system for including minorities in government, or it may cause individuals to reexamine existing values and prejudices regarding minority groups.

Sometimes the very fact that we are willing to tolerate conflict in our interpersonal relationships indicates that we *value the relationship* enough to strive toward harmony and fulfillment. When individual differences are perceived to be great, it is sometimes easier to dissolve the relationship and search for more compatible companions than it is to maintain the relationship. In other words, a valued interpersonal relationship may be characterized by a willingness to manage, or simply deal with, conflict.

In a similar vein, conflict can *clarify* situations and issues. When opinions concerning a specific issue are many and varied, all of the various and sundry dimensions of the issue come to light. Unless ideas are presented in the public forum and subjected to the scrutiny of many, the danger is always present that these ideas are merely a reflection of deluded and self-serving interests. As individuals in society, we cannot judge the veracity of our ideas or the appropriateness of our behavior unless we do so on the basis of objective criteria determined by the society in which we live. We need not be reminded of the injustice to humanity that occurred in Nazi Germany when the absence of conflict failed to clarify values, attitudes, and behaviors.

Conflict also tends to cause *evaluation* of existing and operable systems of society. Foreign leaders frequently have expressed concern over whether the democratic principles representative of the United States really work. The series of events known as the Watergate Scandal and the Iran-Contra Affair (a.k.a. "Iran-a-muck") tested our democratic process, found it wanting, and caused the necessary adjustments to be made. Similarly, conflict can test the strength of interpersonal bonds and determine if the relationship is worthwhile. There is no greater sense of contentment than when two people struggle, find their relationship worthy of the test, and enjoy the security of mutual concern and affection. In this sense, productive conflict interaction results in solutions that lead to a renewed (or sometimes new found) sense of solidarity (Folger, Poole, & Stutman, 1993). Simons (1974) argues that cooperative communication about conflicting perspectives can actually strengthen interpersonal bonds, whereas suppression of conflict can cause irreparable damage.

Conflict can be used as a prime catalyst for *self-improvement*. Whether as individuals or as groups, we often settle into periods of passivity and/or unproductive activity. Sometimes challenge and conflict provide the incentive we need to engage in productive thought and activity. Even individuals whom society labels as "high achievers" sometimes fall into the abyss of complacency or attempt to live off past accomplishments. These individuals are more than willing to defend their reputations from all challenges. Many people, however, develop patterns of resignation and acceptance of their "lot in life." Conflict can be a potent force in spurring groups and individuals to their full potential. The late football coach Vince Lombardi created intense conflict among his players as a regular part of his coaching philosophy. With this group of athletes, some of whom were considered to be mediocre by the experts, he created a football dynasty.

Finally, conflict can be pure *enjoyment* for some. Remember our earlier example of the individual who is not content unless embroiled in some crisis? Some people thrive on competition and challenge. They are not happy unless they are engaged in some sort of activity that provides even a temporary escape from the mundane world. Many professional athletes cite as one of the principal reasons for choosing their profession the pure joy of conflict and combat. America is infatuated with conflict and competition. Conflict is legally sanctioned through athletic competition, and competition is recognized as the only way of reaching the great American dream. Let us quickly point out that we do not endorse conflict on its own merit. Obviously, conflict can become disruptive and dangerous. Many harmless encounters with much ribbing on both sides have degenerated into harsh words, hurt feelings, and sometimes physical injury.

It should be obvious at this point that conflict takes many forms, occurs at many levels, and carries with it both positive and negative consequences. Because we believe that conflict is an inevitable part of the human experience, we feel that it is appropriate to end this chapter with a brief discussion of conflict resolution. We realize that by the time most people have reached college age they already have developed a variety of conflict-resolution strategies. We have also argued that it is often the appropriate response to conflict to engage in communication to reduce conflict. However, we want to stress our belief that there are occasions when we have neither the reserve nor the inclination to "turn the other cheek" when conflict arises. This notion suggests that no one ready-made formula will make conflict disappear and that effective management of conflict requires all the skills required for effective interpersonal relationships. Therefore, we offer the following *possible* strategies for your consideration, with the idea that they may offer insights into how you can improve your conflict management skills.

Strategies for Managing Conflict

Recognizing Conflict

The first step in effectively managing conflict is to *recognize* the type of conflict present and at which level it is operating. You need to ask yourself such questions as: "Is this real or artificial conflict?" "Is this conflict at the interpersonal level or a conflict between groups?" "Is this a conflict of personalities or ideas?" "Does this conflict involve me, or am I simply getting 'sucked in' to someone else's conflict?" As we have discussed previously, attempting to manage conflict when you are uncertain as to the specific type and level present is similar to riding a horse for the first time; you generally know what you are dealing with, but not exactly what to expect.

Dealing With Conflict

If you are able to recognize the nature of the conflict adequately, you need to weigh all the relevant factors in the situation and decide how you want to deal with the conflict. People vary greatly in their ability to tolerate conflict. Many people decide simply to *tolerate* or accept a grievance and not pursue it further. This is colloquially known as "turning the other cheek," "bagging it," "lumping it," or "letting it slide." Toleration, however, is a very effective conflict management strategy when the consequences of engagement into overt conflict are not worth the effort. For example, it would not be uncommon for you to tolerate the barking dog of your next-door neighbors because to confront them would take a lot of effort, and the results might only be hurt feelings and resentment for all parties concerned. In relationships, deeper levels of intimacy have a tendency to cool conflict and lead to toleration. This does not mean that people like the conflict they experience. Much of the crime in this country is tolerated. It is estimated that two thirds of serious crimes are tolerated and not reported. Toleration is perhaps the most frequent response to improper conduct. The danger involved in tolerating conflict is that you no longer have any input in determining if the conflict will disappear.

Another method of managing conflict is to *leave the field* or *avoid* contact with the offender. The most drastic avoidance of conflict is, of course, suicide. In our society, avoidance is readily observed within the middle class (Nader & Todd, 1978). Even within families, people hide in their bedrooms, lock themselves in bathrooms, or go for a walk when conflict arises. People can manage conflict in this manner with one of three strategies. First, they can physically depart— such as walk out of a meeting, leave the house, or move away. Second, they can leave the field psychologically by refusing to verbalize the felt grievance, by insisting that nothing is wrong. A third method of avoidance is to change the topic. If you know that discussing a particular topic has the potential to lead to heated disagreements, it may be wise to stay clear of that issue. Leaving the field does little to "resolve" differences, but it may avoid aggravating the situation.

In general, studies of the effect of communication behavior indicate that during conflict conditions communication becomes polarized (i.e., divided), defensive, restrictive, and highly controlled. Thus *increased use of effective communication* becomes the third strategy for managing conflict. Throughout this text we have been discussing methods of increasing your communication effectiveness whether intended to persuade, to develop and maintain relationships, or to make decisions. Conflict management is no different, and in many ways the same concepts apply. Effective communication in managing conflicts entails constructing messages that are not accusatory; that accurately represent the source of the conflict; and that identify attitudes, values, or behaviors in question. It is ironic that conflict impedes the communication that is so vital in managing the conflict. Understanding the interplay between meaning and language, realizing that your perspective is just that—your perspective—and it should not be projected onto the other person, and "owning" your emotions may increase your chances of effectively communicating your position and ultimately aid in successfully managing your conflict.

A fourth strategy for managing conflict is to *reestablish mutual trust*. As we discussed in the previous chapter, once trust is violated it is difficult to regain. Successful management of conflict necessitates the reestablishment of the trust that was lost owing to the conflict. An adversary must trust that you are sincere, that you will uphold any agreements that are negotiated, and that your motives are genuine if an equitable solution is to be found. Trust can often be established through a compromise posture. This style allows you to acknowledge the other person's goals without completely sacrificing your own needs.

The use of *effective persuasion* is the fifth strategy for managing conflict. We have provided what we consider to be an adequate synthesis of knowledge concerning methods of effective persuasion in Chapters 6 and 7. The techniques suggested will aid greatly in the management of conflict. Because conflicts involve differences in attitudes or behaviors, persuading people to change their behaviors or attitudes may contain the conflict. We suggest you review these chapters with conflict management in mind.

Finally, conflict management through *bargaining and negotiation* represents the sixth possible strategy. These strategies are frequently used for intergroup and organizational conflicts. Negotiation is a process of discussing conflict and seeking an acceptable resolution for all concerned.

Bargaining and negotiation typically involve compromises and changes of position through social persuasion. Bargaining is a type of negotiation that is concerned with generating specific proposals or the trading of proposals to manage the conflict. Often times a neutral third party, or an arbitrator, is used to facilitate a free flow of communication.

Summary

1. Conflict is an inevitable aspect of the human condition. Individuals, groups, and whole societies advance most when conflict is recognized as an inevitable and even healthy aspect of human interaction and when communication is valued as a means of managing conflict. Conflict is manifested only through some type of communication behavior. Although it is possible to communicate without conflict, conflict without some type of communication is impossible.

2. Conflict is an *expressed* struggle between *at least* two parties either of whom perceives incompatible goals and interference from one party, which precludes the other from attainment of some goal. There are many different kinds and intensities of conflict. *Real* conflict results when goals or behaviors are incompatible owing to a struggle for resources. *Artificial* conflict resembles real conflict except it occurs in a non-zero-sum condition. In this situation, gains by one party do not necessarily have to result in losses by another party. When an individual or group creates some conflict for purposes other than the apparent ones, it is *induced* conflict.

3. The difference between *violent* and *nonviolent conflict* is the distinction between the use of force and the use of rhetoric. Whenever a conflict progresses from a verbal exchange to physical aggression, the conflict becomes violent.

4. Most conflict arising among individuals and within small groups is face-to-face as opposed to mediated conflict. Large organizations and institutions can retain legal counsel to settle their disputes in the impersonal and objective atmosphere of the courtroom, whereas individuals and group members rarely can be that detached from their conflict.

5. Every individual brings into each interpersonal and group relationship a set of *values and principles*. Conflict often arises when choosing the principles and values with which to operate in specific situations.

6. There is variety of styles that individuals and groups typically employ in conflict situations. *Avoidance* is a conflict management style in which communication and behavior is unassertive. Adopting an avoidance style has the advantage of giving a person time to think over the situation and not act in haste. Reliance on this style, however, could result in a "backwash" of ill-managed conflicts that have been allowed to fester over time. The *accommodating style* is one in which people in conflict do not assert themselves and try to cooperate with others. A person using this style will generally view the other person's needs and goals as superordinant to their own. A *competitive style* is one in which individuals seek to dominate the situation. This style is characterized by aggressive, assertive, and uncooperative behavior. A person with a competitive style wants to engage others in direct confrontation, trying to "win" at the other's expense. A *compromise style* is characterized by a give-and-take philosophy. People using a compromise style attempt to manage conflict by an equal exchange of concessions and "splitting the difference." A person using a *collaborative style* attempts to manage incompatible goals by working toward the goals of the other. In this way, both people (ideally) end up winning.

7. Generally, conflicts between groups of actors develop in similar ways. *Disagreement, confrontation, escalation, de-escalation, conflict resolution*, and *conflict aftermath* are phases of conflict in most conflict situations.

8. The three major categories of choices that confront people in our society and ultimately cause conflict are *approach-approach* when the two options available are both desirable; *approach-avoidance,* when one option is more favorable than the other; and *avoidance-avoidance,* when the available alternatives are all undesirable.

9. Not all conflict is detrimental to the individual and society. Conflict may breed suspicion and mistrust, impede normal communication, intensify real or imagined differences, or detract from one's self-concept. On the other hand, conflict may precipitate necessary social change, serve to clarify issues, assist in evaluating existing structures of society, generate advances in science and technology, or promote self-improvement.

10. Successful management of conflict necessitates becoming cognizant of the specific type of conflict present and at which level it is operating. With this knowledge in mind, possible strategies include tolerance, leaving the field (avoidance), increased use of effective

communication channels, effective persuasion, bargaining or negotiation, and reestablishing mutual trust.

References

Brown, R. (1965). *Social psychology*. New York: Free Press.

Coser, L. (1956). *The functions of social conflict*. New York: Free Press.

Deutsch, M. (1969). Socially relevant science: Reflections on some studies of interpersonal conflict. *American Psychologist, 24*, 1076-1092.

Folger, J., & Poole, M. S. (1983). *Working through conflict*. Chicago: Scott, Foresman.

Folger, J., Poole, M. S., & Stutman, R. K. (1993). *Working through conflict* (2nd ed.). New York: HarperCollins.

Hocker, J. L., & Wilmot, W. W. (1985). *Interpersonal conflict* (2nd ed.). Dubuque, IA: William C. Brown.

Horney, K. (1937). *The neurotic personality of our time*. New York: Norton.

Nader, L., & Todd, H. F. (1978). *The disputing process—Law in ten societies*. New York: Columbia University Press.

Simons, H. W. (1974). Prologue. In G. R. Miller & H. W. Simmons (Eds.), *Perspectives on communication in social conflict* (pp. 1-13). Englewood Cliffs, NJ: Prentice Hall.

Index

About the Authors

JUDEE K. BURGOON is Professor of Communication and Director of Graduate Studies at the University of Arizona, where she specializes in the areas of nonverbal communication, interpersonal relationship management, and research methods. She has taught previously at West Virginia University, the University of Florida, Hunter College in New York, and Michigan State University, where she was the recipient of the Teacher-Scholar Award. Her research and writing credits include seven books and monographs, three of which relate to nonverbal communication, and more than 110 articles, chapters, and reviews on such subjects on nonverbal and relational communication, dyadic interaction patterns, and deception. Her current research focuses on interpersonal interaction patterns, expectancy violations, and deception. She is the recipient of nine awards for research excellence from national professional associations, has served as Editor for *Communication Monographs*, is a fellow of the International Communication Association, and was recently elected to the Society for Experimental Social Psychology.

MICHAEL BURGOON (Ph.D., Michigan State University, 1970) is Professor of Communication and is also affiliated with the Department of Family and Community Medicine at the University of Arizona, and is a member of the research staff of the Arizona Cancer Center. He directs the basic undergraduate communication core program and teaches in the Executive Development Program in the College of Business and Public Administration at Arizona. He is a Fellow of the International Communication Association and a member of the Society of Experimental Social Psychologists. He has published extensively in scholarly journals in communication, psychology, journalism, management, education, and medicine. In addition to *Human Communication,* he is the author or editor of 13 other texts and scholarly books and more than 25 contributed book chapters. He has also been recognized by national and international professional organizations with outstanding research awards for nine different papers. His major research interests are in social influence, health communication, and the social effects of the mass media. He has received substantial financial support for his academic research from governmental funding agencies, foundations, professional media societies, and private corporations. He is also an active consultant for a number of media organizations in the United States and Canada. He did the original research that resulted in the launch of the first national newspaper, *USA Today.*

EDWIN J. DAWSON is currently a doctoral candidate in Communication at the University of Arizona, Tucson. He received his Master of Arts' Degree in Speech communication from the University of Nebraska at Omaha. He has taught at Creighton University in Omaha; coached intercollegiate forensics; and has taught speech and theater in various high schools across the Midwest. His teaching experience also includes a position at Little Wound School on the Pine Ridge Reservation in South Dakota, where he served as a Speech and Language Arts Specialist. He has contributed articles to academic journals including the *Journal of Nonverbal Behavior, The Basic Course Annual,* and the *Ohio Speech Journal.* In addition, he has authored or coauthored articles at regional and national conventions and has been awarded top paper honors for his work.

His present research interests include communication and health with a special emphasis on HIV/AIDS-intervention strategies for young people and medical adherence among the elderly.

LAURA K. GUERRERO is a doctoral candidate and graduate associate teacher in the Department of Communication at the University of Arizona. Her main areas of interest include relational communication, nonverbal messages, emotional expression, and research methods. She has taught previously at San Diego State University, where she earned her master's degree, and at San Diego Mesa College. Courses she has taught include nonverbal communication, relational communication, communication theory, and advanced public speaking. She has served as course director of an introductory-level interpersonal communication course and as a speech team coach, and has received teaching awards from the International Communication Association and the University of Arizona's New-Traditional Student Association. She has also received several top paper awards for manuscripts presented to regional, national, and international conventions. Her writing credits include book chapters on topics such as jealousy and haptics, and several articles published in communication and social psychology journals.

FRANK G. HUNSAKER (M.A., University of Arizona, 1991) is currently a doctoral candidate and Graduate Associate Teacher in the Department of Communication at the University of Arizona in Tucson. His research interests include health communication, social influence, persuasion, and effects of the mass media. He is Senior Data Manager at the Arizona Cancer Center. In addition to his responsibilities as Assistant Director of the introductory undergraduate communication course, he teaches upper-division courses in persuasion and social relations as well as lower-division classes in small group communication and interpersonal communication. His most recent publications have focused on communication and deception.